Salutogenic Organizations and Change

Georg F. Bauer • Gregor J. Jenny
Editors

Salutogenic Organizations and Change

The Concepts Behind Organizational
Health Intervention Research

 Springer

Editors
Georg F. Bauer
University of Zürich
Zürich, Switzerland

Gregor J. Jenny
University of Zürich
Zürich, Switzerland

ISBN 978-94-007-6469-9   ISBN 978-94-007-6470-5 (eBook)
DOI 10.1007/978-94-007-6470-5
Springer Dordrecht Heidelberg New York London

Library of Congress Control Number: 2013943117

Printed on acid-free paper

Springer is part of Springer Science+Business Media (www.springer.com)

Contents

Chapter 1
From Fidelity to Figuration: Current and Emerging Approaches to Organizational Health Intervention Research

Georg F. Bauer and Gregor J. Jenny

Background

Many professional communities are committed to the issue of organizational health and corresponding intervention research. They are dealing with individuals, teams and organizations, management, leaders and politics, health, well-being and productivity, and change, promotion, and development – for all of which there are experts with focused knowledge and methods. Actors in this scientific field include *stress researchers* moving from individual to organizational stress management, *organizational behavior researchers* concerned with the positive perspective, *public health researchers* considering organizations as root cause of psychosocial determinants of health, *health promotion researchers* dealing with healthy settings, *ergonomics researchers* addressing the macro level through participatory approaches, *organizational change researchers* introducing health as one criterion of successful change, *management researchers* discovering happiness as an additional, legitimate outcome, and so on.

The *range of research traditions* covered by this multiplex field might be roughly and exemplarily illustrated by the two following approaches. On the one hand, there are *stress management interventions* within the larger fields of work and health psychology. Since psychology is primarily concerned with the experience and behavior of humans, these interventions often start with a focus on the individual and follow (quasi-)experimental paradigms common in these fields. The key interest is to assure fidelity of the implementation of (pre-defined) interventions or treatments and to measure their effect size. This research is based on the premises of predictability, linearity, and measurability. On the other hand, there is the *workplace health promotion* (WHP) movement. Whereas one line of WHP

G.F. Bauer (✉) • G.J. Jenny
Division of Public and Organizational Health, Institute of Social and Preventive Medicine,
University of Zürich, Hirschengraben 84, 8001 Zürich, Switzerland
e-mail: gfbauer@ifspm.uzh.ch; gjenny@ifspm.uzh.ch

G.F. Bauer and G.J. Jenny (eds.), *Salutogenic Organizations and Change:*
The Concepts Behind Organizational Health Intervention Research,
DOI 10.1007/978-94-007-6470-5_1, © Springer Science+Business Media Dordrecht 2013

focuses on individual life style factors, another line is rooted in the WHO health promotion and settings approach: Its key interest is to reduce health inequalities through programs aimed at health determinants in settings[1] such as neighborhoods, schools, hospitals, and other workplaces. Changing settings requires involving the entire system with its dynamics, power players, and stakeholders to get a program going. Accordingly, this research accounts for the non-predictable, non-linear, and non-measurable.

Continua and Tensions: Compiling Perspectives to a Dialogue

This range of research traditions could be mapped on various continua, for example from *tailoring to standardization,* from *program to experiment*, from *process to effect*, from *quality to quantity*, from *fundamental change to better functioning*, from *dynamics to stability*, from *subjectivity to objectivity*, from *systemic interactions to mono-causal relationships*. Our field has to deal with the tensions implied by these continua if we intend to build-up a coherent, comprehensible knowledge base over the next years.

This book aims to provide an overview of current approaches to organizational health intervention research (**OHIR**). Each chapter is written by different intervention researchers who – taken together – cover a broad range of the fields and perspectives mentioned above. The authors were invited to elaborate first on their respective concept of a healthy organization, second on their approach to change organizations, and third on how to research corresponding interventions in the field. Also, they were encouraged to refer to the notion of salutogenesis, focusing on resources and positive outcomes of health-oriented organizational change processes.

The authors of the contributions in this book have been self-organizing in recent years to exchange their knowledge and the challenges that they faced when intervening in organizations. Author invitations were sent to participants of the pre-conference meeting of the informal group "Salutogenic organizational health intervention research" (SOHIR) at the European Academy of Occupational Health Psychology (EAOHP) conference 2012, to members of the International Process Evaluation Partnership (IPEP) sponsored by EAWOP, and finally members of the Global Working Group of Salutogenesis of the International Union for Health Promotion and Health Education (IUHPE). The contributions have the character of structured discussion papers and embrace diverse perspectives and ways of proceeding. This compilation of concepts will convey to the reader the mental models as well as applied methods of health researchers intervening in organizations. In its sum, the book is expected to trigger a virtual dialogue between the individual contributions and the reader.

---

[1] Settings are defined as "The place or social context in which people engage in daily activities in which environmental, organizational, and personal factors interact to affect health and wellbeing" (World Health Organization 1998).

Aiming at Common Frames of Reference, Embracing Heterogeneity

In the following, we summarize our perception of common themes emerging from this book. We organize our – certainly subjective – reading along the three key issues covered by each author: *perspectives of organizational health, approaches to changing organizations,* and *approaches to OHIR.* Further, we add some preliminary proposals for future developments within these areas. Given the complexity and diversity of organizational interventions, the diversity of research traditions, and the high need for autonomy of the researchers involved, we do not expect and suggest a set of standardized, agreed-upon concepts, approaches, methods, or measures in future OHIR. However, it would be very desirable to build up a common terminology and frame(s) of reference. This would facilitate relating and contrasting our diverse, distinct approaches. By doing so, we could co-create a coherent evidence base of OHIR over time and increase the scientific and practical credibility of this approach.

We hope that this book contributes to the further discourse in and visibility of the field – helping to *make the case for a working environment full of enjoyment, resources, and positive health.*

Perspectives of Organizational Health

The target of change has shifted from individuals to whole organizations. As in the broader literature on organizational health, in the contributions to the book three main lines of arguments for moving from occupational to organizational health (**OH**) can be found (Bauer and Jenny 2012): (1) health of employees is strongly influenced by the organizational context, (2) health of employees strongly influences the health (i.e., performance, adaptability, innovativeness) of organizations, and (3) both health of employees and performance of organizations are continuously coproduced by the ongoing interaction between employees and the organizational context. In all cases, both employees and the organization need to be simultaneously considered in organizational health interventions.

Localizing the Unit of Interest and Adopting a Systems View

Various authors acknowledge that it is unrealistic to involve the entire organization in interventions. Thus, often the group (team) level is introduced as the unit of intervention, assigning team leaders (middle managers) a key role as change agents. In this case, organizational health emerges from teams going through health improvement processes.

Following this need to consider multiple levels in organizations and their interactions to understand and promote organizational health, several authors refer to systems theory to describe organizations as complex social systems. A systemic conceptualization of organizational health is in line with empirical findings, such as that demanding jobs can impair health and resourceful jobs can enhance motivation simultaneously, that there are cross-lags and reciprocal (gain-/loss-) spirals, all of which impact higher-level outcomes. Yet, we are still searching for *patterns* of how health is created in organizations as complex social systems.

Framing the Individual, Organization, and Processes

A common framework of organizational health might facilitate the search for key patterns of health development and also help map interventions, the expected processes of change and outcomes. Referring to our own work (Bauer and Jenny 2012; Chap. 10 by Jenny and Bauer in this volume) and the work of the authors in this volume, the following elements and interdependencies seem generic to an organizational health framework: *Individual employees* who are the primary actors and beneficiaries of salutogenic health development are of core interest. *Employees with a leadership role* are particularly highlighted: Through their leadership behavior they are crucial for generating health and for steering (health-oriented) change processes. Employees *interact with the organization*; they work within what constitutes their health-relevant environment. Here, *sub-groups* such as divisions or teams are considered as the entity offering identity to employees and constituting a feasible unit of change. The key characteristics on the level of employees (e.g., behavior, motivation, identity) and of organizations (e.g., culture/climate, strategy, structure) considered by various researchers certainly will vary, as illustrated in this volume.

Further, most OH interventions target both *work processes* through job re-design and work organization as well as *social relationship processes* influencing health in organizations. Following the general shift from a pure risk/demand perspective towards resources at work, these processes can be differentiated into health impairing (*pathogenic*) and health enhancing (*salutogenic*) processes – in line with the commonly acknowledged JDR model (Bakker and Demerouti 2007). Finally, most OH interventions presented in this book are processes to improve any one or all three targets of OH: employees/leaders, organization/teams, and the co-generated work and social processes. Thus, this (self-) optimization process is depicted at the center of this generic OH framework (Fig. 1.1).

Defining "Health"

The question of how health is created within organizations naturally leads to the questions of how *health* should be conceptualized and measured. The concept of stress and related negative health (disease) outcomes is still eminent. However, along with the movement towards positive psychology, a call for measures of positive health has emerged. During the preparatory workshop (see above), particularly

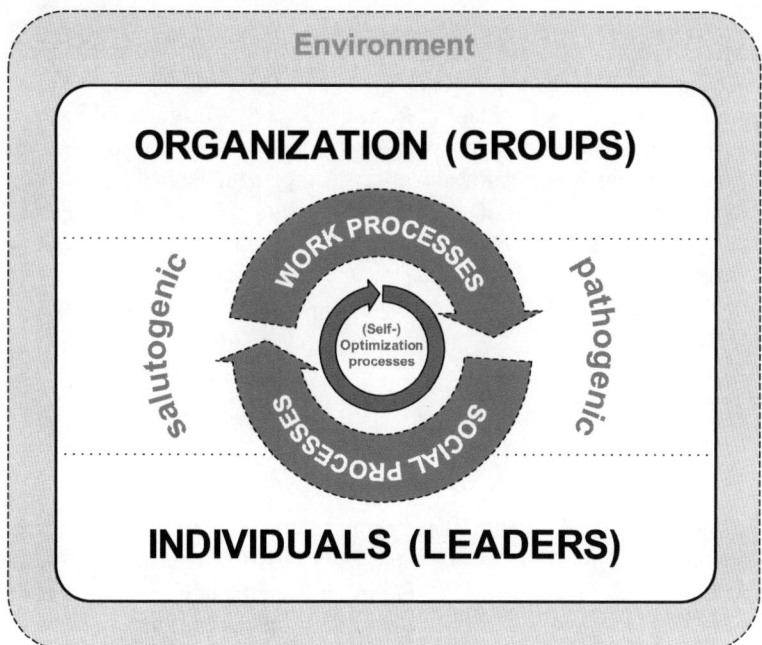

Fig. 1.1 Generic organizational health framework

"happiness," "enjoyment," and "meaningfulness" were repeatedly suggested as appropriate and clearly positive outcomes pointing beyond pure functioning at work. This is also in line with current thinking in the management literature (Blanchflower and Oswald 2011). Several authors in this volume refer to the concept of salutogenesis, which communicates a focus on resources and positive outcomes of health-oriented organizational change processes (Bauer and Jenny 2012). We see a potential in better specifying the concept of salutogenesis with regard to criteria of coherent and salutogenic work, organizations, and change processes. Further, consistent categories of health outcome measures would be needed to compare OHIR results across different studies. In our research, for example, we distinguish 12 categories of health (Bauer et al. 2006; Faltermaier 2005; Brauchli et al. 2012; Keyes 2007): 3 domains of health (physical, mental, social) × 2 qualities of negative vs. positive health × 2 dimensions of experience (well-being) and functioning.

Changing Organizations: From Fidelity to Fit to Figuration

Before translating our perspectives of OH into appropriate interventions, we feel the need to explicate our elementary view of change of and by organizations. The basic assumption underlying the concept of this volume is that we first need to have a clear understanding of how health is created in organizations on an everyday basis, as was summarized in the previous section above. Only then can we reflect on how we, as external change agents, can *link to, build on*, and *improve* this ongoing health production process in organizations. Starting from inside out seems justified based on two arguments: First, ongoing, unintentional health production through existing routines in organizations has much stronger health effects compared to limited power of external, predefined interventions. Thus, improvement of existing routines will have the greatest potential for health gains in organizations. Second, building on and health-oriented improvement of existing organizational structures and processes may lead to long-term institutionalization of the intervention (maintenance) and to sustainable effects.

Universalistic, Contingent and Configurational Approaches

For a comparison of different OH interventions, they may be grouped into the three approaches originally defined as key theories of strategic human resource (**HR**) management in organizations (Delery and Doty 1996): universalistic, contingency, and configurational. Delery and Doty (1996) defined the *universalistic approach* as "that some HR practices are always better than others and that all organizations should adopt these best practices" (p. 803). With regard to the *contingency approach*, they stated: "Contingency theorists argue that, in order to be effective, an organization's HR policies must be consistent with other aspects of the organization" (p. 803). Finally, the *configurational approach* builds on configurational theories that "are concerned with how the pattern of multiple independent variables is related to a dependent variable rather than with how individual independent variables are related to the dependent variable" (p. 804). Originally, Delery and Doty applied the term configurational to indicate specific combinations of HR strategies that achieve both a horizontal fit (i.e., internal consistencies of HR practices) and a vertical fit (i.e., congruence of HR system with organizational strategy).

Origins of (Con-)Figurational Thinking

In sociology, (con-)figuration theory has been conceptualized as a dynamic social network of interdependent individuals (Elias 1939). Elias' (1939) figurational sociology deals with the relationship between power, behavior, emotion, and knowledge over time and is intended to overcome the dichotomy between the individual and society through consideration of interactions between these levels of analysis. This conceptualization is compatible with the basic assumption of the generic OH model outlined above: individuals interacting with the organization as the relevant social environment. In the context of OH interventions, we construe the configurational approach as intentional change of the social system's patterns that are relevant for ongoing reproduction and targeted improvement of OH.

Table 1.1 Approaches to organizational health interventions

Intervention characteristics	Organizational health intervention approaches[a]		
	A. Universalistic	**B. Contingency**	**C. Configurational**
Focus	Fidelity of the intervention	Fit between intervention/ organization	Figuration of the organization
Context organization used	For selection & targeting	For tailoring/fitting	As target & actor of change
Implementation process	Standardized	Tailored/fitted	Co-created
Aim/outcome	Predefined	Predefined or modified	Predefined (health capacities)+emergent
Content	Predefined	Predefined or modified	Emergent
Research object	Effect of static implementation	Process+effect of dynamic implementation	Process+effect of interactive capacity building process
Main change process	Issue-specific individual+group learning	Multi-level learning through participatory problem solving	Capacity building for own ongoing health improvements+increased legitimacy of health

[a]Terminology of universalistic, contingency, configurational based on Delery and Doty (1996)

Characteristics of Universalistic, Contingent, and Configurational Approaches

We apply the three HR approaches to OH interventions to reflect on how they influence characteristics of the intervention, such as its focus, aim, and implementation (Table 1.1).

Accordingly, we characterize the three approaches to OH interventions as follows:

(A) **Universalistic:** The starting point is the predefined, universalistic intervention itself. To assure fidelity of its standardized implementation and its predicted effectiveness, appropriate organizations in need of that intervention are selected. The aim, the content, and the implementation process of the intervention are all predefined. For research, the basic object is the effect of the static implementation, whereas the change process – as it is (seemingly) predictable – is of minor interest.

(B) **Contingency:** Here, the fit between a partly predefined intervention and self- or externally selected organizations in need of that intervention are of primary concern. Accordingly, implementation requires continuous tailoring or fitting of the intervention to the context of the specific organization. Depending on how much control is given to the organization, this adaptation might go so far that finally even the aims and contents of the intervention will no longer be predefined but modified. For research, the process of the dynamic implementation needs to be understood in order to predict and assess potential effects. This change process involves multilevel (organizational) learning, particularly by going through a health-oriented problem solving process in organizations.

(C) **Configurational:** The starting and end point of this approach is the figuration of the organization itself – that is, the pattern of how individual and organizational capacities influence health and how these ongoing processes can be improved. Thus, the context of the organization is not a mere boundary condition for a predefined or fitted intervention but becomes initially the *key target* and finally through continuous capacity building the *key actor* of change. Consequently, the aim and content of the intervention emerge from the organization itself and are co-created with leadership and ownership by the organization, the external OH intervener being less and less involved. Researchers are interested in the process and effect of this interactive capacity building process, including the final capacity of the organization to go through similar improvement processes in the future.

Thinking Outside the Box: Trends in Changing Organizations

Combining Fitting for Buy-in and Tensioning for Disturbing Routines

Applying these approaches to OH interventions to the contributions in this volume makes it clear that they are often used in combination throughout all intervention phases. For example, initially, an analysis using a predefined employee survey instrument might be used, with results presented in a standardized manner *(universalistic approach)*. Later, a predefined workshop to build readiness for change in teams is implemented but tailored to the specific language and needs of the teams involved *(contingency approach)*. Finally, the OH intervention institutionalizes having each team in the organization go through health-oriented improvement cycles regularly, setting their own aims and the contents of their actions *(configurational approach)*.

This raises important questions: In which phase of an OH intervention, how much fitting to the context or alignment with strategic goals is needed to obtain the buy-in of the organization? In which phases is it necessary to induce differences and tensions with current patterns so as to trigger more fundamental change of practices and possibly even priorities and values in organizations, such as moving from economic values (value added) to a broader, employee-oriented set of values (added values)?

Participation for Self-Optimization and Developing Ownership

Across the various chapters in this volume, there is a trend towards OH interventions and tools that enable self-observation and self-optimization on the part of organizations. There is a strong salutogenic focus on building on existing strengths and promoting resources in organizations. As mentioned above, the overall intervention approaches used and particularly the single intervention elements range from universalistic to configurational approaches. Within these approaches, there are shifting degrees of participation of employees. This raises the fundamental question of who owns the process of developing OH and who is allowed to only take part in it. With regard to the degree of participation of organizations and their members in OHIR projects, this can range from researchers who allow employees participate in their research-driven action research to researchers participating in OH-related actions driven by the organizations themselves with the aim to support and evaluate the process. To best realize the many potentially positive effects of participation in OH discussed in different chapters in this volume, it will be important to clarify how to decide upon and implement the appropriate level of participation in future OH intervention studies.

Sustainability Through Building on Existing Structures?

The intervention approaches take different stances regarding the degree of long-term capacity building for and dissemination of a self-optimization approach in organizations. The degree of capacities built up during the intervention partly depends on the intervention architecture used, for example whether a new, parallel structure (e.g., health circles, planning teams) was established for implementation. This might impede successful implementation of action plans developed by these parallel intervention structures, as they might not be considered part of the regular decision-making processes. Thus, joint problem solving and health enhancement skills developed and applied in parallel structures could be more difficult to transfer into regular structures such as team or division meetings. If the parallel structure is not permanently established, the sustainability of such an approach could be questionable. Thus, working with existing power and relationship structures might be more promising with regard to transfer to everyday practice and maintenance. On the other hand, as argued above, difference and tension might be needed to trigger change in (pathogenic) routines, and the difference might be better induced through an intervention that is clearly distinguishable from daily work life. Thus, also the intervention architecture needs to balance fitting with and tensioning of the organization.

Terminology in Organizational Health Intervention Research

Intervention vs. Implementation

We propose to use the term "intervention" for covering all planned, intentional measures by change agents to purposefully improve OH. These measures are often grouped into specific *intervention phases* (e.g., analysis, planning, implementation, evaluation) and apply specific *intervention elements* or measures (e.g., employee surveys, workshops, trainings), which are connected through an appropriate *intervention architecture* (i.e., who is involved in which phase through which element). Whereas an intervention can be planned and described in general terms, its final design will only become clear during its actual implementation. Thus, the term "implementation" refers to all real actions taken to implement the intervention, being best understood as an interaction (or even co-production) between the actors implementing the intervention and the target system.

Process of Implementation and Change Leading to Alterations in Outcomes

We suggest that the term "process" covers both the implementation processes described above (e.g., conducting an employee survey or training course) and the intended and unintended process of change triggered in organizations and their employees, leading to alterations in intermediary outcomes (e.g., knowledge, attitude, behavior, structures, collaborative climate), finally leading to the outcomes of interest (e.g., health). As this volume impressively demonstrates, processes of change can cover a whole range of foci, such as taking over others' perspectives, individual and organizational learning, social processes, realization of jointly developed action plans for improving work, organizational structure, strategy, social processes, etc.

Considering vs. Changing the Context

Finally, if we follow the now common recommendation to consider both process and "*context*" in OHIR, we should clearly conceptualize the latter. The approaches above suggest that the organization as the context of OH interventions might be considered for *selecting and targeting* the intervention (universalistic approach), for *adapting* the intervention to this context (contingency approach), or as the final *target and actor of change* (configurational approach). Each leads to different evaluation questions and strategies.

Approaches to Organizational Health Intervention Research

The overall aim of promoting organizational health can be considered the common ground of all three OH intervention approaches. However, we saw that the approaches differ with regard to the specific aims pursued, the content, main change process of interest, and last not least the research object. These differences have implications concerning how to research the three OH intervention approaches. Table 1.2 shows that the different approaches to OH interventions lead to distinct key evaluation research questions.

Depending on the OH intervention approach chosen and the key research questions of interest, different research paradigms will be of relevance to address these questions appropriately. Providing an overview of the key paradigms of social theory at the time, the "four paradigm model of social theory" (Burrel and Morgan 1979) distinguished two orthogonal axes: (1) theories of the nature of social sciences, ranging from subjectivist to objectivist assumptions, and (2) theories about society, ranging from the sociology of regulation to the sociology of radical change. Taken together, the two orthogonal axes create four fields to which four

Table 1.2 Approaches to organizational health interventions: Implications for key evaluation research questions (RQ)

Evaluation research questions (RQ)	Organizational health intervention approaches[a]		
	A. Universalistic	**B. Contingency**	**C. Configurational**
Outcome evaluation			
Key RQ regarding outcome	Predefined effects of static implementation	Predefined or modified effects of dynamic implementation	Predefined (health capacities) + emergent effects of interactive capacity building process
Process-evaluation			
Key RQ regarding implementation process	Effect dependent on fidelity and adherence?	Effect dependent on fit with organization and reach?	Effect dependent on co-creation and reach?
Key RQ regarding change process	Effect through issue-specific individual + group learning?	Effect through multi-level learning through participatory problem solving?	Effect through capacity building for OH + health gaining legitimacy?
Context evaluation			
Key RQ regarding context (organization)	Representative sample of organizations to assure external validity of results?	Context sufficiently considered for tailoring/fitting? To which contexts are results generalizable?	Context sufficiently considered for capacity building? To which contexts are results generalizable?

[a] Terminology of universalistic, contingency, configurational based on Delery and Doty (1996)

main research paradigms can be assigned: the *functionalist* and *interpretative* vs. the *radical structuralist* and the *radical humanist* paradigms. This frame visualizes opposite paradigmatic assumptions and could facilitate reflection on one's own, value-based position regarding knowledge generation and change in organizations. More generally, it would allow us to map different organizational health intervention (research) approaches, to relate them to each other, and to reflect on implications of the diverse, basic assumptions about knowledge generation and type of change needed. The benefits of applying and contrasting multiple paradigms simultaneously for organizational research has been demonstrated previously (Hassard 1991; Deetz 1996).

Taken together, the chosen intervention approach, the related key research questions, and the overarching research paradigm will help to define a research design or rather a combination of designs "fit for purpose" (Cox et al. 2007; Randall et al. 2005) and the related, mostly mixed methods. As a consequence, currently heterogeneous designs and methods are applied to OHIR as reflected in the diverse contributions in this volume, ranging from experimental to quasi-experimental to large-scale field studies involving entire organizations to small-scale qualitative case studies.

The Logics of Research and Practice Today and Tomorrow

The authors of the contributions in this volume are all researchers who have chosen the object of their studies rather courageously, facing many hazards that researchers normally fear: Their study object (the organization) is a moving target that constantly changes its form and size, operating in a dynamic environment; their study object "health" is usually of low priority on the management's agenda and exposed to not-measurable influences (usually not to the better); their study population tends to mistrust both analysis and change; and their study designs and methods are notorious for being unwieldy and unfit within the logics of fast and competitive business processes and gold standards in experimental research. This is why we are happy to compile the embodied knowledge of so many intrepid intervention researchers and to present their concepts, frameworks, mind maps, methods, and practice.

Given the heterogeneity of OHIR approaches presented in this volume, this last section below will provide a brief overview of the single chapters. To facilitate orientation, we grouped the chapters into sections. Assignment to a section considered the primary focus of the respective contribution, not excluding that it also covers aspects of other sections. The four sections are:

1. **Concepts of organizational health**: These chapters emphasize the relevance of particular aspects or of an entire model of organizational health to clarify our final object and aim of OHIR.
2. **Organizational concepts guiding theory-driven interventions**: These contributions agree upon the importance of a clear model of OH and derive specific intervention and evaluation approaches based on this underlying conceptualization.

3. **Concepts of organizational health interventions and change**: This section contains chapters covering concepts of how to design and implement OH interventions and/or what change processes should be studied to understand their impact on OH.
4. **Intervention and change concepts guiding theory-driven interventions**: These chapters show how clear conceptualizations of OH interventions, their implementation, and the induced changes can guide theory-driven interventions and process evaluations.

Concepts of Organizational Health

Egan elaborates on the term "psychosocial" with regard to psychosocial environment, factors/characteristics, pathways, interventions, and a healthy organizational environment, summarizing from reviews what we know about organizational-level psychosocial interventions. Egan also brings up the issue of outcomes on meso-macro levels, combined with inequality issues, and points to a research bias through the inverse evidence law.

Montgomery, Doulougeri, Georganta, and Panagoupoulou dehierarchize the way of visualizing medical organizations and present a model with Sense of coherence (SOC) and optimization as outcomes and foundation of the organization. Also, they discuss action research as an appropriate approach to organizational health intervention research. They propose three indices – quality, impact, and cost – to quantify healthcare interventions.

Idan, Braun-Lewensohn, and Sagy structure a needs evaluation in a psychiatric inpatient unit, grouping 10 primary themes (leadership of head nurse, patients' diversity, self-fulfillment, etc.) within the three axes of SOC, further distinguishing between their SOC-promoting and SOC-deterring qualities. They build on qualitative data and show how an intervention could target the themes identified within this logic.

Organizational Concepts Guiding Theory-Driven Interventions

Vandraager and Koelen introduce the salutogenic approach to the workplace and the need to strengthen key general resistance resources (job control, task significance, social relations) and sense of coherence. They call for a multilevel interdisciplinary approach, employee participation, and organizational development, and in a side line, reflect on how a salutogenic intervention might "show up" in the system's discourse and documentation.

Llorens, Salanova, Torrente, and Acosta present a persistent focus on collective levels and positive targets. They produce best practice recommendations for positive interventions and show how the HERO model (consisting of healthy organizational resources and practices, healthy employees, and healthy organizational outcomes) provides organizations a useful framework for talking about and acting on the issue of health and well-being.

Von Thiele and Hasson apply the concept of vertical, horizontal, and diagonal alignment to organizational health, interventions, and research. They provide what we could also call a single principle of harmony to guide our discourse on the organization (e.g., Are company goals aligned with the employees competencies?) and on the intervention and its research (e.g., Is the program design aligned with the company's strategy?).

Ipsen and Andersen present a systemic view of organizations as being capable of self-optimization and discuss nine principles of primary interventions. They emphasize, among other things, making tacit knowledge explicit in rooms for reflection and discussion – stimulated by "bricoleurs" – in order to build organizational capabilities to see, talk, and act continuously on the topic of work and health. They outline this approach with three phases and five steps in knowledge intensive companies.

Pelikan, Dietscher, and Schmied pinpoint the terminology of health, health promotion and salutogenesis, and combine it with systems theory according to Luhmann, quality management, and Mintzberg's theory of professional bureaucracies. They apply these schools of thoughts to hospitals, provide an overview of patient, staff and community targeted change strategies, and reflect upon corresponding research as meta-meta activity in organizations.

Jenny and Bauer combine a generic health development model with a management model. The emerging organizational health development (OHD) model is devised as a frame of reference for organizations, consultants, and researchers collaborating in targeted health-optimization projects. The model not only serves as common mind map but is also thought to support systemic thinking and the organization's own ability to reflect and act upon issues related to work and health.

Concepts of Organizational Health Interventions and Change

Mackay and Palferman show how the Management Standards approach is evolving, reflecting many lessons learned from implementation processes (such as the need for management competency or the traps within indicator tools). They also embrace the perspective of a population approach to organizational health.

Hasson and Villaume introduce a web-based assessment tool (HealthWatch), presenting the three target groups (employees, managers, management/HR) and five principles of logic (time efficiency, proactive-reactive, user-driven, monitoring trends, self-help) behind their approach to strengthen healthy organizations. They show how to implement this assessment tool to promote adherence and ultimately long-term sustainability.

Karanika-Murray and Biron characterize the dynamics of change and place targeted organizational health interventions in this setting. They propose amongst others issues to be borne in mind when thinking about health-oriented change and present social mechanisms relevant to change that are of interest to all who use multilevel methods and team-oriented interventions.

Randall examines the important issue of process evaluation, offering six themes to be monitored before and during interventions with a process and context evaluation dashboard. These themes are participation, appraisal, and exposure (with regard to the process of implementation), and organizational resources, psychological resources, and facilitating and obstructing elements (with regard to the context of implementation).

Intervention and Change Concepts Guiding Theory-Driven Interventions

Pedersen and Nielsen present a theory of integrative safety management that complements a bottom-up behavior-based approach with a top-down culture-based approach to change. They contrast the two approaches and show how they operationalized and implemented them by paralleling participatory problem-solving workshops with manager coaching in a multitude of companies.

Milch, Vaag, Giaever, and Saksvik reflect on truly resource-oriented approaches – called "countervailing interventions" – and present a project on spurring positive emotional experiences through music and culture. Their discussion adds to this by reflecting on the causal logics and critical side effects of this kind of interventions, also taking into account that such practices are already quite prevalent but not really researched in the field.

Henning, Reeves, and the CPH-NEW Research Team integrate Antonovsky's postulates into their Participatory Ergonomics × Health Promotion (PE×HP) approach, and provide a look at the growth and development of the PE×HP program in the field. Central to their approach are design teams, which are in dynamic interplay with a steering committee and the program facilitator, all of which are guided by the seven steps of the Intervention Design and Analysis Scorecard (IDEAS).

Nielsen, Stage, Simonson, and Brauer contribute a five-phase participatory intervention approach (PIOP) rooted in the field. They show how employees as active agents craft not only their work environment but also the intervention process, which is thoroughly built up in an intensive initiation phase and continues with two tailored instruments for analysis. They illustrate the building-up of intervention-craftmanship and ownership, leading to the planning and implementation of measures targeted at the individual, group, leader and/or organizational (IGLO) level.

Acknowledgements We thank Annemarie Fridrich, Ph.D. student, Division of Public and Organizational Health, for her valuable support of the editing process.

References

Bakker, A. B., & Demerouti, E. (2007). The job demands-resources model: State of the art. *Journal of Managerial Psychology, 22*, 309–328.

Bauer, G. F., & Jenny, G. J. (2012). Moving towards positive organisational health: Challenges and a proposal for a research model of organisational health development. In J. Houdmont, S. Leka, & R. Sinclair (Eds.), *Occupational health psychology: European perspectives on research, education and practice* (pp. 126–145). Oxford: Wiley-Blackwell.

Bauer, G. F., Davies, J. K., & Pelikan, J. (2006). The EUHPID health development model for the classification of public health indicators. *Health Promotion International, 21*(2), 153–159. doi:10.1093/heapro/dak002.

Blanchflower, D. G., & Oswald, A. J. (2011). International happiness: A new view on the measure of performance. *Academy of Management Perspectives, 25*(1), 6–22.

Brauchli, R., Jenny, G. J., Füllemann, D., & Bauer, G. F. (2012). Developing an expanded job demands-resources model predicting negative and positive health. Manuscript in progress.

Burrel, G., & Morgan, G. (1979). *Sociological paradigms and organisational analysis: Elements of the sociology of corporate life*. London: Heinemann.

Cox, T., Karanika, M., Griffiths, A., & Houdmont, J. (2007). Evaluating organizational-level work stress interventions: Beyond traditional methods. *Work and Stress, 21*(4), 348–362.

Deetz, S. (1996). Crossroads-describing differences in approaches to organization science: Rethinking Burrell and Morgan and their legacy. *Organization Science, 7*(2), 191–207. doi:10.1287/Orsc.7.2.191.

Delery, J. E., & Doty, D. H. (1996). Modes of theorizing in strategic human resource management: Tests of universalistic, contingency, and configurational performance predictions. *The Academy of Management Journal, 39*(4), 802–835.

Elias, N. (1939). *Über den Prozess der Zivilisation. Soziogenetische und psychogenetische Untersuchungen* [The civilizing process]. Basel: Haus zum Falken.

Faltermaier, T. (2005). *Gesundheitspsychologie* [Health psychology]. Stuttgart: Kohlhammer Urban.

Hassard, J. (1991). Multiple paradigms and organizational analysis – A case-study. *Organization Studies, 12*(2), 275–299. doi:10.1177/017084069101200206.

Keyes, C. L. M. (2007). Promoting and protecting mental health as flourishing: A complementary strategy for improving national mental health. *The American Psychologist, 62*(2), 95–108. doi:10.1037/0003-066x.62.2.95.

Randall, R., Griffiths, A., & Cox, T. (2005). Evaluating organizational stress-management interventions using adapted study designs. *European Journal of Work and Organizational Psychology, 14*(1), 23–41.

World Health Organization. (1998). *Health promotion glossary*. Geneva: WHO.

Part I
Concepts of Organizational Health

Chapter 2
Psychosocial Interventions and Salutogenic Organizations: Systematic Review Evidence of Theory, Context, Implementation and Outcome

Matt Egan

Abstract This chapter explores and synthesizes systematic review evidence of the effectiveness of psychosocial interventions in workplace settings, along with broader issues of theory, implementation and context. Evidence from reviews demonstrate that theoretical and empirical research into psychosocial interventions has tended to focus on workplaces, rather than other types or organization or population settings. Furthermore, most of the research evaluates individual-level interventions, despite the fact that organizational-level interventions are arguably preferable as preventative measures. The reviews identified relatively little evidence relating to implementation and contextual factors that may influence the outcomes of organizational interventions. They also illustrate how the research community has generally failed to rise to the challenge of ensuring that social interventions likely to have an impact on health should also be evaluated in terms of their impacts on health inequalities. However, the chapter demonstrates that useful findings can be derived from flawed evidence, and that there is evidence to suggest organizational-level interventions can improve health through psychosocial pathways. This supports the case for recommending that more interventions of this kind should be implemented on both a local and macro scale as health improving measures. Evaluators should use new interventions as opportunities to learn more about implementation, context and the social patterning of health impacts.

Keywords Workplace health • Systematic review • Psychosocial

M. Egan (✉)
MRC/CSO Social and Public Health Sciences Unit, University of Glasgow, UK
e-mail: matthew.egan@glasgow.ac.uk

G.F. Bauer and G.J. Jenny (eds.), *Salutogenic Organizations and Change:* 19
The Concepts Behind Organizational Health Intervention Research,
DOI 10.1007/978-94-007-6470-5_2, © Springer Science+Business Media Dordrecht 2013

Introduction

The term 'psychosocial' describes an intermediary level that bridges individual psychology and social structures (Martikainen et al. 2002). This 'meso-level' helps us conceptualize how social environments influence the way we feel. Psychosocial theories have been particularly prominent in the study of organizational health (Marmot et al. 2006). In fact, organizational psychology was a notable early influence on this subject area, particularly following the work of Karasek and Theorell (1990) and others who have explored psychosocial characteristics such as demands, control, and social support within organizational settings (Johnson and Hall 1988; Siegrist 1996). Salutogenic theories have also been associated with this area of research since their early focus on the personal resources and sense of coherence that, it is hypothesized, help people cope with psychosocial stressors (Antonovsky 1979).

Some doubt has been cast on the strength of evidence supporting theorized psychosocial pathways to health, and on the usefulness of such theories in the development of effective strategies for achieving public health goals (Macleod and Davey Smith 2003a). Evaluations of interventions may provide evidence to test both the validity and utility of theories underpinning psychosocial epidemiology. Indeed, evaluations have been described as "the bullet that psychosocial epidemiology has to bite" to demonstrate its worth (Macleod and Davey Smith 2003b, p. 556).

The question of how best to operationalize psychosocial theories as interventions has been a key issue in this field. In terms of broad strategy, researchers and practitioners have considered the relative merits of aiming interventions at either 'improving' organizational structures and practices, or individual behaviors and coping mechanisms. Karasek (1992) argued the case for organizational-level interventions, justifying this preference on the grounds that it focused more squarely on prevention by attempting to create health enhancing psychosocial environments. In contrast, individual-level interventions have been criticized for relying on people learning how to better cope with environments that could continue to be inherently harmful.

This argument fits readily within public health agendas that prioritize prevention over cure. In a review of interventions designed to improve psychosocial factors for (mainly) patient populations, Glass (2000) concluded that researchers should move beyond evaluating individually focused health service interventions and begin to evaluate attempts to modify social determinants of population health and health inequalities.

Since Glass made his comments there has been an increasing interest in outcome evaluations that aim to assess the health impacts of organizational-level change (Bambra et al. 2010). There also exists a body of theoretical and empirical research that addresses other key issues such as identifying which specific psychosocial characteristics affect health; the kinds of interventions that can plausibly modify those characteristics; and the contextual factors that diminish or enhance the prospects of effective intervention (Egan et al. 2008, 2009).

In response to this growing body of research literature, there has also been a number of systematic reviews that attempt to comprehensively scope out and synthesize different types of evidence on organizational-level psychosocial interventions. Systematic reviews are widely advocated as a robust tool for identifying and synthesizing evidence of interventions affecting health and health inequalities (Wanless 2004). This chapter will explore and synthesize the systematic review evidence of effectiveness of organizational-level psychosocial interventions, along with broader issues of theory, implementation and context.

Defining Organizational Health from a Psychosocial Perspective

Box 2.1 presents some definitions of psychosocial terms, as they have been used in this chapter, and defines a healthy organization from a psychosocial perspective. A healthy organizational environment is assumed here to be characterized by psychosocial factors that are conducive, rather than harmful, to health (Martikainen et al. 2002). Exposure to this positive environment should ideally benefit all those included within the organization. There is a need to reverse a tendency, described in numerous studies, in which differential exposures to beneficial psychosocial environments occur within and between organizational settings to create a social gradient in which lower status groups experience relatively less salutogenic and relatively more harmful psychosocial exposures than higher status groups (Marmot et al. 2006).

The difficulty lies in moving from these general principals to a point where we can describe in detail the psychosocial characteristics that make an organizational environment 'healthy.' To do this, a number of key issues must be resolved. We need to identify which environmental characteristics are 'psychosocial,' which are beneficial or harmful, and which can be modified effectively to make organizations healthier.

None of these issues are simple. Before we categorize psychosocial factors as either salutogenic or harmful it would be helpful to have a reasonably tight definition of what is meant by 'psychosocial' and a list of factors that can be linked to the term. There is also the possibility that the relative harm or benefits of a particular psychosocial factor may be context dependent: for example, influenced by organizational type and/or by the characteristics of people exposed to a particular environment. Even the definition of what constitutes a positive health outcome is open to debate in a health field that still disputes the validity of including positive wellbeing as a health outcome, or of assuming that it amounts to anything more than the absence of ill health (Keyes 2002; Saracci 1997).

The identification of interventions that can successfully modify organizational environments is similarly challenging. Complex social interventions, of which organizational-level improvements are an example, are widely considered to be difficult to evaluate and this has doubtless hindered research activity in this field (Craig et al. 2008). 'Difficult' in this context can mean resource intensive, requiring methodological compromises, multiple stakeholder engagement, and the challenge of studying a changing environment over which the researcher has limited control or no control (Egan et al. 2010). Whilst there has certainly been pioneering work on

Box 2.1 Definitions

The definitions below summarize how the author has used psychosocial terminology in this article. It should be noted that there is a general lack of consensus in the literature about how these concepts should be defined.

Psychosocial: a 'meso-level' concept that bridges individual psychology and social structures to describe how social environments influence the way we feel.

Psychosocial environment: if *environment* refers to the circumstances or conditions that surround people, then the *psychosocial environment* refers more specifically to the circumstances or conditions that interact with the individual psychological characteristics of exposed populations. Organizational and social structures are presumed to be of particular relevance to the psychosocial environment.

Psychosocial factors/characteristics: specific characteristics of the psychosocial environment considered to be particularly likely to interact with individual psychology and influence how people feel. Commonly cited psychosocial factors include control, autonomy, demands, social support, etc.

Psychosocial pathways: this refers to hypothesized causal relationships by which psychosocial factors are assumed to influence the way people feel through a direct effect on their individual psychological characteristics (rather than an indirect effect mediated by more instrumental or material mechanisms).

Psychosocial interventions: an attempt to modify characteristics of the psychosocial environments or modify the way people respond to their psychosocial environment. Psychosocial interventions are often implemented with the aim of improving health and/or wellbeing.

Healthy organizational environments (from a psychosocial perspective): Such environments are characterized by organizational and social structures that promote health and wellbeing through psychosocial pathways. Psychosocial factors that are likely to be health promoting are encouraged, whilst psychosocial factors associated with health risks are limited. To avoid inequalities, exposure to this positive environment should benefit all those included within the organization.

complex intervention evaluation, systematic reviews of such research continue to struggle to find robust evidence of effectiveness (Bambra et al. 2010).

The barriers to producing evidence of 'what works?' in organizational-level health also make it difficult to address the broader set of questions commonly asked by evaluators of 'what works, for whom and in what context?' (Pawson and Tilley 1997). If we lack robust evidence of intervention effectiveness then we necessarily lack robust findings that can show whether an intervention is more or less effective for a particular sub-group, or whether contextual factors act as barriers or facilitators to effectiveness. Furthermore, even when evidence of health impacts is available at the organizational level, evaluators will still face the problem of how to explore impacts on smaller sub-populations within the organization (Craig et al. 2008). Sub-group analysis helps us establish whether or not intervention effects are socially patterned but often it involves working with relatively small samples that may underpower the analysis. This in turn makes it difficult to produce conclusive findings on the extent to which interventions narrow or widen social inequalities.

These, and doubtless other, difficulties help us explain a somewhat contradictory situation: that is, organizational-level psychosocial interventions have been recommended by numerous authoritative commentators across scientific disciplines but research into this field has until recently been sparse. Nonetheless, interest in this field has developed to the extent that it is now possible to identify a range of systematic reviews covering different areas of relevance. This in turn allows us to scope out the current state of knowledge at the level of systematic review.

Aims

This chapter draws on published and unpublished reviews to discuss how 'psychosocial interventions' have been conceptualized, identified, implemented and evaluated. It will demonstrate that theoretical and empirical research into psychosocial interventions has tended to focus on workplaces, rather than other types or organizational or population settings (e.g. schools, communities) and will discuss some implications of this research focus. The chapter will then present a narrative synthesis of findings across several systematic reviews to build a more comprehensive picture of the types of interventions, contexts (macro and micro) and implementation characteristics that can facilitate or hinder the development of more salutogenic organizations. It will summarize evidence of the effectiveness of interventions and the degree to which this evidence considers the social patterning of effects.

Whilst this chapter focuses on psychosocial theories, it is important to remember that there are alternative pathways by which organizations can affect health. These may include material, behavioral and physical mechanisms (Macleod and Davey Smith 2003a). These alternative pathways can operate in addition to psychosocial mechanisms so they do not need to be treated as mutually exclusive rival theories. However, there is a clear need for research to shed more light on the relative importance of these alternative theories in terms of their ability to explain intervention effectiveness and health outcomes. This is one issue, and perhaps the most important one, that this chapter does not explore. The chapter will, however, provide what I believe to be the most comprehensive account currently available of how our understanding of psychosocial organizational health has been developed and synthesized at the level of systematic review.

Psychosocial Theory and Definitions

Identifying 'Psychosocial Factors'

Whilst the psychosocial research literature is rich in theoretical discussions, there remains some contention regarding how the term 'psychosocial' is defined and used. The distinction between 'psychosocial' and 'psychological' has been a particular problem, as commentators have identified numerous examples where there is no obvious difference in the way these two terms have been applied (Egan et al. 2008). Furthermore, psychosocial exposures do not necessarily affect health purely by psychosocial pathways. For example, social support is often assumed to be a 'psychosocial factor' but it can lead to instrumental and material benefits as well as emotional support from friends and family. It has been argued that only the latter path should qualify as a 'psychosocial pathway' (Egan et al. 2008; Martikainen et al. 2002).

There is, therefore, a lack of consistency in the usage of psychosocial terminology and the available definitions can involve rather subtle distinctions. To some extent, different conceptualizations of 'psychosocial' may also reflect the variety of research traditions and subject areas from which researchers have come to take an interest in this field.

For example, research into work and health tends be framed around two well-known theoretical models of the workplace psychosocial environment: the 'demand control support model' (Johnson and Hall 1988; Karasek and Theorell 1990) and the 'effort-reward imbalance model' (Siegrist 1996; Tsutsumi and Kawakami 2004).

However, an alternative research trajectory to that of workplace health emanates from Putnam's (2001) work on social capital, which he defines as features of social organizations, such as networks, norms, and trust, that facilitate action and co-operation for mutual benefit. Social capital theory hypothesizes that strong social interactions between residents of a neighborhood can lead to mutual support systems and increased empowerment. These in turn can lead to more salutogenic environments that may benefit exposed populations through emotional, practical and financial pathways.

Since medical sociologists and epidemiologists became increasingly interested in psychosocial and social capital theories, these ideas have been integrated into broader theories relating to public health. For example, Siegrist and Marmot have emphasized the importance of self-efficacy and self-esteem when they defined the psychosocial environment as the sociostructural range of opportunities that is available to an individual person to meet his or her needs of well being, productivity and positive self-experience (Siegrist and Marmot 2004). Stafford et al.'s work on social cohesion considers a number of different dimensions drawing from both psychosocial and social capital theories (Stafford and McCarthy 2006).

As part of a recent review of psychosocial factors in neighborhood and community settings (Egan et al. 2008), an attempt was made to identify various types of neighborhood characteristics that have been described as 'psychosocial.' Seven main themes were identified, each of which could be further divided to include a range of more specific psychosocial factors. Some of those factors are theorized to be resources that have a positive relationship with wellbeing (e.g. autonomy and control), while others are treated as risk factors with an inverse relationship to well-being (e.g. demands and role conflict). The main themes were:

(a) autonomy and control,
(b) involvement, participation and empowerment,
(c) social capital, social cohesion, trust and belonging,
(d) social support (including specific types of support: e.g. emotional), social networks and receiving positive feedback
(e) social diversity and tolerance,
(f) vulnerability, security or safety, and
(g) demands, role conflicts or role imbalance.

The review concluded that most of the identified evidence of psychosocial risk factors in neighborhood and community settings related to social support and net-works. In comparison, there was relatively little evidence identified on the other types of risk factor. This provides a notable contrast with the literature on workplace health, in which control is often posited as the factor with the strongest health asso-ciations (Marmot et al. 2006). Furthermore, we lack overarching models to describe how items from the broader list of psychosocial factors included in the seven themes listed above might interact with one another to affect health. Again, this contrasts with workplace theoretical models (van Vegchel et al. 2005). For example, the effort-reward imbalance model posits that adverse health consequences at work result from an unfavorable interaction whereby employees feel that their jobs involve both a high degree of effort and relatively low rewards (Siegrist 1996).

Identifying 'Psychosocial Interventions'

As there is no single agreed definition of what is meant by 'psychosocial', it follows that we also lack a consistent definition of what a 'psychosocial intervention' might be. A scoping exercise was conducted in 2006 by the author of this chapter and col-leagues to identify the different types of psychosocial interventions identified from systematic reviews of community interventions. The reviewers focused on commu-nity rather than health service interventions and categorized studies identified from the reviews by setting, whether they referred to a specific psychosocial theory or model, and whether the interventions were delivered at the individual- or setting-level (i.e. at the level of a workplace, school etc).

Twenty-six relevant reviews were identified from the search. Only 11 of these defined or referred to any theory describing what was meant by 'psychosocial'. Most of those that did had workplace settings (n = 7) and the most commonly cited psychosocial theory was the demand control support model.

From the 26 reviews, a total of 598 included studies were identified as being evaluations of psychosocial interventions. Most of the interventions (80 %) could be

Table 2.1 Findings from a scoping review of 'psychosocial interventions'

Level of intervention	Settings			
	Workplace	School/college	Home/community	All settings
Individual	151	184	146	481
Setting	61	0	0	61
Both[a]	42	0	14	56
All studies	254	184	160	598

[a]Both = individual and setting level interventions

described as individual-level health promotion initiatives that involved psychosocial skills training in issues such as stress management, communication, self-efficacy, empowerment, social support and (in the case of risky behavior interventions) resisting the negative influence of peers. Research into these types of intervention was found to be relatively evenly spread between workplace, educational and home/community settings (see Table 2.1).

In contrast, only 10 % of the 598 identified studies were setting-level interventions and all of these focused on organizational workplace change. Some of these interventions were developed explicitly to achieve psychosocial improvements. Most typically, these involved the creation of new workplace structures such as committees that enabled employees to participate more in decision-making affecting their working environment. In other cases the improved psychosocial factors appeared to be of secondary or no importance to the managers who implemented the changes, but had nonetheless been hypothesized by researchers to potentially affect health through psychosocial pathways. A further 9 % of studies included interventions with both individual and setting level dimensions and again most of these were set in the workplace.

In summary, this scoping of the literature provides evidence of a research bias favoring psychosocial interventions delivered at the individual-level over attempts to improve the health of populations through socio-environmental modification. Workplace health research has led the way in the development of evaluations that counter this trend. However, even amongst the workplace studies, the research focus still appears to prioritize individual-level interventions. This is despite the fact that some of the leading researchers in this field have expressed a clear preference for interventions that attempt to improve organizational structures and environments (Glass 2000; Karasek 1992; Karasek and Theorell 1990). This contrast between the kinds of interventions researchers advocate and the kinds of interventions researchers evaluate is clearly an anomaly that should be redressed.

Outcomes from Organizational-Level Psychosocial Interventions

Although the number of studies evaluating organizational-level interventions is small, relative to other types of intervention, the evidence base is still sufficient to be the topic of several systematic reviews that focus on workplace health. In 2009,

Bambra et al. synthesized evidence from systematic reviews on the health effects of organizational changes to the psychosocial work environment (Bambra et al. 2009). Seven reviews were identified. Most of the studies included in these reviews evaluated modifications to the way in which specific workplaces were managed and so can be described as examples of local interventions. However, two of the reviews focused on interventions that originated from economic policy and government legislation, and in this sense can be described as resulting from macro-level decision-making.

Two reviews identified by Bambra et al. examined the health effects of interventions that increased employee participation in workplace decision-making (Aust and Ducki 2004; Egan et al. 2007a). The first of these focused on employee health circles, a form of staff discussion group that aims to improve potentially harmful working conditions (Aust and Ducki 2004). The review found mixed results, with one controlled study reporting an increase in sickness absence whilst four uncontrolled studies reported improvements in psychosocial factors. The second review included any kind of workplace intervention that aimed to increase employee control or participation, providing the study measured changes to both psychosocial factors and health outcomes (so that hypothesized psychosocial pathways to health could be explored) (Egan et al. 2007a). This review found that interventions that increased employee control had a consistent and positive impact on self-reported health. There was less consistent evidence that changes in social support or workplace demands were related to health outcomes in ways suggested by the demand control support model.

Another review also focused on psychosocial pathways to health, this time by examining the health effects of task restructuring interventions such as increasing task variety, modifying team working structures and the creation of autonomous working groups (Bambra et al. 2007). The review found that few of the interventions altered any measured characteristic of the psychosocial work environment significantly. However, those that increased demand and decreased control tended to have an adverse effect on mental health, while those that decreased demand and increased control resulted in improved health, although some effects were minimal.

Two reviews examined the health impacts of changes to working shift schedules. One looked at the effects of the Compressed Working Week on the health and work-life balance of shift workers (e.g. changing from an 8 h, 5 day week to a 12 or 10 h, 4 day week) (Bambra et al. 2008b). The other review scoped out a broader range of approaches to changing shift work schedules (Bambra et al. 2008a). Whilst the health effects of introducing Compressed Working Weeks were found to be inconclusive, the review did identify some evidence of psychosocial benefits around improved work-life balance. The second review found evidence that changing from slow to fast shift rotation; from backward to forward shift rotation; and introducing self-scheduling of shifts could benefit health (particularly mental health) and work-life balance.

Outcomes from Macro-/National Psychosocial Interventions

Research is necessarily selective, in that some topics become the focus of more research activity than others. However some commentators have observed that research selectivity appears to follow the pattern of an "inverse evidence law," whereby we know least about the effects of those interventions most likely to influence the largest populations (Ogilvie et al. 2005). Research into workplace health demonstrates this 'law.' There are more evaluations of interventions aimed at individual rather than organizational change. Furthermore, the organizational interventions are likely to be local initiatives rather than the result of national or regional policies or programs.

Hence, systematic reviews have identified relatively little evidence on the effects of broader economic, legal and political interventions that may affect workplace psychosocial environments. A review did focus on one type of macro-level intervention that became a feature of late twentieth and early twenty-first century politics: namely, privatization. The review identified 11 studies of the effects on psychosocial factors, general health, health inequalities, and injury rates of privatization of public utilities and industries (Egan et al. 2007b). Most of these focused on injury data and/or were of low methodological quality. However, one higher quality study suggested that the job insecurity and unemployment resulting from privatization had an adverse impact on psychosocial and health outcomes. A second review found some evidence that increased enforcement of health and safety legislation was associated with a decrease in injury rates, but little to suggest that benefits occurred directly through psychosocial pathways (Rivara and Thompson 2000).

In addition to these published reviews identified by Bambra and colleagues in 2009 (Bambra et al. 2009), the author of this chapter conducted an initial scope for a proposed systematic review on the health impacts of government subsidies to businesses in 2003. However, the search failed to identify relevant studies despite an extremely broad inclusion criteria and a multi-disciplinary electronic search of over 10,000 titles and abstracts across 15 databases. The contrast between the potential impacts and political importance of macro interventions on the one hand, and the paucity of evidence available to inform decision-making on the other is striking.

Research on Implementation and Context

The case has been made for providing detailed and robust accounts of the implementation of effective interventions (Armstrong et al. 2008). Implementation is not a new concern: for example clinical trials for medical health technologies such as drugs and other treatments have traditionally devoted attention to the questions of how to deliver interventions safely and in a form that best encourages practitioner and patient adherence to guidelines (Dusenbury et al. 2003).

More recently, methodologists interested in evaluations of complex interventions have stressed the importance of describing and promoting effective implementation (Craig et al. 2008). As complex interventions are likely to vary depending on local circumstances, there is a need to keep track of how particular interventions are rolled out. Doing so can help us answer the fundamental, but sometimes elusive, question of what exactly is it that we are evaluating? It can also aid replicability either of the whole intervention or, in more complex circumstances, of specific features of interventions judged to be transferable to new contexts (Pawson and Tilley 1997). In addition, the way an intervention is implemented may influence its outcomes. Evaluations that fail to take this into account cannot distinguish negative outcomes that result from poor implementation (implementation failure) from interventions that are inherently ineffective (theory failure) (Dobson and Cook 1980).

In response to these issues, four of the systematic reviews described in the previous section included an appraisal of issues relating to planning and implementation (Bambra et al. 2007, 2008a, b; Egan et al. 2007a). The reviewers, who included the author of the current chapter, developed a checklist that covered intervention planning; aims; underlying theory; macro and local contexts; personnel; consultations and collaborations at the planning and delivery stages; management and employee support for the intervention; resources; and demographic characteristics of the workforce (focusing on sub-groups differentially exposed to and affected by the intervention).

This list of factors is broad and clearly extends beyond what might strictly be considered to be 'implementation' to include issues related to planning, theory, context and differential impacts. Like other types of literature appraisal, the process was highly dependent on the quality of reporting. In fact it was arguably the reporting rather than the actual implementation that was really being appraised, on the assumption that good reporting was a precondition to being able to assess whether implementation was problematic or not (Egan et al. 2009).

Despite the checklists' breadth of scope, the reviewers identified relatively little information from any of the studies to populate it. Only the aims and motivations of deliverers, and whether or not there was employee support for the interventions, received any sort of mention from over half the studies identified across the four reviews. Reporting of the other characteristics on the checklist was rare. Furthermore, such reports tended to take the form of brief anecdotes of uncertain origin or credibility. Hence, the reviewers often found it difficult to determine (a) what exactly the intervention entailed; (b) whether the intervention was implemented fully or adhered to good practice guidelines; and (c) whether there were confounding factors in the wider social context that would affect the outcome of the intervention (Egan et al. 2009). Until researchers' reporting of these issues improves substantially, a checklist approach to implementation appraisal is likely to yield unsatisfactory results.

Furthermore, the reviewers became concerned that developing an a priori list of important implementation and context issues might not be the most effective way of appraising complex interventions that are, by definition, likely to experience unexpected and idiosyncratic developments when rolled out. In response to this concern, we also carried out a more inductive assessment of implementation and context issues based on a careful reading of the included studies, conducted independently by two reviewers.

It was this inductive approach that yielded the most useful information on implementation and context, albeit from a relatively small number of included studies. For example, in the participation review we found that the only two interventions with negative health outcomes had both been implemented in the context of workplaces undergoing organizational downsizing (Egan et al. 2007a). We found that in the "task structure" review, negative health outcomes were more likely to result from interventions that were motivated for business reasons (managerial efficiency, productivity, cost etc) rather than by employee health concerns (Bambra et al. 2007). However the studies identified for the compressed working week and the shift work reviews provide evidence of both positive, negative or 'little change' outcomes resulting from interventions regardless of whether they were motivated by business concerns, health concerns or pressure from employees (Bambra et al. 2008a, b). Again, these issues were usually described anecdotally within the studies, yet they often provided the most plausible explanations for negative outcomes available to reviewers.

(In)Equalities – What Works for Whom?

For many researchers, policy-makers and practitioners involved in public health, the reduction of social inequalities in health is the number one priority (Marmot et al. 2010). Unfortunately, as an extension to the inverse evidence law, it appears that that the political importance attached to a public health issue is inversely related to the quantity and quality of evidence on that issue. At least this seems to be the case for evidence on the social patterning of health impacts that result from organizational level interventions.

Bambra et al.'s 2009 synthesis of evidence from workplace reviews specifically aimed to identify evidence that could potentially inform strategies to reduce health inequalities (Bambra et al. 2009). The authors concluded that "disappointingly, very few relevant reviews have been conducted". Similarly, there appear to be relatively few primary studies that address this issue. In one review (Egan et al. 2007a), a single uncontrolled study of a participatory intervention found improvements in terms of mental health outcomes among manual workers but not managers or clerical employees. In the review of task restructuring (Bambra et al. 2007), an uncontrolled study found that a team-working intervention adversely affected the health of employees from the lowest grade, but not those from higher grades. The review of privatization also identified a single study that provided weak evidence of privatization leading to occupational stress among clerical and administrative staff, but not among manual workers or managers (Egan et al. 2007b). The other reviews identified relatively little evidence no evidence of differential effects that could be plausibly linked to psychosocial pathways (Bambra et al. 2009).

So at the systematic review level, the phrase 'absence of evidence' largely sums up the current state of knowledge regarding aims to reduce inequalities by modifying psychosocial environments at work. This should not, of course, be confused with evidence of absence of effect. In fact, those few studies described above that did seek out evidence of differential health impacts did indeed find such evidence. This suggests that future studies should explore this issue further, as a matter of urgency.

Discussion

Strengths and Limitations

In this chapter, a series of systematic reviews have been synthesized to map out various issues relevant to the development of healthier organizations through psychosocial interventions. Our decision to focus on reviews makes the task of synthesizing such a broad subject area more manageable. Systematic reviews also have advantages of transparency and comprehensiveness, although both of these qualities remain ideals to strive for rather than wholly achievable aims.

There are a number of limitations inherent to this chapter's approach. For example, publication bias may affect the findings on a number of levels. Most of the included reviews were published within the last 5 years but many of the literature searches were conducted earlier than that and therefore have not included recent primary research. In addition, if publishers favor articles that report positive findings (as is commonly believed), the publication of literature reviews and the publication of primary studies included in those literature reviews may reflect this positive bias. We have also been reliant on the authors of reviews to accurately report findings and other relevant information from the studies they have synthesized, just as those reviewers were themselves reliant upon the authors of primary studies maintaining high standards of reporting. We know that for some issues (e.g. implementation and context), reporting was often poor. Some of the findings also need to be framed within a wider discussion about the problems of using systematic reviews to inform decision makers about issues that have been poorly researched.

Key Messages

None the less, there is a case to be made that even flawed studies and flawed reviews can provide information that is potentially useful. This is particularly the case in poorly researched fields where the choice is between the best available evidence, which may be of variable quality, or offering no evidence at all to guide decision-making (Ogilvie et al. 2005). The reviews summarized here do have findings that are potentially useful to research, practitioner and policy audiences.

From a theoretical perspective, this chapter has aimed to progress attempts to build a consensus regarding how the term 'psychosocial' should be conceptualized. In particular, much of the work reported here has been influenced by, and lends support to, the 'meso-level' definition suggested by Martikainen et al. (2002). The chapter categorizes a relatively broad list of psychosocial factors into a number of key themes to help researchers identify which kinds of characteristics might be included in this meso-level. In addition I have suggested a definition of a 'healthy organizational environment' that emphasizes equity of exposure to positive psychosocial characteristics.

The chapter shows that organizational-level psychosocial theories are generally more developed and tend to be translated into practice more in workplaces compared to other types of community setting. However, even in the field of workplace health, there appears to be a research bias towards individual-level interventions. This is despite the fact that organizational-level initiatives are preferred as preventative measures. In line with a pattern predicted by the inverse evidence law, there is also evidence that organizational interventions tend to be evaluated more frequently and more robustly when they are delivered on a local rather than a macro scale.

The health outcomes of organizational modifications appear to be mixed, but findings are often consistent with those predicted by the demand control support model. In particular, improved control has been found to be the psychosocial modification most consistently associated with improved health outcomes, especially mental health. Hence, interventions that encourage greater employee autonomy and participation in decision-making are particularly recommended. The two shift work reviews also identified positive impacts on work-life balance. However, interventions that appeared to have a negative effect on the psychosocial environment (e.g. by decreasing control, increasing demands or creating stress related to job insecurity) were found to be potentially harmful to employee health.

Systematic review level findings on implementation, context and differential impacts were particularly sparse. However, even with these issues the reviews were able to identify some useful messages. Organizational downsizing, lack of management support, and the aim of increasing individual productivity without regard to employee wellbeing were all offered as explanations for negative impacts. Some evidence also indicated that organizational-level workplace interventions may have the potential to reduce health inequalities amongst employees through psychosocial pathways. However these are areas of evidence that urgently require more research.

Conclusion

Findings from these reviews support concerns raised by researchers and policymakers that the literature on public health research is often biased towards what can be measured easily rather than on the immensely more complex issues of the broader social forces that also affect health, directly or indirectly (Beaglehole et al. 2004). They also illustrate how the research community has generally failed to rise to the challenge of ensuring that social and policy interventions likely to have an impact on health are evaluated in terms of impacts on health inequalities (UK Department of Health 1998). However, the reviews do present evidence to suggest that organizational interventions can improve health through psychosocial pathways. We therefore recommend that more interventions of this kind should be implemented on a local and macro scale as health improving measures. Evaluators should use new interventions as opportunities to learn more about implementation, context and the social patterning of health impacts (Box 2.2).

> **Box 2.2 What the Reviews Tell Us About Organizational-Level Psychosocial Interventions**
>
> **Theory**: The dominant theories in this field tend to have emerged from research on workplace health. The demand control support model is the most commonly referred to theory.
>
> **Context**: Most of the interventions described as 'psychosocial' had workplace settings. Detrimental organizational circumstances (e.g. downsizing, efficiency drives) were potential barriers to intervention effectiveness.
>
> **Implementation**: Evidence of effectiveness was particularly consistent amongst interventions that explicitly aimed to improve psychosocial characteristics, especially those that improved control and participation.
>
> **Outcomes**: There is evidence to suggest organizational interventions can improve health, particularly mental health, through psychosocial pathways.
>
> **Inequalities**: The potential for such interventions to reduce health inequalities has not been adequately researched, although the reviews did identify some evidence that health impacts could be socially patterned.

Acknowledgement Hilary Thomson co-reviewed the literature summarized in Table 2.1. Lyndal Bond commented on this chapter.

References

Antonovsky, A. (1979). *Health, stress and coping*. San Francisco: Jossey-Bass Publishers.

Armstrong, R., Waters, E., Moore, L., Riggs, E., Cuervo, L. G., Lumbiganon, P., et al. (2008). Improving the reporting of public health intervention research: Advancing TREND and CONSORT. *Journal of Public Health, 30*, 103–109.

Aust, B., & Ducki, A. (2004). Comprehensive health promotion interventions at the workplace: Experiences with health circles in Germany. *Journal of Occupational Health Psychology, 9*, 258–270.

Bambra, C., Egan, M., Thomas, S., Petticrew, M., & Whitehead, M. (2007). The psychosocial and health effects of workplace reorganisation 2: A systematic review of task restructuring interventions. *Journal of Epidemiology Community Health, 61*, 1028–1037.

Bambra, C., Whitehead, M., Sowden, A., Akers, J., & Petticrew, M. (2008a). Shifting schedules: The health effects of reorganising shift work. *American Journal of Preventive Medicine, 34*, 427–434.

Bambra, C., Whitehead, M., Sowden, A., Akers, J., & Petticrew, M. (2008b). A hard day's night? The effects of compressed work week interventions on the health and wellbeing of shift workers: A systematic review. *Journal of Epidemiology and Community Health, 62*, 764–777.

Bambra, C., Gibson, M., Sowden, A., Wright, K., Whitehead, M., & Petticrew, M. (2009). Working for health? Evidence from systematic reviews on the effects on health and health inequalities of organisational changes to the work environment. *Preventive Medicine, 48*, 454–461.

Bambra, C., Gibson, M., Sowden, A., Wright, K., Whitehead, M., & Petticrew, M. (2010). Tackling the wider social determinants of health and health inequalities: Evidence from systematic reviews. *Journal of Epidemiology and Community Health, 64*, 284–289.

Beaglehole, R., Bonita, R., Horton, R., Adams, O., & McKee, M. (2004). Public health in the new era: Improving health through collective action. *The Lancet, 363*, 2084–2086.

Craig, P., Dieppe, P., Macintyre, S., Michie, S., Nazareth, I., & Petticrew, M. (2008). Developing and evaluating complex interventions: The new Medical Research Council guidance. *British Medical Journal, 337*, a1655.

Dobson, L., & Cook, T. (1980). Avoiding Type III error in program evaluation: Results from a field experiment. *Evaluation and Program Planning, 3*, 269–276.

Dusenbury, L., Brannigan, R., & Falco, M. (2003). A review of research on fidelity of implementation: Implications for drug abuse prevention in school settings. *Health Education Research, 18*, 237–256.

Egan, M., Bambra, C., Thomas, S., Petticrew, M., Whitehead, M., & Thomson, H. (2007a). The psychosocial and health effects of workplace reorganisation 1: A systematic review of organisational-level interventions that aim to increase employee control. *Journal of Epidemiology and Community Health, 61*, 945–954.

Egan, M., Petticrew, M., Ogilvie, D., Hamilton, V., & Drever, F. (2007b). Profits before people? A systematic review of the health and safety impacts of privatising public utilities and industries in developed countries. *Journal of Epidemiology and Community Health, 61*, 862–870.

Egan, M., Tannahill, C., Petticrew, M., & Thomas, S. (2008). Psychosocial risk factors in home and community settings and their associations with population health and health inequalities: A systematic meta-review. *BMC Public Health, 8*, 239.

Egan, M., Bambra, C., Petticrew, M., & Whitehead, M. (2009). Reviewing evidence on complex social interventions: Appraising implementation in systematic reviews of the health effects of organisational-level workplace interventions. *Journal of Epidemiology and Community Health, 63*, 4–11.

Egan, M., Beck, S., Bond, L., Coyle, J., Crawford, F., Kearns, A., et al. (2010). Protocol for a mixed methods study investigating the impact of investment in housing, regeneration and neighbourhood renewal on the health and wellbeing of residents: The GoWell programme. *BMC Medical Research Methodology, 10*, 41.

Glass, T. (2000). Psychosocial intervention. In L. Berkman & I. Kawachi (Eds.), *Social epidemiology* (pp. 267–305). Oxford: Oxford University Press.

Johnson, J., & Hall, E. (1988). Job strain, work place social support, and cardiovascular disease: A cross-sectional study of a random sample of the Swedish working population. *American Journal of Public Health, 78*, 1336–1342.

Karasek, R. (1992). Stress prevention through work reorganisation: A summary of 19 case studies. *Conditions of Work Digest, 11*, 23–42.

Karasek, R., & Theorell, T. (1990). *Healthy work: Stress, productivity and the reconstruction of working life*. New York: Basic Books.

Keyes, C. (2002). The mental health continuum: From languishing to flourishing in life. *Journal of Health and Social Behaviour, 43*, 207–222.

Macleod, J., & Davey Smith, G. (2003a). Psychosocial factors and public health: A suitable case for treatment? *Journal of Epidemiology and Community Health, 57*, 565–570.

Macleod, J., & Davey Smith, G. (2003b). Psychosocial factors and public health: Authors' reply. *Journal of Epidemiology and Community Health, 57*, 553–556.

Marmot, M., Siegrist, J., & Theorell, T. (2006). Health and the psychosocial environment at work. In M. Marmot & R. Wilkinson (Eds.), *Social determinants of health* (2nd ed., pp. 97–130). Oxford: Oxford University Press.

Marmot, M., Allen, J., Goldblatt, P., Boyce, T., McNeish, D., Grady, M., et al. (2010). *Fair society, healthy lives: Strategic review of health inequalities in England post-2010*. London: The Marmot Review.

Martikainen, P., Bartley, M., & Lahelma, E. (2002). Psychosocial determinants of health. *International Journal of Epidemiology, 31*, 1091–1093.

Ogilvie, D., Egan, M., Hamilton, V., & Petticrew, M. (2005). Systematic reviews of health effects of social interventions: 2. Best available evidence: How low should you go? *Journal of Epidemiology and Community Health, 59*, 886–892.

Pawson, R., & Tilley, N. (1997). *Realistic evaluation*. London: Sage.

Putnam, R. D. (2001). *Bowling alone: The collapse and revival of American community*. New York: Touchstone.

Rivara, F., & Thompson, D. (2000). Prevention of falls in the construction industry: Evidence for program effectiveness. *American Journal of Preventive Medicine, 18*(4s), 23–26.

Saracci, R. (1997). The World Health Organization needs to reconsider its definition of health. *British Medical Journal, 314*, 1409–1410.

Siegrist, J. (1996). Adverse health effects of high effort/low-reward conditions. *Journal of Occupational Health Psychology, 1*, 127–141.

Siegrist, J., & Marmot, M. (2004). Health inequalities and the psychosocial environment – Two scientific challenges. *Social Science & Medicine, 58*, 1463–1473.

Stafford, M., & McCarthy, M. (2006). Neighbourhoods, housing and health. In M. Marmot & R. Wilkinson (Eds.), *Social determinants of health* (2nd ed., pp. 297–317). Oxford: Oxford University Press.

Tsutsumi, A., & Kawakami, N. (2004). Review of empirical studies on the model of effort-reward imbalance at work. *Social Science & Medicine, 59*, 2335–2359.

UK Department of Health. (1998). *Independent inquiry into inequalities in health report*. London.

van Vegchel, N., de Jonge, J., & Lansbergis, P. (2005). Occupational stress in (inter)action: The interplay between job demands and job resources. *Journal of Organizational Behaviour, 26*, 535–560.

Wanless, D. (2004). *Securing good health for the whole population: Final report*. London: HM Treasury.

Chapter 3
Organizational Health Intervention Research in Medical Settings

Anthony Montgomery, Karolina Doulougeri, Katerina Georganta, and Efharis Panagopoulou

Abstract Medical settings, especially hospitals, represent a challenging environment in which to conduct organizational health interventions. This is due to the fact that healthcare professionals tend to hold pathogenic rather than salutogenic views about health and well-being. Additionally, healthcare professional identity and sense of coherence is deeply embedded in role behaviors (i.e., I am a doctor) rather than organizational awareness (i.e., The purpose of the hospital is…). Worksite health promotion interventions in medical settings, despite their prominent character, have yielded mixed results regarding their effectiveness. One of the major challenges is to be both theoretically sound and, at the same time, context appropriate. The proposed chapter will; (1) conceptualize what a health medical organization (hospital) should look like, (2) review organizational health interventions in medical settings in terms of theoretical focus and practical outcomes, (3) identify the salutogenic factors that promote well-being, (4) review the cultural and contextual factors that are barriers to interventions, and (5) reflect on how health intervention researchers can address process and context (intervention) issues in medical setting. All medical settings will be reviewed, but special focus will be given to hospitals and the use of action research which has been extensively used in medical settings.

Keywords Medicine • Healthcare professionals • Interventions • Salutogenic

A. Montgomery (✉) • K. Doulougeri • K. Georganta
Department of Educational and Social Policy, University of Macedonia,
Thessaloniki, Greece
e-mail: antmont@uom.gr

E. Panagopoulou
Medical School, Aristotle University of Thessaloniki, Thessaloniki, Greece

G.F. Bauer and G.J. Jenny (eds.), *Salutogenic Organizations and Change:*
The Concepts Behind Organizational Health Intervention Research,
DOI 10.1007/978-94-007-6470-5_3, © Springer Science+Business Media Dordrecht 2013

Relevance of Organizational Health Intervention Research in Medical Settings

Hospitals are organizations under considerable stress. In the UK surveys show that continuity of care for the patient is being compromised (Hawkes 2012). This is not surprising when one considers that healthcare professionals are expected to handle structural changes and technical developments, are required to be accessible, provide holistic patient-centered and patient-managed care, develop their own evidence-based competence and achieve an appropriate balance between their work and private life. Put simply, staff well-being moderates the relationship between organizational health and the quality of health care delivered (Cox and Leiter 1992). However, the majority of interventions target the individual physician with little attention given to the organizational and social context within which the physician is practicing (Dunn et al. 2007). Indeed, this focus on the individual over the organization is consistent with interventions conducted with other professions (Kompier and Kristensen 2001). Karasek, the author of the Job-Demand Control model has argued that organizational interventions are preferable as preventative measures, because they address the causes of unhealthy working environments (Karasek 1992).

The arguments favoring an organizational approach to staff well-being are rooted in the symbiotic way that both healthcare professionals and patients experience the organization. Healthcare organizations are unique in the sense that "bad" physicians/nurses can contribute to medical errors, while "bad" patients can contribute to more burnout among staff, again leading to errors. Without too much effort, the purpose of the organization can become self-preservation and not healing. Additionally, trying to position patients as clients in this system runs the risk of simplifying the way that they become part of the organization (for a specified period). According to Cox and Leiter (1992), the absence of support at the level of primary *task completion* for strongly espoused organizational values may reflect unresolved conflicts regarding policy throughout the organization. For example, patient-centered care may be 'paid significant lip-service' in the organization, but in reality decreasing resources and defensive medicine may be the real drivers of patient care. Differences between espoused values and actual practice are symptoms of serious organizational dysfunction (Argyris 1982). This dysfunction in the medical setting is most evident in the occurrence of job burnout (Montgomery et al. 2011). The link between physician burnout and quality of care is set to become increasingly important in the twenty-first century, as the general trend taking place in most of the industrialized countries is a decrease in organizational resources and an increase in individual demands. The duration and harshness of budgetary constraints and organizational restructuring suffered by the health care sector are exercising a cumulative and heavy burden on the quality of everyday work in health care institutions. Thus, performance improvements and cost reductions will probably not continue to occur, in the long term, without considering provider characteristics and then focusing on topics such as burnout, fatigue, and shared cultural values (Minvielle et al. 2008; Rotondi et al.

2000). Healthcare professionals represent a significant proportion of the workforce in every developed country, and the need to support them will only increase as we go forward into the future. Indeed, in 2008, it was estimated that 70 % of the health budget in Europe was allocated to salaries and employment related costs (Commission of the European Communities 2008).

The Hospital: A Unique Organizational Environment

Organizational culture determines how individuals behave, what people pay attention to, how they respond to different situations, and how they socialize with new members and exclude those who do not fit in (Spataro 2005). The Institute of Medicine (IOM) in the USA has repeatedly highlighted the link between patient safety, physician well-being and organizational culture (Institute of Medicine 1999, 2001). Hospitals represent a unique organizational environment and relatively little systematic research exists with regard to how this unique environment contributes to job burnout and/or quality of care (Montgomery et al. 2011). Hospitals are populated by a range of professionals, both medical and non-medical, and the stressors/strains experienced by healthcare professionals is a combination of patient driven demands and the organizational factors specific to the hospital environment. To date, workplace interventions aimed at physician well-being has focused on the professional role rather than the organizational context. Not surprisingly, progress in the field of what aspects of organizational culture increase performance within healthcare has been slow. There is little consistent and reliable evidence as to what represents the most effective strategies to change organizational culture to improve healthcare performance (Parmelli et al. 2011).

This represents an interesting gap for healthcare professionals globally, but it may have special resonance for developing countries. Van Wyk and Pillay-Van Wyk (2010) note that intervention research is notably missing for low and middle income countries, where there is an acknowledged crisis in human resources for health. Developing countries have problems with retaining or attracting staff. Retention problems are rooted in both indigenous organizational culture problems and attractive alternatives, one feeding into the other. For example, recent research from Romania highlights the way that working and living abroad can become a 'normative' part of one's career trajectory for health care professionals (Spânu et al. 2012). Such phenomena have their roots in organizational culture as a reflection of wider community values. For example, in a comparison of Turkish public and private hospitals, Seren and Baykal (2007) found that healthcare professionals in hospitals dominated by power cultures were less likely to accept change compared to individuals working in collaborative cultures. Not surprisingly, the collaborative culture was more likely to be found in private hospitals, as opposed to public. Equally, Türköz (2004), in a private hospital, found that a positive attitude towards organizational change could be encouraged by participation in quality circles, commission studies and project teams. In studies among Slovenian healthcare professionals, researchers have found that healthcare professionals report low levels of personal involvement in the hospitals where they work, and they tend to view the culture in their hospitals as being stable, having an internal focus and controlling (Skela Savič and Pagon 2008; Skela Savič et al. 2007). Overall, the trend in Europe is towards more privatisation and there is a growing movement towards making hospitals more self-managed and a greater emphasis on attracting patients and improving efficiency, quality, and the responsiveness of services (Busse et al. 2002). It's probably too early to make predictions about the impact on hospitals in developing countries, but already in Greece, private hospitals are increasing their market share compared with public hospitals, mainly because of the perceived shortcomings of the public health care system.

Stress management interventions for healthcare professionals are informed by work stress theories that place particular emphasis on job control/job autonomy, as informed by the Karasek Job-Demands-Control Model (Karasek 1979), and which undervalue the role that the hospital culture can play. Interestingly, in a recent study evaluating work stress among eight hospitals in the European Union, Pisljar et al. (2011) found that both work control and job/time autonomy were not associated with the health of hospital employees. Pisljar et al. (2011) conclude that interventions to prevent work stress must look more closely at interventions that will help all hospital employees cope with their growing workload, longer hours and unsocial schedules. This is in agreement with research that shows that work control reduces the impact of work stress on health only when employees cope actively with work stress (de Jonge and Kompier 1997). Indeed, Egan et al. (2007) in a review of organization-level interventions that aimed specifically to increase employee control found some evidence to support the demand-control-support model, but control did not protect employees from generally poor working conditions. Overall, the review identified 18 studies of which 8 focused on healthcare professionals. Reviewing these 8 studies indicates that improvement in psychological and health outcomes were marginal. According to a review by Michie and Williams (2003), regarding sickness absence among healthcare workers, intervention studies have focused mainly on staff training, to the detriment of employment practices and management style. Finally, a review of the interventions aimed at the reduction of burnout among physicians (McCray et al. 2008) highlights that there is a paucity of evidence on what actually works. All the aforementioned suggests that understanding and preventing job stress among physicians can be aided by looking at the organization (hospital) as a unique point of analysis. For example, the growing literature on disruptions in the operating theatre in hospitals (Rivera-Rodriguez and Karsh 2010) is an added stressor that has the potential to contribute to errors (Sevdalis et al. 2008). Such a stressor is hospital specific, and it would be valuable to have data on interruptions in developing countries. We can speculate that interruptions are probably more intense in environments with close family relationships and more fluid professional boundaries.

Hospitals and medical settings in general, require us to take a more nuanced approach to accounting for their impact upon themselves and the individuals who use the hospital. Well-being intervention research is dominated by scales, which are reliable and valid, but can have little clinical significance. Therefore, we have to recommend to a different approach to comparing organizational health interventions across medical settings.

Adopting a Salutogenic Approach to Medical Settings

Not surprisingly, the pathogenic approach has dominated our approach to health. We have a tendency to focus on disease and illness, which prompts us to think in terms of risk factors and disease amelioration. Such a tendency is even stronger in healthcare professionals, who are continuously reinforced to view health through a pathogenic prism. Antonovsky (1996) has questioned the objective of health promotion as being severely limited, in that it has "exposed the 'bias of the downstream focus', i.e. the devotion of the disease care system to saving swimmers drowning by heroic measures, rather than asking 'Who or what is pushing them into the river in the first place?' (p. 12)". Antonovsky urges researchers to view health on a continuum model, which sees each of us, at a given point in time, somewhere along a 'healthy/disease continuum'.

The basic idea behind his salutogenic approach to health is that we should work towards facilitating health rather than limiting disease. This approach represents an interesting way for us to look at organizations, and healthcare settings in particular. The salutogenic model proposes that the goal of health research should be to identify, define, and describe pathways, factors, and causes of positive health to supplement our knowledge about how to prevent, treat, and manage negative health (pathogenesis) (Antonovsky 1979). Congruently, in the field of organizational psychology, we have amassed considerable data on the causes and consequences of depression, anxiety and stress, without identifying any "magic bullets". Thus, a salutogenic approach can focus our attention on the organizational factors that contribute to engagement with the organization, such as dedication and vigour.

For example, the salutogenic research places great importance on the sense of coherence (SOC), that people experience. Interestingly, SOC is positioned as a dependant variable. SOC as an outcome should prompt us to look at organizational functioning differently. In terms of healthcare professionals, the idea that one's SOC is shaped by three kinds of life experiences: consistency, underload-overload balance, and participation in socially valued decision making, represents a richer approach in comparison with the demand-control-support one. In addition to SOC, generalized resistance resources (GRRs) are positioned as important mechanisms to promoting health among individuals. GRRs can be biological, material and psychosocial factors which make it easier for people to cope and be resilient. Examples of GRRs are money, support, knowledge, experience, intelligence and traditions, and the existence of these resources contribute to SOC. GRRs and SOC are consistent with more recent theories of job stress, such as the Job-Demand-Resources Model (Bakker and Demerouti 2007) that view different kinds of resources as protecting and contributing positively to the motivation of individuals.

Fig. 3.1 Typical organizational chart for a hospital

At a practical level, we can adapt the guidance offered by Antonovsky (1987) for use in an organizational medical setting. He recommended three ways to take a salutogenic approach: (1) look at the data differently: instead of looking at those who have succumbed to a problem to find out why, look at those who are succeeding and try to find out why they are doing well; (2) persuade practitioners and researchers to ask about the factors related to success, not just factors related to problems; and finally (3) stimulate the formation of unique hypotheses generated to explain desired outcomes. Ultimately, it is an approach that emphasizes what works.

Another interesting idea from the saultogenic perspective is Optimization, which refers to the idea that work in health would focus on determining and creating the most favorable conditions and factors responsible for measurable positive outcomes such as high levels of performance (Becker et al. 2010). For example, an important strategic step would be to add the concepts of positive health and salutogenesis to the curriculums and textbooks used to train health professionals (Becker et al. 2010). Inherent in the ideas proposed by Becker et al. (2010) is the idea that if we train healthcare professionals to focus on pathogenic processes and outcomes, then they will understand well-being in this particular way, which has important implications for how they view their organization.

Evidence that the time for a saultogenic approach has come in healthcare is indicated by the title of a WHO/EC report (Wiskow et al. 2010) titled *How to create an attractive and supportive working environment for health professionals*. The fact that words like 'effective', 'cost-efficient' or 'competitive' do not appear in the title is revealing. The authors of the report conclude that an off-the-shelf list of solutions are not possible, however they do recommend that; (1) we focus on process and content issues, and (2) many factors impacting on the work environment of health professionals are beyond the scope of influence of health policy-makers. In other words, we need to view health care settings as organizational settings (process), and their relationship with the other actors in the community needs to be taken into account.

The organizational charts that can be found in the websites of hospitals reveal a good deal about their vision. Typically, the organizational charts are two dimensional and hierarchical (see Fig. 3.1). They convey content and status, but little about process or relationships. Indeed, even the lines that connect the various departments and roles within the organization seem weak and tenuous.

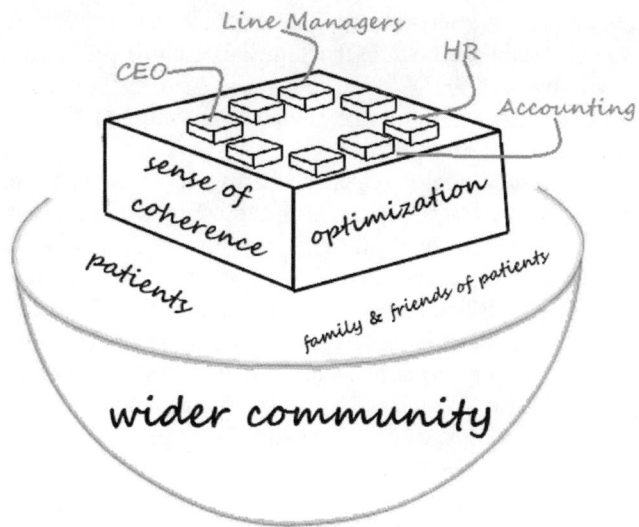

Fig. 3.2   3-D organizational chart for a hospital

Therefore, we would like to propose a more dynamic 3-D model that attempts to capture the essential salutogenic elements that should be found in a healthy medical organization. Figure 3.2 emphasizes the importance of sense of coherence (SOC) and optimization as the appropriate outcomes, and these are embedded in a larger system of patients, families, and the wider community. The different levels of embedding are intended to alert one to the idea that SOC and optimization are contextualized or 'fit' into the prevailing environment. Congruently, one should think of the SOC/optimization cube as being embedded within smaller cubes. Thus, these smaller cubes represent various individuals/departments in the organization that are embedded in the unit. Some of the smaller cubes are empty, indicating that (1) hospital management cannot realistically attend to all the dimensions of a complex organization/entity, and (2) empty cubes equals opportunities and openness to new stakeholders who may (unexpectedly) contribute positively to SOC and/or optimization. The fact that the unit and individuals are represented by cubes and the stakeholders by a semi-circle is intentional and should alert one to the notion that the stakeholders are more fluid but more influential, in that all the other aspects needed to be embedded within them. Our conceptualization is influenced by the ecological systems approach of Bronfenbrener (1979) and the Force-Field Analysis approach of Kurt Lewin (1951).

Interventions in the Medical Setting: What Works?

Many articles identify the causes of decreased well-being among healthcare professionals, and such studies behoove us to develop interventions. Not surprisingly, the number of analytic studies looking at causes far outweighs the number of actual studies evaluating interventions. This imbalance reflects the fact that the problems are well established, while the solutions are difficult to operationalize, evaluate or even imagine.

To date, organizational intervention research has suffered from a number of problems; from a focus on strengthening employees (e.g., skills development) rather than improving work conditions (Cooper and Cartwright 1994), from being directed predominately at individuals and/or small groups (Larsson and Setterlind 1991), and from a paucity of methodological rigor. However, the lack of suitable control-group comparison is complicated for two reasons; firstly, it is difficult to have a strict control group in real life, and secondly, in real life, the effects of an intervention are difficult to distinguish from effects of intervening events.

The studies that have been carried out present a mixed picture. The work of Bunce and West (1996), one of the earliest studies in the field, compared traditional stress management methods with an organizational improvement program for health care professionals. The results indicated that interventions focusing on the process and promoting work quality seemed to increase work productivity and efficiency and to encourage staff to more actively handle the work stressors. However, the study was less successful regarding gains in psychological well-being. Petterson and Arnetz (1998) evaluated the impact of an intervention on Swedish healthcare professionals. The intervention research assessed both wellbeing and performance indicators and each department formulated their own improvement goals. They also made their own decisions on relevant improvement activities. Despite an overall worsening in most of the measures most likely due to a notice of a 20 % staff reduction prior to the follow-up assessment, the intervention appeared to have attenuated negative changes in the high activity group as compared with the low activity group. The study is noteworthy in highlighting the impact of bottom-up approaches to constructing interventions and the lack of dramatic changes in dependant variables.

One of the most exhaustive approaches to developing and evaluating a health intervention can be found in the work of Bourbonnais and his colleagues (Bourbonnais et al. 2006a, b). In two sequential papers, the authors describe the development and implementation of a health intervention. In the first paper (Bourbonnais et al. 2006a), they described the process of developing and implementing a participative health intervention for healthcare workers in an acute hospital. In the second paper (Bourbonnais et al. 2006b), the authors report on the results (after 12 months) of the intervention. There was a reduction of several adverse psychosocial factors in the experimental group, whereas no such reduction was found in the control group. However, there was a significant deterioration of decision latitude and social support from supervisors in both experimental and control groups. More recently, Dunn et al. (2007) developed a program comprising three components: (1) leadership valuing physician well-being equal to quality of care and financial stewardship; (2) physicians identifying factors that influenced well-being, followed by plans for improvement with accountability; and (3) measuring the well-being of physicians regularly using validated instruments. The intervention used in primary care groups resulted in some reductions of emotional and work-related exhaustion.

The aforementioned mixed pictures are borne out by a number of reviews in the area of healthcare staff well-being. For example, Gilbody et al. (2006), in a review of interventions to boost morale among psychiatric staff, found that methodological rigor was weak, while interventions were dominated by educational interventions designed to enhance skill and competency. Moreover, analysis occurred at the level of the individual healthcare worker without accounting for within group clustering. In a recent review of preventive staff-support measures for health care workers, van Wyk and Pillay-Van Wyk (2010) conclude that the majority of studies have serious methodological weaknesses, making it difficult to conclude that interventions have sustainability. Deeper reading of this review highlights the reluctance among researchers to view hospital as an organizational system, in that 8/10 of studies involved stress management training (predominately among nurses) and only one study targeted the healthcare team as a unit (Weir et al. 1997). Additionally, the variability of both the duration and intensity of the interventions strongly suggests that we are in the dark when it comes to knowing how much of an intervention is needed. The dominance of nurses in worksite health intervention reviews (see Jones and Johnston 2000; Mimura and Griffiths 2003 for examples of reviews on nursing staff) suggests that interventions focused on physicians or other staff are seriously lacking.

There is relatively little methodologically rigorous intervention research carried out in medical settings, and this makes it difficult to identify what works per se. One issue that does emerge is the need to integrate interventions with regard to well-being and performance. The salutogenic approach has the potential to shift the focus from reactive and self-preservation tendencies towards more holistic approaches to organizational functioning. The need to view medical settings as an organizational system has been recognized by the medical community, especially when it comes to errors (Institute of Medicine 1999). With regard to the salutogenic approach, there is a growing body research that examines how positive factors contribute to well-being in organizations. For example, in a longitudinal study among Finnish dentists, Hakanen et al. (2008) found a positive link between job engagement on the one hand, and personal initiative and innovation on the other. Moreover, engaged dentists were more likely to do more than they are asked to do, and tried to be actively involved in organizational matters.

Action Research in Medical Settings: A Salutogenic Approach?

Action Research (AR) is increasingly gaining popularity within health care (East and Robinson 1994). It comprises a useful methodological approach, able to facilitate changes within health care settings and support health service delivery development (Hampshire 2000; Tanna 2005). Two of the key elements of AR are the cyclical process and the collaborative element (Waterman et al. 2001). In AR, researcher and practitioners are working closely, in every stage of the process, to systematically identify issues and problems and to improve professional practice and quality of care (Waterman et al. 2001). The cyclical process of AR includes problem identification-planning of action-implementation of action-evaluation and reflection (Waterman et al. 2001).

Unlike other research approaches aimed only at generating knowledge and understanding of specific problems, AR focuses on facilitating action and generating knowledge about that action (Meyer 2000). AR attempts to bridge the gap between theory and practice (Holter and Schwartz-Barcott 1993; Rolfe 1996), is problem-focused (Hart and Bond 1995) and informed by the reality of practice (Waterman et al. 1995). While it has not been identified as salutogenic method per se, it represents a more holistic approach to working in medical settings.

We believe that AR is particularly relevant to the principles and goals of a healthy organization and it can inform effective organization health interventions. The participatory element that characterizes AR seems to be important in organizational interventions aimed at promoting employees well-being (Mikkelsen and Gundersen 2003; Mikkelsen and Saksvik 1999).

AR has been used in health care settings to promote organizational changes, improve professional practice and service delivery development (Hampshire 2000). According to a review of (Munn-Giddings et al. 2008) on the use of AR in nursing, 87 % of AR studies were focused on organizational/professional development, or the education of practitioners. Problems in the aforementioned areas are associated with increased stress and burnout among health workers and decreased well-being (Firth-Cozens 2001). Subsequently, identifying and implementing changes in those areas by means of AR, may affect indirectly health workers well-being. Thus, AR has the potential to address the roots of stress and burnout. Interestingly, our lack of success in "treating" burnout might mean that indirect approaches are the way forward.

To date, only two studies have used AR as a methodology to promote directly the well-being of health workers. Shaha and Rabenschlag (2007) aimed at identifying everyday burdensome situations in nursing care associated with stress and burnout among nurses, by means of qualitative action research. Based on the findings of the initial phase, they implemented an intervention to facilitate practice oriented problem solving. The interventions adopted a team and problem based learning approach. After the implementation of the intervention nurses provided verbal feedback for the evaluation of the intervention and they reported that the nursing team was benefitted as a whole from the AR. Another study that used AR as a methodology for a team base burnout intervention program was conducted by Le Blanc et al. (2007). They conducted a quasi experimental study among staff of 29 oncology wards in order to evaluate their program. The work situation and well- being of participants was measured with a questionnaire in three points of time, namely, before the initiation of the program, immediately after and 6 months later. The program included introductory meetings with the team counselors where the main stressors were identified, the training component and the evaluation. In the educational part, topics such as communication and feedback, building social support networks were discussed with the counselor. In the action part participants created problem-solving teams and they designed, implemented, evaluated, and reformulated plans of action for the most important stressors in their working environment. The results of the evaluation indicated that participants in the experimental wards experienced significantly less emotional exhaustion immediately after the implementation of the program and 6 months later and less depersonalization immediately after the program, compared with the control wards. The study showed that a team based burnout intervention informed by participatory action research approach can be an effective strategy to bring changes in the health care setting and mitigate the effect of work related stress and burnout.

Munn-Giddings et al. (2005) used participatory AR in order to promote wellbeing within two organizations, namely Healthcare Trust and Social Services Organization. They recruited staff who participated in five participatory workshops concerning key aspects of stress. The insights that resulted from the workshop were composed into a final strategy document which was further presented to senior managers. Two strategies were proposed as appropriate for well-being promotion namely, a returnees' support group and a self management pack. The first strategy aimed at supporting employees who returned to work after prolonged absence and the latter aimed at facilitating the reflection and insight of individuals participating in the group regarding health promotion strategies. The process enabled staff to identify primary stressors and suggest short-medium and long-term solutions. The solutions were specific and context/organizational specific. Unfortunately the very small number of participants did not allow drawing firm conclusions regarding the effectiveness of the program.

Despite the lack of existing studies focusing on promoting health workers' well-being through AR, we believe that AR is an appropriate methodology for this objective. AR empowers employees to identify problems create and implement solutions and this leads to a healthy working environment (Clark 2009).

Evaluation Approaches for Intervention Research in Medical Settings

Effectiveness across interventions can be assessed by measuring indicators that are relevant to healthcare settings. Indicators can be produced for each intervention, regarding three factors; quality, impact and cost. Additionally, these three indicators can be supplemented by a context-sensitive approach that evaluates 'success stories' in more detail. This approach has been developed via a European Union Framework Seven funded ORCAB project (ORCAB 2012). The project is concerned with improving quality and safety in the hospital via the link between organizational culture, burnout and quality of care. This multicentre study among hospitals in nine European countries utilized systematic reviews, focus groups, surveys and action research to identify the key mechanisms within quality of care. The three indicators were identified as key to components to evaluating interventions.

Firstly, the *quality index* consists of the following criteria:

(a) theory/OR evidence based (0: not based, 1: based on a theoretical model, or evidence)
(b) well-defined objectives (0,1)
(c) well-defined target groups (0,1)
(d) Consistency of the delivery (0,1)

Secondly, the *impact index* consists of the following criteria:

(a) The outcomes that were measured (whether they were individual out-comes, quality of care measures and organizational outcomes)
(b) The recipients of the intervention (whether it is an individual, selected groups of professionals or all the healthcare professionals in the organization)

Thirdly, the *cost index* will include the following costs:

(a) Direct costs (personnel and material costs, office rents and other supplies)
(b) Indirect costs
(c) Opportunity costs

These three indexes provide a methodology to quantify relevant aspects of healthcare interventions. Additionally, the data collected can be integrated in the following formula:

$$\text{Effectiveness} = \left(\text{Impact} / \text{Cost}\right) \times \text{Sustainability} \times \text{Generalisibility}$$

The formula is intended to be conceptual, and needs to be interpreted in each particular context. Sustainability should be assessed in terms of how sustainable the effects were after the end of the intervention. Generalizability should be assessed in terms of how many different settings and health systems the intervention was found to be effective. The quality index should be treated independently.

This quantitative approach should be supplemented by a qualitative one that seeks to account for what actually works. Thus, *Profiling Success Stories* refers to an in-depth assessment of interventions that have proved efficacious and should be analyzed further. To do this one should seek to obtain data other than those presented in the relevant publications. This could be achieved by direct contact with the authors and by accessing the site of the interventions. One could attempt to obtain information from the target organization, regarding the implementation and evaluation of the intervention. Details that might have not been published could be documented.

The aforementioned evaluation approach is a complementary one that seeks to assess interventions at different levels. Attempting to account for the impact of an intervention at different levels is consistent with organizational researchers who recommend that we seek to combine micro and macro aspects of the organization, the so-called Meso-Paradigm approach (House et al. 1995). The evaluation approach recommended needs to be embedded within an action research approach to organizational interventions (see previous section).

Conclusions and Recommendations

Our ability to reach strong conclusions about health interventions is severely limited by the mixed results and heterogeneity of study designs. Using RCTs is desirable, but problematic given the need to study real life organizations. On the one hand, the use of observational studies might introduce one form of bias, as noted by a recent systematic review of worksite wellness programs (Osilla et al. 2012), which found that when evaluations used observational designs, positive effects were found for three-fourths of the outcomes, whereas positive effects were found for only about half of the outcomes evaluated with RCTs. On the other hand, the use of experimental or quasi-experimental designs can result in demand or Hawthorne effects among individuals (Bourbonnais et al. 2006a, b).

With regard to the salutogenic approach, two types of intervention approaches were discernible in the literature; approaches aimed at strengthening resources (e.g. self-management skills, community networks) and approaches aimed at creating meaning and order (e.g. interventions to increase perceptions of control and therapy interventions) (Harrop et al. 2007). However, both approaches underestimate the importance of either career transitions of the employees or organizational change upon the work group. For example, career transitions influence burnout levels among individuals, especially emotional exhaustion and depersonalization (Dunford et al. 2012). Equally, organizational change impacts upon organizational climate and staff relations.

Overall, there is no compelling evidence that either the Karasek or Siegrist models of job stress feed directly into interventions. This suggests that we need to take a broader or more salutogenic approach to organizational health interventions targeting healthcare professionals. Väänänen et al. (2012) in a recent history of work stress recommend to researchers that there is a need to consider more information on cultural factors, social structures, and broader working life/value shifts when studying occupational health. The ability of cultural activities to increase well-being is an emerging field in occupational health. For example, among healthcare professionals, studies show that arts in the work environment is linked with better satisfaction (Liikanen 2003), reduced burnout and better coping in oncology workers (Italia et al. 2008), the promotion of social functioning and vitality (Bygren et al. 2009), and lower anxiety/depression (Cuypers et al. 2012). The implications for creativity at work are obvious, and recent work has shown the interrelationships between cultural activities in the workplace, creative work performance and well-being (Tuisku et al. 2012).

We are left with the problem of what guidelines or recommendations we can provide for medical settings. Our future models of healthy organizations for healthcare professionals need to be bottom-up and acknowledge the reality of interdependence between the main actors. According to the American Association of Critical-Care Nurses (AACCN 2005), the standards for establishing and sustaining healthy work environments are: skilled communication, true collaboration, effective decision making, appropriate staffing, meaningful recognition and authentic leadership. The standards are intended to provide a functional yardstick for development and performance. The interesting and pragmatic aspect of these recommendations is the fact that they are highly interdependent and salutogenic, in that they are focusing on what works. However, it is noteworthy that they are prefixed, and refer to true collaboration and skilled communication, suggesting that knowledge alone will not suffice. The emphasis of the AACCN guidelines are on true collaboration are (unfortunately) highlighted by what happens when things go wrong in healthcare and the subsequent; reports (Institute of Medicine 1999), enquiries (*Final Report of the Special Commission of Inquiry into Campbelltown and Camden Hospitals* 2004) and studies (Forster et al. 2004) which all collectively show that a predetermining factor is that patient care is delivered in a fragmented, isolated way, with health-care professionals having failed to collaborate effectively.

Hospitals are very interesting organizations, in that the culture of medicine is similar across the globe, and physicians (especially) are educated to take a very specific role in an organization. Mintzberg (1997) has written directly on the issue of the hospital cultures in Toward a Healthier Hospital, and strongly insists that real organizational change can be effected only by a gradual bottom up approach that doesn't threaten the roles that individuals have established within the organization. The advice offered by Mintzberg is further evidence that a salutogenic approach is the most pragmatic way for us to design organizational interventions in medical settings.

References

AACCN. (2005). AACN standards for establishing and sustaining healthy work environments: A journey to excellence. *American Journal of Critical Care, 14*(3), 187–197.

Antonovsky, A. (1979). *Health, stress and coping*. San Francisco: Jossey-Bass.

Antonovsky, A. (1987). The salutogenic perspective: Toward a new view of health and illness. *Advances, 4*(1), 47–55.

Antonovsky, A. (1996). The salutogenic model as a theory to guide health promotion. *Health Promotion International, 11*(1), 11–18. doi:10.1093/heapro/11.1.11.

Argyris, C. (1982). *Reasoning, learning, and action: Individual and organizational*. San Francisco: Jossey-Bass.

Bakker, A. B., & Demerouti, E. (2007). The job demands-resources model: State of the art. *Journal of Managerial Psychology, 22*(3), 309–328. doi:10.1108/02683940710733115.

Becker, C. M., Glascoff, M. A., & Felts, W. M. (2010). Salutogenesis 30 years later: Where do we go from here? *The International Electronic Journal of Health Education, 13*, 25–32.

Bourbonnais, R., Brisson, C., Vinet, A., Vézina, M., & Lower, A. (2006a). Development and implementation of a participative intervention to improve the psychosocial work environment and mental health in an acute care hospital. *Occupational and Environmental Medicine, 63*(5), 326–334. doi:10.1136/oem.2004.018069.

Bourbonnais, R., Brisson, C., Vinet, A., Vézina, M., Abdous, B., & Gaudet, M. (2006b). Effectiveness of a participative intervention on psychosocial work factors to prevent mental health problems in a hospital setting. *Occupational and Environmental Medicine, 63*(5), 335–342. doi:10.1136/oem.2004.018077.

Bronfenbrenner, U. (1979). *The ecology of human development.* Cambridge, MA: Harvard University Press.

Bunce, D., & West, M. A. (1996). Stress management and innovation interventions at work. *Human Relations, 49*(2), 209–232. doi:10.1177/001872679604900205.

Busse, R., Grinter, T., & Svensson, P. G. (2002). Regulating entrepreneurial behaviour in hospitals: Theory and practice. In R. B. Saltman (Ed.), *Regulating entrepreneurial behaviour in European health care systems* (European observatory on health care systems series, pp. 126–145). Maidenhead: Open University Press.

Bygren, L. O., Weissglas, G., Wikström, B. M., Konlaan, B. B., Grjibovski, A., Karlsson, A. B., Andersson, S. O., et al. (2009). Cultural participation and health: A randomized controlled trial among medical care staff. *Psychosomatic Medicine, 71*(4), 469–473. doi:10.1097/PSY.0b013e31819e47d4.

Clark, P. R. (2009). Teamwork: Building healthier workplaces and providing safer patient care. *Critical Care Nursing Quarterly, 32*(3), 221–231. doi:10.1097/CNQ.0b013e3181ab923f.

Commission of the European Communities. (2008). *Green paper on the European workforce for health* (COM (2008) 725 final). Brussels: Commission of the European Communities. http://ec.europa.eu/health/ph_systems/docs/workforce_gp_en.pdf. Accessed 29 Nov 2012.

Cooper, C. L., & Cartwright, S. (1994). Healthy mind; Healthy organization – A proactive approach to occupational stress. *Human Relations, 47*(4), 455–471. doi:10.1177/001872679404700405.

Cox, T., & Leiter, M. (1992). The health of health care organizations. *Work and Stress, 6*(3), 219–227. doi:10.1080/02678379208259954.

Cuypers, K., Krokstad, S., Holmen, T. L., Knudtsen, M. S., Bygren, L. O., & Holmen, J. (2012). Patterns of receptive and creative cultural activities and their association with perceived health, anxiety, depression and satisfaction with life among adults: the HUNT study, Norway. *Journal of Epidemiology and Community Health, 66*, 698–703. doi:10.1136/jech.2010.113571.

de Jonge, J., & Kompier, M. A. J. (1997). A critical examination of the demand-control-support model from a work psychological perspective. *International Journal of Stress Management, 4*(4), 235–258. doi:10.1023/B:IJSM.0000008152.85798.90.

Dunford, B. B., Shipp, A. J., Boss, R. W., Angermeier, I., & Boss, A. D. (2012). Is burnout static or dynamic? A career transition perspective of employee burnout trajectories. *The Journal of Applied Psychology, 97*(3), 637–650. doi:10.1037/a0027060.

Dunn, P. M., Arnetz, B. B., Christensen, J. F., & Homer, L. (2007). Meeting the imperative to improve physician well-being: Assessment of an innovative program. *Journal of General Internal Medicine, 22*(11), 1544–1552. doi:10.1007/s11606-007-0363-5.

East, L., & Robinson, J. (1994). Change in process: Bringing about change in health care through action research. *Journal of Clinical Nursing, 3*(1), 57–61.

Egan, M., Bambra, C., Thomas, S., Petticrew, M., Whitehead, M., & Thomson, H. (2007). The psychosocial and health effects of workplace reorganisation. 1. A systematic review of organisational-level interventions that aim to increase employee control. *Journal of Epidemiology and Community Health, 61*(11), 945–954. doi:10.1136/jech.2006.054965.

Firth-Cozens, J. (2001). Interventions to improve physicians' well-being and patient care. *Social Science & Medicine, 52*(2), 215–222. doi:10.1016/S0277-9536(00)00221-5.

Forster, A. J., Clark, H. D., Menard, A., Dupuis, N., Chernish, R., Chandok, N., Khan, A., et al. (2004). Adverse events among medical patients after discharge from hospital. *Canadian Medical Association Journal, 170*(3), 345–349.

Gilbody, S., Cahill, J., Barkham, M., Richards, D., Bee, P., & Glanville, J. (2006). Can we improve the morale of staff working in psychiatric units? A systematic review. *Journal of Mental Health, 15*(1), 7–17. doi:10.1080/09638230500512482.

Hakanen, J. J., Perhoniemi, R., & Toppinen-Tanner, S. (2008). Positive gain spirals at work: From job resources to work engagement, personal initiative and work-unit innovativeness. *Journal of Vocational Behavior, 73*(1), 78–91.

Hampshire, A. J. (2000). What is action research and can it promote change in primary care? *Journal of Evaluation in Clinical Practice, 6*(4), 337–343.

Harrop, E., Addis, S., Elliott, E., & Williams, G. (2007). *Resilience, coping and salutogenic approaches to maintaining and generating health: A review*. London: National Institute for Health and Clinical Excellence (NICE).

Hart, F., & Bond, M. (1995). *Action research for health and social care: A guide to practice*. Buckingham: Open University Press.

Hawkes, N. (2012). Almost a quarter of Royal College fellows say their hospitals cannot deliver continuity of care. *BMJ (Clinical Research ed.)*, *345*, 4942.

Holter, I. M., & Schwartz-Barcott, D. (1993). Action research: What is it? How has it been used and how can it be used in nursing? *Journal of Advanced Nursing*, *18*(2), 298–304.

House, R., Rousseau, D. M., & Thomas-Hunt, M. (1995). The meso paradigm: A framework for the integration of micro and macro organizational behavior. *Research in Organizational Behavior*, *17*, 71–114.

Institute of Medicine. (1999). *To err is human. Building a safer health system*. Washington, DC: National Academy Press.

Institute of Medicine. (2001). *Crossing the quality chasm: A new health system for the 21st century*. Washington, DC: National Academy Press.

Italia, S., Favara-Scacco, C., Di Cataldo, A., & Russo, G. (2008). Evaluation and art therapy treatment of the burnout syndrome in oncology units. *Psycho-Oncology*, *17*(7), 676–680.

Jones, M. C., & Johnston, D. W. (2000). Reducing distress in first level and student nurses: A review of the applied stress management literature. *Journal of Advanced Nursing*, *32*(1), 66–74. doi:10.1046/j.1365-2648.2000.01421.x.

Karasek, R. A. (1979). Job demands, job decision latitude, and mental strain: Implications for job redesign. *Administrative Science Quarterly*, *24*(2), 285–308. doi:10.2307/2392498.

Karasek, R. A. (1992). Stress prevention through work reorganisation: A summary of 19 international case studies. *Conditions of Work Digest; Preventing Stress at Work*, *11*(2), 23–42.

Kompier, M., & Kristensen, T. S. (2001). Organizational work stress interventions in a theoretical, methodological and practical context. In J. Dunham (Ed.), *Stress in the workplace: Past, present and future* (pp. 169–190). London/Philadelphia: Whurr Publishers.

Larsson, G., & Setterlind, S. (1991). A stress reduction program led by health care personnel: Effects on health and well-being. *European Journal of Public Health*, *1*(2), 90–93. doi:10.1093/eurpub/1.2.90.

Le Blanc, P. M., Hox, J. J., Schaufeli, W. B., Taris, T. W., & Peeters, M. C. W. (2007). Take care! The evaluation of a team-based burnout intervention program for oncology care providers. *The Journal of Applied Psychology*, *92*(1), 213–227.

Lewin, K. Z. (1951). *Field theory in social science*. New York: Harper.

Liikanen, H. L. (2003). *Art meets life – The arts in hospital initiative and cultural activities in the everyday life and festivities of care units in Eastern Finland*. Doctoral Dissertation, University of Helsinki.

McCray, L. W., Cronholm, P. F., Bogner, H. R., Gallo, J. J., & Neill, R. A. (2008). Resident physician burnout: Is there hope? *Family Medicine*, *40*(9), 626–632.

Meyer, J. (2000). Qualitative research in health care: Using qualitative methods in health related action research. *BMJ*, *320*, 178–181. doi:10.1136/bmj.320.7228.178.

Michie, S., & Williams, S. (2003). Reducing work related psychological ill health and sickness absence: A systematic literature review. *Occupational and Environmental Medicine*, *60*(1), 3–9. doi:10.1136/oem.60.1.3.

Mikkelsen, A., & Gundersen, M. (2003). The effect of a participatory organizational intervention on work environment, job stress, and subjective health complaints. *Journal of Stress Management*, *10*(2), 91–110.

Mikkelsen, A., & Saksvik, P. O. (1999). Impact of a participatory organizational intervention on job characteristics and job stress. *International Journal of Health Services: Planning, Administration, Evaluation*, *29*(4), 871–893.

Mimura, C., & Griffiths, P. (2003). The effectiveness of current approaches to workplace stress management in the nursing profession: An evidence based literature review. *Occupational and Environmental Medicine*, *60*(1), 10–15. doi:10.1136/oem.60.1.10.

Mintzberg, H. (1997). Toward healthier hospitals. *Health Care Management Review, 22*(4), 9–18.

Minvielle, E., Aegerter, P., Dervaux, B., Boumendil, A., Retbi, A., Jars-Guincestre, M. C., & Guidet, B. (2008). Assessing organizational performance in intensive care units: A French experience. *Journal of Critical Care, 23*(2), 236–244. doi:10.1016/j.jcrc.2007.11.006.

Montgomery, A., Panagopoulou, E., Kehoe, I., & Valkanos, E. (2011). Connecting organisational culture and quality of care in the hospital: Is job burnout the missing link? *Journal of Health Organization and Management, 25*(1), 108–123.

Munn-Giddings, C., Hart, C., & Ramon, S. (2005). A participatory approach to the promotion of well-being in the workplace: Lessons from empirical research. *International Review of Psychiatry, 17*(5), 409–417. doi:10.1080/09540260500238546.

Munn-Giddings, C., McVicar, A., & Smith, L. (2008). Systematic review of the uptake and design of action research in published nursing research, 2000–2005. *Journal of Research in Nursing, 13*(6), 465–477. doi:10.1177/1744987108090297.

New South Wales. Special Commission of Inquiry into Campbelltown and Camden, & Walker, B. (2004). *Final report of the special commission of inquiry into Campbelltown and Camden hospitals*. Sydney: NSW Government, Special Commission of Inquiry.

ORCAB. (2012). *Indicators to evaluate effectiveness of health care interventions*. http://orcab.web.auth.gr/. Accessed 6 June 2013.

Osilla, K. C., Van Busum, K., Schnyer, C., Larkin, J. W., Eibner, C., & Mattke, S. (2012). Systematic review of the impact of worksite wellness programs. *The American Journal of Managed Care, 18*(2), 68–81.

Parmelli, E., Flodgren, G., Beyer, F., Baillie, N., Schaafsma, M. E., & Eccles, M. P. (2011). The effectiveness of strategies to change organisational culture to improve healthcare performance: A systematic review. *Implementation Science, 6*, 33. doi:10.1186/1748-5908-6-33.

Petterson, I. L., & Arnetz, B. B. (1998). Psychosocial stressors and well-being in health care workers. The impact of an intervention program. *Social Science & Medicine, 47*(11), 1763–1772.

Pisljar, T., van der Lippe, T., & den Dulk, L. (2011). Health among hospital employees in Europe: A cross-national study of the impact of work stress and work control. *Social Science & Medicine, 72*(6), 899–906. doi:10.1016/j.socscimed.2010.12.017.

Rivera-Rodriguez, A. J., & Karsh, B. T. (2010). Interruptions and distractions in healthcare: Review and reappraisal. *Quality & Safety in Health Care, 19*(4), 304–312. doi:10.1136/qshc.2009.033282.

Rolfe, G. (1996). Going to extremes: Action research, grounded practice and the theory-practice gap in nursing. *Journal of Advanced Nursing, 24*(6), 1315–1320.

Rotondi, A. J., Angus, D. C., Sirio, C. A., & Pinsky, M. R. (2000). Assessing intensive care unit performance: A new conceptual framework. *Current Opinion in Critical Care, 6*(3), 155–157.

Seren, S., & Baykal, U. (2007). Relationships between change and organizational culture in hospitals. *Journal of Nursing Scholarship, 39*(2), 191–197. doi:10.1111/j.1547-5069.2007.00166.x.

Sevdalis, N., Forrest, D., Undre, S., Darzi, A., & Vincent, C. A. (2008). Annoyances, disruptions, and interruptions in surgery: The disruptions in surgery index (Disi). *World Journal of Surgery, 32*, 1643–1650.

Shaha, M., & Rabenschlag, F. (2007). Burdensome situations in everyday nursing: An explorative qualitative action research on a medical ward. *Nursing Administration Quarterly, 31*(2), 134–145. doi:10.1097/01.NAQ.0000264862.87335.e4.

Skela Savič, B., & Pagon, M. (2008). Relationship between nurses and physicians in terms of organizational culture: Who is responsible for subordination of nurses? *Croatian Medical Journal, 49*(3), 334–343.

Skela Savič, B., Pagon, M., & Robida, A. (2007). Predictors of the level of personal involvement in an organization: A study of Slovene hospitals. *Health Care Management Review, 32*(3), 271–283. doi:10.1097/01.HMR.0000281628.22526.0a.

Spânu, F., Băban, A., Bria, M., & Dumitrascu, D. L. (2012). What happens to health professionals when the ill patient is the health care system? Understanding the experience of practising medicine in the Romanian socio-cultural context. *British Journal of Health Psychology*. doi:10.1111/bjhp.12010.

Spataro, S. E. (2005). Diversity in context: How organizational culture shapes reactions to workers with disabilities and others who are demographically different. *Behavioral Sciences & the Law, 23*(1), 21–38. doi:10.1002/bsl.623.

Tanna, N. K. (2005). Action research: A valuable research technique for service delivery development. *Pharmacy World & Science, 27*(1), 4–6.

Tuisku, K., Pulkki-RåBack, L., Ahola, K., Hakanen, J., & Virtanen, M. (2012). Cultural leisure activities and well-being at work: A study among health care professionals. *Journal of Applied Arts & Health, 2*(3), 273–287. doi:10.1386/jaah.2.3.273_1.

Türköz, Y. (2004). *Relationships between the participation of a private hospital's employees in quality studies and their attitudes towards work and institution.* http://www.merih.net/m1/ wyturk04.htm. Accessed 5 Sept 2012.

Väänänen, A., Anttila, E., Turtiainen, J., & Varje, P. (2012). Formulation of work stress in 1960-2000: Analysis of scientific works from the perspective of historical sociology. *Social Science & Medicine, 75*(5), 784–794. doi:10.1016/j.socscimed.2012.04.014.

van Wyk, B. E., & Pillay-Van Wyk, V. (2010). Preventive staff-support interventions for health workers. *Cochrane Database of Systematic Reviews* (Online), *17*(3), CD003541. doi:10.1002/14651858.CD003541.pub2.

Waterman, H., Webb, C., & Williams, A. (1995). Parallels and contradictions in the theory and practice of action research and nursing. *Journal of Advanced Nursing, 22*(4), 779–784.

Waterman, H., Tillen, D., Dickson, R., & de Koning, K. (2001). Action research: A systematic review and guidance for assessment. *Health Technology Assessment, 5*(23), iii–157.

Weir, R., Stewart, L., Browne, G., Roberts, J., Gafni, A., Easton, S., & Seymour, L. (1997). The efficacy and effectiveness of process consultation in improving staff morale and absenteeism. *Medical Care, 35*(4), 334–353.

Wiskow, C., Albreht, T., & de Pietro, C. (2010). *How to create an attractive and supportive working environment for health professionals.* World Health Organization 2010 and World Health Organization, on behalf of the European Observatory on Health Systems and Policies 2010: http://www.euro.who.int/__data/assets/pdf_file/0018/124416/e94293.pdf. Accessed 13 Sept 2012.

Chapter 4
Qualitative, Sense of Coherence-Based Assessment of Working Conditions in a Psychiatric In-Patient Unit to Guide Salutogenic Interventions

Orly Idan, Orna Braun-Lewensohn, and Shifra Sagy

Abstract Following a joint initiation by the Salutogenic Research Center at Ben Gurion University and a mental health center in southern Israel of an intervention program based on the salutogenic model for the mental health center's acute psychiatric in-patient unit, the current qualitative sense of coherence-based assessment aimed at assessing the unit's needs for the purpose of developing the rationale and goals of the intervention. The intervention, subject to the current study's assessment, aims at creating a health promoting community focusing on the advancement of the staff's individual and collective Sense of Coherence (SOC). The questions addressed during the assessment were aimed at (a) identifying key working conditions and their relation to the three dimensions of SOC; (b) characterizing the SOC grouped working conditions; and (c) deriving recommendations for interventions. Meetings with the Unit's administrative and professional management were held and fifteen unstructured interviews with the unit's staff were carried out. The three thematic axes, around which the core ten themes revealed in the interviews revolved, disclosed a salutogenic model of individual and collective SOC, as follows: (1) The comprehensibility axis, comprised of leadership of head nurse; lack of expertise in treatment of patients with mental retardation; lack of attention to the staff's and unit's concerns; (2) The environment axis (manageability), comprised of lack of social and academic activities outside the hospital; impossible living and working conditions; patients suffering from diverse problems (retarded, psychotic and retarded and psychotic); (3) The motivation/emotion axis (meaningfulness), comprised of self- fulfillment; Occupational Self-Efficacy; professional/job satisfaction; devotion to the unit and its patients and a strong sense of belonging. An in-depth examination of the three axes revealed two discrete fields: promoting and deterring, in which the motivation/emotion axis encompassed promoting factors, the

O. Idan (✉) • O. Braun-Lewensohn • S. Sagy
Conflict Management and Conflict Resolution Program, Department of Interdisciplinary Studies, Ben-Gurion University of the Negev, POB 653, Beer Sheva, Israel
e-mail: oidan@idc.ac.il; ornabl@bgu.ac.il; shifra@bgu.ac.il

G.F. Bauer and G.J. Jenny (eds.), *Salutogenic Organizations and Change:*
The Concepts Behind Organizational Health Intervention Research,
DOI 10.1007/978-94-007-6470-5_4, © Springer Science+Business Media Dordrecht 2013

environment axis encompassed deterring factors, and the comprehensibility axis encompassed both promoting and deterring factors. Furthermore, the interviews were perceived as empowering. Consequently, the intervention, in line with the salutogenic approach, aims at supporting the three dimensions of SOC at individual as well as collective levels, enhancing the staff's communal SOC which, in turn, could promote the patients' health and the well-being of their families.

Keywords Salutogenic intervention • Mental health staff • Sense of coherence • Health promoting community • Qualitative assessment

Introduction

Professional staff in the mental health services caring for patients with long term acute psychiatric illnesses may be frequently exposed to hardships and stressful emotional situations which may lead to a decline in the quality of the workers and, in turn, a decline in the quality of patient care (Thomsen et al. 1999). The aim of the present study was to evaluate the acute psychiatric in-patient unit in a mental health center in southern Israel for the purpose of developing an intervention program based on the salutogenic model. The current qualitative sense of coherence-based assessment aimed at assessing the unit's needs, towards the development of an intervention, integrating the concepts of Sense of Coherence, health promotion, Occupational Self-Efficacy, and job satisfaction.

Sense of Coherence (SOC)

Human beings have resources to survive and grow alongside abilities to resist adversities and experience a life of well-being. The manner in which people succeed in overcoming adversaries, such as illness, decline in functioning, and loss, vary according to their personal resources and inner strengths. Research has increasingly focused on adults' resilience and the interrelated components that constitute it. The contribution of the salutogenic paradigm in explaining successful coping with stressors and health promotion was initially introduced by Antonovsky (1987; Griffiths 2009), with a focus on adults' functioning and adjustment. Antonovsky (1979, 1987) was interested in the impact of resistant resources on health promotion, in an attempt to explain why people stay healthy despite the fact that they face a multitude of stressors. Antonovsky formulated the Sense of Coherence (SOC) concept; a global life orientation shaped by the individual's life experiences, and established the relation between a strong Sense of Coherence and health (Eriksson and Lindstrom 2006).

SoC is defined as a global orientation that expresses the extent to which one has a pervasive enduring (though dynamic) feeling of confidence that the stimuli deriving from one's internal and external environment are structured, predictable, and explicable (comprehensibility); that resources are available to meet the demands posed by these stimuli (manageability); and that these demands are challenges, worthy of investment and engagement (meaningfulness) (Antonovsky 1987; Lindstrom and Eriksson 2006; Eriksson and Lindstrom 2007). Antonovsky (1987) considered Sense of Coherence as an inner personal resource that develops during childhood and becomes established during adolescence or early adulthood. The Sense of Coherence Questionnaire was developed with adults' samples in mind, although the roots of Sense of Coherence were identified by patterns of life experiences during developmental stages. A person with a strong sense of comprehensibility believes that events experienced are structured, ordered and explicable, rather than chaotic or random; a person with a strong sense of manageability does not feel victimized by life and has confidence that resources are available to meet given demands; and, a person with a strong sense of meaningfulness perceives demands as challenges, finding meaning in that which facilitates individual ability to be effective (Stanton 2000). In reference to the relations among the three components of comprehensibility, manageability and meaningfulness, Antonovsky (1987) concluded that the motivational component of meaningfulness seemed the most crucial for without the latter comprehensibility (understanding) and manageability (resources) were likely to be impermanent.

A strong Sense of Coherence has been related to the availability of a wide and varied repertoire of *coping strategies* and to flexibility in selecting the particular coping strategy that seems most appropriate at certain times and environmental conditions. Eriksson and Lindstrom's review (2006) of 458 scientific publications that used Sense of Coherence to assess people's reactions to stress revealed that SOC was linked to psychological problems including psychological aspects or health measures. However, for individuals with a higher level of SOC, SOC seemed to be a better predictor of stress and health related symptoms, whereas its role for those with moderate or low SOC was unclear (Eriksson and Lindstrom 2005). Wiesmann and Hannich (2011) examined salutogenic predictors of multiple *health behaviors* in a sample of healthy "third age" individuals and, in accordance with Antonovsky's (1987) hypothesis, found that meaningfulness was the most distinguishing among the Sense of Coherence components. Moreover, the aging individuals reported that their lives made sense and were worthy of commitment and engagement. The Sense of Coherence components were significantly associated with multiple health behaviors and were also significantly interrelated. In accordance with the salutogenic theory, the strong correlations among the components explained their overlapping and yet distinct character. Furthermore, meaningfulness mediated self-esteem and self-efficacy influences on multiple health behaviors and advanced age was associated with a higher extent of comprehensibility of the world. The latter supported the salutogenic assumption that psychological resources such as self-esteem and self-efficacy created life experiences that contributed to the individual's meaningful world.

Collective Sense of Coherence, according to Antonovsky (1996), is conveyed when the members of a group perceive the group as an entity that considers the world or their own lives to be comprehensible, manageable and meaningful, and if there is a high degree of agreement regarding this point among the group members. Challenged with a stressor, the person or collective with a strong SOC will be motivated to cope (meaningfulness); trust that the challenge is understood (comprehensibility); and, believe that resources to manage are available (manageability).

Health Promotion in Mental Health Services

In order to respond better and faster to the challenges of a changing world, the World Health Organization (WHO) emphasized the need to develop and support effective strategies and multi-professional approaches for the promotion of health-enhancing activities and the enhancing of equal health opportunities (WHO Europe 2005). WHO (2005) proposed that health promoting activities should be advanced and *integrated into health care services* as an essential part of any treatment. Antonovsky (1996) perceived the salutogenic orientation as the basis for health promotion, directing research and action efforts to include everyone, wherever they are on the health/disease continuum, and to focus on salutary issues. The concept of health promotion has received increased attention in recent years in terms of health care policy making, health care practice and health care research (Svedberg 2007). Recent research has focused on health promotion within health services in general (Malach Pines 2002; Posadzki et al. 2010; Rabin et al. 2005; Wennerberg et al. 2012) and within mental health services, in particular (Edwards et al. 2000; Lloyd and King 2004; Morse et al. 2012; Jormfeldt 2010; Reid et al. 1999; Richards et al. 2006; Svedberg 2007).

Research on *health promoting interventions in the mental health field* is scare, in particular with regards to the relations between the staff and the patients. In the past decade the necessity of an alliance (McGuire et al. 2006) between the staff and the patients in health promoting interventions has been studied, emphasizing the significance of the staff's empathic qualities alongside their ability to be understanding and respectful toward their patients. Furthermore, concerns regarding recent changes in acute in-patient mental healthcare environments have led to apprehensions relating to staff stress and low morale in acute in-patient mental healthcare staff and demands to ameliorate occupational stress and improve staff recruitment in this group (Richards et al. 2006). Improving the workplace environment within psychiatric services was found to be one of the most important factors in staff burnout prevention strategies, suggesting potential benefits for the patients (Lasalvia et al. 2009).

Studies have demonstrated that the *potential sources of stress* for community mental health nursing are stressors intrinsic to the job itself (increases in workload, problems relating to time management, safety issues dealing with potentially violent and suicidal patients), role based stressors (role conflict), and stressors concerning relationships with others (staff, supervision) (Edwards et al. 2000). Contrary to research focusing on understanding the origin and nature of stressors in nursing, Malach Pines (2004) used an existential approach to explain the relatively lower levels of stress and burnout in Israeli nurses. Empowered nurses reported higher levels of autonomy, job satisfaction and commitment and lower levels of job stress. Malach Pines asserted that the primary sense of existential significance within the medical professions, in general, derived from their daily confrontation with life and death issues.

In a systematic review (Richards et al. 2006) of 34 studies on the *prevalence of nursing staff* stress on adult acute psychiatric in patient units, occupational stress, job satisfaction, burnout, psychological ill health, and sickness rates were examined. The review did not support the argument that staff in in-patient mental health services experienced very high levels of stress and poor morale. Furthermore, in two cross sectional studies, one found that occupational stress in acute units were significantly less than in a general nurse comparison group and two reported reasonably high levels of job satisfaction.

Occupational Self-Efficacy

The beliefs that individuals possess about themselves are critical in the exercise of control and individual agency (Bandura 1997). "Perceived self-efficacy is defined as individuals' beliefs about their capabilities to produce designated levels of performance that exercise influence over events that affect their lives (…), determining how individuals feel, think, motivate themselves, and behave" (Bandura 1994, p. 71). Human accomplishment and individual well-being are enhanced by a strong sense of self-efficacy, wherein individuals with a strong sense of self-efficacy approach difficulties as a challenge rather than a threat to be avoided. These individuals set high goals for themselves and are committed to them. For this reason, individuals' beliefs about their abilities may often explain their behavior. Self-efficacy beliefs assist in determining the outcomes one anticipates. Individuals who possess confidence will expect successful outcomes; individuals who are more socially inclined will expect successful social encounters; and, individuals who are academically successful will expect to continue receiving high marks (Schunk and Pajares 2002).

Self-efficacy has been defined and assessed as a global construct generalized over a number of domains (Schwarzer 1994); a domain-linked knowledge structure that varies across spheres of functioning, rather than a global trait (Caprara et al. 2004) and a task specific variable that refers to specific and situational judgments of abilities (Pajares 1996). It has been examined in organizational research. On the one hand, research has focused on outcomes of self-efficacy in the working environment, such as performance (Stajkovic and Luthans 1998), commitment (Tracey et al. 2001), and job satisfaction (Judge and Bono 2001). On the other hand, antecedents of efficacy expectations were hypothesized to be acquired and modified through four major routes: past performance accomplishment; exposure to and identification with efficacious models (vicarious learning); access to verbal persuasion and support from others; and, experience of emotional or physiological arousal in the context of task performance (Bandura 1997). These four sources of efficacy information continually and reciprocally interact to affect performance judgments that may in turn influence performance and effort (Linnenbrink and Pintrich 2003).

Job Satisfaction in Mental Health Professions

Job satisfaction, defined as a pleasurable or positive emotional state resulting from one's job (Locke 1976), reflects one's hedonic experiences together with one's cognitive beliefs relating to job experiences (Weiss and Cropanzano 1996) in which the nature of the hedonic experiences derive from motivation (Carver and Scheier 1998). Job satisfaction was also found to be related to core self-assessment (Brown et al. 2007), a latent construct accounting for shared variance among self-esteem, generalized self-efficacy, emotional stability, and locus of control (Judge and Bono 2001).

Onyett et al. (1997) found high levels of emotional exhaustion accompanied by high levels of job satisfaction and personal accomplishment in professional staff within community mental health teams. Similarly, Prosser et al. (1996) found emotional exhaustion and general health scores at high levels alongside satisfaction and personal accomplishment. However, community based staff scored significantly higher than hospital based staff in general health and emotional exhaustion; whereas, satisfaction did not vary between the settings.

Research on health promoting interventions in the mental health field is scarce, in particular with regards to the mental health professional staff. This scarcity has accentuated the need for a comprehensive intervention in a mental health environment, subject to an evaluative needs assessment study.

Purpose of the Study

The aim of the present study was a qualitative, sense of coherence-based assessment of working conditions in a psychiatric in-patient unit in a mental health center in southern Israel, as a data basis for developing an intervention program based on the salutogenic model. Following the joint initiation by the Salutogenic Research Center at Ben Gurion University and a mental health center in southern Israel of an intervention program for the unit, the questions addressed during the assessment were aimed at (a) identifying key working conditions and their relation to the three dimensions of SOC; (b) characterizing the SOC grouped working conditions; and (c) deriving recommendations for interventions. Meetings with the Unit's administrative and professional management were held and 15 unstructured interviews with the unit's staff were carried out. The qualitative assessment presented in the current study was embedded in a comprehensive mixed methods study which will be reported in a separate study.

Method

Sample and Procedure

The sample of 15 mental health professionals (aged 34–60; 11 females and 4 males) was drawn from the inpatient adult unit, housing approximately 40 patients above 18 years of age requiring intensive care within a closed area, within the mental health center in southern Israel. The Center provides mental health services to the population of Southern Israel and the Negev area, providing clinical teaching for students in all mental health related academic programs. Treatment at the Center is based on the bio-psycho-social model of psychiatry aimed for patients of all ages at different levels of clinical severity. The staff included psychiatric nurses and ward nurses (one a senior charge nurse) who had been working in the profession an average of 19 years; at the Center an average of 17 years; and, in the given unit an average of 6 years in full time positions. The staff employed at the Center is required for the most to rotate between the various sectors of the Center in order, according to the interviewees, "to avoid burnout and habituation".

The interviews were held in two sessions at the health center at the office of the head nurse of the Unit and scheduled by the head nurse. The staff of the Unit was not informed regarding the purpose or content of the interview. Interviews were recorded (half of them agreed to be recorded) on audiotape and transcribed verbatim. For those who were not recorded, notes were taken during the interview by the interviewer. Following each of the interviews, questionnaires were completed by each one of the staff members while the interviewer was present, enabling the participants to ask questions relating to the content of the questionnaires. The quantitative part of the assessment was embedded in a comprehensive mixed methods study and will be reported in a separate study.

Qualitative Analysis Approach

Qualitative research strives to study in detail the complexity of lived experience and human practices. There is not a single standard for qualitative data, for the data is required to serve the aims of the research. Descriptions and experiences are often elicited through reports of personal events, accounts or other types of first hand expressions (Wertz et al. 2011). At present, a variety of interview approaches and procedures exist within the qualitative movement: structured interview, semi-structured interviews and unstructured interviews (Zhang and Wildemuth 2009). In the current study a qualitative method of unstructured interviews was employed and reported (see following section).

The current qualitative analysis employed for developing an intervention program based on the salutogenic model was embedded within a more comprehensive mixed methods assessment that will be reported separately in an evaluative study following the outcomes and process of the intervention. The more comprehensive study adopted the Convergent Parallel Design approach to mixing methods in order to illustrate quantitative results with those of qualitative; synthesizing corresponding quantitative and qualitative results to develop a more multifaceted and insightful understanding (Creswell and Plano Clark 2011) than would be obtained by analyzing either type of data separately.

Unstructured Interviews

The current study employed unstructured interviews as a qualitative research method for data collection. Unstructured interviews were developed in the disciplines of anthropology and sociology in order to elicit people's social realities (Zhang and Wildemuth 2009). Punch (1998) described unstructured interviews as a way of comprehending people's behavior patterns without imposing any prior categorization which might narrow the field of inquiry. Patton (2002) defined unstructured interviews as a natural extension of participant observation, relying on the spontaneous generation of questions in the natural flow of an interaction. The interviewer generates questions in response to the interviewee's narration. The intention is to expose the interviewer to unanticipated themes and to assist in developing an in-depth understanding of the staff's reality from their perspective. The interviewer is aware of the purpose of the interview and the general scope of the issues that he/she wishes to discuss (Fife 2005) while maintaining an open mind and creating a secure environment for the interviewee. The interviewer's control of the interview is intended to be minimal. However, he/she tries to encourage the interviewees to relate experiences and issues related to the purpose of the interview (Burgess 1995). In the current assessment, the interviewer did not approach the interviews with any social realities and therefore no specific questions were designed beforehand, but rather had conversations with the interviewees and generated questions in response to the conveyed narrations. As evaluators, we wanted the interview to be as open as possible in order to enable the interviewee to express his or her perceptions and feelings freely. As a result, each interview generated data in a different pattern and from diverse perspectives. The subjectivity of the interviewee was more apparent due to the fact that the interview was not structured in advance. In the current study, where appropriate, and when unanticipated themes arose, additional probe questions were asked to elicit further details and amplify answers (Rubin and Rubin 1995).

The analysis of the interviews was done according to the following guidelines: (1) generating themes and categories which conveyed the interviewees' meaning in an attempt to identify links between the themes; (2) producing a list of main themes which captured the interviewees' main concerns; and, (3) presenting evidence in words from the interview. The analysis of the interviews was based on the Sense of Coherence construct and its three dimensions of comprehensibility, manageability and meaningfulness. In line with theory based analysis, the resultant model emerged from the data itself in which it was grounded. The subsequent core themes were identified disclosing the three thematic axes of Sense of Coherence around which they revolved.

Results: Assessment of Salutogenic Motivational (Promoting) and Environmental (Deterring) Themes

Interview Results

Data analysis of the interviews generated the following ten primary themes: leadership of head nurse; lack of expertise in treatment of patients with mental retardation and their integration with the mentally ill; disappointment from the hospital management's lack of attention to the staff's and unit's concerns; lack of social and academic activities outside the hospital grounds; near to impossible living and working conditions (large number of patients versus an insufficient number of staff, lack of furniture, etc.); patients suffering from diverse problems (retarded, psychotic and retarded and psychotic); self- fulfillment; Occupational Self-Efficacy; professional/job satisfaction; devotion to the unit and its patients and a strong sense of belonging.

The three thematic axes, around which the core ten themes revealed in the interviews revolved, disclosed a salutogenic model of individual and collective SOC, as visualized in Fig. 4.1: (1) The *comprehensibility* axis; (2) The *environment* axis (manageability); and (3) The *motivation/emotion* axis (meaningfulness). An in-depth examination of the three axes revealed two discrete fields: *promoting and deterring*, in which the motivation/emotion axis encompassed promoting and constructive factors, the environment axis encompassed deterring and negative factors, and the comprehensibility axis encompassed both promoting and deterring factors.

Comprehensibility

The level of comprehensibility; pervasive, enduring and dynamic feeling (or lack of feeling) of confidence that the stimuli deriving from one's internal and external environment were structured, predictable, and explicable (Antonovsky 1987); was conveyed in the staff's individual and collective SOC within three themes:

Leadership of Head Nurse

The staff acknowledged the leadership qualities of the head nurse as responsible for structuring their working environment and duties. They conveyed their comprehensibility on a personal level and on a collective level.

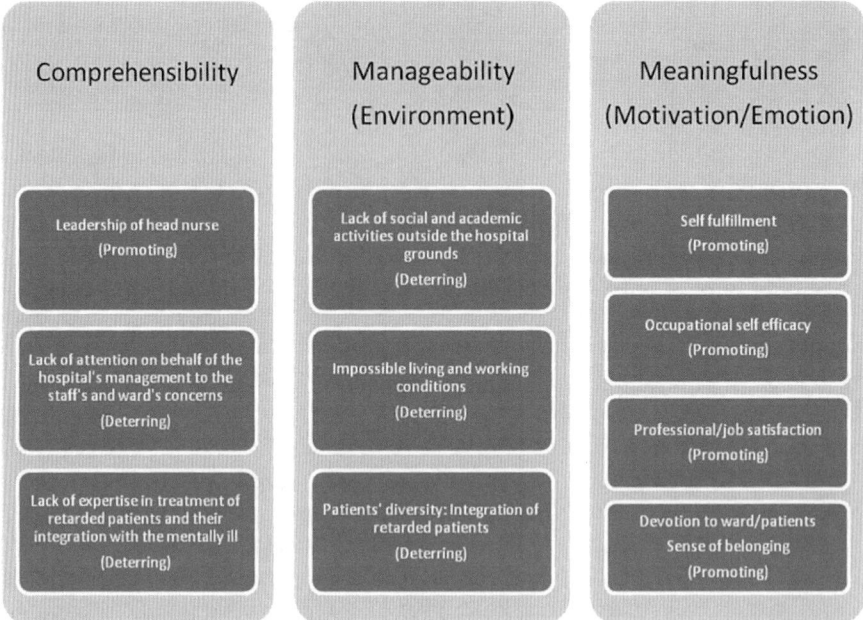

Fig. 4.1 A salutogenic model of sense of coherence

I understand my position, responsibilities, and duties in the unit. (Tom)
My functions as part of a staff are clear. (Dan)
The head nurse sets an example for us and we want to carry out what she expects of us. (Lee)
The head nurse understands our needs and addresses the management on our behalf. She does not always succeed, but we know that she tries. (Gal)
The head nurse always explains why she asks me to do something and this makes the task much easier to perform. (Ella)

Lack of Expertise in Treating Patients with Mental Retardation

The staff expressed their frustration due to their lack of knowledge and understanding regarding the treatment of patients with mental retardation that are hospitalized alongside patients with acute psychiatric disorders. The staff was not trained to treat patients with mental retardation and was aware that the lack of professional knowledge was damaging to all the patients in the unit and to the staff's quality of care.

The patients with mental retardation have different needs than the patients with acute psychotic problems. (Tom)
Sometimes I don't know what to do with patients with mental retardation. (Dan)
The patients with mental retardation require my constant attention and the other patients are therefore neglected. (Lee)
We were not trained to treat patients with mental retardation. Our lack of knowledge evokes frustration and aggravation. (Gal)
The hospital management is aware of the problem, but nothing is being done because the patients with mental retardation have nowhere to go to. (Ella)

Hospital Management's Lack of Attention to the Staff's Concerns

The staff expressed their frustration with the management's lack of attention to their concerns and needs. Although they were given the opportunity to convey their concerns via the head nurse, they felt that the issues that they had presented were not properly attended to. This lack of attention caused individual and collective disorientation and perplexity among the staff members.

> We feel that the management disregards our needs and requests. (Tom)
> I know that the head nurse has tried to no avail to address our needs. We represent the needs of the patients first and foremost. Our needs are secondary. The patients come first. (Dan)
> The management has promised over the years to renovate our unit, but this has not occurred. Other units are given first priority over our unit. It seems that the patients that are severely ill are regarded as second class compared to patients from other units. (Lee)
> We feel that our concerns are less important because we are treating patients that are not aware of their personal and collective environment. (Gal)

The interviews revealed *promoting and deterring themes* within the component of comprehensibility. The staff's high regard of their head nurse was a promoting factor in their daily routine and persisting hardships within the unit. In fact, the head nurse was the cause for the staff's sense of order and regularity within the unit. The interviews expressed the staff's recognition of the head nurse's leadership qualities and the head nurse's role in preserving their individual and collective comprehensibility. The latter had a significant role in balancing the factors which were regarded by the staff as deterring: lack of expertise in treatment of patients with mental retardation and their integration with the mentally ill; disappointment from the hospital management's lack of attention to the staff's and unit's concerns.

Manageability: The Environment Axis

The level of manageability; availability of sources to meet the demands posed by the stimuli deriving from one's internal and external environment (Antonovsky 1987), was articulated by the staff with extreme reservations with regards to three primary issues:

Lack of Social and Academic Activities Outside the Hospital Grounds

The staff expressed their desire to participate in activities outside the mental health center. For the most, they conveyed their desire to take part in joint activities, both social and academic, and emphasized that they take place outside the hospital grounds. Due to the poor facilities and the intense and stressful work, they felt that they did not have the opportunity to actually socially interact and exchange experiences, whether professional or personal. Their sense of belonging to a group, being part of a team, enhanced their wish to create personal interactions exceeding the boundaries of the unit.

On the one hand, we are very close to each other; spending many hours together in an intense and closed environment; On the other hand, we do not have the opportunity to share our experiences and thoughts. (Dan)

There is a need to hold activities for the well-being of the staff. Sometimes we have in training activities, but they are within the hospital and we do not experience a change in our environment. (Tal)

Aside from educational activities, we need to do pleasurable activities together. The management should realize that we need to enjoy ourselves as a group and experience positive emotions jointly. (Ben)

Patients Suffering from Diverse Problems

Within the unit they categorized the patients into three kinds: patients suffering from acute psychiatric conditions, patients suffering from mental retardation and those comorbid patients suffering from both acute psychiatric conditions and mental retardation. Their frustration lay in the fact that they were experienced and knowledgably in treating patients with acute psychiatric conditions and not patients with mental retardation. They felt that the time that they were spending on "trial and error" actions regarding the treatment of the patients with mental retardation was at the expense of all the patients, consuming both the staff's time and emotional energy. The realization that the patients with mental retardation were hospitalized in a psychiatric unit due to lack of proper facilities was evident and a cause for disorder and malfunctioning.

The unit specializes in acute cases of psychiatric conditions. However, due to lack of facilities in the southern region of Israel, the unit treats patients with mental retardation as well. We were not trained to treat patients with mental retardation and realize that their needs are different from the needs of patients with acute psychiatric illnesses. Our lack of training and the fact that the two populations are in one unit, affects our quality of work and the patients pay a heavy price as well. (Sonia)

It is very hard to manage patients suffering with such a diverse range of illnesses. (Gal)

We should have three separate units – one for patients with acute psychiatric conditions; one for patients with mental retardation and one for patients with both conditions. (Dan)

The time that we spend in "trial and error" activities is also energy consuming and not fair to the patients. (Doron)

Poor Living and Working Facilities

The staff expressed their concern regarding the insufficient size of the acute in patient unit. The unit had not been intended to contain 34 patients and the staff. The dining room cannot serve meals to everyone at the same time due to lack of space and meals are served in shifts. The living rooms are very small and with minimal facilities. There is one area for toilets that is intended for both the female and male patients. Due to an insufficient number of toilets, the patients sometimes use the inner court when the toilets are occupied by other patients for longer periods of time. Furthermore, the unit is in desperate need of renovation and care. The staff expressed their frustration with the fact that other units at the hospital had been renovated (due to a large contribution that was given to the hospital) and their unit had been neglected. An example of negligence was the long broken water cooler that served both the patients and the staff in the unit.

> It is impossible to provide maximum care when we are so few and they are so many. (Ella)
> The management thinks that the patients who are in severe mental states do not notice the terrible conditions that they live in. (Gal)
> During the winter when it is too cold to be outdoors (within the inner court), all the patients and staff are in the lobby of the unit which is the size of a standard bedroom. There are not enough chairs and the patients start to fight with each other only because of lack of space. (Bella)
> We need to clean the inner court because patients use the court as toilets when the toilets inside the unit are occupied. These are not conditions fit for human beings. (Dan)
> The staff has a small room for itself. We wish we had a better place for resting and cleaning our minds. (Ben)
> In the past we were told that there was no money. However, now we know that a large donation was made and we don't understand why nothing is being done. (Katie)

The interviews revealed *deterring themes* within the component of manageability. It was apparent from each and every one of the interviewees that the low level of manageability was a significant drawback, interfering with the flow and quality of the staff's work.

Meaningfulness: The Motivation/Emotion Axis

A strong sense of meaningfulness was a significant underlying characteristic within the staff's narratives. The demands of the staff's functions were perceived as challenges, worthy of investment and engagement. Meaningfulness was conveyed in the staff's individual and collective SOC within four themes: Self- fulfillment; Occupational Self-Efficacy; professional/job satisfaction; devotion to the unit and its patients and a strong sense of belonging. The staff expressed the significance of their work to the advancement and security of their patients' lives. Their importance as primary emotional and physical supporters of the patients was very coherent to them. They perceived themselves as the patients' sole caretakers, filling the roles of parents, siblings and other close relationships. The sense that they were contributing to the well-being of their patients was highly apparent in the tone, the choice of words and the gestures employed by the staff members. The realization that they were working under poor conditions with patients suffering from acute psychiatric illnesses and patients with mental retardation, at times paying a personal price, did not weaken them or reduce their level of motivation. On the contrary, their high regard for their own work provided them with a deep understanding that they were actually making a difference, increasing their sense of self-worth. Each one of the staff members expressed their enthusiasm and excitement with their profession in general and their work in "the most difficult unit of all", in particular. They recognized that their level of commitment to their patients was overwhelming and unique. This sense of being special on both functional and emotional levels provided the staff members with a meaningful existence, finding meaning in that which facilitates individual ability to be effective.

Self-Fulfillment

The staff described their high sense of self-fulfillment due to their work in the acute psychiatric in-patient unit. All of them said that they had previous experience in other psychiatric units in the hospital and in other hospitals. However, the highest level of self-fulfillment was experienced in this particular unit because of the severity of the patients' conditions and their total dependence on the staff.

> I feel that the patients need me for everything and this strengthens the important role I have in their lives. (Stav)
> I have worked in other units in this hospital due to the rotation regulation, but I don't want to move to another unit because of the strong sense of fulfillment that I feel here. (Gal)
> The reason for choosing my profession receives confirmation in the sense of fulfillment that I experience almost on a daily basis. (Ella)

Occupational Self-Efficacy

The staff's narratives communicated a strong Occupational Self-Efficacy (demonstrated in the results of the quantitative analysis as well), conveying their feeling of accomplishment in performing the unit's required tasks. They expressed their Occupational Self-Efficacy by conveying their work values, the commitment to their profession and their willingness to do what is required of them in accordance with the patients' needs. Moreover, the staff's ability to ask for and receive support from their colleagues enhanced their Occupational Self-Efficacy. The staff recognized the importance of working together as a team in order to strengthen both their individual and their collective Occupational Self-Efficacy.

> I am very proud of my occupation. (Ben)
> I know that I am very good at what I do. (Gal)
> At times, we carry out the impossible and this sense of accomplishment is very rewarding (May)
> I am happy that I can fulfill the needs of the patients. (Dror)

Professional/Job Satisfaction

The staff's narratives conveyed the result of their strong sense of self-fulfillment and Occupational Self-Efficacy – a high level of job satisfaction (demonstrated in the results of the quantitative analysis as well). The staff conveyed their satisfaction which, according to their self-analysis, derived from pleasurable experiences with the patients, cognitive beliefs related to the significance of their job, and a high level of motivation to continue to promote the well-being of their patients. Supporting this analysis, significant positive correlations (quantitative analysis) were found between hospital Sense of Coherence and Occupational Self-Efficacy and Occupational Self-Efficacy and professional satisfaction.

> I am very satisfied with my job. (Ben)
> I do not want to leave this unit, even though it is the most difficult one to work in. (Gal)
> We are satisfied as a team because we know that we are doing a good job. (Dan)
> The head nurse is a leading factor in my job satisfaction. I think that the entire staff feels the same. (May)

Devotion to Unit/Sense of Belonging

The staff communicated a very high sense of belonging to a group, a team, a setting. The understanding that each and every one of them was working toward a common goal and the ability to place the patients' needs above their own, established, a strong sense of joint activity towards enhancing the well-being of their patients.

> The head nurse's devotion to us and her constant dedication to our patients enhance our devotion to the unit. (Guy)
> We all want the same thing – our patients' well-being. This joint endeavor creates a sense of belonging. We are all loyal to a common goal. (Ella)
> There is a strong sense of team effort. We all try to comply with each other's needs. We know that if we help each other, we will all profit. (Dorin)

The interviews revealed *promoting themes* within the component of meaningfulness. Self-fulfillment; Occupational Self-Efficacy; professional/job satisfaction; devotion to the unit and its patients and a strong sense of belonging were considered by the staff as contributing to their individual and collective quality of work and to their patients' well-being.

Discussion and Recommendations for Interventions

The aim of the present study was to evaluate an acute psychiatric in-patient unit in a mental health center in southern Israel for the purpose of developing an intervention program based on the salutogenic model. Following the initiation of an intervention program for the unit by the Salutogenic Research Center at Ben Gurion University and a mental health center in southern Israel, the current study aimed at assessing the unit's needs in order to develop the rationale and goals of the intervention for the advancement of the staff's individual and collective Sense of Coherence.

The Comprehensibility Axis

The *comprehensibility axis* revealed promoting and deterring themes. The staff's high regard of their head nurse was a promoting factor in their daily routine and persisting hardships within the unit. In fact, the head nurse was the cause for the staff's sense of order and regularity within the unit. The latter had a significant role in balancing the factors which were regarded by the staff as deterring: lack of expertise in treatment of patients with mental retardation and their integration with the mentally ill; disappointment from the hospital management's lack of attention to the staff's and unit's concerns. This finding accentuates the importance of having a strong and respected management in preserving the staff's individual and collective comprehensibility, in particular, and Sense of Coherence, in general.

Furthermore, the integration of patients with mental retardation in one unit with patients suffering from psychiatric illnesses has been shown in the current assessment as a deterring factor that interferes with the effectiveness of the workforce and the wellbeing of the patients. It is recommended that the staff receive professional training on the treatment of patients with mental retardation and the treatment of patients suffering from a diverse range of illnesses hospitalized in the same unit. In addition, the management should consider moving the patients with mental retardation to a different unit with staff that has appropriate training, which could address the patients' needs better.

Finally, it is suggested that meetings between the staff and the hospital management be held on a regular basis, enabling the staff to share their individual and collective concerns with the management and establish a platform for communication with the management.

The Manageability Axis

The *environment axis* (manageability) revealed deterring themes. The low level of manageability was a significant drawback, interfering with the flow and quality of the staff's work. Following the staff's aspiration for joint social and academic activities outside the health center, it is suggested that resources for at least four annual joint activities be recruited. These activities may be an integral part of the intervention, including psychological, academic and cultural modules.

Furthermore, it is essential to improve the near to impossible living and working conditions in order to create a more effective and pleasurable working and living environment. Improving the workplace environment within psychiatric services was found to be one of the most important factors in staff burnout prevention strategies, suggesting potential benefits for the patients (Lasalvia et al. 2009). The intervention may consider integrating professional financial consultants in an attempt to make use of the existing financial resources available for upgrading the unit's physical surroundings. The current assessment emphasized the importance of renovating the unit in order to provide a respectful home for those long term patients that may never know another environment alternative to the current mental health center.

The Meaningfulness Axis

The *motivation/emotion axis* (meaningfulness) was considered by the staff as contributing (promoting) to their individual and collective quality of work and to their patients' well-being. The relationship between individual and staff meaningfulness, Occupational Self-Efficacy and job satisfaction was conveyed by the staff, calling attention to their outstanding sense of fulfillment and meaning. The latter supported the salutogenic assumption that psychological resources such as self-esteem and self-efficacy created life experiences that contributed to the individual's meaningful world (Wiesmann and Hannich 2011). Furthermore, the staff's high levels of commitment and their strong sense of professional meaning and purpose echoed previous research on the impact of meaningfulness on the quality of patient care (Ablett and Jones 2007).

Consequently, the intervention should attempt to accentuate this strength by holding staff meetings on individual and collective meaningfulness. The staff may not be fully aware of their individual and collective meaningfulness and moreover, they may need assistance in making use of this asset in the unit's daily functioning and effectiveness.

The staff's narratives communicated a strong Occupational Self-Efficacy, conveying their recognition of past performance accomplishment and exposure to and identification with efficacious models (vicarious learning). The staff's ability to ask for and receive support from their colleagues enhanced their Occupational Self-Efficacy. These sources of efficacy information continually and reciprocally interact to affect performance judgments that in turn influence their performance and effort (Linnenbrink and Pintrich 2003).

Interviews as Part of the Intervention

Furthermore, an interesting result of the interviews was noted during the interviewer's meeting with the head nurse. The latter reported that the staff members that were interviewed felt as if they had gone through a psychological session. The interviews were perceived as an empowering and beneficial experience; a "ventilation point", enabling them to express their perceptions and emotions. This may derive from the opportunity that they had to convey their thoughts and feelings in a secure and pleasant setting to someone who was not a part of the mental health center. Patton (2002) perceived this secure setting as one of the merits of an unstructured interview. The interviewer is able to be highly responsive to individual differences and situational changes. In a recent study (Wennerberg et al. 2012) examining informal caregivers' resources to health using the salutogenic approach, participating in salutogenic interviewing was an enlightening experience due to the focus on health and positive aspects in a situation that usually employs the pathological approach.

As a result, the current assessment views the interviews not only as a stage in the assessment process, but also as a stage in the intervention program. In this case, the interviewer is not only an integral part of the research procedure, but a part of the entire assessment and intervention process. In light of the interview's therapeutic role, it is recommended to integrate, in the planned intervention, sessions in which the mental health professionals have the opportunity to openly convey their thoughts and emotions on a regular basis, providing a setting, and a sitting, that enables relief, reflection and empowerment.

Limitations and Conclusions

The findings of the current evaluative study should be treated in light of several limitations. The cross-sectional nature of this study demonstrates that causal relations and longitudinal research that addresses reciprocal effects over time may add valuable knowledge to understanding the needs of the unit towards planning an intervention that intends to be effective over a long period of time. Furthermore, future research should evaluate a larger sample of professional and administrative staff and compare various psychiatric units in diverse mental health centers. Finally, the interviews' "therapeutic role" in the current assessment should be taken into consideration when analyzing the questionnaires that were submitted to the staff from the acute in patient unit following the interviews.

A recent study found that the Sense of Coherence model lends support to tailoring rehabilitation programs to the individual patient's holistic needs and personal goals. Evidence in support of this approach provided insight into rehabilitation practice, focusing both on reducing obstacles preventing the highest level of personal and social functioning and on building and strengthening external and internal resources (Griffiths 2009). It is suggested that the planned intervention incorporate goals and programs for the staff, the patients and their families with the Sense of Coherence concept as part of their foundation.

In conclusion, the assessment presented here based on the salutogenic model, has significant implications for the impending intervention. Consequently, the intervention program aims at creating a health promoting community based on the salutogenic approach, focusing on the advancement of the staff's individual and collective Sense of Coherence: the extent to which one has a persuasive, enduring, dynamic feeling of confidence that the stimuli deriving from one's internal and external environment are structured, predictable, and explicable (comprehensibility); that resources are available to meet the demands posed by these stimuli (manageability); and that these demands are challenges, worthy of investment and engagement (meaningfulness) (Antonovsky 1987). Supporting these three dimensions at individual as well as collective levels is believed to improve the staff's communal Sense of Coherence which, in turn, will promote the patients' health and the well-being of their families.

References

Ablett, J. R., & Jones, R. S. P. (2007). Resilience and well-being in palliative care staff: A qualitative study of hospice nurses' experience of work. *Psycho-Oncology, 16*, 733–740.

Antonovsky, A. (1979). *Health, stress, and coping: New perspectives on mental and physical wellbeing*. San Francisco: Jossey-Bass.

Antonovsky, A. (1987). *Unraveling the mystery of health*. San Francisco: Jossey-Bass.

Antonovsky, A. (1996). The salutogenic model as a theory to guide health promotion. *Health Promotion International, 11*(1), 11–18.

Bandura, A. (1994). Self-efficacy. In V. S. Ramachaudran (Ed.), *Encyclopedia of human behavior* (pp. 71–81). New York: Academic Press.

Bandura, A. (1997). *Self-efficacy: The exercise of control*. New York: Freeman.

Brown, D. J., Ferris, D. L., Heller, D., & Keeping, L. M. (2007). Antecedents and consequences of the frequency of upward and downward social comparisons at work. *Organizational Behavior and Human Decision Processes, 102*, 59–75.

Burgess, R. G. (1995). *In the field: An introduction to field research*. London: Routledge.

Caprara, G. V., Regalia, C., Scabini, E., Barbaranelli, C., & Bandura, A. (2004). Assessment of filial, parental, marital, and collective family efficacy beliefs. *European Journal of Psychological Assessment, 20*, 247–261.

Carver, C. S., & Scheier, M. F. (1998). *On the self-regulation of behavior*. New York: Cambridge University Press.

Creswell, J. W., & Plano Clark, V. L. (2011). *Designing and conducting mixed methods research*. Los Angeles: Sage.

Edwards, D., Burnard, P., Coyle, D., Fothergill, A., & Hannigan, B. (2000). Stress and burnout in community mental health nursing: A review of literature. *Journal of Psychiatric and Mental Health Nursing, 7*, 7–14.

Eriksson, M., & Lindstrom, B. (2005). Validity of Antonovsky's sense of coherence scale: A systematic review. *Journal of Epidemiology and Community Health, 59*, 460–466.

Eriksson, M., & Lindstrom, B. (2006). Antonovsky's sense of coherence scale and the relation with health: A systematic review. *Journal of Epidemiological Community Health, 60*, 376–381.

Eriksson, M., & Lindstrom, B. (2007). Antonovsky's sense of coherence scale and its relation with quality of life: A systematic review. *Journal of Epidemiology and Community Health, 61*, 938–944.

Fife, W. (2005). *Doing fieldwork: Ethnographic methods for research in developing countries and beyond*. New York: Palgrave Macmillan.

Griffiths, C. A. (2009). Sense of coherence and mental health rehabilitation. *Clinical Rehabilitation, 23*, 72–78.

Jormfeldt, H. (2010). Attitudes towards health among patients and staff in mental health services: A comparison of ratings of importance of different items of health. *Social Psychiatry and Psychiatric Epidemiology, 34*(45), 225–231.

Judge, T. A., & Bono, J. E. (2001). Relationship of core self-assessment traits – Self-esteem, generalized self-efficacy, locus of control, and emotional stability – With job satisfaction and job performance: A meta-analysis. *The Journal of Applied Psychology, 86*, 80–92.

Lasalvia, A., Bonetto, C., Bertani, M., Bissoli, S., Cristofalo, D., Marrella, G., Ceccato, E., Cremonese, C., De Rossi, M., Lazzarotto, L., Marangon, V., Morandin, I., Zucchetto, M., Tansella, M., & Ruggeri, M. (2009). Influence of perceived organizational factors on job burnout: Survey of community mental health staff. *The British Journal of Psychiatry, 195*, 537–544.

Lindstrom, B., & Eriksson, M. (2006). Contextualizing salutogenesis and Antonovsky in public health development. *Health Promotion International, 21*, 238–244.

Linnenbrink, E. A., & Pintrich, P. R. (2003). The role of self-efficacy beliefs in student engagement and learning in the classroom. *Reading & Writing Quarterly, 19*, 119–137.

Lloyd, C., & King, R. (2004). A survey of burnout among Australian mental health occupational therapists and social workers. *Social Psychiatry and Psychiatric Epidemiology, 39*, 752–757.

Locke, E. A. (1976). The nature and causes of job satisfaction. In M. D. Dunnette (Ed.), *Handbook of industrial and organizational psychology* (pp. 1297–1343). Chicago: Rand McNally.

Malach Pines, A. (2002). A psychoanalytic existential approach to burnout: Demonstrated in the cases of a nurse, a teacher and a manager. *Psychotherapy, 39*(1), 103–113.

Malach Pines, A. (2004). Why are Israelis less burned out? *European Psychologist, 9*(2), 69–77.

McGuire, D. B., Correa, M. E. P., Johnson, J., & Wienandts, P. (2006). The role of basic oral care and clinical practice principles in the management of oral mucositis. *Supportive Care in Cancer, 14*, 541–547.

Morse, G., Salyers, M. P., Rollins, A. L., Monroe-DeVita, M., & Pfahler, C. (2012). Burnout in mental health services: A review of the problem and its remediation. *Administration and Policy in Mental Health, 39*(5), 341–352. doi:10.1007/s10488011035 21.

Onyett, S., Pillinger, T., & Muijen, M. (1997). Job satisfaction and burnout among members of community mental health teams. *Journal of Mental Health, 6*, 55–66.

Pajares, F. (1996). Self-efficacy beliefs in academic settings. *Review of Educational Research, 6*, 543–578.

Patton, M. Q. (2002). *Qualitative research and assessment methods.* Thousand Oaks: Sage.

Posadzki, P., Stockl, A., Musonda, P., & Tsouroufli, M. (2010). A mixed method approach to sense of coherence, health behaviors, self-efficacy and optimism: Towards the operationalization of positive health attitudes. *Scandinavian Journal of Psychology, 51*, 246–252.

Prosser, D., Johnson, S., Kuipers, E., Szmukler, G., Bebbington, P., & Thornicroft, G. (1996). Mental health, "burnout" and job satisfaction among hospital and community-based mental health staff. *The British Journal of Psychiatry, 169*, 334–337.

Punch, K. F. (1998). *Introduction to social research: Quantitative and qualitative approaches.* Thousand Oaks: Sage.

Rabin, S., Matalon, A., Maoz, B., & Shiber, A. (2005). Keeping doctors healthy: A salutogenic perspective. *Families, Systems & Health, 23*(1), 94–102.

Reid, Y., Johnson, S., Morant, N., Kuipers, E., Szmukler, G., Thornicroft, G., Bebbington, P., & Prosser, D. (1999). Explanations for stress and satisfaction in mental health professionals: A qualitative study. *Social Psychiatry and Psychiatric Epidemiology, 34*, 301–308.

Richards, D. A., Bee, P., Barkham, M., Gilbody, S. M., Cahill, J., & Glanville, J. (2006). The prevalence of nursing staff stress on adult acute psychiatric in-patient wards. *Social Psychiatry and Psychiatric Epidemiology, 34*(41), 34–43.

Rubin, H., & Rubin, I. (1995). *Qualitative interviewing: The art of hearing data.* Thousand Oaks: Sage.

Schunk, D. H., & Pajares, F. (2002). The development of academic self-efficacy. In A. Wigfield & J. Eccles (Eds.), *Development of achievement motivation* (pp. 16–31). San Diego: Academic.

Schwarzer, R. (1994). Optimistische Kompetenzerwartung: Zur Erfassung einer personellenBewältigungsressource [Optimistic expectation of competence: The assessment of personnelcoping resource]. *Diagnostica, 40*, 105–123.

Stajkovic, A. D., & Luthans, F. (1998). Self-efficacy and work-related performance: A metaanalysis. *Psychological Bulletin, 124*, 240–261.

Stanton, M. (2000). Stress, coping, and health in families: SOC and resiliency. *Family Relations, 49*(3), 350–351.

Svedberg, P. (2007). Health promotion intervention in mental health services. Doctoral dissertation, Department of Health Sciences, Faculty of Medicine, Lund University, Sweden).

Thomsen, S., Soares, J., Nolan, P., Dallender, J., & Arnetz, B. (1999). Feelings of professional fulfillment and exhaustion in mental health personnel: The importance of organizational and individual factors. *Psychotherapy and Psychosomatics, 68*, 157–164.

Tracey, J. B., Hinkin, T. R., Tannenbaum, S., & Mathieu, J. E. (2001). The influence on individual characteristics and the work environment on varying levels of training outcomes. *Human Resource Development Quarterly, 12*, 5–23.

Weiss, H. M., & Cropanzano, R. (1996). Affective events theory: A theoretical discussion of the structure, causes, and consequences of affective experiences at work. In B. M. Staw & L. L. Cummings (Eds.), *Research in organizational behavior* (Vol. 18, pp. 1–74). Greenwich: JAI Press.

Wennerberg, M. M. T., Lundgren, S. M., & Danielson, E. (2012). Using the salutogenic approach to unravel informal caregivers' resources to health: Theory and methodology. *Aging & Mental Health, 16*(3), 391–402.

Wertz, F. J., Charmaz, K., McMullen, L. M., Josselson, R., Anderson, R., & McSpadden, E. (2011). *Five ways of doing qualitative analysis.* New York: The Guilford Press.

Wiesmann, U., & Hannich, H.-J. (2011). Salutogenic perspectives on health maintenance: The role of resistance resources and meaningfulness. *Geropsychology, 24*(3), 127–135.

World Health Organization Europe. (2005). *Mental health: Facing the challenges, building solutions.* Report from the WHO European Ministerial Conference. Copenhagen: World Health Organization, Regional Office for Europe.

Zhang, Y., & Wildemuth, B. M. (2009). Unstructured interviews. In B. M. Wildemuth (Ed.), *Applications of social research methods to questions in information and library science.* Westport: Libraries Unlimited.

Part II
Organizational Concepts Guiding Theory-Driven Interventions

Chapter 5
Salutogenesis in the Workplace: Building General Resistance Resources and Sense of Coherence

Lenneke Vaandrager and Maria Koelen

Abstract Companies and work organisations nowadays are dependent on well-trained, highly qualified, and motivated employees. At the same time, the potential of the workforce and its ability to develop have become the subject of a new understanding of health, which encompasses both physical and mental well-being, quality of life, and learning. From a salutogenic perspective, workplace health can be defined as the ability of the workforce to participate and be productive in a sustainable and meaningful way. Implementing a salutogenic approach at work requires keen employee involvement and interdisciplinary collaboration between, e.g., management, HRM, safety, environmental and health professionals. A salutogenic organisation provides personal, social, and environmental resources (general resistance resources) that offer coherent (comprehensible, manageable, and meaningful) working experiences and sustainable organisational outcomes. It promotes the development of the capacities of employees and employers to use these resources. Workplaces can be considered as complex ecological systems. Implementing a salutogenic intervention may be seen as a critical event in the history of a workplace system, leading to new structures of interaction, new resources, and individual, social, and organisational learning. These types of outcomes are therefore of interest when a salutogenic approach in the workplace is being evaluated.

Keywords Salutogenesis • General resistance resources (GRRs) • Workplace system • Individual • Social, and organisational learning

L. Vaandrager (✉) • M. Koelen
Health and Society, Department of Social Sciences,
Wageningen University, Wageningen, The Netherlands
e-mail: lenneke.vaandrager@wur.nl; maria.koelen@wur.nl

G.F. Bauer and G.J. Jenny (eds.), *Salutogenic Organizations and Change:*
The Concepts Behind Organizational Health Intervention Research,
DOI 10.1007/978-94-007-6470-5_5, © Springer Science+Business Media Dordrecht 2013

Introduction

In present-day society, organisations as well as individuals are confronted with the increasing need to compete in a changing environment (Carroll and Edmondson 2002; Nauta et al. 2009). Employers are challenged to increase productivity and efficiency and at the same time maintain the quality of the working environment and enhance organisational learning. Organisational learning is a process that increases the capacity for effective organisational action through knowledge and understanding (Carroll and Edmondson 2002). Workplaces shape daily experiences and provide many options for organisational learning because they represent social systems with specific norms, values, beliefs, and attitudes (Graeser 2011). Organisations need qualified, motivated, and efficient workers. It is therefore of prime interest for an organisation that employees remain physically and mentally healthy. This has led to a trend towards recognising health as an important business value (Zwetsloot et al. 2010).

Health in the workplace can be approached from a pathogenic perspective, which looks at organisational shortcomings, illness, stress, occupational accidents, or chronic diseases. Despite the importance of this pathogenic perspective, it is also worthwhile to look at factors or resources that create health in the workplace, such as an inspiring working environment or sufficient opportunities for learning, the so-called salutogenic perspective (Lindström and Eriksson 2010). In this chapter, we start by defining workplace health from a salutogenic perspective and then unravel what it means to implement this salutogenic approach to work and health. The chapter concludes with implications for the evaluation of the effectiveness of such an approach.

Defining Workplace Health

Definition of Health

It is difficult to define health in terms of objective, measurable criteria. Views regarding what should be understood by health differ across and within different disciplines (Koelen and van den Ban 2004). "Health," like "justice" and "happiness," is a very general concept and difficult to define (Callahan 1973). In 1946, when the World Health Organisation (WHO) was created, health was defined as the complete state of mental, physical, and social well-being, and not merely the absence of disease or infirmity (WHO 1992). With this definition, health was placed in a broad context referring to the interaction between the body and the mind and the importance of the social environment (including affectionate relationships and group membership).

This definition must be historically contextualised in the years following two world wars and a major economic crisis. The belief behind the formation of the WHO was that improving world health would make an important contribution to world peace; health and peace were seen as inseparable. For at least three decades, this definition was used rather generally. It was hardly debated; the main point of debate concerned the problem created by the word "complete" (Callahan 1973). In 1986, the WHO presented a new definition: "health is a resource for everyday life, not the object of living" to stress that health is not a state, but a process on a continuum with a dynamic nature since physical and mental functioning and participation in society can differ over time and place. It was also added that "Health is a positive concept emphasizing social and personal resources, as well as physical capacities" (WHO 1986). Health develops in the context of everyday life, in reciprocal interaction between individuals and their socio-ecological environment. The socio-ecological environment of the workplace includes the social environment (e.g., social relationships, socio-economic position, and social institutions); the physical environment (e.g., working conditions and safety measures), and lifestyle (e.g., healthy nutrition and exercise), which is considered as a function of the reciprocal interaction between individuals and their environment. This broader and more process-oriented definition fitted well with the development of the welfare state.

Workplace Health

Following the 1986 definition, health is an important prerequisite for being able to work, and it encompasses both physical and mental well-being, the quality of life, and learning. In this vein, workplace health can be defined as *the ability of the workforce to participate and be productive in a sustainable and meaningful way*. It also fits with the notion that in the workplace many employees with a chronic disease or disability are able to function with fulfilment and a feeling of well-being (Huber et al. 2011). Even more interestingly, work in itself creates health: we may speak of circular causation, with several interconnected causes and effects. Work has impacts on self-esteem and social recognition. Employment provides time structure, social contact, collective effort and purpose, social identity, and regular activity. Therefore, re-employment has been shown to be one of the most effective ways of promoting the (mental) health of the unemployed (Harnois and Gabiel 2000).

As the workplace forms part of a wider social context, the salutogenic approach to work and health challenges us to look beyond the organisational setting to explore all societal forces and their synergy that contribute to the overall production of healthy learning within the work environment. While recognising this wider focus, in this chapter we restrict our focus to the workplace level.

Salutogenic Perspective: SOC and GRRs

To understand a salutogenic approach to work and health on a workplace level, we first need to explain the salutogenic perspective. The salutogenic perspective focuses attention on health generation as compared to a pathogenesis focus on disease generation. The perspective introduces two fundamental concepts: general resistance resources (GRRs) and the sense of coherence (SOC). GRRs are the internal and external resources that enable individuals to deal with challenges in life. Examples of GRRs include social support, knowledge, self-esteem, traditions, money (Antonovsky 1987). The SOC has been conceptualised as a global orientation in life. Having a strong SOC enables people to view life (or work) as coherent, comprehensible, manageable, and meaningful. A strong SOC gives trust and confidence to an individual to identify resources within themselves and in the immediate environment, and the ability to use and reuse these resources in a health-promoting manner. The comprehensibility component refers to the belief that life events (or working life experiences) are structured, predictable, and explicable. Manageability relates to the belief that life events (or working life experiences) are within one's control. Meaningfulness refers to the belief that life events (or work events) are worthy of investment and a source of satisfaction. Together, they form the cognitive, instrumental, and motivational base necessary to move in a health promoting direction. The stronger the SOC, the greater the capacity of individuals to identify, mobilise, and use their GRRs: according to Antonovsky, the GRRs maintain a dynamic and reciprocal relationship with SOC (Lindström and Eriksson 2010).

Across the literature, the SOC is usually considered as an orientation on an individual level (Graeser 2011), but there have also been attempts to explore the collective meaning of SOC. Antonovsky was the first to propose this idea through his research on family adaptation and health (Antonovsky and Sourani 1988). This research demonstrated that a strong SOC, shared by family members, was predictive of successful adaptation towards conflicts posed by family stressors. This idea can also be applied to a collective SOC in the workplace, shared amongst employees and their managers (the actors in the workplace). Making changes that promote workplace health thus requires an organisational understanding that reaches beyond individual responsibility. Or, in other words, workplace health depends on everyday technical, social, and personal resources (GRRs) as well as employees' capacities to use these resources (the SOC) (Antonovsky 1993; Hanson 2007). Measures which are (only) directed at the individual level (e.g., promotion of healthy lifestyles) are of great importance but cannot suffice in creating a healthy working life. Increasingly, attention is shifting towards organisational resources in diagnosing and improving organisations. In line with Antonovsky's reasoning, the fit between employees and these organisational resources should be considered, rather than the resources alone.

Key GRRs at Work

Amongst others, Nilsson and colleagues (2012) have suggested that the SOC theory can be directly related and applied to a work context. Several researchers have started to investigate specific GRRs in the workplace (Bringsén et al. 2011, 2012; Feldt et al. 2000; Graeser 2011; Nilsson et al. 2012; Wilson et al. 2004). On the basis of this literature, and practical experience in workplace health promotion projects, the GRRs *job control*, *task significance*, and *social relations* are selected here as they have been found to promote health in various studies and projects and also seem to make sense in light of the salutogenic perspective.

Job Control

Job control is a recurrent theme in the literature on workplace health promotion. Job control involves employees' authority to make decisions concerning their jobs and the use of skills regarding task variety and options to develop and learn new things (Lindfors 2012). Job control has also been shown to contribute to an experience of 'distancing' as it increases the ability of the employee to balance the working and non-working life (Bringsén et al. 2012). In light of the SOC dimensions, working conditions supporting greater job control may enhance the perception of manageability as the individual is given the opportunity to exercise more control over aspects of the work. The fact that the worker participates in shaping the working process and has a responsibility for work outcomes also generates an experience of meaningfulness at work (Gagnon and Vaandrager 2012).

Task Significance

Task significance is defined as the perception that one's job has a positive impact on other people (Grant 2008), or, in other words, the meaningfulness and importance of the work, and whether it really matters. Bringsén et al.'s (2012) study on nurses' opinions with regard to what constitutes a health-promoting workplace showed that tasks that had to do with the provision of immediate care to patients were positively linked to meaningful work. Moreover, tasks that fell outside the realm of direct care, such as administrative tasks and development work, were also found to provide positive feelings at work. In fact, they offered an opportunity for nurses to explore new areas of responsibility and to integrate diversity into their work.

Task significance has been linked to a positive experience of congruence between personal values and work activities (Clausen and Borg 2010), which is accompanied by strong feelings of identification with the attitudes, values, or goals of the working tasks (Clausen and Borg 2010) and feelings of motivation and involvement (Kulik et al. 1987). This work-related characteristic influences the meaningfulness component of the SOC as it fosters the belief that the work is worthy of investment.

Predictability is related to task significance. Predictability is referred to in the literature as the extent to which a job provides sufficient and consistent information to enable the employee to do the work well, and to foster awareness of the important decisions and actions taken within the organisation (Kristensen et al. 2005). In accordance with the SOC dimensions, predictability can improve comprehensibility as it provides the boundaries and the necessary information that enable the employee to undertake the work in a predictable manner. Consequently, it may also strengthen the manageability dimension (Gagnon and Vaandrager 2012).

Social Relations

Well-being at work also relates to good social relationships among co-workers and between employees, organisational leadership, and management (Feldt et al. 2000; Lindfors 2012; Whitehead 2006). According to the study by Bringsén et al. (2012) on opinions of healthcare workers with regard to workplace health resources, being part of a team and working in small groups pairing the expertise of staff members from the same or different professions was recognised as an important source of improved quality of work performance.

One special aspect of social relations is social support, in terms of the frequency of opportunities to get help from direct colleagues and managers, as well as the frequency of situations where colleagues are willing to listen and reflect. With respect to the SOC dimensions, social networks and trust can represent strong coping resources to *manage* demands, either within or outside the workplace. Social relations also relate to the meaningfulness component because a collective sense of belonging has a powerful emotional and motivational impact on individuals (Gagnon and Vaandrager 2012).

Another aspect of social relations is feedback at work. As a consequence of the feedback one receives from doing the work, greater knowledge is achieved about results of the work activities. Besides colleagues, managers play an important role in giving feedback by rewarding and encouraging employees. Studies have associated job feedback with an experience of confirmation (Bringsén et al. 2012). To draw a parallel with the SOC dimensions, consistent feedback at work may influence one's perception of comprehensibility with regard to the work situation. In fact, on-going feedback and input can help maintain cognitive clarity and a feeling that things happen in a predictable and explicable manner (Gagnon and Vaandrager 2012).

Principles for Implementing a Salutogenic Approach at Work

Many authors stress that the promotion of capacity development – the creation and improvement of social and physical working conditions – should be treated as a shared task and responsibility between employers and employees (Whitehead 2006). To enhance job control and task significance and to foster social relations, three principles need to be in place: a *multilevel interdisciplinary approach*, *employee participation* and *organisational development*. These factors are based on the Ottawa action areas (WHO 1986) and the Luxembourg declaration on workplace health promotion (ENWHP 1997).

Multilevel Interdisciplinary Approach

As stated in the first section, a salutogenic workplace is not only free of hazards, but also provides an environment that is stimulating and satisfying for those who work there. The 'ownership of health' is distributed over a variety of workplace actors, from different disciplines. By involving and connecting these actors, services of medicine, human resource management, sustainability, well-being, and safety policies are integrated to develop health and well-being (Hanson 2007). These professionals need to learn to work together and integrate their efforts (Koelen et al. 2012). Workplaces can be considered as complex ecological systems. If we examine workplaces from this systemic perspective, we are interested in the connectedness, interrelations, and interdependence of all the parts involved (Hanson 2007; Naaldenberg et al. 2009). Creating a healthy workplace (the innovation or new system) is about network building and/or reconfiguring existing networks in the workplace (Vaandrager et al. 2013). Key tasks and activities to that effect are social learning and negotiation, as well as process management (Koelen et al. 2012). Successful collaboration is therefore a key success factor of salutogenic workplace health promotion. As such, a salutogenic approach takes the complexity and dynamics of health and well-being at the workplace into account, rather than trying to control for it. It regards employees not in isolation but as part of their environment, paying explicit attention to this context. Implementing a salutogenic approach at work can be perceived as a system innovation. The effectiveness of measures or interventions increases if all aspects of salutogenic workplace health, i.e. safety, physical, mental, and social, are integrated into a complex whole (Naaldenberg et al. 2009). Therefore, it is generally advocated to use a multilevel and interdisciplinary approach to integrate individual and organisational strategies and to build the GRRs of job control, task significance, and social relations. Ensuring the presence of these GRRs at the workplace and strengthening employees' capacities to use them are complementary to health safety measures or health protecting equipment. Capacity building and strengthening employees' SOC contribute to managing the challenging business of everyday life and work with their multitudinous stimuli, deadlines, and information.

Employee Participation

Participation is seen as a key success factor for implementing a salutogenic approach at work (Dugdill and Springett 2001; Hanson 2007; Inauen et al. 2012). Knowledge and capacities of different stakeholders, such as employees, members of the executive board, and human resource and occupational health managers, play an important role in salutogenic workplace health. A central role should be given to employees. Employees themselves know very well what they need in their work situation and what is best for their health. Resources which are health promoting for some employees might have no relevance to others, even if these employees are working in the same workplace and so their involvement is vital. A salutogenic approach to work and health is about a good fit between an individual and a particular working environment. For the workforce to be able to participate and be productive, we therefore need to find this fit between the person and the environment, matching the characteristics of jobs to the abilities and needs of jobholders

(Kulik et al. 1987). The strategy of empowerment – fostering the ability and desire of employees to act in empowered ways and to have the autonomy to take part in decision-making processes – is perhaps the most important prerequisite in the implementation process. Empowering employees to control the determinants of their health means that the structures governing working life have to be tailored to promote good health.

Organisational Development

Traditionally, healthcare in the workplace is aimed at improving individual health. From the salutogenic perspective however, health promotion becomes a strategy that supports organisational learning, development, and performance, and consequently it influences the organisation's capacity to carry out its mission (Hanson 2007). The potential of the workforce and its ability to develop have become the subject of a new understanding of managing workplace health, namely, as managing 'fitness for the job' in addition to managing absenteeism and applying safety measures to prevent workplace accidents. Job control, for example, can be enhanced by educational training and career development programmes (Bringsén et al. 2012). Task significance can grow by discussing personal values and how they can play a role in that person's job. Social relations can, for instance, be enhanced by creating trust and by teambuilding activities. A workplace 'fitness for the job' health policy is important because organisations need to mobilise the full potential of their employees, and the workforce needs skills and health to perform in the best possible way. Improving skills can enhance the ability to gain and maintain physical, mental, and emotional fitness for the job. Within this understanding, the promotion of health becomes a strategic issue that supports organisational development and strengthens business performance (Baart et al. 2003).

We assume that the principles for implementing a salutogenic approach relate to the learning experiences which increase people's SOC: participation facilitates individual learning, multilevel and interdisciplinary work facilitates social learning, and organisational development facilitates organisational learning. The GRRs and principles for implementing a salutogenic approach at work are visualised in Fig. 5.1. It should be noted, though, that the description of the relation between the GRRs and the SOC dimensions within the work context as depicted in Fig. 5.1 are theoretical assumptions which should be further tested in empirical research.

Evaluating a Salutogenic Approach at Work

A salutogenic perspective on workplace health has consequences not just for health promotion programmes but also for the way we evaluate these programmes. The dominant approach in research is to analyse origins of problems with a focus on

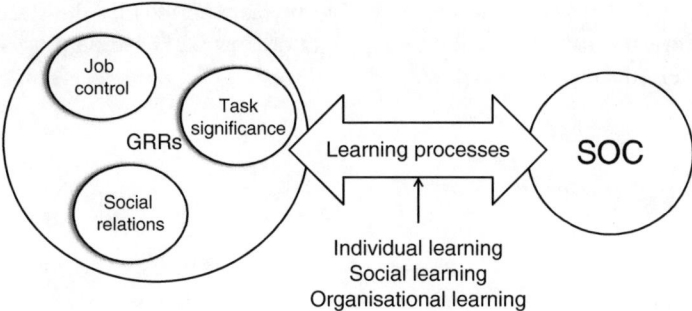

Fig. 5.1 Salutogenesis in the workplace: building GRRs and SOC

deficits, such as unachieved aims and objectives, problematic relations, and other weaknesses, and the aim is to find and implement solutions to 'fix' them. However, as Cooperider et al. (2001) argue, compulsive concern with what is not working and why things are going wrong demoralises members of an organisation, reduces the speed of learning, and undermines relationships and forward movement. That is to say, for evaluation, it is central to shift the focus away from organisational shortcomings, illness, and stress, towards organisational evaluation research with a more positive reference point (Bringsén et al. 2011). The principles of *appreciative inquiry* (Cooperider and Srivasta 1987; Cooperrider et al. 2005) fit very well with this. Appreciative inquiry is an organisational development method which focuses on strengthening what an organisation does well rather than on eliminating what goes wrong. These principles can be applied in both *process evaluation* and *outcome evaluation*.

Process Evaluation

A good theoretical understanding is needed of how salutogenic workplace interventions induce change. Antonovsky's (1987) salutogenic perspective offers such an understanding, but it is difficult to precisely demarcate the boundary between a workplace intervention and its context. Interventions are realised by combining elements such as theory, action plans and materials such as posters, websites, gadgets, with elements situated in the local context, e.g., specific competences, funding, existing collaboration with the workplace (Kok et al. 2012). Process measures signal what worked well and what did not, and in what context. Moreover, since multilevel and interdisciplinary collaboration and employee participation are important processes in workplace health promotion, they need regular assessment too. Regular assessment of how these processes function in practice, and discussion among the participants about their experiences of collective action, can facilitate and support the process. Assessment of these processes has a double function: (1) to evaluate the state of the art and (2) to enable the participants to identify the strengths for moving forward. It is important to get insight on how participation processes have been perceived and appreciated.

Outcome Evaluation

Of course, individual level outcomes such as SOC changes (individual learning, ability to participate and be productive) are of interest when salutogenic workplace health promotion is being evaluated. However, on the basis of the multilevel approach, a range of measures, including measures on the social and organisational level, can help to understand the broader picture, the unintended consequences, and the underlying mechanisms of change. Implementing a salutogenic intervention may be seen as a critical event in the history of a workplace system, leading to new structures of interaction, new resources, and individual, social, and organisational learning. Hawe et al. (2009, p. 270), who introduced this view on evaluation, describe examples such as "Does it exist on the organisation's website? Is it in the orientation package given to new staff? Does it get mentioned in Board Minutes? Is it mentioned in regular staff meetings? Does it exist in the conversations during lunch breaks? Is there time and space regularly allocated for it to take place? Is it part of the organisational mission? Is it funded in the regular budget of the organisation?" These multilevel and systemic success factors can be used looking back to monitor how the intervention has 'shown up' in the organisation, documenting changes in communication, signs and symbols, and behaviours. Hence, the way a salutogenic workplace intervention comes to seep into or saturate its context becomes a way to view the extent of its implementation (Hawe et al. 2009).

Gathering Evaluation Data: Action Research

The fluid nature of the workplace setting requires a holistic and innovative evaluation approach, drawing on a paradigm that places change at the centre of research design. Such an approach comes from the field of action-oriented methodologies, which fully engage participants (in this case the employees and managers of an organisation) in the process. They are well known in business research and management science (Dugdill and Springett 2001). Appreciative inquiry matches with action research approaches.

Action research is a collaborative approach to research that equitably involves employees, organisational representatives, and researchers in all aspects of the research process. The partners contribute unique strengths and shared responsibilities to enhance understanding of a given phenomenon and the social and cultural dynamics of the workplace, and they integrate the knowledge gained with action to improve the health and well-being of the workplace.

Action research also involves an iterative process: data are collected and analysed and immediately fed back into the organisation to see whether the interpretation makes sense in the light of a new experience (new data) in order to be able to refine the interpretation. Consequently, it contributes to organisational learning.

Conclusion

Workplaces can benefit from salutogenic workplace interventions because in the long term they can result in a higher quality of products and services, more innovation, and a rise in productivity.

Employees play a central role, and their participation is a core principle. Furthermore, a salutogenic perspective results in finding a good fit between the aspirations, capacities, and passions of employees and their working environment. Organising work in a salutogenic way is also a prestige factor which helps to improve the public image of a company and makes it become more attractive as an employer (Vaandrager et al. 2013). There are many benefits for employees as well. In the first place, it leads to increased job satisfaction. As mentioned in the first section, work is important for the creation of individual and collective identities. Membership of social groupings provides a point of reference from which individuals make meaning of their work and manage identity. Besides good social relationships, salutogenic interventions in the workplace produce safe and healthy work environments, leading to enhanced job control and task significance.

References

Antonovsky, A. (1987). *Unraveling the mystery of health: How people manage stress and stay well*. San Francisco: Jossey-Bass.

Antonovsky, A. (1993). The structure and properties of the sense of coherence scale. *Social Science & Medicine, 36*(6), 725–733.

Antonovsky, A., & Sourani, T. (1988). Family sense of coherence and family adaptation. *Journal of Marriage and Family, 50*(1), 79–92.

Baart, P., van Capelleveen, C., Iedema, P., Raaijmakers, T., Vaandrager, L., & der Weduwe, K. (2003). *Workplace health promotion*. Woerden: NIGZ.

Bringsén, A., Ejlertsson, G., & Andersson, I. (2011). Flow situations during everyday practice in a medical hospital ward. Results from a study based on experience sampling method. *BMC Nursing, 10*(1), 3. doi:10.1186/1472-6955-10-3.

Bringsén, Å., Andersson, H. I., Ejlertsson, G., & Troein, M. (2012). Exploring workplace related health resources from a salutogenic perspective: Results from a focus group study among healthcare workers in Sweden. *Work: A Journal of Prevention, Assessment and Rehabilitation, 42*(3), 403–414. doi:10.3233/wor-2012-1356.

Callahan, D. (1973). The WHO definition of 'health'. *The Hastings Center Studies, 1*(3), 77–87.

Carroll, J. S., & Edmondson, A. C. (2002). Leading organisational learning in health care. *Quality & Safety in Health Care, 11*(1), 51–56. doi:10.1136/qhc.11.1.51.

Clausen, T., & Borg, V. (2010). Do positive work-related states mediate the association between psychosocial work characteristics and turnover? A longitudinal analysis. *International Journal of Stress Management, 17*(4), 308–324. doi:10.1037/a0021069.

Cooperider, D. L., & Srivasta, S. (1987). Appreciative enquiry in organizational life. *Research in Organizational Change and Development, 1*, 129–169.

Cooperider, D. L., Sorensen, P., Yeager, T., & Whitney, D. (2001). *Appreciative inquiry: An emerging direction for organization development*. Champaign: Stipes.

Cooperrider, D. L., Whitney, D., & Stavros, J. M. (2005). *Appreciative inquiry handbook*. Brunswick: Crown Custom Publishing.

Dugdill, L., & Springett, J. (2001). Evaluating health promotion programmes in the workplace. In I. Rootman, M. Goodstadt, et al. (Eds.), *Evaluation in health promotion: Principles and perspectives*. Copenhagen: WHO.

ENWHP. (1997). *The Luxembourg declaration for workplace health promotion*. Luxembourg: European Network for Workplace Health Promotion.

Feldt, T., Kinnunen, U., & Mauno, S. (2000). A mediational model of sense of coherence in the work context: A one-year follow-up study. *Journal of Organizational Behavior, 21*(4), 461–476.

Gagnon, E., & Vaandrager, L. (2012). *Salutogenic indicators for workplace health promotion, an internship report*. Wageningen: Chairgroup Health & Society of Wageningen University.

Graeser, S. (2011). Salutogenic factors for mental health promotion in work settings and organizations. *International Review of Psychiatry, 23*(6), 508–515. doi:10.3109/09540261.2011.637909.

Grant, A. M. (2008). The significance of task significance: Job performance effects, relational mechanisms, and boundary conditions. *The Journal of Applied Psychology, 93*(1), 108–124. doi:10.1037/0021-9010.93.1.108.

Hanson, A. (2007). *Workplace health promotion: A salutogenic approach*. Bloomington: Author House.

Harnois, G., & Gabiel, P. (2000). *Mental health and work: Impact issues and good practices*. Geneva: ILO.

Hawe, P., Shiell, A., & Riley, T. (2009). Theorising interventions as events in systems. *American Journal of Community Psychology, 43*(3–4), 267–276. doi:10.1007/s10464-009-9229-9.

Huber, M., Knottnerus, J. A., et al. (2011). How should we define health? *BMJ, 343*(4163), 235–287. doi:10.1136/bmj.d4163.

Inauen, A., Jenny, G. J., & Bauer, G. F. (2012). Design principles for data- and change-oriented organisational analysis in workplace health promotion. *Health Promotion International, 27*(2), 275–283. doi:10.1093/heapro/dar030.

Koelen, M. A., & van den Ban, A. W. (2004). *Health education and health promotion*. Wageningen: Wageningen Academic Publishers.

Koelen, M. A., Vaandrager, L., & Wagemakers, A. (2012). The healthy alliances (HALL) framework: Prerequisites for success. *Family Practice, 29*(Suppl 1), i132–i138. doi:10.1093/fampra/cmr088.

Kok, M. O., Vaandrager, L., Bal, R., & Schuit, J. (2012). Practitioner opinions on health promotion interventions that work: Opening the 'black box' of a linear evidence-based approach. *Social Science & Medicine, 74*(5), 715–723.

Kristensen, T. S., Hannerz, H., Høgh, A., & Borg, V. (2005). The Copenhagen Psychosocial Questionnaire – A tool for the assessment and improvement of the psychosocial work environment. *Scandinavian Journal of Work, Environment & Health, 31*(6), 438–449.

Kulik, C. T., Oldham, G. R., & Hackman, J. R. (1987). Work design as an approach to person-environment fit. *Journal of Vocational Behaviour, 31*(3), 278–296.

Lindfors, P. (2012). Reducing stress and enhancing well-being at work: Are we looking at the right indicators? *European Journal of Anaesthesiology, 29*(7), 309–310.

Lindström, B., & Eriksson, M. (2010). *The hitchhiker's guide to salutogenesis*. Helsinki: Folkhälsan Research Centre and GWG-SAL.

Naaldenberg, J., Vaandrager, L., Koelen, M., Wagemakers, A. M., Saan, H., & de Hoog, K. (2009). Elaborating on systems thinking in health promotion practice. *Global Health Promotion, 16*(1), 39–47. doi:10.1177/1757975908100749.

Nauta, A., van Vianen, A., van der Heijden, B., van Dam, K., & Willemsen, M. (2009). Understanding the factors that promote employability orientation: The impact of employability culture, career satisfaction, and role breadth self-efficacy. *Journal of Occupational and Organizational Psychology, 82*(2), 233–251. doi:10.1348/096317908x320147.

Nilsson, P., Andersson, I. H., Ejlertsson, G., & Troein, M. (2012). Workplace health resources based on sense of coherence. *International Journal of Workplace Health Management, 5*(3), 156–167.

Vaandrager, L., Bakker, I., Koelen, M. A., Baart, P., & Raaijmakers, T. (2013). System innovation: Health promotion in the workplace. In E. W. Broerse & J. Grin (Eds.), *Towards system innovations in health systems*. New York/London: Routledge (Forthcoming).

Whitehead, D. (2006). Workplace health promotion: The role and responsibility of health care managers. *Journal of Nursing Management, 14*(1), 59–68. doi:10.1111/j.1365-2934.2005.00599.x.

WHO. (1986). *Ottawa charter of health promotion*. Copenhagen: WHO.

WHO. (1992). *Basic documents* (39th ed.). Geneva: WHO.

Wilson, M. G., Dejoy, D. M., Vandenberg, R. J., Richardson, H. A., & McGrath, A. L. (2004). Work characteristics and employee health and well-being: Test of a model of healthy work organization. *Journal of Occupational and Organizational Psychology, 77*(4), 565–588. doi:10.1348/0963179042596522.

Zwetsloot, G. I. J. M., Van Scheppingen, A. R., Dijkman, A. J., Heinrich, J., & Den Besten, H. (2010). The organizational benefits of investing in workplace health. *International Journal of Workplace Health Management, 3*(2), 143–159. doi:10.1108/17538351011055032.

Chapter 6
Interventions to Promote Healthy & Resilient Organizations (HERO) from Positive Psychology

Susana Llorens, Marisa Salanova, Pedro Torrente, and Hedy Acosta

Abstract The development of the concept of HEalthy and Resilient Organization (HERO) is a milestone in research and practice aimed at promoting health among employees, teams, and organizations. HERO is thus conceptualized as an organization that makes systematic, planned, and proactive efforts to improve employees' and organizational processes and outcomes. These efforts involve fostering healthy organizational resources and practices intended to improve the work environment at the task, interpersonal, and organizational levels, especially during times of change and crisis. Despite its relevance in modern societies, research on the subject is scarce, particularly in terms of the effects of interventions focused on Positive Psychology. Consequently, the objective of this chapter is to present an overview of intervention effectiveness based on Positive Psychology. First, we focus on the concept, its relationship with salutogenesis, and the measurement of HEROs. Second, we review the literature on interventions to promote HEROs based on Positive Psychology. Third, we analyze methodological questions concerning the way to test the effectiveness of interventions in order to obtain criteria with which to develop a set of best practices. Finally, we address future research, professional practice, and teaching/training on positive interventions in organizations.

Keywords Health • Resilience • Positive interventions

S. Llorens (✉) • M. Salanova • P. Torrente • H. Acosta
WONT (Work & Organization NeTwork) Research Team,
Universitat Jaume I, Castellón, Spain
e-mail: llorgum@uji.es; salanova@uji.es; torrente@uji.es; hacosta@uji.es

G.F. Bauer and G.J. Jenny (eds.), *Salutogenic Organizations and Change:*
The Concepts Behind Organizational Health Intervention Research,
DOI 10.1007/978-94-007-6470-5_6, © Springer Science+Business Media Dordrecht 2013

Conceptualizing and Measuring HEROs

Modern societies are characterized by recurring periods of crisis, and social and economic change. This situation requires modern organizations to be focused on healthy employees, teams, and organizations. In this scenario, Occupational Health Psychology (OHP) calls for Integral Health Management in the development and promotion of health at work. Research has shown the importance of: (1) focusing on a more comprehensive, interdisciplinary, and multicausal approach that establishes the role of different stakeholders (e.g., Chief Executive Officers – CEOs, teams' immediate supervisors, employees, and customers) in the intervention process, and (2) integrating healthy programs in the companies' policies and culture as a benefit itself (Salanova et al. 2009a, b).

Therefore, HEROs constitute a key element within the framework of Positive Organizational Psychology. As stated above, Salanova et al. (2012) stressed that a HERO is an organization that make systematic, planned, and proactive efforts to improve employees', teams', and organizational processes and outcomes. Moreover, these organizations are "resilient" because they: maintain positive adjustment under challenging conditions, bounce back from untoward events, and maintain desirable functions and outcomes in the midst of strain. These efforts involve implementing healthy organizational resources and practices aimed at improving the work environment at the task (e.g., autonomy), interpersonal (e.g., transformational leadership styles), and organizational (e.g., Human Resources – HR – practices) levels, especially during times of turbulence and change.

Multilevel and Mixed-Method Measurement of HEROs

The so-called *HERO Model* is a heuristic theoretical model that integrates results from empirical and theoretically-based evidence on topics such as job stress, Human Resource Management (HRM), organizational behavior, and positive OHP. Specifically, the HERO Model has been developed based on previous research from 2004 until now. The studies of Wilson, DeJoy and colleagues stressed that a direct and systematic test of a comprehensive model of healthy work organization is needed (DeJoy et al. 2010; Wilson et al. 2004). These authors attempted to develop and test heuristic models of healthy organizations, which included employees' health as well as variables referring to the organizational context (e.g., work demands, tools and technologies, or social environment) and business performance. Both studies represent a preliminary approach towards understanding how organizational practices are related to employees' health. However, the validation of these first comprehensive models of healthy work organization (DeJoy et al. 2010; Wilson et al. 2004) had several limitations: (1) data were collected from the same respondents (employees) using the same measure instruments, thus making common method variance a potential bias in the dataset; and

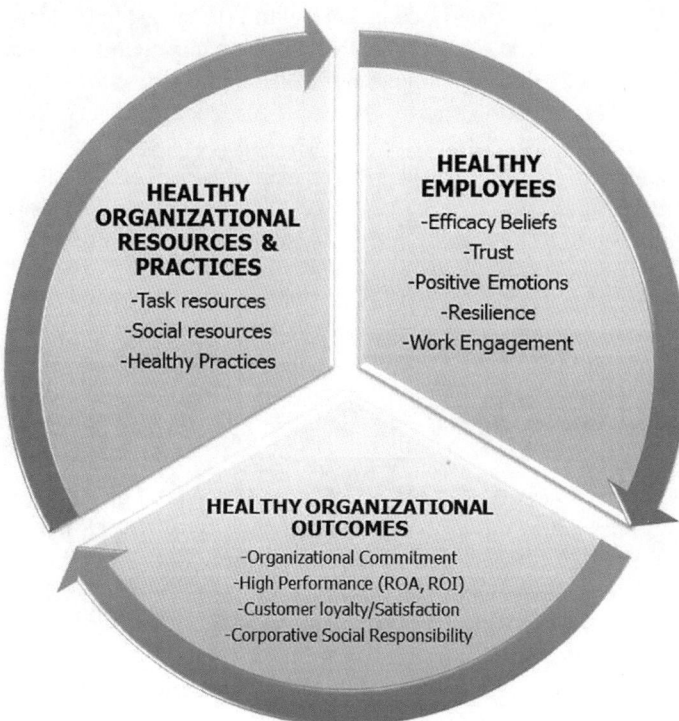

Fig. 6.1 HEalthy & Resilient Organizations (HERO) model (Salanova et al. 2012)

(2) constructs were tested at the individual level of analysis though the underlying conceptual premises of a healthy organization suggest the need to examine the model at the collective level of analysis.

In order to overcome these limitations, a HERO (Salanova 2008, 2009; Salanova et al. 2011, 2012) refers to a combination of three main interrelated components: healthy organizational resources and practices (e.g., job resources, healthy organizational practices) as strategies to structure and organize the work; healthy employees/teams (e.g., trust, work engagement), who show high levels of psychosocial well-being; and healthy organizational outcomes (e.g., high performance, corporate social responsibility). The HERO Model has mainly two advantages which are related to data collection and analyses. First, data are collected from different respondents (e.g., CEOs, teams' immediate supervisors, employees and customers) and from objective financial performance indicators (e.g., Return Of Assets – ROA) using both quantitative (questionnaires) and qualitative (interviews) methodologies. Secondly, data analyses are computed at the collective level following a multilevel perspective (i.e., individuals, teams, and organizations) (see Fig. 6.1).

Results from a validity study conducted with 303 teams and their immediate supervisors (Salanova et al. 2012) show that when organizations have healthy practices and resources (team autonomy, team feedback, supportive team climate, team working, team coordination, transformational leadership), teams feel healthier (more efficacious, engaged, and resilient to adversity), which in turn leads to healthier organizational outcomes (team in-role and extra-role performance as assessed by their immediate supervisors). Employees' excellent job performance also positively predicted customer loyalty and satisfaction with the company. Further evidence for the HERO Model is shown in other research (Acosta et al. 2012; Cruz et al. 2013; Torrente et al. 2012).

HEROs and Salutogenesis

Given the positive essence of the HERO Model, it could be integrated within the theoretical framework of *salutogenesis* (see Antonovsky 1979, 1996). Salutogenesis is related to the developing, testing, and implementing of plans and practices in order to enhance health and well-being by making use of the key elements: sense of coherence, optimization, and continuous improvement. Research provides evidence that sense of coherence and optimization are positively associated to better health, enjoyment (Eriksson and Lindström 2005; Hakanen et al. 2007), and the effective use of coping (McCrae and Costa 1990).

There are a number of different reasons showing that HEROs and salutogenesis share interests regarding: (1) health development and promotion rather than pathogenic factors, illness-focused approaches and/or the biomedical model; (2) the discovery of the precursors (e.g., communication practices, social support) and causes of health or beneficial factors regarding the person as a whole, immersed in their social and biographical context; (3) the strategies to create, enhance, and improve psychosocial factors that influence a person's ability to keep healthy; (4) the role of resources (personal, social, and organizational) as drivers of healthy settings; and (5) the key impact of HRM plans and practices, which are shown as health promoters (by implementing healthy organizational resources and practices) to build and maintain healthy work places as a whole (Becker et al. 2010; Rabin et al. 2005).

Promoting HEROs: Interventions from Positive Psychology

The relevance of developing theoretical models, valid methodologies, and positive interventions for enhancing HEROs despite crises is a milestone in OHP. It is time for a shift of focus and the moment to improve the strengths of teams and the optimal and positive functioning of organizations (Nielsen et al. 2010a; Schaufeli and Salanova 2007).

Intervention Strategies

Positive interventions refer to strategies implemented in teams and organizations in order to improve the performance and satisfaction of teams and organizations with the ultimate goal of promoting health, quality of work life, and organizational excellence. They could be split into primary (for achieving optimal functioning and the satisfaction of individuals, teams, and organizations) and secondary (further efforts over time to achieve peak functioning, health and satisfaction of teams and organizations) (Snyder et al. 2000). Thus, secondary improvement only occurs when the basic levels of functioning, health, and satisfaction are guaranteed.

Finally, Schaufeli and Salanova (2010) went a step further by arguing that we are entering into a novel phase of development known as *amplition*, which is based on the principle of improvement or betterment (Seligman and Csikszentmihalyi 2000). Amplition is defined as "positive" interventions that promote, increase, and improve health and well-being (e.g., engagement) at the collective level (teams and organizations) and includes three characteristics: (1) comprehension: the focus of interventions is oriented toward improving the health and wellness of teams and organizations; (2) inclusion of the *entire* workforce: employees, teams, and organizations that are not sick or distressed; and (3) it constitutes a long mission that requires continuous and sustained effort. Based on these features, positive interventions at the collective level (teams and organization) constitute the essence of amplifying strategies to develop HEROs. Research suggests that healthy organizational resources and practices are responsible for increasing the health of employees and healthy organizational outcomes (Acosta et al. 2012; Cruz et al. 2013; Salanova et al. 2012; Torrente et al. 2012).

A review of collective intervention highlights the benefits of using the following strategies: (1) assessment and evaluation of HEROs (talent attraction, recruitment, selection and retention, establishing and monitoring the psychological contract, periodical HERO audits, and workshops on positive experiences); (2) job and organization (re)design and changing work places (investing in task and social resources, organizational practices, and work changes); (3) developing transformational leadership; (4) work training in efficacy beliefs; and (5) career management (see Salanova et al. 2013; Schaufeli and Salanova 2010).

Optimization Targets

Despite the advances in the concept, models, and strategies of amplition programs, less empirical research has been conducted on the effectiveness of positive programs, above all when they are applied at the collective level. We conducted a review of the scholarly publications in the PsycInfo database following these criteria:

(1) publication date (from 2000 to 2012) and (2) "psychosocial intervention" and "organization" as subject terms in abstract. Results reveal that 66 articles (90 %) are related to intervention programs at work (training, participation, team re-design, workshop) that are oriented, for example, toward the reduction of: (1) mental and psychosocial health problems (Milnea et al. 2000); (2) burnout at the individual and organizational levels (Awa et al. 2010); (3) job stress, learning climate, and leadership style (Mikkelsen et al. 2000); and (4) anxiety and stress in university students (Bresó et al. 2011).

However, only seven of the articles (10 %) are based on current interventions from Positive Psychology, which are focused on developing the personal strengths, teams, and the optimal functioning of organizations. A deeper revision reveals that interventions are generally oriented toward optimizing: (1) self-confidence, self-consciousness, communication, skills for resolving conflicts, and personal resilience (McDonald et al. 2012); (2) individual performance, team collaboration, and team effectiveness (Robertson and Huang 2006); (3) learning and the improvement of the quality of service with patients (Phillips 2005); (4) psychological capital (hope, optimism, self-efficacy, and resilience), economic impact and revenues (Luthans et al. 2006); (5) positive feelings, behaviors, cognitions, and well-being (see Sin and Lyubomirsky's meta-analysis 2009); (6) self-efficacy, work engagement, and job performance (Carter et al. 2010); and (7) participation, problem-solving skills, and organizational healthiness (satisfaction, commitment, and well-being) in teams (DeJoy et al. 2010). Moreover, in the WONT Research Team we also carried out an intervention to boost emotional intelligence in nurses (Rodríguez et al. 2006; Salanova et al. 2007).

Methodology Issues of Positive Interventions

A deeper review of previous research reveals that interventions at work based on Positive Psychology differ in their focus, design, and data analyses. Firstly, interventions are focused on organizations and individuals, and consider a number of different stakeholders: employees (DeJoy et al. 2010; McDonald et al. 2012; Salanova et al. 2007), employees, managers, and supervisors (Carter et al. 2010; Luthans et al. 2006, 2008; Robertson and Huang 2006).

Secondly, participants are mainly distributed in intervened (experimental, pilot) and non-intervened (non-experimental, control) groups either by random selection (Carter et al. 2010; Luthans et al. 2006, 2008) or by assigning them to intervention and non-intervention conditions, which are comparable groups in terms of location, demographics, or employee characteristics (DeJoy et al. 2010). Different alternatives are also used: non-random selection with one group intervened and no control group (McDonald et al. 2012; Robertson and Huang 2006), and "natural" selection with intervened (participants who voluntarily participated in the intervention) and non-intervened groups (Salanova et al. 2007).

Procedures of Positive Interventions

In terms of the procedure, interventions are largely focused on case studies (e.g., Carter et al. 2010; McDonald et al. 2012; Rodríguez et al. 2006) with quasi-experimental designs, but also on different organizations (DeJoy et al. 2010). They are mainly divided into pre- and post-interventions with different strategies, and time schedules. Interventions are focused above all on different strategies: (1) feedback survey (Rodríguez et al. 2006); (2) workshops and training on learning goals, ergonomics or emotional intelligence (McDonald et al. 2012; Rodríguez et al. 2006); (3) micro-interventions (exercises, videos, small team talks) (Luthans et al. 2006); (4) web-based interventions in Psychological Capital (Luthans et al. 2008); (5) theatre-based interventions to increase self-efficacy (Carter et al. 2010); and (6) problem-solving processes to increase the healthiness of organizations (DeJoy et al. 2010). A review of the different interventions shows significant differences in time schedules, which range from one session (1–3 h; Luthans et al. 2006) to six sessions (McDonald et al. 2012). Generally, the interventions mainly involve a pre- and post-assessment with different time lags in order to measure the progress of the interventions. These post-evaluations range from a final assessment conducted immediately after the last intervention sessions (Rodríguez et al. 2006) to 3 days (Luthans et al. 2008), 8 months (Carter et al. 2010) or 6 and even 18 months after the last session (DeJoy et al. 2010).

Analytical Issues

Regarding methodology, positive interventions were largely quantitative and involved questionnaires that were completed by different stakeholders (employees, managers, supervisors, and customers). Pre- and post-intervention scores for the variables intervened were compared using independent t-tests for the control and intervened teams (Carter et al. 2010; Luthans et al. 2006; Robertson and Huang 2006), Analysis of Variance (ANOVA), Analysis of Covariance (ANCOVA) (e.g., Luthans et al. 2008), and multilevel random coefficient models (DeJoy et al. 2010). Other interventions were based on interviews about participants' reflections and field notes (which were completed after each workshop), and the participation ratio (McDonald et al. 2012). Finally, other authors combine the qualitative and quantitative methodologies by collecting data from validated questionnaires and from interviews about the positive and improved aspects as a result of the intervention (Salanova et al. 2009a).

Although Positive interventions at work are still in an early phase of development, previous results show that researchers and practitioners are endeavoring to implement strategies to promote psychosocial health, well-being, and positive outcomes in organizations. Although more research is needed, above all on interventions at the organizational level, the existing set of interventions that are currently being conducted provide some insight and good practices regarding positive interventions at work. In the following, we propose a set of best practices for designing positive interventions in job settings in order to conduct successful interventions. They are also intended to open up future avenues of study on the issue by means of an example of a positive intervention leading to the development of HEROs.

The Best Practices in Positive Interventions in HEROs

The underlying Scientific-Professional Model is the one proposed (e.g., Dunnette 1990; Fleishman 1990) by the European Network of Organizational and Work Psychologists (ENOP 1998). Based on the idea that Work and Organizational Psychology is both a scientific discipline and a profession, this model stresses the significance of integrating the scientific and practical dimensions of the psychologist specialized in work and organizational Psychology. By applying this model to positive interventions, the Scientific-Professional Model should focus on not only the scientific aspects related to the design interventions, but also the procedure in order to obtain the effectiveness of the interventions. Despite the relevance of positive intervention to promote HEROs, it is not exempt of future challenges. One of the main challenges that the promotion of HEROs will face is the need of evidence-based protocols that bridges the gap between science and practice as a key element to intervene. Following this rationale, research has offered a list of advices, basically based on stress interventions, that could be extended to develop HEROs from a Positive Psychology perspective (see Macik-Frey et al. 2007; Nytrø et al. 2000; Salanova et al. 2009a). In the following section we attempt to build up a set of best practices in interventions to promote HEROs.

Recommendation # 1

Preparing the Work Settings: *Thinking About the Story...*

- *All for one and one for all!* Incorporate interventions into the general policies of the organization. By including interventions in the commonly implemented practices, they will become a natural procedure, thus being easily prompted when required.
- *All aboard!* Ensure full commitment of the whole organization. Engaging CEOs and immediate supervisors requires providing them with full information about the project and the expected gains. Their implication will start a top-down process running through the whole organization, from middle managers to baseline employees via team supervisors.
- *Tell me!* Promote information and participation mechanisms for different agents in the organization: CEOs, supervisors, employees (teams), and customers in order to actively encourage their participation in the interventions. By sharing

accurate information about the procedures and the objective of the intervention anxiety and obstacles will be reduced, and motivators of change and positive experiences are developed.

- *Take your time!* Take advantage of wisdom and experience within the organization. Every organization has among the members of its workforce experienced collaborators who can act as facilitators. They can provide support in the design and in the implementation process by spreading information, acting as mentors or solving specific problems.

Recommendation # 2

Design of the Intervention: *Once Upon a Time…*

- *Step by step!* Plan the positive interventions, which should be realistic and take into account the possibility of unexpected events; the aim is to avoid unnecessary delays in the application of the intervention strategies and to generate a culture of positivity at work.
- *Please don't forget me!* Objectives and hypotheses should be based on scientific, valid, and robust theories (e.g., HERO Model; Salanova et al. 2012). The general objective should include three interrelated elements: (1) the design, (2) the implementation, and (3) how to test the effectiveness of team/organizational positive intervention. In addition to the general objective, specific objectives and hypotheses should also be included.
- *We are the 'sample', my friend!* The sample is composed of the "top organizations", which are characterized by showing the best organizational resources and practices. The intervention should be oriented toward organizations/teams that are randomly distributed as either intervened or non-intervened. To guarantee ethical tenets, the intervention should be implemented in the non-intervened organizations/teams after finishing the intervention process (www.apa.com).
- *Take a picture!* The focus of the strategies is on the collective level (organizations and teams). Specific strategies should be conducted to capture the collective nature of the work in organizations. The specific strategies to be implemented depend on the previous results obtained in the evaluation of the HEROs, in which different perspectives are gathered from different stakeholders (CEOs, supervisors, employees, and customers) (Chan 1998).

Recommendation #3

Development in the Work Setting and Testing Effectiveness: *Telling the Story…*

- *Divide and conquer!* The design should include a field and quasi-experimental study (intervened and non-intervened groups), with a longitudinal design and multiple levels of analyses (individuals, teams, organizations), and multiple stakeholders

(CEOs, supervisors, employees, and customers). This makes it possible to understand the dynamic processes (antecedents, processes, and results) and positive spirals among the intervened constructs (Chan 1998; Lindsley et al. 1995; Mathieu and Taylor 2006) through different time lags: pre-intervention and three post-intervention evaluations (immediately after finishing the intervention, and at 6 and 12 months after the intervention).

- *The power of collectivity!* Perform a comprehensive global analysis of the information based on the specific real results. The main goal is to propose collective intervention strategies (e.g., developing transformational leadership) based on optimization targets (e.g. collective efficacy) at the organizational and team level.
- *Put the meat on the grill!* Different data analyses could be computed based on the specific hypothesis. First, quantitative analyses could be carried out (by SPSS, AMOS, LISREL, MPlus): (1) descriptive analyses, chi-square, MANOVA, ANCOVAs or t-test to check whether there are significant differences between intervened and non-intervened teams/organizations from the pre- to the post-evaluations; (2) Structural Equation Modeling, to test the causal and reciprocal impact of intervention strategies on healthy organizational resources and practices, healthy employees (teams), and healthy organizational outcomes; and (3) multilevel analyses by hierarchical linear modeling to test the impact of intervention strategies at the organizational (level 2) and temporal levels (level 3) on team-level variables (level 1). Furthermore, qualitative analyses (by SPSS, ATLAS.Ti, N-Vivo) could be computed to analyze the perceptions, and positive aspects of improvement assessed by the intervened teams/organizations in order to increase the quality of the intervention in the future. These could include criteria on inter-judge validity (Cohen's Kappa), the Concordance Index (CI), and the Intraclass Correlation Coefficient (ICC).

Recommendation #4

Maintenance Over Time: *To Be Continued...*

- *Speed up the process!* Assess the actual impact of the intervention in the short, medium and long term in order to increase the benefits of its effectiveness by checking for significant increases in the variables over time. It also includes comparing non-intervened groups with subjective (perceived performance) and objective measures of effectiveness (e.g., financial returns or cost reduction).
- *And what else?* Focus on the actual transferability of the intervention to the current jobs. An important part of the intervention process has to do with putting knowledge into practice and exercising how to transfer it into daily work procedures.

- *Top secret, please!* Guarantee data protection and the confidentiality of the organizations and teams which participate in the process of evaluation-intervention.
- *The show must go on!* Institutionalize HERO services by creating and strengthening support services to promote the overall health of the organization at the collective level. This involves the proactive assessment of future needs, the anticipation of economic and social changes, and monitoring the primary and secondary enhancement interventions as a strategic goal of the organization.

Future Avenues in Positive Interventions at Work

Research Methods

Focusing on *research*, the future avenues in positive interventions imply a change in focus so as to intervene in teams and organizations and to get the different key agents involved (CEOs, teams, immediate supervisors, and the customers themselves), given the collective and multilevel nature of organizations (Whitman et al. 2010; Wilson et al. 2004). Furthermore, it is obviously necessary to continue the development of well-articulated theoretical models and validated instruments, which integrate the focus of collectivism and shared experiences ("*My team...*"; "*My organization...*" instead of "*I...*"), as well as the use of objective indicators (e.g., ROA) to avoid possible sources of common-method variance. In terms of design, research should also include empirical evidence and an agreement on the optimal time schedule and temporal patterns (3 months, 6 months, a year or even further) to test the effectiveness of positive interventions in HEROs (Rappaport 1977; Swerissen and Crisp 2004). Researchers are also strongly encouraged to report in-depth information about details regarding the implementation and evaluation of the intervention in order to identify the most suitable situations for a particular intervention to succeed (i.e., generalizability). They should also be on the lookout for factors that threaten an optimal implementation (Nielsen and Randall 2012; Nielsen et al. 2010b). As regards statistical procedures, the effectiveness of the positive intervention should be tested using a broader range of statistical procedures, by combining multiple qualitative (e.g., interviews, focus teams) and quantitative methodologies (e.g., diary studies, and multi-trait multi-method matrices) to ensure that the intervention is successful throughout different situations and circumstances.

Professional Practice

The second future line of research is related to professional practice, with the application of the procedure and the results from the intervention to *real* practice in *real* organizations. The immediate future will require occupational health psychologists to be familiar with strategies for optimizing people, teams, and organizations in the long term. Salanova et al. (2005) pointed out that the literature about how to manage interventions from Positive Psychology is scarce but interest is growing – above all in times of crisis. Despite its relevance, practice intervention in Positive Psychology is still in an incipient phase, and in fact the evaluations and interventions of the vast majority of companies are mainly focused on "risks" (Salanova et al. 2009a). More efforts should be made to integrate positive intervention in organizations and to test their effectiveness by means of methodological safeguards. One of these efforts would be the use of web- or software-based platforms in the e-design and e-implementation of positive interventions at the workplace (Luthans et al. 2008). These virtual environments are more flexible and make it easier to adapt and to implement the interventions to different populations at different times and places. Of course, all of these aspects make sense if strategic HRM is integrated with business policies for developing HEROs and everyone in the company (including the customers) is allowed to participate (Boselie 2010; Marks et al. 1986; Verburg et al. 2007). Finally, the future of positive interventions implies the refining of evidence-based protocols for optimizing teams and organizations from a global perspective.

Teaching/Training

The last future line of research is related to training in Positive Psychology interventions. Specific positive training should be implemented in universities and training centers from the positive and scientific-professional paradigms. With this specialized training, psychologists will undertake holistic and comprehensive training that complements their training grounded on the traditional illness-based model. This perspective facilitates the implementation of interventions that are focused not only on the "bad" side – it also makes it easier to promote the optimization of employees, teams, and organizations. A positive intervention has been implemented at the Universitat Jaume I through the Master's Degree in Work, Organizational and Human Resources Psychology, which has been available to students since the academic year 2007–2008. It includes a dual perspective and prepares master's degree students in professional competencies, as well as researchers specialized in OHP with special emphasis on Positive evaluation and interventions in different organizational settings. Furthermore, students can also study a PhD in a Occupational Health Psychology doctoral degree program. In this regard, it is worth highlighting the efforts made by different European and international institutions to hold specific conferences on Positive Psychology, such as *European Network for Positive Psychology, International Positive Psychology Association, Pennsylvania's Positive Psychology Center,* and *Spanish Society for Positive Psychology.*

A General Overview of the Chapter and Conclusions

The aim of this chapter was to provide an overview of interventions based on Positive Psychology, especially during times of turbulence and change, focused on the concept and measurement of HERO (Salanova et al. 2012). Likewise, its purpose was to discuss methodological questions with the aim of developing a set of best practices for organizational interventions based on Positive Psychology.

The present chapter makes different key contributions to the field of OHP. First, it shows the strengths of the *HERO Model* as a guide for data collection and analysis involved in the evaluation and promotion of HEROs based on Positive Psychology. Despite the relevance of this new approach (Nielsen et al. 2010a, b) to cope with current demands and crises, there is lack of research about positive interventions focused on HEROs.

The second contribution is related to the state-of-the art of positive interventions. Based on the *Research to Practice (R2P)* premise and on the Professional-Scientific Model, the chapter offers a revision of the main interventions strategies, optimization targets, and methodological issues to improve health and well-being at the collective level (teams and organizations) (Salanova et al. 2012; Schaufeli and Salanova 2010). These contributions are reflected in a set of best practices to develop and design successful interventions.

The final contribution of this chapter deals with future challenges in positive interventions at work, particularly concerning to the research methods, professional practice and teaching/training. The chapter illustrates the needs to (1) change the focus of interventions given the collective and multi-level nature of organizations (e.g., Whitman et al. 2010; Wilson et al. 2004), (2) integrate positive interventions within the organizations' policies, and (3) train in positive psychology interventions by means of masters' degrees and PhDs in Occupational Health Psychology Interventions.

References

Acosta, H., Salanova, S., & Llorens, S. (2012). How organizational practices predict team work engagement: The role of organizational trust [Special issue in work engagement]. *Ciencia & Trabajo, 14*, 7–15.

Antonovsky, A. (1979). *Health, stress and coping.* San Francisco: Jossey-Bass.

Antonovsky, A. (1996). The salutogenic modes as a theory to guide health promotion. *Health Promotion International, 11*(1), 11–18. doi:10.1093/heapro/11.1.11.

Awa, W. L., Plaumann, M., & Walter, U. (2010). Burnout prevention: A review of intervention programs. *Patient Education and Counseling, 78*(2), 184–190. doi:10.1016/j.bbr.2011.03.031.

Becker, C. M., Glascoff, M. A., & Felts, W. (2010). Salutogenesis 30 years later: Where do we go from here? *The International Electronic Journal of Health Education, 13*, 25–32.

Boselie, P. (2010). *Strategic human resource management. A balanced approach.* Glasgow: McGraw-Hill.

Bresó, E., Schaufeli, W. B., & Salanova, M. (2011). Can a self-efficacy-based intervention decrease burnout, increase engagement, and enhance performance? A quasi-experimental study. *Higher Education, 61*(4), 339–355. doi:10.1007/s10734-010-9334-6.

Carter, A., Nesbit, P., & Joy, M. (2010). Using theatre-based interventions to increase employee self-efficacy and engagement. In S. L. Albrecht (Ed.), *Handbook of employee engagement* (pp. 416–424). Northampton: Edward Elgar Publishing.

Chan, D. (1998). Functional relations among constructs in the same content domain at different levels of analysis: A typology of composition models. *The Journal of Applied Psychology, 83*(2), 234–246. doi:10.1037/0021-9010.83.2.234.

Cruz, V., Salanova, M., & Martínez, I. M. (2013). Liderazgo transformacional y desempeño grupal: unidos por el engagement grupal [Transformational leadership and group performance: linked by team work engagement]. *Revista de Psicología Social, 28*(2), 183–196.

DeJoy, D. M., Wilson, M. G., Vandenberg, R. J., McGrath-Higgins, A. L., & Griffin-Blake, C. S. (2010). Assessing the impact of healthy work organization intervention. *Journal of Occupational and Organizational Psychology, 83*(1), 139–165. doi:10.1348/096317908X398773.

Dunnette, M. D. (1990). Blending the science and practice of industrial and organizational psychology: Where are we and where are we going? In M. D. Dunnette & L. M. Hough (Eds.), *Handbook of industrial and organizational psychology* (Vol. 1, pp. 1–27). Palo Alto: Consulting Psychologists Press.

Eriksson, M., & Lindström, B. (2005). Validity of Antonovsky's sense of coherence scale: A systematic review. *Journal of Epidemiology and Community Health, 59*(6), 460–466. doi:10.1136/jech.2003.018085.

European Network of Organizational and Work Psychologists. (1998). *European curriculum in W & O Psychology*. Reference model and minimal standards. http://www.ucm.es/info/Psyap/enop/rmodel.html. Accessed 17 Nov 2012.

Fleishman, E. A. (1990). Prologue. In K. R. Murphy & F. E. Saal (Eds.), *Psychology in organizations: Integrating science and practice*. Hillsdale: Lawrence Erlbaum Associates.

Hakanen, J., Feldt, T., & Leskinen, E. (2007). Change and stability of sense of coherence in adulthood: Longitudinal evidence from the healthy child study. *Journal of Research in Personality, 41*(3), 602–617. doi:10.1016/j.bbr.2011.03.031.

Lindsley, D. H., Brass, D. J., & Thomas, J. B. (1995). Efficacy-performance spirals: A multilevel perspective. *The Academy of Management Review, 20*(3), 645–678. doi:10.2307/258790.

Luthans, F., Avey, J. B., Avolio, B. J., Norman, S. M., & Combs, G. M. (2006). Psychological capital development: Toward a micro-intervention. *Journal of Organizational Behaviour, 27*(3), 387–393. doi:10.1002/job.373.

Luthans, F., Avey, J. B., & Patera, J. L. (2008). Experimental analysis of a web-based training intervention to develop positive psychological capital. *The Academy of Management Learning and Education, 7*(2), 209–221. doi:10.5465/AMLE.2008.32712618.

Macik-Frey, M., Quick, J. C., & Nelson, D. (2007). Advances in occupational health: From a stressful beginning to a positive future. *Journal of Management, 33*(6), 809–840. doi:10.1177/0149206307307634.

Marks, M. L., Mirvis, P. H., Hackett, E. J., & Grady, J. (1986). Employee participation in a quality circle program: Impact on quality of work life, productivity, and absenteeism. *The Journal of Applied Psychology, 71*(1), 61–69. doi:10.1037/0021-9010.71.1.61.

Mathieu, J. E., & Taylor, S. R. (2006). Clarifying conditions and decision points for mediational type inferences in organizational behavior. *Journal of Organizational Behavior, 27*(8), 1031–1056. doi:10.1002/job.406.

McCrae, R. R., & Costa, P. T. J. (1990). *Personality in adulthood*. New York: Guilford Press.

McDonald, G., Jackson, D., Wilkes, L., & Vickers, M. H. (2012). A work-based educational intervention to support the development of personal resilience in nurses and midwives. *Nurse Education Today, 32*(4), 378–384. doi:10.1016/j.nedt.2011.04.012.

Mikkelsen, A., Saksvik, P. Ø., & Landsbergis, P. (2000). The impact of a participatory organizational intervention on job stress in community health care institutions. *Work and Stress, 14*(2), 156–170. doi:10.1080/026783700750051667.

Milnea, D. L., Keegan, D., Westerman, C., & Dudley, M. (2000). Systematic process and outcome evaluation of brief staff training in psychosocial interventions for severe mental illness. *Journal of Behaviour Therapy and Experimental Psychiatric, 31*(2), 87–101. doi:10.1016/S0005-7916 (00)00013-6.

Nielsen, K., & Randall, R. (2012). Opening the black box: Presenting a model for evaluation organizational-level interventions. *European Journal of Work and Organizational Psychology*, ifirst, 1–17. doi:10.1080/1359432X.2012.690556.

Nielsen, K., Randall, R., Holten, A. L., & Rial, E. (2010a). Conducting organizational-level occupational health interventions: What works? *Work and Stress, 24*(3), 234–259. doi:10.1080/026 78373.2010.515393.

Nielsen, K., Taris, T. W., & Cox, T. (2010b). The future of organizational interventions: Addressing the challenges of today's organizations. *Work and Stress, 24*(3), 219–233. doi:10.1080/026783 73.2010.519176.

Nytrø, K., Saksvik, P. O., Mikkelsen, A., Bohle, P., & Quinlan, M. (2000). An appraisal of key factors in the implementation of occupational stress interventions. *Work and Stress, 14*(3), 213–225. doi:10.1080/02678370010024749.

Phillips, J. (2005). Knowledge is power: Using nursing information management and leadership interventions to improve services to patients, clients and users. *Journal of Nursing Management, 13*(6), 524–536. doi:10.1111/j.1365-2934.2005.00607.x.

Rabin, S., Matalon, A., Maoz, B., & Shiber, A. (2005). Keeping doctors healthy: A salutogenic perspective. *Families, Systems & Health, 23*(1), 94–102. doi:10.1037/1091-7527.23.1.94.

Rappaport, J. (1977). *Community psychology: Values, research and action*. New York: Holt, Rinchart & Winston.

Robertson, M. M., & Huang, Y. H. (2006). Effect of a workplace design and training intervention on individual performance, group effectiveness and collaboration: The role of environmental control. *Work, 27*(1), 3–12.

Rodríguez, A. M., Llorens, S., & Salanova, M. (2006). Taller de trabajo sobre inteligencia emocional en enfermeras: Eficacia a corto plazo [Workshop on emotional intelligence in nurses: Short time efficacy]. *Gestión Práctica de Riesgos Laborales, 29*, 46–51.

Salanova, M. (2008). Organizaciones saludables y desarrollo de recursos humanos [Healthy organizations and human resource development]. *Estudios Financieros, 303*, 179–214.

Salanova, M. (2009). Organizaciones saludables, organizaciones resilientes [Healthy organizations, resilient organizations]. *Gestión Práctica de Riesgos Laborales, 58*, 18–23.

Salanova, M., Martínez, I. M., & Llorens, S. (2005). Psicología Organizacional Positiva [Positive Organizational Psychology]. In F. J. Palací (Coord.) (Ed.), *Psicología de la Organización* (pp. 349–376). Madrid: Pearson, Prentice-Hall.

Salanova, M., Cifre, E., Martínez, I., & Llorens, S. (2007). *Caso a caso en la prevención de riesgos psicosociales. Metodología WONT para una organización saludable* [Case by case in the psychosocial risk prevention: WONT methodology for a healthy organization]. Bilbao: Lettera Publicaciones.

Salanova, M., Llorens, S., & Rodríguez, A. (2009a). Hacia una psicología de la salud ocupacional más positiva [Towards a more positive occupational health psychology]. In M. Salanova (Dir.), *Psicología de la Salud Ocupacional* (pp. 247–284). Madrid: Editorial Síntesis.

Salanova, M., Martínez, I. M., Cifre, E., & Llorens, S. (2009b). La salud ocupacional desde la perspectiva psicosocial: Aspectos teóricos y conceptuales [The occupational health from the psychosocial perspective: Theoretical and conceptual aspects]. In M. Salanova (Dir.), *Psicología de la Salud Ocupacional* (pp. 27–62). Madrid: Editorial Síntesis.

Salanova, M., Cifre, E., Llorens, S., Martínez, I. M., & Lorente, L. (2011). Psychosocial risks and positive factors among construction workers. In R. Burke, S. Clarke, & C. Cooper (Eds.), *Occupational health and safety: Psychological and behavioral challenges* (pp. 295–322). Surrey: Gower.

Salanova, M., Llorens, S., Torrente, P., & Acosta, H. (2013). *Positive interventions in positive organizations. Terapia Psicológica, 31*(1), 101–113. doi: 10.4067/S0718-48082013000100010.

Salanova, M., Llorens, S., Cifre, E., & Martínez, I. M. (2012). We need a HERO! Towards a validation of the Healthy & Resilient Organization (HERO) model. *Group & Organization Management, 37*(6), 785–822. doi:10.1177/1059601112470405.

Schaufeli, W. B., & Salanova, M. (2007). Efficacy or inefficacy, that's the question: Burnout and engagement, and their relationships with efficacy beliefs. *Anxiety, Coping & Stress, 20*(2), 177–196. doi:10.1080/10615800701217878.

Schaufeli, W. B., & Salanova, M. (2010). How to improve work engagement? In S. L. Albrecht (Ed.), *Handbook of employee engagement. Perspectives, issues, research and practice* (pp. 399–415). Northampton: Edward Elgar.

Seligman, M. E. P., & Csikszentmihalyi, M. (2000). Positive psychology: An introduction. *The American Psychologist, 55*(1), 5–14. doi:10.1037/0003-066X.55.1.5.

Sin, N. L., & Lyubomirsky, S. (2009). Enhancing well-being and alleviating depressive symptoms with positive psychology interventions: A practice-friendly meta-analysis. *Journal of Clinical Psychology: In Session, 65*(5), 467–487. doi:10.1002/jclp.20593.

Snyder, C. R., Feldman, D. B., Taylor, J. D., Schroeder, L. L., & Adams, V. (2000). The roles of hopeful thinking in preventing problems and promoting strengths. *Applied and Preventive Psychology: Current Scientific Perspectives, 9*(4), 249–269. doi:10.1016/S0962-1849(00)80003-7.

Swerissen, H., & Crisp, B. R. (2004). The sustainability of health promotion interventions for different levels of social organization. *Health Promotion International, 19*(1), 123–130. doi:10.1093/heapro/dah113.

Torrente, P., Salanova, S., Llorens, S., & Schaufeli, W. B. (2012). Teams make it work: How team work engagement mediates between social resources and performance in teams. *Psicothema, 24*(1), 106–112.

Verburg, R. M., Den Hartog, D. N., & Koopman, P. L. (2007). Configurations of human resource management practices: A model and test of internal fit. *International Journal of Human Resource Management, 18*(2), 184–208. doi:10.1080/09585190601102349.

Whitman, D. S., Van Rooy, D. L., & Viswesvaran, C. (2010). Satisfaction, citizenship behaviors, and performance in work units: A meta-analysis of collective construct relations. *Personnel Psychology, 63*(1), 41–81. doi:10.1111/j.1744-6570.2009.01162.x.

Wilson, M. G., DeJoy, D. M., Vandenberg, R. J., Richardson, H. A., & McGrath, A. L. (2004). Work characteristics and employee health and well-being: Test of a model of healthy work organization. *Journal of Occupational and Organizational Psychology, 77*(4), 565–588. doi:10.1348/0963179042596522.

Chapter 7
Alignment for Achieving a Healthy Organization

Ulrica von Thiele Schwarz and Henna Hasson

Abstract Modern working life is characterized by change and competiveness. It is also characterized by a drift away from low-skilled work to more complex jobs and increased social interaction. This means that the human resources – employees and their skills, competencies, engagement and motivation – are the greatest asset of many organizations. This has implications for how an organization can be healthy, i.e. create an environment that will contribute to employee health, wellbeing and motivation as well as achieve business outcomes. In this chapter, we will draw on theories from work and organizational psychology and behavioral psychology, and our own research, to describe what we believe to be the fundament of a healthy organization. We will do this by introducing the concept of alignment, which will be used to illuminate the healthy organization. Alignment can be described as the lining up of different aspects of what is going on in an organization so that they create a common thread. This cuts across different layers and processes in the organization; thus vertical, horizontal and diagonal alignments will be described. In the second part, we will use the framework of alignment to illuminate why occupational health interventions need to be integrated with the organization's strategy and systems in order to create sustainable change. Implications of alignment for participatory approaches, intervention fit, program theories, the role of management and more will be discussed. In the third part, we will describe the implications of our view of an aligned, healthy organization for designing and evaluating interventions

U. von Thiele Schwarz (✉)
Department of Psychology, Stockholm University, Stockholm, Sweden

Medical Management Centre, Karolinska Institutet, Solna, Sweden
e-mail: ulrica.schwarz@ki.se

H. Hasson
Medical Management Centre, Karolinska Institutet, Solna, Sweden

Vårdal Institute, The Swedish Institute for Health Sciences, Lund University, Lund, Sweden
e-mail: henna.hasson@ki.se

G.F. Bauer and G.J. Jenny (eds.), *Salutogenic Organizations and Change:*
The Concepts Behind Organizational Health Intervention Research,
DOI 10.1007/978-94-007-6470-5_7, © Springer Science+Business Media Dordrecht 2013

in organizations. This includes arguing for changing the roles and responsibilities of researchers and practitioners, and how this change can be beneficial to the organization as well as the quality of the research.

Keywords Organizational behavior management • Participatory approach • Health • Performance • Strategic goals

Conceptualization of a Healthy Organization: Creating Healthy Organizations Through Alignment

Every organization has a core mission that motivates its existence. In order to stay in business, it needs to succeed in delivering value to its customers, patients, owners and other key stakeholders. Employees are one of the most important resources for creating and sustaining performance in an organization (Wright et al. 2001). It is through the employees' behaviors that the organization's business goals as well as its missions are achieved. This ties the human and the business perspectives closely together. We argue that the "health" of an organization and the health of its employees are mutually dependent. Here, we use a broad definition of employee health involving absence due to ill health and disease as well as psychological wellbeing and job motivation. As we see it, there are many reasons why business issues and employee health should be approached as being intertwined. Not least, we believe that both organizations and employees benefit from closing the gap between strategic goals, productivity and employee health issues. Thus, we define healthy organizations as those in which employees are seen as a prerequisite for reaching strategic goals.

In our conceptualization of a healthy organization, alignment is a central concept. Alignment can be described as different aspects of an organization – people, processes and structures – being organized so that it forms a common, stable entity. To illustrate this, we can use how atoms bind to other atoms to form molecules as an analogy. Molecule structures can be very complex both in terms of number of atoms (entities) and internal relations. Importantly, the stability of molecules is, to a large extent, determined by the strength of the bond between the atoms (see Fig. 7.1). The alignment of organization can be thought of as the binding strength between different parts of the organization. However, in contrast to molecules, organizations also need to have a direction. Thus, the stability that alignment creates aims at improving the organization's ability to achieve target outcomes.

Within the management literature, alignment denotes how strategic practices and systems, such as overall human resource practice and IT management, need to be aligned with overall business goals. Alignment is also used in management practices that take a behavioral approach to understanding organizations, organizational behavior management (OBM). In OBM, alignment involves ensuring that processes and structures give employees the opportunity for high motivation to perform in line with the organization's strategic goals. In this chapter, we will apply and extend the

Fig. 7.1 Alignment as a
central concept in the healthy
organization, illustrated as a
molecule. Like molecules, the
different aspects of an
organization need to form a
common entity. However,
unlike molecules, the
alignment of entities should
not only create stability but
also a direction toward target
outcomes

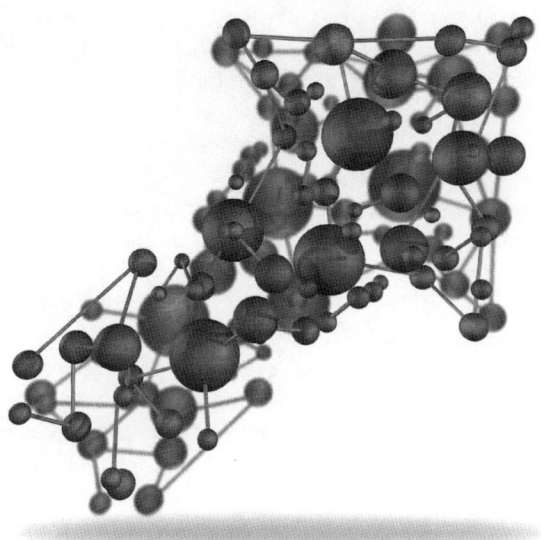

concept of alignment as it is used in the management literature in general, and in OBM in particular, to occupational health. We will do this by discussing alignment in three different dimensions: vertical, horizontal and diagonal.

Vertical Alignment: Visions, Goals and Behaviors

The first thing that needs to be aligned is the organization's vision, the goals for departments and work groups and the key behaviors each employee needs to perform in order to achieve the goals. This is sometimes referred to as "the method of cascading objectives" (Abernathy 2008) or "the line of sight" (Boswell 2006; Buller and McEvoy 2012). Thus, in a vertically aligned organization all employees know what they are expected to do, and how they contribute to their team or workgroup as well as to the strategic goals of the department and the visions of the organization. Understanding how one contributes to the strategic goals is more important than understanding the goals per se (Boswell 2006). This does not imply a top-down approach. It is often the employees, not the managers, who have intimate knowledge about which behaviors drive key results. Vertical alignment, therefore, needs to be created in continuous, iterative processes in which both management and employees participate. The participatory approach also taps into motivational processes. High employee participation is consistently linked to improved performance and productivity, as well as employee health and job satisfaction (Batt and Appelbaum 1995; Jacobsen et al. 2008; Lawler et al. 1995).

The more employees participate in organizational processes, the higher the performance in the organization (Wagner 1994). Given this, it is not surprising that what we call vertical alignment has been linked to positive employee outcomes, including increased job satisfaction and decreased turnover (Buller and McEvoy 2012). The mechanism in this relationship between alignment and positive employee outcomes is not entirely clear. However, greater job clarity and task significance have been used to explain it (Buller and McEvoy 2012). Task significance, in turn, may increase the sense of meaningfulness, which has been suggested to be a critical psychological need linked to job motivation and job satisfaction (Hackman and Oldham 1976). Concurrently with positive employee effects, alignment has also been linked to organizational performance (Buller and McEvoy 2012). Taking a behavioral perspective, this is not surprising: alignment means that the employees spend time on tasks that are relevant to the organization's strategic goals. Therefore, in a healthy organization, employees as well as leaders are aware of what is most important to do, and how this relates to the goals and vision of the organization.

To this chain (vision-goals-behaviors), another dimension needs to be added: competence and skills. In our description of a healthy organization, competence is seen as an important strategic issue: the organization acknowledges that it needs the competencies to function. It also acknowledges that the way the organization functions affects the learning opportunities of its employees, and thereby there competencies. Aligning competence with the organization's goals and the employees' behavior is likely to have a positive effect on both organizational performance and employee outcomes. A more efficient use of the organization's human resources is likely to contribute to organizational performance. Increased skill discretion may contribute to improved employee health (Rafferty et al. 2001); and increased learning opportunities to improved psychological functioning (Mikkelsen et al. 1999). In other words, in a healthy organization there is a common understanding that both individuals and the organization benefit from arranging the work and the organization so that each individual is allowed to use – and develop – his or her competence. Practically, this means that competence development plans are made based on gap analysis between the current state and the goals of the organization. The aim of competence development is a change in behaviors and processes. Thereby, competence development is a strategy for continuous improvement. This is not always the case. For example, our recent study of a comprehensive competence development program within older people's care showed that despite some initial positive effects on attitudes and knowledge, very little change in clinical practice was seen (Augustsson et al. 2013). Interviews showed that this was partly due to the fact that as employees went through the program and gradually gained new knowledge and skills, they were still in the same environment, with the same expectations. Hence, there were no changes to the organizational structures and processes, which would have been necessary for the program to lead to behavioral changes. The organization seemed to have thought that the program was a time-limited project that would only be beneficial on the individual level. They were not aware of the need to – or prepared to – align the outcome of the competence development program with any necessary organizational changes. Thus, the organization saw it as a single intervention, unrelated to its strategic goals. In sum, for employees, having the possibility to use their knowledge and skills, and learn, at work is an important determinant of employee health (Fried and Ferris 1987; Hackman and Oldham 1976). Also, it is obviously an essential dimension from an organizational perspective, as it will ensure that the most important resource is used efficiently and strategically.

Horizontal Alignment: Antecedents – Behaviors – Consequences

Often when horizontal alignment is discussed, it is described as the alignment of different processes – and departments, such as sales, administration or production – within an organization. However, it is the behaviors of the employees that make up the processes. Therefore, we will focus our discussion of horizontal alignment on behavior. In OBM, a basic assumption is that the frequency of a behavior is determined by circumstances under which the behavior takes place (Wilder et al. 2009). For employees to be able to work efficiently, the antecedents that precede the key behaviors, and the consequences that follow the behaviors, need to be aligned. This is the A – B – C (antecedents – behaviors – consequences) of alignment. More specifically, antecedents such as instructions, guidelines, routines, work descriptions and other information and tools that tell employees what they should do should be in line with what follows from these behaviors. Consequences can take many different forms, but in order to influence the reoccurrence of a behavior they need to follow soon after it, and with a certain degree of certainty. We do more of the behaviors we gain something from, and that helps us avoid things we want to avoid. For example, it is not sufficient to simply ask staff to be active at meetings. Instead, this will occur more frequently if questions and suggestions are followed by immediate positive consequences such as being listened to and acknowledged. Many organizations think merely of consequences in terms of tangible rewards, such as the incitement system. Some also realize that social interaction is an important influence, and increasingly so, as employees are often interdependent (Humphrey et al. 2007; Oldham and Hackman 2010). However, a healthy organization also understands that characteristics of job tasks can be powerful motivators – e.g. seeing the result of one's work, doing something meaningful, being in control or helping someone. They also see the potential of a participatory approach. Employees are generally more aware of the circumstances that affect their behavior than managers are. A high degree of participation and the autonomy it can create are powerful reinforcers in themselves. A close collaboration between employees and managers, in other words, is as important for horizontal alignment as for vertical alignment.

From this system perspective on employee motivation and performance follows that an organization will have more of what it reinforces. In a healthy organization, there is an understanding that this system links employee behaviors to the environment the organization creates. There is an awareness of the need to focus on consequences rather than just antecedents. Antecedents are prioritized in many organizations – possibly because they are temptingly easy to administrate. However, focusing on consequences is more effective in sustaining behaviors over time. Motivation is not something that can be injected or recruited, but is rather created and sustained within the organization. In essence, a healthy organization sees employee intrinsic motivation as a key to long-term productivity as well as employee health. From this follows that it is an organizational objective to provide a situation that will allow employees to be motivated, rather than considering motivation an individual trait.

Given the importance of employee motivation, a healthy organization relies on positive rather than negative reinforcement. This means that it strives to motivate employee behaviors by making sure that key behaviors are followed by consequences that increase the behavior. The opposite involves organizations that motivate employees to do things or act in a certain way in order to avoid potential negative consequences. Positive reinforcement strategies have a positive effect on organizational performance as well as employee health and motivation. Under the influence of negative reinforcement, employees will only continue a behavior until the threat of negative consequences is no longer obvious. For example, an employee will do what is asked of him or her to avoid being singled out but will stop when this level is reached, as nothing motivates pursuing the behavior further. This means that negative reinforcement automatically introduces a ceiling effect for employee behavior and performance. Concurrently, negative reinforcement is likely to be related to negative mood, experiences of stress and dissatisfaction. With positive reinforcement, on the other hand, employees do things because it is stimulating and rewarding. This will lead to a discretionary effort among the employees: they will do more than is demanded of them. In organizational psychology, discretionary effort is part of the concept of organizational citizenship behavior, which has been related to positive outcome on both the organizational and the individual level (Podsakoff and MacKenzie 1997). Hence, organizational citizenship behavior is an essential characteristic of an organization that wants to promote both individual and organizational health.

Diagonal Alignment: Interlocking

A third form of alignment is between different managerial levels in an organization. In OBM this is referred to as interlocking (Glenn and Malott 2004). Since it involves both the vertical alignment of missions, visions, department goals and individual behaviors as well the horizontal alignment around key behaviors, we call it diagonal alignment. The focus is on making sure the behaviors of superiors create horizontal alignment, e.g. encourage and support the key behaviors of their direct subordinates. When this is done at each managerial level, in line with the visions, goals and behaviors, it contributes to vertical alignment as well. The first-line manager, then, should make sure to align his or hers own behavior so as to facilitate and support the key behaviors he or she wants the work group to perform. This is done by providing the appropriate antecedents and making sure the consequences that follow a behavior reinforce rather than contradict it. For example, imagine an employee who is expected to safely turn a machine off before making an adjustment to it. Often, this safe behavior may result in productivity losses, take longer time and be more inconvenient than the unsafe behavior (e.g. making the adjustment without stopping the machine). This tips the reinforcement balance towards the unsafe behavior, which the organization needs to acknowledge and counterbalance. First, the first-line manager needs to make sure that instructions and routines encompass the safe behavior and that it is possible to perform (physically as well as in terms of employee competence and skill). Then, the manager needs to look closely at what happens when the employee turns the machine off, and ensure that the behavior is reinforced, e.g. acknowledged. Similarly, middle and higher managers need to adjust their behavior so that they facilitate the behaviors they request of their direct subordinates. In this case, the most important part would be to make sure safety is a strategic goal. Behaviorally, this could mean to give equal attention to safety issues as to production in their communication with their subordinates. Thereby, the behavior of managers at each level is important for every employee behavior.

Approaching Interventions in Organizations

Above, we presented a conceptualization of a healthy organization where alignment is a central concept, and where occupational health issues and strategic goals are knit closely together. Traditionally, occupational health interventions have been conducted without paying much attention to the business perspective (Miller and Haslam 2009). The opposite is true of other types of organizational developments, which are often done without sufficient acknowledgement of employee issues. In this section, we will describe how occupational health interventions can be approached with the principals of alignment in mind to close this gap.

Vertical Alignment in Organizational Change: Linking Occupational Health Interventions to Organizational Strategy

Occupational health interventions can involve individual as well as organiza- tional level interventions, the first of which refers to interventions aiming to increase the individual's resources, and the second to changes in the design, organization and management of work (European Agency for Safety and Health at Work 2010a; Nielsen and Randall 2012; Van der Klink et al. 2001). This means that organizational level interventions are intertwined with the organizational systems and processes, and therefore, that these kinds of interventions require changes to organizational structures in order to be effective (Mikkelsen 2005; Semmer 2003). This links organizational level health interventions to the overall aim of the organization. Traditionally, organizational level health interventions have often used top-down approaches (Nielsen et al. 2010b, c). However, partici-patory approaches to interventions have several advantages. This includes using the expertise the employees have about the organization to design better and more suitable interventions. Also, the implementation of the intervention is facil-itated because employees can see how the intervention relates to the organiza-tion's strategic goals. This has been described as a prerequisite for getting buy-in from employees (Zink et al. 2008).

When an intervention is aligned with the strategic goals of an organization and involves changes in organizational structures and process, these kinds of interventions are no longer time-limited projects. They become ongoing activities (Landsbergis and Vivona-Vaughan 1995). Some suggest that we approach them as part of an evolu-tionary process, which would actually make the use of the word "intervention" seem out of place (Kuorinka et al. 1995). In any case, we argue that occupational health interventions should not be considered discrete events that can be clearly distinguished in time and content from other activities in the organization. Rather, they should be considered as an organization's continuous effort to improve its long-term commit-ments to different stakeholders through a holistic approach to its human resources.

Integration of Occupational Health with Management Systems

Several authors have proposed that occupational health and safety (OHS) should be integrated with health promotion (Baker et al. 1996; Hymel et al. 2011; NIOSH 2012). Going one step further, others have suggested that OHS and health promo-tion need to be integrated with other systems as well, primarily quality improvement and production systems (Jørgensen et al. 2006; Wilkinson and Dale 1999, 2002; Zwetsloot 1995). This would be a way of bridging the gap that otherwise often exists between these areas. In terms of alignment, integrated systems can be thought of as a way of making OHS and health promotion part of the strategic goals and of ensuring that OHS processes are aligned with other processes in the organization. It has been suggested that integrated systems have several advantages. For example, having multiple systems for issues that are, or should be, interdependent is likely to be counterproductive as it increases the risk of complex administration, conflicting procedures and accelerated costs (European Agency for Safety and Health at Work 2010b). This implies that integrated systems can save resources and increase the efficiency of the organization. In addition, integrated systems may facilitate that both business aspects and health aspects are considered simultaneously, with atten-tion to productivity and quality as well as environment and health. This minimizes the risk of the systems working in isolation from each other (Smith 2002). In other words, it ensures that the different systems are aligned.

An example of how OHS and health promotion can be integrated with quality improvement and production systems can be taken from an ongoing research project called LeanHealth (Stenfors-Hayes et al. 2013). At a regional hospital in Sweden, a structured, participatory problem-solving method called kaizen (which is a Lean tool), initially only used for quality improvement, is now being used for OHS and health promotion as well. Each department has staff members functioning as kaizen representatives, i.e. motors for the kaizen work, engaging staff in identifying problems at work and documenting it on a kaizen note, and regularly (at least monthly, often weekly) holding kaizen meetings. The integration involves two dimensions: (1) the preparation of kaizen notes on issues related to health and safety, thereby ensuring that these issues are handled the same way as quality improvement and production issues and (2) all issues identified on kaizen notes, whether initially considered health-related or not, are analyzed from an employee health perspective. Hence, the first dimension is concerned with making OHS interventions part of continuous improvements and the second with making OHS one of the strategic perspectives that needs to be considered for all kinds of organizational development. In sum, this example shows how an integrated approach to OHS and health promotion and issues relating to other types of organizational performance can be implemented in practice.

For some OHS interventions, e.g. individual-level interventions with employee health improvement as their main goal, it may seem out of reach to link the intervention to the organization's strategic goals. However, we believe it is merely a matter of the depth of the integration. For example, even individual-level OHS interventions can be linked to business outcomes. In one of our research projects on physical exercise during work hours (von Thiele Schwarz and Hasson 2011, 2012; von Thiele Schwarz et al. 2008), we did this by showing how the health effects achieved among employees were related to organizational outcomes such as number of treated patients and costs associated with sickness absence. Thus, it was possible to illustrate how and why the intervention was valuable for the organization's strategic goals.

Aligning Intervention Components with the Outcomes

An important part of vertical alignment is the creating of a clear line of sight, e.g. that it is clear to each person how his or her tasks and goals are related to the company's strategic goals. An analog in interventions and change is the importance of creating a line of sight for how the intervention, or change, will produce the desired outcome. Thus, we propose that the logic of the intervention, e.g. the program theory, needs to be illuminated. This involves identifying the core intervention components. These are the aspects of an intervention that are instrumental for achieving the expected outcomes. It also involves illuminating the logic steps between these components, the outcomes (immediate and intermediate) and the impact (Hasson 2010; Steckler et al. 2002). This should be done before the intervention is launched to make sure the right interventions and changes are put in place and the right outcomes measured. Using a participatory approach will allow managers and employees to elaborate on the logics of the intervention, and will likely increase commitment to it. Logic descriptions of how the intervention affects the target outcomes are an important selling point for the intervention (Nytrø et al. 2000). The lack of a logic link (or a lack of the communication of a logic link) can have the opposite effect. For example, a belief that the intervention is unlikely to lead to a particular outcome will demotivate participation. For instance, a manager or employee who does not believe teamwork in emergency departments will lead to shorter lead times is less likely to be committed to the implementation, when shortened lead times are the main outcome. If the mechanism linking teamwork to shortened lead times is not made explicit, it may not matter that the intervention itself is perceived as reasonable. Knowledge about the mechanism is central to understanding the aim of the change, which, in turn, is central to commitment to the intervention (Nielsen and Randall 2012; Nytrø et al. 2000; Randall et al. 2007).

Horizontal Alignment: Antecedents, Behaviors and Consequences in Interventions

OHS interventions, on the individual as well as the organizational level, require changes in employee behavior in order to take place. This, in turn, requires three things: (1) that the behaviors are made explicit, (2) that changes in the environment are made so that the new behaviors are possible to perform and (3) that the new behaviors are more rewarding than "business as usual". In other words, appropriate antecedents as well as consequences need to be put in place. This holds true regardless of the kind of change – e.g. whether it is a new work practice, taking the stairs rather than the elevator, or working with web-based exercises. This may sound simple enough, but is often more challenging than expected.

First, it means that the intervention or change needs to be defined on a very concrete level, in terms of employee behaviors. Stating that "we should show each other respect" is one thing; describing what this means in terms of key behavior another. What does it mean that you should do? Say hello to your colleagues when you get to work in the morning? Help someone out? Be more responsive to complaints from colleagues? In our experience, many change initiatives fail because this step, describing the change in key behaviors, is not undertaken or is done too shallowly. Another common mistake is to try to pursue it without a participatory approach. Second, the organization needs to understand the circumstances that will increase the likelihood of the targeted behavior. It must also understand what behaviors the change should replace, and the behaviors the new behavior may collide with. Thus, an analysis of contingences affecting key behaviors needs to be performed. Third, actions need to be taken so that the results of the analysis come to use; e.g. by making sure the new behavior is more reinforced than those it replaces.

Alignment of Interventions to Employee and Organizational Needs

In occupational health interventions, one size does not fit all. This means that for an intervention to be effective, it needs to be the right solution in relation to the needs of the organization. It also needs to adapt to the practical circumstances of both organization and employees. In other words, the alignment of intervention to organization is concerned with both choosing the right intervention and adapting that chosen intervention to the specific needs of the organization and the employees. Thorough analyses of organizational needs should guide which type of intervention is chosen. For example, an individual-level stress intervention could be appropriate when the main problem is individuals showing poor coping skills, whereas an organizational level intervention may be used to target factors in the organization that cause stress (Burke 1993). Another example is from emergency care, where teamwork has traditionally been approached through staff training. However, in one or our studies, the TEPPP study (Mazzocato et al. 2011), teamwork was instead approached through job redesign. This meant that the intervention involved continuously and deliberately ensuring that teamwork behaviors were easier, faster and more convenient to perform than the behaviors associated with the traditional work process. The choice of intervention type and implementation strategy should be guided by a need analysis. Training and competence development, for example, is the right choice if there is a competence gap or lack of skills among staff. Job redesign, on the other hand, is suitable when the staff is unable to perform the target behavior because they are not given the opportunity to do so, as in the example of competence development in the first part of this chapter.

When the right intervention has been chosen, it may also need to be adapted according to the needs of the organization and the employees (Nielsen and Randall 2012). In the analogy in Fig. 7.1, this corresponds to how there must be an attraction between the atoms in the molecule to form bindings that keep the molecules together. If a planned intervention does not fit the organization or its employees, the risk of failure increases. A challenge when it comes to allowing local adaptation is to define which aspects of the intervention are open for adaptation and which ones are non-negotiable, e.g. what the core intervention components are (Carroll et al. 2007; Hurrell and Murphy 1998). Hence, it is a balancing act between the need to align the intervention to the organization and the employees in order to make it useful in practice (e.g. ensure the effectiveness of the intervention) and the need to implement the elements of the intervention that ensure its efficacy.

An intervention consists of several aspects that can be varied. In the Conceptual Framework for Implementation Fidelity (Carroll et al. 2007; Hasson 2010; Hasson et al. 2012), these are described as (1) the content of the intervention, (2) the dose delivered/received (including both frequency and duration, and possibly intensity), (3) coverage (whether all those who should participate actually do so). Here, we add a fourth component, namely timeliness; i.e. if the intervention is done at the right time. In OHS interventions, the analyses of whether to adhere or adapt needs to take into account the different levels of the organization: e.g. the individual (employee), the department and the organization. For example, in the intervention involving physical exercise during work hours, each workplace was allowed to decide when during the work week the physical exercise sessions would be scheduled (timeliness, department level). This was done to ensure that each department had the possibility to find the best possible fit between the intervention and their business needs. However, they were not allowed to vary the frequency (twice a week), as this would threaten the integrity of the intervention (the possibility to reach its goal). On the individual level, the same intervention allowed variance within the content category: each individual was allowed to choose the type of physical exercise, is long as it met an intensity criterion (middle to high intensity). Coverage is often one of the most challenging aspects of physical exercise interventions, since they often attract those who already exercise and not others. In the current project, coverage was considered a non-negotiable aspect of the intervention at the departmental level. Therefore, after the employees at the participating departments had jointly agreed to participate in the project, all employees were obligated to do physical exercise, which was considered a work task during the project time. At the individual level, each individual was given the choice to work at another department during the project time (an option no employee pursued).

Diagonal Alignment in Occupational Health Interventions

The support and involvement of managers at all organizational levels are central to the implementation of occupational health interventions (Nielsen and Randall 2009; Nytrø et al. 2000). Middle managers are often subsequently responsible for communicating and implementing the intervention as well as being involved in the practical integration of the intervention with "the ordinary work" (Saksvik et al. 2002). Higher management provides financing, lends legitimacy to the intervention, and illuminates how it is related to the strategic goals of the organization (Nielsen and Randall 2012; Randall et al. 2007). Upper management also needs to demonstrate ownership of the intervention, which will be more likely to happen when the intervention is aligned with the strategic goals of the organization and is thus perceived as more strategically important.

In sum, several important managerial activities have been described, including motivating employees, giving feedback and supporting the initiative (Øvretveit 2009). However, less is known about the function of these management activities, e.g. how they affect employee behavior. In terms of alignment, the activities can be understood as making it possible for others to perform their key behaviors (horizontal alignment) as well as providing a line of sight for how the intervention relates to important outcomes (vertical alignment). This involves several different functions, including providing direction, assuring that necessary competence development and training take place, creating opportunities for the change to happen, and assuring that the results are visualized and that the intervention is related to reinforcing consequences. For example, in the TEPPP study described previously, first-line managers gave feedback on work processes. For employees, this filled different functions at different occasions. Feedback sometimes provided information about the aim of the intervention (e.g. provided feedback), and at other times was purely motivational (e.g. perceived as positive consequences that followed the key behaviors). We suggest that, since it is the function of the activity that determines the influences on key behaviors, it is the function rather than the activity that should be analyzed and understood. This same logic applies to employee participation. For example, participating in terms of being able to influence the design and the implementation of an intervention may have the function of creating a sense of direction, by illuminating a line of sight. However, it may also have other functions such as ensuring that the content of the intervention is intrinsically motivating, or optimizing the implementation process by engaging in troubleshooting. In any case, we believe that a participatory approach is a necessity in order to succeed with interventions as well as to create the healthy organization we have outlined in this chapter.

Implications of Alignment for Researching Interventions

In previous parts of this chapter, we have painted a picture of how OHS interventions can be aligned with the organization in the modern working life. Here, we will discuss the implications of this on how OHS interventions can be researched.

Research Implications of Vertical Alignment

When interventions are aligned with the organization, and embedded with the overall strategies, this has implications for the collaboration between researchers and practitioners. Importantly, the organization (not the researcher) needs to determine the aim of the intervention, and what problem or opportunity it should target. This should then guide what intervention is implemented. Thus, the role of researcher (and consultant) at this stage is to help conduct need analysis and inform the organization about current evidence; it is not to implement a specific pre-determined solution. After the researcher and the organization have settled on a specific intervention, the role of the researcher is to facilitate the implementation of the intervention – either themselves or by cooperating with those that do. In this, the research becomes part of the intervention. The degree of involvement of the researcher will differ depending on the intervention and the implementation strategy. This means that the researcher may affect the outcome. In contrast to the golden standard of experimental studies and randomized control trials (RCTs), we do not necessarily consider this negative. However, it is essential that the researcher carefully consider his or her role and involvement and, when appropriate, describe these as intervention components.

Design Implications

For studies of aligned interventions, traditional efficacy studies using RCT designs are often inadequate, due to difficulties in randomizing, lack of power for cluster randomization, a lack of control over spurious variables, etc. (Nielsen et al. 2010a). Instead, natural experiments and adaptive study designs may be more appropriate (Randall et al. 2005). These designs utilize the natural variation between intervention groups as important information for understanding the process by which an intervention can potentially have an effect, rather than treating it as nuisance. This widens the scope of the research questions from "Does this intervention work?" to "Under what circumstances, for whom, does what work?" In other words, these designs try to explain the variation within organizations and interventions, instead of trying to control it (Griffiths 1999). In most organizations, change happens all the time. It may even be difficult to determine when an intervention has started. For example, has an intervention started when most employees have heard of it? When the strategic decision to start it was made? When a specific intervention component was launched? Or was it when a certain level of change in line with the intervention (e.g. when it had been implemented to a certain extent)? Thus, the research should be designed to make use of the variation within the organization rather than trying to control it. This makes the collection of process and context data very important (Murta et al. 2007). Moreover, through the combination of process and outcome data (what we call "procome studies") the significance of various process components for intervention effects can be evaluated. This way, it is still possible to perform studies that will separate implementation effects from intervention effects, and implementation failure from theory failure (Fixsen et al. 2005).

Using Program Theory to Guide Measurements

Complex interventions often require complex evaluations. Program theory can be useful as a guide in formulating the hypothesis to be tested, and to inform the choice of data sources. In our experience, multiple data sources and analytic methods are often necessary in order to capture both process and multiple effects. For example, we frequently use interviews to highlight perceptions of an intervention and its implementation; organizational documents to inform about formal decision-making and policies; observations to understand what is implemented in practice; and questionnaires for statistical analysis of process as well as outcome data. Also, multiple data sources and analytic strategies help in validating the findings by comparing the results from analyses of different data, e.g. triangulation (Yin 2003). A participatory approach is also, as always, important. For example, employees can very well be involved in the collection of data, such as following up on register data or keeping diaries. The diary is an example of a data collection method that can have multiple functions: it can form part of the intervention, for example by increasing self-reflection or being part of a risk assessment, but can also be used by researchers for the evaluation of intervention activities.

Program theory is also useful in establishing the appropriate times points for data collection. This is because program theory outlines when specific effects theoretically would occur, and how they relate to each other. From this follows that different outcomes would optimally be measured at different time points. The problem is that for many interventions and outcomes, the optimal time lag is unknown; and in addition, under most circumstances several measurements at different time points would be practically impossible. Therefore, in practice, the time points will often be chosen based on several, competing objectives. However, this does not justify measuring the right thing at the wrong time. For example, it is common in Swedish organizations to follow up the effects of occupational health interventions with company-level sickness absence data. Often, this is measured as the percentage of work days missed due to sickness absence in relation to the available work days. This measure may be valid as an end outcome, a couple of years down the line; however, it can seldom be regarded as an immediate or intermediate outcome in intervention studies.

Measuring Important Strategic Output

A consequence of research on interventions that are aligned with an organization's strategic goals is that measures relevant to the strategic goals should be included in the evaluation. For example, in health care, quality of care and patient outcomes may be relevant measures; in industry, it may be safety. Generally, productivity is a central part of strategic goals. Measuring productivity is challenging; both objective and self-rated productivity measures are often needed, as they complement each other. Collaboration with the organization will help in choosing the productivity measures that are most relevant for the particular organization. The drawback of this is that as the validity of the productivity measures for the specific organization increases, comparison between organizations becomes more difficult. In such cases, self-ratings can offer possibilities for cross-organizational comparisons.

Research Implications of Horizontal Alignment

Interventions need to be aligned with the needs of the organization and the individual in order to be effective. They need to address the right problems, and the actions that make up the intervention must be possible to perform in practice. This makes adaptability an important feature of an organizational intervention; subsequently, as argued above, the research design has to be adaptive as well. Moreover, this has implications for how measurements are performed. First, data should be used for learning and improvement. Thus, we suggest a formative research approach, whereby data are used systematically to make modifications to the intervention (Nastasi et al. 2007). We believe this approach is helpful in making sure that the organization assumes responsibility for the intervention, since evaluation is essential in the continuous improvement work we want all interventions to be part of. Second, being able to see the results of one's efforts is an important reinforcer of behavior. Therefore, data gathered for research purposes should be available to those participating in the intervention. Practically, this means prioritizing data that are easy to gather, give feedback on and interpret. For example, in the TEPPP study the teams gathered after each shift and reviewed performance data (number of patients treated by the team). This helped them visualize a positive effect of teamwork that was not immediately obvious to them without the feedback.

Research Implications of Diagonal Alignment

Given the importance of leaders for the successful implementation of interventions, research on intervention in aligned organizations means working with managers at all levels. The involvement of top management ensures commitment to the research process – and project. Their commitment will also – in line with the concept of alignment – show the organization that the research project is important and should be prioritized. The fact that it is they, not the researchers, who are responsible for the intervention is important in this. Upper management will also provide access to key resources, such as documentation, managers, employees and the physical workplace. Middle and first-line managers have a similar role of giving the mandate to the researchers to gain access to the workplace and the work groups. They also have a great deal of hands-on information about the intervention, along with their central role in implementation. We believe that a close collaboration between researcher and the organization is important not only for the success of the intervention at hand; it may also be important from a larger perspective, in that it can help achieve alignment between research and practice, which in the long run may help bridge the gap that often exists between these two entities.

Summary

In this chapter, we provide a system perspective on healthy organizations by expanding the concept of alignment and applying it to occupational health. In this, we have discussed employee participation and management's role in health interventions from a functional perspective. It is suggested that program theory should guide the selection of intervention as well as its evaluation. We provide a framework for balancing adaptation and adherence in order achieve fit between intervention and organization while maintaining the intervention's theoretical soundness. The overall aim of the presented approach is to close the gap between occupational health and the organization's strategic goals.

References

Abernathy, W. B. (2008). Implications and applications of a behavior systems perspective. *Journal of Organizational Behavior Management, 28*(2), 123–138.

Augustsson, H., Törnquist, A., & Hasson, H. (2013). Challenges in transferring individual learning to organizational learning in residential care for older people. *Journal of Health Organization and Management, 27*(3).

Baker, E., Israel, B. A., & Schurman, S. (1996). The integrated model: Implications for worksite health promotion and occupational health and safety practice. *Health Education & Behavior, 23*(2), 175–190.

Batt, R., & Appelbaum, E. (1995). Worker participation in diverse settings: Does the form affect the outcome, and, if so, who benefits? *British Journal of Industrial Relations, 33*(3), 353–378.

Boswell, W. (2006). Aligning employees with the organization's strategic objectives: Out of 'line of sight', out of mind. *International Journal of Human Resource Management, 17*(9), 1489–1511.

Buller, P. F., & McEvoy, G. M. (2012). Strategy, human resource management and performance: Sharpening line of sight. *Human Resource Management Review, 22*(1), 43–56.

Burke, R. J. (1993). Organizational-level interventions to reduce occupational stressors. *Work and Stress, 7*(1), 77–87.

Carroll, C., Patterson, M., Wood, S., Booth, A., Rick, J., & Balain, S. (2007). A conceptual framework for implementation fidelity. *Implementation Science, 2*(1), 40.

European Agency for Safety and Health at Work. (2010a). *European Survey of Enterprises on New and Emerging Risks: Managing Safety and Health at Work*. Luxembourg: Publications Office of the European Union. http://osha.europa.eu/en/publications/reports/esener1_osh_management. pdf. Accessed 27 Nov 2012.

European Agency for Safety and Health at Work. (2010b). *Mainstreaming OSH into business management*. Luxembourg: European Agency for Safety and Health at Work. http://osha.europa.eu/ en/publications/reports/mainstreaming_osh_business.pdf. Accessed 28 Nov 2012.

Fixsen, D. L., Naoom, S. F., Blase, K. A., Friedman, R. M., & Wallace, F. (2005). *Implementation research: A synthesis of the literature* (Vol. 125). Tampa: University of South Florida, Louis de la Parte Florida Mental Health Institute, The National Implementation Research Network (FMHI Publication 231).

Fried, Y., & Ferris, G. R. (1987). The validity of the job characteristics model: A review and meta-analysis. *Personnel Psychology, 40*(2), 287–322.

Glenn, S. S., & Malott, M. E. (2004). Lead article complexity and selection: Implications for organizational change. *Behavior and Social Issues, 13*, 89–106.

Griffiths, A. (1999). Organizational interventions: Facing the limits of the natural science paradigm. *Scandinavian Journal of Work, Environment & Health, 25*(6), 589–596.

Hackman, J. R., & Oldham, G. R. (1976). Motivation through the design of work: Test of a theory. *Organizational Behavior and Human Performance, 16*(2), 250–279.

Hasson, H. (2010). Study protocol: Systematic evaluation of implementation fidelity of complex interventions in health and social care. *Implement Science, 5*, 67.

Hasson, H., Blomberg, S., & Dunér, A. (2012). Fidelity and moderating factors in complex interventions: A case study of a continuum of care program for frail elderly people in health and social care. *Implementation Science, 7*, 23.

Humphrey, S. E., Nahrgang, J. D., & Morgeson, F. P. (2007). Integrating motivational, social, and contextual work design features: A meta-analytic summary and theoretical extension of the work design literature. *The Journal of Applied Psychology, 92*(5), 1332.

Hurrell, J. J., & Murphy, L. R. (1998). Occupational stress intervention. *American Journal of Industrial Medicine, 29*(4), 338–341.

Hymel, P. A., Loeppke, R. R., Baase, C. M., Burton, W. N., Hartenbaum, N. P., Hudson, T. W., et al. (2011). Workplace health protection and promotion: A new pathway for a healthier—And safer—Workforce. *Journal of Occupational and Environmental Medicine, 53*(6), 695–702.

Jacobsen, D. I., Thorsvik, J., Sandberg, A., & Sandin, G. (2008). *Hur moderna organisationer fungerar: Introduktion I organisation och ledarskap*. Lund: Studentlitteratur.

Jørgensen, T. H., Remmen, A., & Mellado, M. D. (2006). Integrated management systems: Three different levels of integration. *Journal of Cleaner Production, 14*(8), 713–722.

Kuorinka, I., Forcier, L., Hagberg, M., Silverstein, B., Wells, R., Smith, M., et al. (1995). *Work related musculoskeletal disorders (WMSDs): A reference book for prevention*. London: Taylor & Francis.

Landsbergis, P. A., & Vivona-Vaughan, E. (1995). Evaluation of an occupational stress intervention in a public agency. *Journal of Organizational Behavior, 16*(1), 29–48.

Lawler, E. E., Mohrman, S. A., & Ledford, G. E. (1995). *Creating high performance organizations: Practices and results of employee involvement and total quality management in Fortune 1000 companies*. San Francisco: Jossey-Bass.

Mazzocato, P., Hvitfeldt Forsberg, H., & von Thiele Schwarz, U. (2011). Team behaviors in emergency care: A qualitative study using behavior analysis of what makes team work. *Scandinavian Journal of Trauma, Resuscitation and Emergency Medicine, 19*(1), 1–8.

Mikkelsen, A. (2005). Methodological challenges in the study of organizational interventions in flexible organizations. In A. M. Fuglseth & I. A. Kleppe (Eds.), *Anthology for Kjell Grønhaug in celebration of his 70th birthday* (pp. 150–178). Bergen: Fagbokforlaget.

Mikkelsen, A., Saksvik, P. O., Eriksen, H. R., & Ursin, H. (1999). The impact of learning opportunities and decision authority on occupational health. *Work and Stress, 13*(1), 20–31.

Miller, P., & Haslam, C. (2009). Why employers spend money on employee health: Interviews with occupational health and safety professionals from British Industry. *Safety Science, 47*(2), 163–169.

Murta, S. G., Sanderson, K., & Oldenburg, B. (2007). Process evaluation in occupational stress management programs: A systematic review. *American Journal of Health Promotion, 21*(4), 248–254.

Nastasi, B. K., Hitchcock, J., Sarkar, S., Burkholder, G., Varjas, K., & Jayasena, A. (2007). Mixed methods in intervention research: Theory to adaptation. *Journal of Mixed Methods Research, 1*(2), 164–182.

Nielsen, K., & Randall, R. (2009). Managers' active support when implementing teams: The impact on employee well-being. *Applied Psychology: Health and Well Being, 1*(3), 374–390.

Nielsen, K., & Randall, R. (2012). Opening the black box: Presenting a model for evaluating organizational-level interventions. *European Journal of Work and Organizational Psychology,* 1–17.

Nielsen, K., Randall, R., & Christensen, K. B. (2010a). Developing new ways of evaluating organizational-level interventions. In J. Houdmont & S. Leka (Eds.), *Contemporary occupational health psychology: Global perspectives on research and practice* (pp. 21–45). Chichester: Wiley-Blackwell.

Nielsen, K., Randall, R., Holten, A., & Rial Gonzalez, E. (2010b). Conducting organizational-level occupational health interventions: What works? *Work and Stress, 24*(3), 234–259.

Nielsen, K., Taris, T. W., & Cox, T. (2010c). The future of organizational interventions: Addressing the challenges of today's organizations. *Work and Stress, 24*(3), 219–233.

NIOSH. (2012). *Research compendium: The NIOSH Total Worker HealthTM Program: Seminal Research Papers 2012* (Vol. DHHS (NIOSH) Publication No. 2012–146). Washington, DC: Department of Health and Human Services, PublicHealth Service, Centers for Disease Control and Prevention, National Institute for Occupational Safety and Health. http://www.cdc.gov/niosh/docs/2012-146/pdfs/2012-146.pdf. Accessed 28 Nov 2013.

Nytrø, K., Saksvik, P., Mikkelsen, A., Bohle, P., & Quinlan, M. (2000). An appraisal of key factors in the implementation of occupational stress interventions. *Work and Stress, 14*(3), 213–225.

Oldham, G. R., & Hackman, J. R. (2010). Not what it was and not what it will be: The future of job design research. *Journal of Organizational Behavior, 31*(2–3), 463–479.

Øvretveit, J. (2009). Effective leadership of improvement: The research. *The International Journal of Clinical Leadership, 16*(2), 97–105.

Podsakoff, P. M., & MacKenzie, S. B. (1997). Impact of organizational citizenship behavior on organizational performance: A review and suggestion for future research. *Human Performance, 10*(2), 133–151.

Rafferty, Y., Friend, R., & Landsbergis, P. A. (2001). The association between job skill discretion, decision authority and burnout. *Work and Stress, 15*(1), 73–85.

Randall, R., Griffiths, A., & Cox, T. (2005). Evaluating organizational stress-management interventions using adapted study designs. *European Journal of Work and Organizational Psychology, 14*(1), 23–41.

Randall, R., Cox, T., & Griffiths, A. (2007). Participants' accounts of a stress management intervention. *Human Relations, 60*(8), 1181.

Saksvik, P., Nytrø, K., Dahl-Jørgensen, C., & Mikkelsen, A. (2002). A process evaluation of individual and organizational occupational stress and health interventions. *Work and Stress, 16*(1), 37–57.

Semmer, N. K. (2003). Job stress interventions and organization of work. In J. C. Quick & L. E. Tetrick (Eds.), *Handbook of occupational health psychology* (pp. 325–353). Washington, DC: American Psychological Association.

Smith, D. (2002). *IMS: Implementing and operating*. London: BSI British Standards Institution.

Steckler, A. B., Linnan, L., & Israel, B. A. (2002). *Process evaluation for public health interventions and research*. San Francisco: Jossey-Bass.

Stenfors-Hayes, T., Hasson, H., Augustsson, H., Hvitfeldt Forsberg, H., & von Thiele Schwarz, U. (2013). *Merging occupational health, safety and health promotion with Lean: An integrated systems approach* (the LeanHealth project) (Vol. Submitted). Gower Publishing.

Van der Klink, J., Blonk, R., Schene, A. H., & Van Dijk, F. (2001). The benefits of interventions for work-related stress. *American Journal of Public Health, 91*(2), 270.

von Thiele Schwarz, U., & Hasson, H. (2011). Employee self-rated productivity and objective organizational production levels: Effects of worksite health interventions involving reduced work hours and physical exercise. *Journal of Occupational and Environmental Medicine, 53*(8), 838–844.

von Thiele Schwarz, U., & Hasson, H. (2012). Effects of worksite health interventions involving reduced work hours and physical exercise on sickness absence costs. *Journal of Occupational and Environmental Medicine, 54*(5), 538.

von Thiele Schwarz, U., Lindfors, P., & Lundberg, U. (2008). Health-related effects of worksite interventions involving physical exercise and reduced workhours. *Scandinavian Journal of Work, Environment & Health, 34*(3), 179–188.

Wagner, J. A., III. (1994). Participation's effects on performance and satisfaction: A reconsideration of research evidence. *The Academy of Management Review, 19*(2), 312–330.

Wilder, D. A., Austin, J., & Casella, S. (2009). Applying behavior analysis in organizations: Organizational behavior management. *Psychological Services, 6*(3), 202.

Wilkinson, G., & Dale, B. G. (1999). Integrated management systems: An examination of the concept and theory. *The TQM Magazine, 11*(2), 95–104.

Wilkinson, G., & Dale, B. G. (2002). An examination of the ISO 9001: 2000 standard and its influence on the integration of management systems. *Production Planning & Control, 13*(3), 284–297.

Wright, P. M., Dunford, B. B., & Snell, S. A. (2001). Human resources and the resource based view of the firm. *Journal of Management, 27*(6), 701–721.

Yin, R. K. (2003). *Case study research: Design and methods*. Thousand Oaks: Sage.

Zink, K. J., Steimle, U., & Schröder, D. (2008). Comprehensive change management concepts: Development of a participatory approach. *Applied Ergonomics, 39*(4), 527–538.

Zwetsloot, G. I. J. M. (1995). Improving cleaner production by integration into the management of quality, environment and working conditions. *Journal of Cleaner Production, 3*(1), 61–66.

Chapter 8
A Multi-level and Participatory Model for Prevention of Work-Related Stress in Knowledge Work

Christine Ipsen and Vibeke Andersen

Abstract Work-related stress is an increasing problem for knowledge workers, despite employee control and influence. As a consequence, the knowledge industry has expressed the need for new knowledge and approaches regarding how to support sustainable preventive action and assure productivity and well-being. A healthy organization has its starting point in the organization, and with a salutogenic approach, focus is on how the organization and work system can be designed in order to improve productivity and working conditions for the individuals involved. Two consecutive research and development projects building on a mixed-method approach have been conducted where organizational- level interventions were implemented in 10 knowledge-intensive companies. The aim was to re-design the daily work practices by using a multi-level, participatory and salutogenic approach. Participants from multi-organizational levels were thus seen as an integrated part of the whole process, including development, design and implementation, and not merely objects exposed to the intervention. The springboard for the changes was thus the local, shared understanding of the workplace and the externalization of individual knowledge regarding problems and potential solutions. The findings suggest that it is possible to prevent work-related stress in knowledge work by adapting a multi-level, collaborative and participatory model which comprises a set of approaches, capabilities and activities that we find to be of key importance in primary interventions. These include managerial support, externalization of tacit

C. Ipsen, Ph.D. (✉)
Department of Management Engineering Production and Service Management,
Technical University of Denmark, Kongens Lyngby, Denmark
e-mail: chip@dtu.dk

V. Andersen
Department of Learning and Philosophy, Aalborg University Copenhagen (AAU-CPH),
Copenhagen, Denmark
e-mail: vian@learning.aau.dk

G.F. Bauer and G.J. Jenny (eds.), *Salutogenic Organizations and Change:*
The Concepts Behind Organizational Health Intervention Research,
DOI 10.1007/978-94-007-6470-5_8, © Springer Science+Business Media Dordrecht 2013

knowledge, collective evaluations, adjustments and decisions, visualization of progress and current status, appointed facilitators and a number of defined phases and activities.

Keywords Knowledge work • Intervention • Prevention • Re-design • Organizational design • Multi-level collaboration • Participatory • Salutogenic

Introduction

Work-related stress is an increasing problem for knowledge workers, despite employee control and influence (Griffiths 1999; Ipsen and Jensen 2012; McClenahan et al. 2007; Stavroula et al. 2003; WHO 1999). A Danish study has made it clear that the prevailing stress management practice in knowledge-intensive companies (KICs) in Denmark has had an individual rather than organizational focus, and has resulted in short-sighted solutions and recurring incidents, as well as new cases (Ipsen and Jensen 2012).

As a consequence of this increasing and unsolved problem, knowledge intensive companies have expressed the need for new knowledge and approaches that can support sustainable preventive actions and assure productivity and well-being.

Two consecutive explorative research and development projects with a mixed-method approach were formulated with the aim to develop and implement primary interventions in knowledge-intensive companies. The organizational level interventions were to use a multi-level, participatory and salutogenic approach.

This chapter presents some of our research findings presented in three sections: our understanding of a healthy organization, the principles and content of a primary intervention in a knowledge-intensive company, and the results of interventions across 10 knowledge intensive companies in Denmark. In closing, we present our research approach to interventions.

Concept of a Healthy Organization

The core of our work is to understand transformation processes within an organization and how they affect individuals and their behavior. In continuation of this, we need to understand how an organizational design – i.e. the deliberate process of creating an effective organization capable of achieving its strategy (Kates and Galbraith 2007) – can be developed in order to create both productivity and well-being. This means that our understanding of a healthy organization has its starting point in the organization (see Fig. 8.1).

Using a salutogenic approach, focus is on how the organization and work system can be designed to improve productivity and working conditions for the individuals involved.

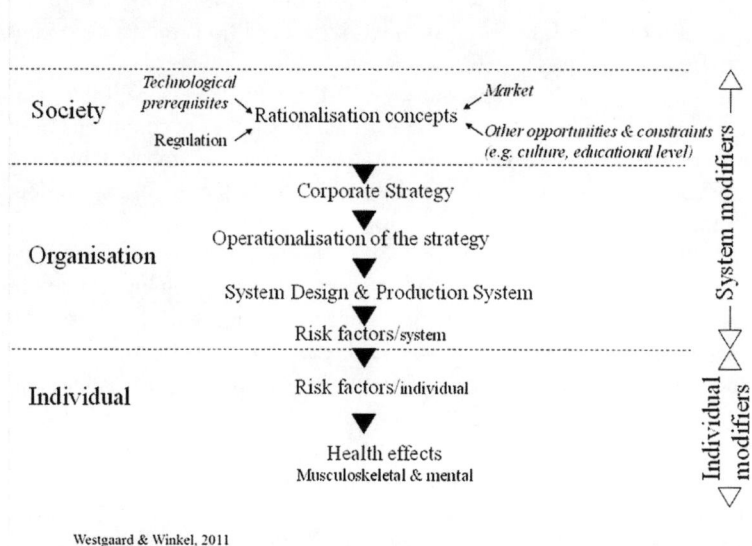

Westgaard & Winkel, 2011

Fig. 8.1 The organization – our starting point for a healthy organization (Westgaard and Winkel 2011)

A healthy organization is also characterized by an organization with a well-designed and well-managed organizational design, where both managers and employees have a sense of coherence and the capability to monitor, reflect and act on disparities. A well-designed organization is thus not a stable solution achieved once and for all. It involves a developmental process that must be kept active (Weick 2001, p. 60).

An organizational design with these characteristics has the capability to improve productivity and well-being, as well as a mature preventive stress management practice. Here, both managers and employees are capable of both reflecting on the existing work and management practices and acting upon them, initiating primary interventions based on a participatory, collective, salutogenic and structured process.

Accordingly, in its everyday operations, a healthy organization has both the individual and organizational process-related capability to reflect, learn and act upon local knowledge on work-related problems and issues in a participatory and multi-level way.

The Characteristics of a Healthy Knowledge-Intensive Company

Work as an academic, which involves knowledge work, is perceived to offer a satisfying and developing job. Working conditions in such jobs are characterized by a high level of influence, control, flexibility and autonomy (Kompier and Cooper

1999; Parker and Wall 1999). Karasek and Theorell, in their work with their Job Decision Latitude model, find that such working conditions reflect a good psychosocial environment (Karasek 1979, 1990).

Newer empirical studies and surveys (Buch and Andersen 2008; Ipsen and Jensen 2012; McClenahan et al. 2007) indicate that working conditions that create enthusiasm can also create stress and strain; therefore, if stressors in knowledge work are removed or reduced, the result would also be the removal or reduction of the working conditions that create enthusiasm.

An example is variation and predictability. Knowledge workers are enthusiastic about the variety of tasks, which differ daily and offer exciting, new and unfamiliar challenges. It can be frustrating however not to know whether there are projects in the pipeline and whether the complex problems can be solved on a satisfactory level. Increasing predictability and simpler tasks are not an option, since this could reduce the work-related enthusiasm.

This is a clear distinction from industrial work, where the overall aim is to remove or reduce strain at work. This new understanding of the working environment and its management influences the stress management practice in relation to knowledge work and is thus a new capability that needs to be achieved.

A Salutogenic Systems Model

Instead, a salutogenic approach can be used in order to understand the factors that actively promote health (Antonovsky 1996). In an organizational setting and with the aim to address stress-preventive actions in knowledge work through organizational development, it is necessary to understand the relationship between the sources of work-related problems and the workplace's organizational design. This will make it possible to point out salutary factors (Antonovsky 1996; Dettinger and Smith 2006; Ipsen and Jensen 2012; Smith and Sainfort 1989; Sørensen and Holman 2010).

Galbraith's organizational design model, The Star Model, is an example of a system model that identifies the linkages between five different organizational conditions. It also focuses on the importance of fundamental organizational issues and work processes as the underlying variables (Galbraith 2002). Kates and Galbraith (2007) point out that *"a strategy implies a set of capabilities at which an organization must excel in order to achieve the strategic goals"* (p. 3).

The capabilities needed to achieve a healthy organization strategy are as follows:

- The ability to reflect and act based on a participatory approach
- The ability to acknowledge that a change in the organizational design in knowledge work can support the development of sound and healthy work and a mature stress management practice, which again promotes both well-being and productivity
- The ability to involve and apply in-house resources and knowledge

- The ability to initiate and implement interventions based on a collective, salutogenic and structured process
- The ability to apply a systemic view of the organization and workplace.

This list reflects the experiences and results achieved in connection with our research projects on interventions (Buch et al. 2009; Ipsen and Andersen 2011; Ipsen and Jensen 2012; Sørensen and Holman 2010) and what works, based on theories on systems design, salutogenesis, the learning organization, and participatory and primary interventions (Antonovsky 1996; Argyris and Schön 1996; Galbraith 2002; Murphy 1988; Rosskam 2009).

By using Galbraith's Star Model, it is possible to address the mutual interdependencies and their relation to the basic elements in the organizational design. The organizational design model consists of five interrelated elements (Galbraith 2002; Kates and Galbraith 2007):

- Strategy – sets the organization's direction and encompasses the company's vision and mission, short-term and long-term goals. The strategy is the cornerstone of the organization design process.
- People – have the necessary and fundamental set of competencies to interact, participate and make decisions within the organization.
- Structure – determines where formal power and authority are located in the organization.
- Rewards – align individual behaviors and performance with the organization's goals and motivate employees.
- Processes – a series of connected activities that move information up, down and across the organization, comprise both work and management processes.

The idea of alignment is fundamental to the model. Each element of the organization represented by a point on the model (see below) should work to support the strategy. When aligned, the five elements form the foundation for organizational behavior, productivity and performance. The model shows that by changing the organizational design, it is possible to change the behavior of the employees and managers and the company's performance. It is thus important to acknowledge the interrelation of the elements and make an attempt to align all five of them in order to obtain the desired effect (Fig. 8.2).

A salutogenic approach can thus be used to understand which factors actively promote health.

The whole description above constitutes our concept of a healthy organization, the strategy of which is to secure a healthy workplace, productivity and well-being, and where all parties acknowledge that organizational and managerial changes contribute to well-being and productivity. It is thus not an individual problem. The healthy organization is also capable of preventing work-related stress in a collaborative process that focuses on the daily practices and the organizational design. The initiated primary interventions are based on a participatory, collective, salutogenic and structured approach and result in both productivity and well-being.

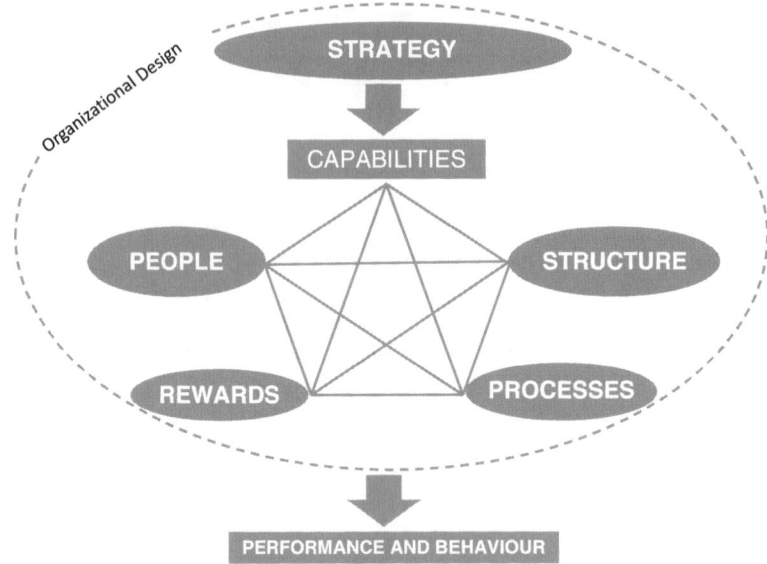

Fig. 8.2 The star model (Kates and Galbraith 2007)

Principles of Primary Interventions – Re-designing the Organizational Design in a Multi-level and Participatory Process

With our starting point for preventive intervention research in the organization and salutary factors – i.e. factors which actively promote health (Antonovsky 1996, p. 14) – our concept of primary interventions is about re-designing work processes and daily activities as part of a company's organizational design in a multi-level and participatory process (Hurrell and Murphy 1996; Ipsen et al. 2010; Murphy 1988; Murphy and Sauter 2003; Rosskam 2009).

The principles for primary preventions listed below concern the target and content of the intervention process. Our findings show these to be of key importance for supporting the re-design of the organizational design in a multi-level, participatory process (Buch and Andersen 2008; Ipsen et al. 2010; Ipsen and Andersen 2011; Ipsen 2011; Ipsen and Jensen 2012; Sørensen and Holman 2010):

Target of the intervention:

1. A primary prevention approach – i.e. organizational-level interventions
2. The outset is the organizational design and daily activities based on a salutogenic approach.

The intervention process requires:

3. Multi-level collaborative approach
4. Active support from managers

5. Explication of tacit knowledge among employees and managers regarding work-related problems and potential solutions
6. Continuous collective evaluations and adjustments of the intervention, based on collective reflections and decisions.
7. Visualization of the process and results to promote awareness and commitment
8. Appointment of one facilitator for each intervention to be the "ears of the organization"
9. A project period with a number of defined phases and activities, a start and finish time

The principles are detailed further below, followed by an outline for an actual intervention in knowledge-intensive companies.

Primary Interventions

Murphy points at primary stress management interventions as the most efficient way to prevent work-related stress (Hurrell and Murphy 1996; Murphy 1988). The interventions aim at stress-related workplace conditions; it is therefore important to understand the relationship between the sources of work-related problems and the organizational design of the workplace (Dettinger and Smith 2006; Ipsen and Jensen 2012; Smith and Sainfort 1989; Sørensen and Holman 2010).

Elkin and Rosch (1990) point to a number of initiatives that can be implemented as part of primary interventions: reorganizing authority lines and restructuring organizational units, changing decision-making processes, re-designing tasks and establishing a reward system (Elkin and Rosch 1990).

Changes in Daily Practices and Organizational Design

If the intervention is to have the desired effect on productivity and well-being, it must result in changes that relate to daily practice and the organizational design.

The systemic approach is thus applied in order to develop an understanding of the basic organizational causes behind the risk of work-related stress in knowledge work and potential options, and to support development of primary stress-preventive changes (Murphy 1988). As Rosskam points out: *"Employing a holistic and systems view is concordant with the reality that improvement in working conditions takes place in a wider organizational context of worker and management relations"*(Rosskam 2009, p. 216).

In an organizational setting, it is important to understand the relationship between the sources of work-related problems and the organizational design of the workplace in order to be able to point out the salutary factors.

In addition, the systemic approach ensures that changes become embedded and rooted in daily practice through re-design of the organizational design so that it is aligned and supports a sustainable effect.

Participation – A Multi-level Collaborative Approach

Participation is one of the most frequently mentioned factors of importance in interventions and intervention processes (Randall et al. 2009). Collective reflection and action must be an integrated part of this process in order to secure sustainability for the new activities. As a responsible unit and as generators of ideas in a development process, the collective can contribute more to the process than the individual (Kompier et al. 1998).

To ensure that all interests, requests and knowledge become explicit, a participatory approach to development activities provides a means to gain access to knowledge and experiences related to a given topic from all relevant parties and groups in the organization in the various stages of the process. This approach thus provides the opportunity to discuss and decide collectively with regard to the development and direction of the research (Hurrell and Murphy 1996; Ipsen et al. 2010; Ivancevich et al. 1990; Reason 1994; Rosskam 2009).

A participatory approach is also a way to establish ownership and secure a sustainable intervention and outcome (Kompier et al. 2000) as well as a sense of coherence (Antonovsky 1996). Finally, both employees and managers have the power and authority to affect the intervention (Greene 1997).

Management Support and Equal Status of the Intervention

Our research shows that primary interventions need active support from management during the whole process, whether it is a leader of the department involved or of the whole corporation. More specifically, management has to agree to the terms on which the project design is based, such as allocation of resources, changes in daily practices and the participatory approach.

In order to ensure that the intervention is carried out, the allocated resources, in terms of time, staff and resources for the parties involved, are crucial. Otherwise, the intervention is likely to be yet another unfulfilled project. Through the allocation of resources, the intervention is secured equal status with other daily, value-creating activities, and the intervention-related activities are more likely to be implemented.

Making Tacit Knowledge Regarding Work and Working Conditions Explicit

Another reason to employ a participatory approach is that it is a way to gain access to knowledge and experiences on a given topic. A study by Ipsen and Jensen (2012) shows that tacit knowledge of problems and possible solutions exists within the organization, but is rarely made explicit so that it can inform stress-preventing activities. If collective tacit knowledge were made explicit through a formalized participatory process of collective reflection, it could form the basis for the formulation of sustainable preventive changes and support their implementation on the organizational level (Ipsen and Jensen 2012; Mogensen et al. 2008). However, knowledge-intensive companies often lack possibilities that could allow collective systematic reflection and development in relation to prevention of work-related stress in the individual departments. Other relevant actors, such as the HR department and/or the safety organization, do not undertake this role either (Ipsen and Jensen 2012).

There is therefore a need for collective space for reflection, which can facilitate making tacit knowledge explicit in an externalization process (Nonaka et al. 2002) and establish a mutual learning process (Argyris and Schön 1996). Collective space for reflection would also support local collective understanding of workplace-related problems and their causes. Such reflection should focus on daily practice and involve the affected employees and managers. The knowledge that needs to be made explicit concerns working conditions, work practices, related problems and organizational causality. To support this process, explorative tools such as Ishikawa's Fish-Bone diagram can be used (Gray et al. 2010; Ishikawa 1968).

Participation by both employees and managers in two workshops has two purposes. First, it clarifies the differences in perceptions of work that exist among employees and managers; and second, it secures a sense of ownership and commitment to the future intervention. During the workshops, it is important to start with the positive aspects of the work and the workplace, since people who experience positive feelings will open their perspective so they are able to gain an overview of relationships and the larger picture (Fredericksons 1998).

The explicated new knowledge can then be used in development, implementation and continuous evaluation of preventive organizational changes and form the basis for adjustments.

Continuous Evaluation and Adjustments of the Intervention

In order to minimize the gap between the planned and actual implementation, Dahler-Larsen (2001) has formulated Program Theory, where the outcomes of an intervention (program) are continuously evaluated by the stakeholders. In line with Dahler-Larsen, Greene (1997) states that the results of an evaluation or intervention are more likely to be used, if the users, through their participation, have become invested in the process, which thus creates a sense of ownership and commitment (Greene 1997).

To secure commitment, Dahler-Larsen suggests that the stakeholders develop a plan for the intervention. The idea is for participants to decide on their program goals and theory, which can be evaluated step by step throughout the intervention. The evaluation thus makes it possible to identify implementation failures and the changes to be made. The aim of the evaluation is to gain increased insight into which factors are important for securing the expected outcomes, so the stakeholders can respond to this and develop a new theory of how the goal can be met, thereby increasing the chance for success.

Dahler-Larsen therefore points to the importance of developing a Program Theory, which can justify the intervention in terms of its expected outcomes and effects and involve the relevant parties (Dahler-Larsen 2001).

Visualization – Process and Results

Visualization is an important principle for an intervention. This means that the involved participants employ physical artifacts in the form of an object that holds information about the intervention's progress and/or results. By tracking the process and securing a picture of the current state of the intervention, there is less risk of fading interest.

Inspired by the Lean Concept (Womack et al. 2007), visualization in this context is a recommended tool to raise awareness at the specific workplace, as well as within the organization and outside it, and to ensure commitment to the intervention.

There are numerous ways to visualize progress and the current state of the intervention. It is up to the individual company to choose the form that is most suitable (Gray et al. 2010).

Facilitators – The Ears of the Organization

A key condition for succeeding with an intervention and securing anchorage is that the process is supported and facilitated by local actors. Rosskam (2009) states that involving workers in the research process can promote organizational learning and can catalyze organizational change from within, without any stimulation by outside researchers (Rosskam 2009, p. 215).

Weick points to the "bricoleur" as the informal change agent who is characterized by using what is at hand (bricolage) (Weick 2001). In this project, we have tried to formalize the bricoleur by appointing employees who naturally engage in change processes, regardless of position and role. Instead of using shop stewards and/or a work environment representative, an ordinary employee is appointed to facilitate the process, and also to act as the *"ears of the organization"* and provide access to stories about what works and does not work in relation to the intervention.

The facilitators' role is to gain insight into the process through interviewing and listening to their colleagues and managers about the intervention, using appropriate methods. This means applying a questioning technique, using an appreciative approach, moving focus from problems to "What do you/we want?" by focusing on what makes sense for the individual and for the department. Besides, they are to facilitate the visualization of the progress and current state of the intervention.

In order to become a facilitator, the person must be trusted. It is not a role one can assume. A facilitator is appointed by colleagues and managers. It is also desirable to have process knowledge and be committed.

The Phase Model – A Number of Arranged Activities

The last principle of an intervention in knowledge-intensive companies is that it consists of a number of defined phases and a set of activities in which both employees and managers participate, based on a salutogenic, multi-level and participatory approach used in a meaningful and manageable manner.

However, this is not a classic change management approach, but rather a dynamic development process similar to "Design Thinking", which is a practical, creative process of creating ideas through cooperation, systems understanding, visualization, testing and adjustment (Brown 2008; Simon 1981). This approach is reflected in the intervention activities, which are conducted in three phases:

1. Assessing the need for a primary intervention
2. Exploring the work and workplace
3. Implementing organizational-level changes and continuous evaluation and adjustments

The sum of the principles for organizational-level interventions is a process model in which both managers and employees participate step by step in order to explore their workplace and, in collaboration, re-design their work practices and organizational design and implement change.

Step-Wise Implementation: Example of an Intervention in a Knowledge-Intensive Company

It is important to acknowledge that the described process tool is not a list of concrete changes to be initiated by any company, nor is it a quick fix. It is a tool that can assist managers and employees to focus on changing their work processes and practices in a participatory and multi-level process. In the following, each step of the process is described as part of three phases. The description is based on experience gained from the six case companies (Fig. 8.3).

Phase 1 – Assessing the Need

Experience shows that companies that want to initiate primary interventions typically have experienced a number of stress-related cases and recognize that new

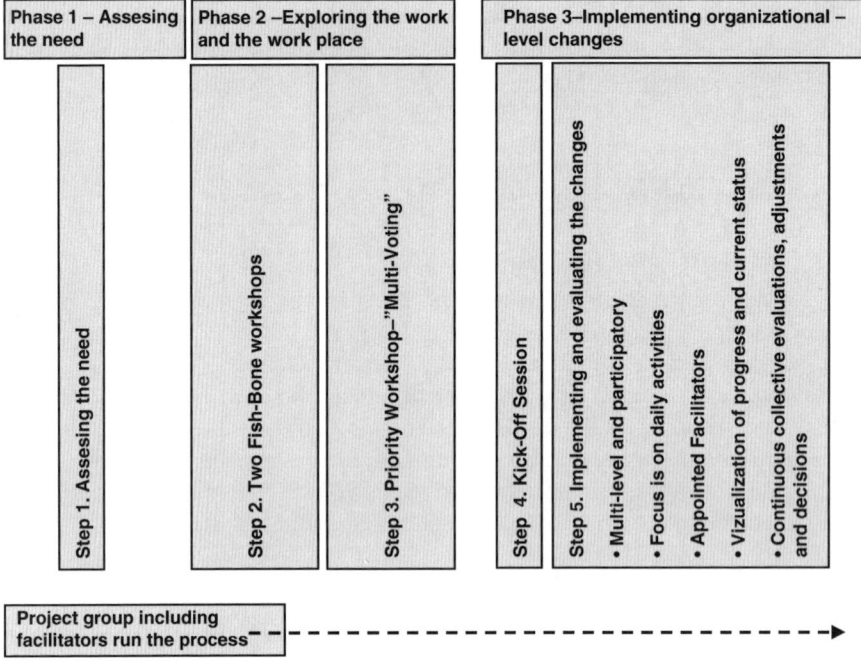

Fig. 8.3 Phase model – a multi-level and participatory model

cases continue to occur, even though the companies have stress policies and EAPs. It is also possible that a job satisfaction survey indicates that a problem exists. A need is thus identified that requires initiating activities with a different perspective. Our research shows that the following six conditions are important to recognize as central, if the intervention is to succeed:

1. The interventions are seen as a development project.
2. Changes are given equal status with other daily activities and changes.
3. Time and resources are allocated.
4. People are designated to be responsible for the project and its progress.
5. Clear goals are set, which can be evaluated continuously.
6. Changes and related activities are integrated in existing activities.

At this point, a project group is constituted. It should have four to five members. One member should be a manager, who acts as project manager; one or two persons of importance to the process are appointed; and two coordinators/facilitators are appointed. The latter have the role of the "organization's ears" and help to ensure that everyone is continuously involved and listened to.

The group meets regularly during the project to evaluate the process and the results, allocate resources, make sure that the right activities are initiated to ensure continued progress and that the project runs according to plan. The group typically presents their observations and conclusions at departmental meetings, followed by a collective discussion with the rest of the department.

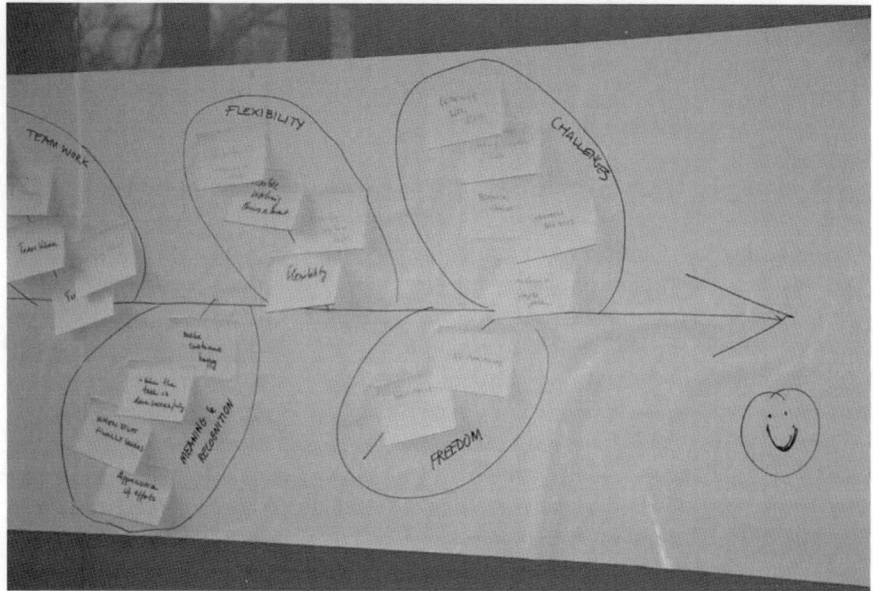

Fig. 8.4 FishBone diagram (Enthusiasm, employees, IT company)

Once the project group is set, it is time to explore what creates enthusiasm and strain at the particular workplace.

Phase 2 – Exploring the Work and Workplace

Two FishBone Workshops

A Fishbone workshop is conducted using Fishbone charts inspired by Ishikawa to map the experiences of the employees in relation to work practices and conditions (Ishikawa 1968). A corresponding workshop is carried out among line and project/ team managers. Here, focus is still on the employees and their working life. The participants at the employee workshop are asked the question: *"What creates enthusiasm in your work?"*

Each person's answers (three) are each written on post-it notes and posted on a Fishbone chart labeled "Enthusiasm", which is hung on the wall. When posting a note, each person is asked to read the note aloud and comment on it, if necessary. Gradually, the first chart is filled out, and when all participants have presented their notes, an image emerges of the factors that create enthusiasm at this particular workplace.

The participants are then asked: *"What creates stress and strain in your work?"* The answers are posted on a new chart labeled "Strain". In cases where there is correlation among the answers, the post-it notes are to be clustered on one "bone" of the Fishbone (Fig. 8.4).

Fig. 8.5 Multi-voting results   •Better project management
– top 5 priorities   •Enough time to do the tasks
                                          •More recognition and feedback
                                          •Our future – more security
                                          •Improved communication with international colleagues.

When the two charts are filled out, the workshop's outcome is a set of working conditions that create enthusiasm or cause stress and strain in the daily work. In this way, everyone has the opportunity to express themselves, and tacit knowledge of problems is made explicit by being visualized and structured. The Fishbone chart thus constitutes a framework for structuring a joint brainstorm.

In the second work shop the managers are asked: *"What do you think creates enthusiasm for your employees?"* and then *"What do you think causes strain and stress for your employees?"*

The collective reflections and visualization of tacit knowledge about the workplace – thus making it explicit – provides the basis for the next step. From the workshops' fishbones, it is evident that each side bone expresses different themes e.g. *"good colleagues"*, *"challenging tasks"*, *"recognition"* or *"unclear goals"*, *"bad project management"*.

Priority Workshop

Immediately following the Fishbone workshops, a participatory Priority workshop is initiated, so the department can assign priorities to the suggested problems and improvements. The aim of the workshop is to build consensus through a collective dialogue about priorities and the number of interventions to be implemented during the following months.

In a Priority workshop, everyone participates, both employees and managers. Jointly, they examine each other's Fishbone charts and discuss where there are similarities and differences. This discussion provides the basis for a better understanding of the employees' experience. Then it is decided which topics should be prioritized, for example by using a "Multi-Voting" process (Gray et al. 2010; Jungk and Müllert 1981).

This provides the basis for a new collective negotiation of the statements from the Fishbone workshop. Each participant, both managers and employees, have three votes. One can vote on all the conditions that create enthusiasm and strain; and all three votes can be cast on a single factor, or they can be distributed. When the votes have been cast and counted, they form the basis for a list of prioritized conditions that have been decided in a participatory and multi-level manner. Figure 8.5 illustrates the result of the multi-voting in a medium-sized IT-company.

Phase 3 – Implementing Organizational-Level Changes

During the following weeks, the project group discusses which of the five themes are to be realized. The aim is to prioritize further to two issues. The two facilitators' task is now to uncover the meaning and understanding of each theme on the list by interviewing their colleagues and managers. The result of the interviews is input to further concretization of the issues that the project group is to work with. The interviews also ensure that everyone continues to be involved.

The two issues are then presented at a department meeting to allow joint discussion. Thereafter, further discussion is carried out among facilitators, daily management and colleagues regarding which specific daily activities can support the realization of the issues.

In the example above (see Fig. 8.5), the meaning and concretization process resulted in two top priorities: *"Better project management"* and *"Feedback and recognition"*. The activities to support these issues were then elaborated in order to make it clear which work processes and activities are to be changed in order to achieve better project management.

In the particular example of *"Better project management"*, the participants agreed that *"weekly project status meetings"*, *"refinement of project checklist"* and *"creation of project plans"* were necessary activities to be initiated or changed in order to ensure better project management.

In the next step, the project group prepares a joint plan, preferably using tools that the group and the workplace are already familiar with. The plan concerns implementing the activities as well as status meetings in the project group, interviews with colleagues, visualization for tracking the process and securing a picture of the current state of the intervention, and finally progress meetings.

The aim of the latter is threefold: to ensure that both managers and employees work with the issues and support activities; to ensure strong focus on the process' progress, for which the manager is responsible; and finally, to revise the activities and initiate adjustments and supporting changes.

Kick-Off Session

It is now time to kick off the implementation. The aim of the Kick-Off session is to highlight the start of the change process regarding the two top priorities and the supporting activities. The Kick-Off session can be conducted in many different ways, depending on how new initiatives are usually celebrated and launched in the department or company. The session should also make clear what resources are available and who is primarily responsible for the process. It is our experience that the Kick-Off session can naturally be associated with a department meeting, thus making it clear that the initiative's purpose is to improve daily work processes.

Implementing and Evaluating Organizational-Level Changes

The changes are implemented during the next 6–9 months. The department accomplishes this by systematically investigating, initiating and implementing the chosen changes. It is of key importance in order to secure primary preventive changes that all members participate in the intervention and that the changes are integrated into existing activities at the workplace. This integration can occur in connection with department meetings, project start-ups and task planning, to name a few examples.

At this point, it is the responsibility of the project group and facilitators to initiate activities that can ensure momentum and secure focus and adjustment, with the overall aim to ensure that the intervention succeeds.

It is during this part of the intervention that continuous evaluation plays a central role. Are the changes working as expected? If not, why? Can adjustments be made that can make the changes work and become an integrated part of the work? By frequently posing these questions to the participants, it is possible to secure commitment and create a foundation for concrete, sustainable and usable preventive solutions.

The Facilitators – The Ears of the Organization

As the cornerstone of the intervention, the job of the facilitators is to make sure that the issues and related activities for which they are responsible are uncovered systematically. By continuously interviewing colleagues and managers during the implementation, views and opinions related to the interventions are made clear and visible to them. For this to function, they need to be trusted. During the process, they must be loyal to all the contributions and anonymize the information, views and opinions that emerge throughout the process.

Visualization – Progress and Current State

The results of the facilitators' interviews are presented regularly at department meetings, i.e. as themes and best practices. Each issue and its supporting activities are discussed and adjustments of the supporting activities are made in a collective process among all participants. In addition, participants highlight how they experience progress and the current state of the changes as shown by the common visualization object. The idea is that both managers and employees continuously communicate how they experience the progress of each particular intervention (see Fig. 8.6).

There are many ways to visualize progress and the current state of the intervention, and each individual company or department can choose the most suitable and informative format. This can be done, for example, in conjunction with department meetings or at other times in accordance with the existing work pattern.

Benefits of the Model

Using the process tool allows both managers and employees to reflect on the existing work and management practice and act upon it, initiating primary interventions based on a participatory, collective, salutogenic and structured process. The outcome of the intervention is thus an individual and organizational process-related capacity

Fig. 8.6 Visualization of
"Better project management"

to reflect on, learn about and act upon local knowledge regarding work-related problems and issues in a participatory and multi-level way, and apply this outcome in future initiatives.

We conclude the presentation of the model with two statements from two people participating in the project:

> We now have a method that we can use again, which makes it easier for us to start up a new change process and which has a starting point in what we experience in our daily work – enthusiasm and strains. The model has also led to an increased awareness of us as a work place. (Director of an IT-company)

> We note that absenteeism is reduced during the interventions, and we can see a reduction in employee turnover. Based on a questionnaire survey before and after the implementation of the project, we can see significant improvements in the areas dealing with leadership and well-being (HR-Partner in an engineering consultancy) (Cited and translated from Ipsen and Andersen 2011, p. 88)

The Research Approach to Interventions in Organizations

In the two projects, researching interventions was about examining managers' and employees' options for preventing work-related problems based on a participatory, multi-level, salutogenic approach, and uncovering which conditions are necessary during the intervention in order to make it work. The point of departure was thus hermeneutic (Alvesson and Sköldberg 2000). The aim was to analyze, explore and thus gain insight into the characteristics of interventions in knowledge work and pragmatics (Peirce 1992). The newest project is still ongoing and will finish September 2012.

The projects have been conducted by researchers representing various fields in collaboration with 10 knowledge-intensive companies (Table 8.1).

The companies were selected on the basis of their interest in issues related to work-related stress. In the selected work places, both tangible and intangible knowledge production (Alvesson 2004) was carried out by self-managed, highly skilled knowledge workers. The selected departments within the companies and work places were typical for the industry.

Data Collection and Continuous Evaluation of What Makes the Intervention Work

In the initial phase, the researchers explored the workplace contexts, and the principles for participation were outlined in terms of multi-level participation, budget and planning in order to adapt expectations and secure the effectiveness of the interventions. In addition, the project plan and activities were presented to the members of the participating departments. During the companies' change process, the researchers acted as organizers and sparring partners at workshops and meetings but did not participate in the day-to-day implementation of the selected interventions.

The effect of the interventions was assessed on the basis of a mixed-methods approach, using quantitative and qualitative methods (Johnson and Onwuegbuzie 2004; Johnson et al. 2007).

In the first project pre- and post-measurements were conducted based on the COPSOQ questionnaire on mental health (Kristensen et al. 2005). The pre-measurement (baseline) consisted of a questionnaire survey of the participating

Table 8.1 Overview of the 10 KICs participating in the projects

Small and medium sized KICs	Larger KICs
IT-Companies (2)	Manufacturing (1)
Manufacturing (2)	Engineering consultancies (2)
	Knowledge-producing institutions (2)
	Social service administration (1)

department just before the first dialogue workshop. This questionnaire measures the psychological aspects of work, including employees' self-perceived stress. To avoid that the results of the survey should influence the intervention, the results were reported after the conclusion of the intervention. Post-measurement was a repetition of the initial questionnaire.

In the second project the companies were asked to formulate a number of goals and effects which they wanted to achieve based on the interventions. To avoid that the goals should influence the research group, the goals are only to be made known to us after the conclusion of the interventions. The listed goals will provide information about the companies' motivation for participating and whether the interventions have had the desired effect from a company point of view.

During the interventions four online surveys are conducted in the participating company or department just after the Fishbone and Priority workshop, the Kick-Off session, halfway through the project and at the end. The questionnaires measure the level of participation, commitment and perceived effects of the interventions and support the identification of implementation failures.

In order to understand the conditions supporting the process, the research team studied and evaluated the process and its results systematically to identify and understand what supported progress and what caused barriers. Semi-structured qualitative interviews were conducted with managers and employees in the departments with the aim of uncovering their understanding and appraisal of the developed Program Theory, the process, measures and potential hidden agendas. The results of the qualitative research activities were also used to inform the quantitative analysis and explain the results. Observations and reflections were documented in a log.

All in all, the process evaluation was based on continuous observation, informant interviews, the participants' Program Theory, and the companies' self-selected measures.

Data Analysis

The purpose of the data analysis in both projects was twofold: first, to identify and outline the work-related experiences of knowledge work by searching for patterns of relationships between personal work experiences and the characteristics of knowledge work through a cross-case analysis.

The second purpose was to identify the factors influencing primary interventions through the externalization of the participants' Program Theory. Together, the results provide answers regarding the overall objective of the study.

Data were analyzed in NVIVO using a template analysis approach (Crabtree and Miller 1999), and were structured according to a list of categories. The outcome of the analysis was verified via a first-order communicative validity process in which several relevant, experienced actors within the field of practice were presented with the results and asked to comment on them. This research activity was carried out in order to clarify the credibility and authenticity of the observations and conclusions

(Dahler-Larsen 2001). The results were presented in different academic forums with the aim to test the validity of the analysis in relation to the theoretical and methodological scope of the study.

The sum of data and results provided input to the development of a multi-level and participatory model for interventions in knowledge-intensive companies, developed in the first project and tested and refined in the second. The principles and components of the model are outlined in the previous sections.

Conclusion

Work-related stress is an increasing problem for knowledge workers, despite employee control and influence. Using a mixed-method approach, two consecutive research and development projects have been conducted in 10 knowledge-intensive companies where organizational level interventions have been implemented with the aim to re-design daily work practices using a multi-level, participatory, salutogenic approach. This chapter presents the principles, the intervention and the evaluation approaches of the development project, which provides new knowledge about how organizational-level preventive changes can be developed and implemented to benefit knowledge work and workers, and what it requires to make the intervention work.

Acknowledgement We would like to offer our special thanks to Senior Researcher Ole Henning Sørensen, University of Aalborg, Denmark, Senior Researcher Anders Buch, University of Aalborg, Denmark, and post.doc Liv Gish, Technical University of Denmark, for their valuable and constructive work during the planning, development and implementation of this research work. This project could not have succeeded without such a joint effort, which is very much appreciated.

References

Alvesson, M. (2004). *Knowledge work and knowledge-intensive firms*. New York: Oxford University Press.

Alvesson, M., & Sköldberg, K. (2000). *Reflexive methodology. New vistas for qualitative research*. SAGE Publications Ltd., London, UK.

Antonovsky, A. (1996). The salutogenic model as a theory to guide health promotion. *Health Promotion International, 11*(1).

Argyris, C., & Schön, D. (1996). *Organizational learning II. Theory, method and practice*. Addison-Wesley Publishing Company.

Brown, T. (2008, June). Design thinking. *Harvard Business Review*, 1–10.

Buch, A., & Andersen, V. (2008). *Knowledge work and stress – Beyond the job-strain model*. In Conference proceeding from ODAM IX, International symposium on human factors in organizational design and management. Sao Paolo, Brazil.

Buch, A., Andersen, V., & Sørensen, O. H. (2009). Videnarbejde og stress – mellem begejstring og belastning. Jurist- og Økonomforbundets Forlag.

Crabtree, B., & Miller, W. (1999). *Doing qualitative research* (2nd ed.). London: Sage.

Dahler-Larsen, P. (2001). From programme theory to constructivism. *Evaluation, 7*(3), 331.

Dettinger, K. M., & Smith, M. J. (2006). Human factors in organizational design and management. In G. Salvendy (Ed.), *Handbook of human factors and ergonomics* (3rd ed.). John Wiley & Sons, Inc. Hoboken: New Jersey. p. 513.

Elkin, A. J., & Rosch, P. J. (1990). Promoting mental health at the workplace: The prevention side of stress management. *Occupational Medicine: State of the Art Review, 5*, 739–754.

Fredericksons, B. (1998). What good are positive emotions? *Review of General Psychology, 2*(3), 300–319.

Galbraith, J. R. (2002). *Designing organizations. An executive guide to strategy, structure and process.* San Francisco: Jossey-Bass.

Gray, D., Brown, S., & Macanufo, J. (2010). *Gamestorming: A playbook for innovators, rulebreaker, and changemakers* (1st ed.). Gray & Brown: O'Reilly Media, Inc. Sebastopol, CA, USA.

Greene, J. C. (1997). Participatory evaluation. In R. E. Stake & L. Mabry (Eds.), *Advances in program evaluation* (pp. 171–189). Greenwich: JAI Press Inc.

Griffiths, A. (1999). Organizational interventions. Facing the limits of the natural science paradigm. *Scandinavian Journal of Work, Environment & Health, 25*(6), 589–596.

Hurrell, J. J., & Murphy, L. R. (1996). Occupational stress intervention. *American Journal of Industrial Medicine, 29*(4), 338–341.

Ipsen, C. (2011). *A participatory stress intervention process – The core of a self-help tool to successful preventive changes.* Work and Well-being in an Economic Context, Orlando, USA.

Ipsen, C., & Andersen, V. (2011). *Forebyg stress – i en fælles proces.* København: DJØF's forlag.

Ipsen, C., & Jensen, P. L. (2012). Organizational options for preventing work-related stress in knowledge work. *International Journal of Industrial Ergonomics, 42*(1), 325–334.

Ipsen, C., Jensen, P. L., & Andersen, V. (2010). Prevention of work-related stress – A participatory approach. In P. Vink & J. Kantola (Eds.), *Advances in occupational, social and organizational ergonomics* (pp. 305–314). Boca Raton, FL, USA: CRC Press.

Ishikawa, K. (1968). *Guide to quality control.* Tokyo: JUSE Press, Ltd.

Ivancevich, J. M., Matteson, M. T., Freedman, S., & Phillips, J. S. (1990). Worksite stress management interventions. *The American Psychologist, 45*(2), 252.

Johnson, R. B., & Onwuegbuzie, A. J. (2004). Mixed methods research: A research paradigm whose time has come. *Educational Researcher, 33*(7), 14–26. 3700093.

Johnson, R. B., Onwuegbuzie, A. J., & Turner, L. A. (2007). Toward a definition of mixed methods research. *Journal of Mixed Methods Research, 1*(2), 112–133.

Jungk, R., & Müllert, N. R. (1981). *Zukunftswerkstätten.* Hamburg: Hoffmann und Campe.

Karasek, R. (1979). Job demands, job decision latitude, and mental strain: Implications for job redesign. *Administrative Science Quarterly, 24*, 285–308.

Karasek, R. (1990). Lower health risk with increase job control among white collar workers. *Journal of Organizational Behaviour, 11*, 171–185.

Kates, A., & Galbraith, J. R. (2007). *Designing your organization: Using the star model to solve 5 critical design challenges.* San Francisco: Jossey-Bass. A Wiley Imprint.

Kompier, M., & Cooper, C. (Eds.). (1999). *Preventing stress, improving productivity. European case studies in the workplace.* London: Routledge.

Kompier, M., Geurts, S. A. E., Gründemann, R. W. M., Vink, P., & Smulders, P. G. W. (1998). Cases in stress prevention: The success of a participative and stepwise approach. *Stress Medicine, 14*, 155–168.

Kompier, M., Cooper, C., & Geurts, S. A. E. (2000). A multiple case study approach to work stress prevention in Europe. *European Journal of Work and Organizational Psychology, 9*(3), 371.

Kristensen, T. S., Hannerz, H., Høegh, A., & Borg, V. (2005). The Copenhagen psychosocial questionnaire – A tool for assessment and improvement of the psychosocial work environment. *Scandinavian Journal of Work, Environment & Health, 31*, 438–449.

McClenahan, C. A., Giles, M. L., & Mallet, J. (2007). The importance of context specificity in work stress research: A test of the demand-control-support model in academics. *Work and Stress, 21*(1), 85–95.

Mogensen, M., Andersen, V., & Ipsen, C. (2008). Ambiguity, identity construction and stress amongst knowledge workers: Developing collective coping strategies through negotiations of meaning. International conference on Organizational Learning, Knowledge and Capabilities, Copenhagen, Denmark.

Murphy, L. R. (1988). Workplace interventions for stress reduction and prevention. In C. Cooper & R. Payne (Eds.), *Causes, coping & consequences of stress at work* (pp. 301–339). Chichester/ New York: John Wiley & Sons Ltd.

Murphy, L. R., & Sauter, S. L. (2003). The USA perspective: Current issues and trends in the management of work stress. *Australian Psychologist, 38*(2), 151–157.

Nonaka, I., Toyama, R., & Konno, N. (2002). SECI, ba, and leadership. In I. Nonaka & D. Teece (Eds.), *Managing industrial knowledge – Creation, transfer and utilization* (pp. 13–43). London, UK: SAGE Publications Ltd.

Parker, S. K., & Wall, T. D. (1999). *Job and work design* (1st ed.). London: Sage.

Peirce, C. S. (1992). How to make our ideas clear. In N. Houser & C. Kloesel (Eds.), *The essential Peirce: Vol. 1. Selected philosophical writings, (1867–1893)* (pp. 124–141). Bloomington: Indiana University Press.

Randall, R., Nielsen, K., & Tvedt, S. D. (2009). The development of five scales to measure employees' appraisals of organizational-level stress management interventions. *Work and Stress, 23*(1), 1–23.

Reason, P. (1994). Three approaches to participative inquiry. In N. K. Denzin & Y. S. Lincoln (Eds.), *Handbook of qualitative research* (pp. 324–340). USA: Sage Publications Ltd.

Rosskam, E. (2009). Using participatory action research methodology to improve worker health. In P. L. Schnall, M. Dobson, & E. Rosskam (Eds.), *Unhealthy work: Causes, consequences, cures* (1st ed., pp. 211–228). Amityville: Baywood Publishing Company.

Simon, H. A. (1981). *The sciences of the artificial* (2nd ed.). Cambridge, MA: MIT Press.

Smith, M. J., & Sainfort, P. (1989). A balance theory of job design for stress reduction. *International Journal of Industrial Ergonomics, 4*(1), 67–79.

Sørensen, O. H., & Holman, D. (2010). Job-redesign in knowledge work. In P. Vink & J. Kantola (Eds.), *Advances in occupation, social, and organizational ergonomics* (pp. 111–120). Boca Raton, FL, USA: CRC Press/Taylor & Francis Group.

Stavroula, L., Griffiths, A., & Cox, T. (2003). *Work organisation & stress*. UK: Nottingham.

Weick, K. E. (2001). Organizational redesign as improvisation. In *Making sense of the organization* (1st ed., pp. 57–91). Malden, USA: Blackwell Publishing.

Westgaard, R. H., & Winkel, J. (2011). Occupation musculoskeletal and mental health: Significance of rationalization and opportunities to create sustainable production systems – A systematic review. *Applied Ergonomics, 42*, 261–296.

WHO. (1999). *The burden of occupational illness*. Office of Press and Public Relations. Geneva: WHO.

Womack, J. P., Jones, D. T., & Roos, D. (2007). *The machine that changed the world: The story of lean production, Toyota's secret weapon in the global car wars that is revolutionizing world industry* (New Ed.). London: Simon & Schuster.

Chapter 9
In How Far Is the Health Promoting Hospital a Salutogenic Hospital, and How Can It Be Developed?

Jürgen M. Pelikan, Christina Dietscher, and Hermann Schmied

Abstract Our contribution to this book focuses on applying concepts of "salutogenic" or "health promoting" to a specific type of organization, namely the hospital, by drawing on experiences from the International Network of Health Promoting Hospitals and Health Services (HPH). We differentiate between "healthy", "health promoting" and "salutogenic" perspectives towards organizational health interventions. Against this background we address three questions: First, what is a health promoting or salutogenic organization or hospital? Second, how can hospitals as a specific type of organization be developed in this direction? Third, how can interventions aiming at achieving this kind of change be researched? To answer these questions, we use concepts from three theoretical paradigms: the theory of autopoietic social systems, especially organizations, in the tradition of Niklas Luhmann; organizational quality models; and organizational theories of relevance to understanding hospitals, especially Mintzberg's theory of professional bureaucracies. From our systems theory orientation follows that organizational health interventions and their effects cannot be understood in a simple input-output manner but have to follow a more complex model taking autopoiesis of involved systems into account. Following quality concepts, health promoting or salutogenic organizations can be conceived of as organizations that (have to) meet specific health promoting or salutogenic quality criteria for their structures, processes and outcomes. From the cited organizational theories follows that (local) organizational management, in hospitals, has only limited impact on or control over the performance of core processes by professionals. Therefore, attempts to change professional performance need to go beyond classical change interventions into organizations.

J.M. Pelikan (✉) • C. Dietscher • H. Schmied
WHO-CC for Health Promotion in Hospitals and Health Care, Ludwig Boltzmann Institut
Health Promotion Research, Untere Donaustraße 47, 1020, Vienna, Austria
e-mail: juergen.pelikan@lbihpr.lbg.ac.at; christina.dietscher@lbihpr.lbg.ac.at;
hermann.schmied@lbihpr.lbg.ac.at

G.F. Bauer and G.J. Jenny (eds.), *Salutogenic Organizations and Change:*
The Concepts Behind Organizational Health Intervention Research,
DOI 10.1007/978-94-007-6470-5_9, © Springer Science+Business Media Dordrecht 2013

Keywords Health promotion • Organizational change • Hospitals • Systems theory • Professional bureaucracies • Quality models

Introduction

Our contribution to this book will focus on applying concepts of "salutogenic" or "health promoting" or "healthy" to a specific type of organization, namely the hospital, by drawing on experiences from the International Network of Health Promoting Hospitals and Health Services (HPH). First, we will clarify how we understand the concepts healthy, health promoting or salutogenic and by what kind of theoretical concepts we conceive of organizations in general and of hospitals specifically. Then we will outline how hospitals pose specific challenges in relation to developing a health promoting or salutogenic organization and how these challenges can be met by change-oriented organizational health interventions. Finally, we will discuss the consequences for research.

Healthy, Health Promoting and Salutogenic

Of the three concepts, "**healthy**" is the most common or everyday language one. It relates to health ("Health is the level of functional or metabolic efficiency of a living being", Wikipedia) as a quality which can be attributed to or observed in objects (a "healthy body" or "healthy food") or activities ("healthy eating" or "healthy life-style"). Therefore its meaning is multivalent. Applied to a living organism it can denote the *state* or *quality* of the organism's actual fitness and wellness, or functional or metabolic efficiency, and by that also have some prognostic value in relation to the future quantitative or qualitative survival of this organism. But "healthy" can also be used to characterize the health *consequences* (impacts or effects) of an object, system or activity on the health of other objects or systems in its environment. While "health" or "healthy" originally relate to living organisms, both qualities can be metaphorically attributed also to other kinds of systems, such as social systems, like "healthy organizations" or "healthy regions". In either case, a phrase like "healthy organization" can refer to the (direct or indirect) health consequences of "healthy" to the system itself, to other systems or objects in its environment, or to both.

As far as "**health promoting**" is concerned, there is less ambivalence of meaning. This qualifier indirectly also relates to health, but more directly to "health promotion" as a specific *strategy* to intentionally and proactively influence the health of people in a positive way and direction, in contrast to other health related strategies for people, such as "health care" or "disease prevention" or "health protection" (some, including us, would have a broader understanding of health promotion comprising also health protection and disease prevention). Health promotion as a strategy of public health has been promoted by WHO, starting with the Alma

Ata Declaration (1978) and in more detail by its Ottawa Charter (WHO 1986) which defines health promotion as the "process of enabling people to increase control over, and to improve, their health". In the context of health promotion, health is understood as a "state of complete physical, mental and social well-being of an individual", following the WHO definition of "health" from 1948. A "health promoting organization", therefore, can be understood as an organization that enables and empowers the people it affects "to increase control over, and to improve, their health" (relating to its somato-psycho-social dimensions).

And there are specific defined criteria or principles, e.g. "empowering" or "participatory", which health promoting interventions have to fulfill (Rootman 2001). Thus, health promotion basically is a normative *strategy* for improving the health of people and *not* an analytic *model* to better understand health. However, health promotion is based on specific assumptions about health, the most important of which is that health is a comprehensive and positive quality that has to be maintained or reproduced by people themselves in their everyday living. But this process can be supported by societally enabling or empowering health promoting interventions.

While "healthy" and "health promoting" use everyday English language terms, **salutogenic** is related to salutogenesis, an artificial anglicized Latin (*salus*=health) and Greek (*genesis*=origin) hybrid neologism, coined by Aaron Antonovsky (1923–1994) in analogy to and as a counterpart to pathogenesis or "pathogenic". Antonovsky formulated a "salutogenic model", in contrast to the dominant pathogenic orientation of (curative and also preventive) medicine (Antonovsky 1979, 1987). This model basically offers different assumptions on the functioning of the human organism and on the resulting consequences for action. Basically the salutogenic model assumes that "the human system (so as all living systems) is *inherently* flawed, subject to unavoidable entropic processes and unavoidable final death" and not that "the human organism is a splendid system, a marvel of mechanical organization, which is now and then attacked by a pathogen and damaged, acutely or chronically or fatally". Therefore, it does not make sense to use the "dichotomous classification of persons into those who have succumbed, temporarily, permanently or fatally to some disease …. and the residual category …, those who are safely on shore." Rather, "a more powerful and more accurate conception of reality" is "a continuum model, which sees each of us, at a given point in time, somewhere along a 'healthy/dis-ease' continuum" (Antonovsky 1996). More specifically, Antonovsky assumes that adequate coping with ubiquitous stress is fundamental for maintaining health. This brings coping capacities into focus. Antonovsky suggests looking for Generalized and Specific Resistance Resources which are important for the development of a personal orientation or feeling of confidence, which he calls "sense of coherence" (SOC). As the three components of this concept, he describes comprehensibility, manageability and meaningfulness and developed a 29 item SOC "Orientation of Life" scale for measuring the concept. Together, the three components of the SOC determine how much harm existing stress factors will cause in an individual. Thus, salutogenesis depends on experiencing a strong sense of coherence. Following from that, instead of a mere concentration on risk factors, we should also concentrate on "salutary factors" which also could be named "'health-promoting' factors or any other term, as long as the concept is clear: factors which are negentropic, actively promote health, rather than just being low on risk factors." "A salutogenic orientation, then, as the basis for health promotion, directs both research and action efforts to encompass *all* persons, wherever they are on the continuum, and to focus on salutary factors." And from that also follows, instead of focusing "on a particular diagnostic category", as specialized curative medicine is notorious for, health promotion "is pressured to be concerned with the person … or all aspect of the person." Thus Antonovsky firstly offers a more realistic *model* to understand health and disease, and, secondly, uses this model to deduct a normative salutogenic *orientation* to improve health. He also explicitly links salutogenesis and health promotion by offering "The salutogenic model as a theory to guide health promotion" because he is "critical of a field in which exciting and important work has been done but one which is in danger of unfulfilled promise because it lacks a theoretical foundation" (Antonovsky 1996).

The theme of this book now is to apply the term "salutogenic" to social systems, in the sense of "salutogenic organizations", in a descriptive and also a prescriptive manner. As far as we know, a "salutogenic organization" can be understood in the same way as a "health promoting organization", i.e. as an organization that, when trying to maintain or promote people's health, considers the salutogenesis and not just the pathogenesis of the human beings it affects, and which concentrates its health-oriented interventions not only on organization-related risk factors, but also on organizational salutary factors.

Taking this understanding into account, we do not use the multivalent term "healthy organization", but stick to the more technical and clearly defined terms "health promoting organization" or "salutogenic organization", which seem to have a rather similar or overlapping general meaning, even if they come from somewhat differing traditions. While "salutogenic" relies more on an underlying model, "health promoting" rather refers to an underlying strategy. In this sense, the two concepts are rather complementary. "Salutogenic" is based on a mainly psychological model of reproduction of individual human health, while "health promoting" relates to a set of defined social strategies and principles of promoting comprehensive health by social means. In this perspective, "salutogenic" can be understood as a more specific subset of the broader concept of "health promoting". Therefore, a health promoting hospital is likely, but does not have to be, a salutogenic hospital.

Since neither the salutogenesis nor the health promotion traditions offer an explicit model of organizations, we first need a better understanding of the functioning of organizations in general and of hospitals in particular in order to apply these terms to organizations in more detail.

Understanding the Functioning and Changing of Organizations

For understanding the functioning and changing of organizations in general, and of hospitals in particular, we follow a specific kind of general **social systems theory** established by the German sociologist Niklas Luhmann (1927–1998). This theory implies a paradigm shift in systems theory from a "first order systems theory", with an understanding of systems as trivial or mechanistic machines functioning on an input–output basis, to a second-order systems theory (or "second-order cybernetics" or "second order emergence") with an understanding of systems as "nontrivial" or "complex machines" whose input and output are interconnected through feedback loops, and therefore are less predictable and cannot be easily steered (Moeller 2012).

The basic distinction in this theory is the distinction between a **system** and its relevant **environment(s)**. Systems are seen as entities emerging or out-differentiating from an environment. And it is the system that has to manage and maintain the difference of system and environment to (re)produce its identity, i.e. its boundaries, structures and processes within, by use of, and partly in demarcation to its relevant environments. Thus, Luhmann's theory is a "systems-environment theory" or an "ecological systems theory" (Moeller 2012).

To specify the process of reproduction of a complex system, Luhmann borrowed from the theory of **autopoiesis** (self-generation) which the Chilean neuro-scientists Varela and Maturana offered for biological living systems (Varela et al. 1974; Maturana and Varela 1980). This theory states that autopoietic (self-generating) systems have to reproduce the elements they consist of, by the network of elements they consist of, and by that they achieve "operational closure". But living systems are not only operationally closed, but also **structurally coupled** to relevant systems in their environment of which they are existentially dependent. Because of their operational closure, autopoietic or second-order systems "do not change in a 'creationist' way – in which all change is created from without, but in an evolutionary way, where change is created from within" (Moeller 2012, p. 129).

Luhmann took essential assumptions of this theory and applied these to social systems and psychic systems as well, and contrasted three types of autopoietic systems (living, psychic, social) with allopoietic (externally generated) systems, e.g. machines (Luhmann 1984). The **elements** of autopoietic systems are understood as specific **operations** in time, which therefore have to be followed/continued by further operations to keep the system in existence. For the reproduction of social systems in general, Luhmann proposed **communications** as the specific operation of reproduction. This general theory of social systems (Luhmann 1984, 1997) was specified by Luhmann himself (Luhmann 2000) and by others (Bakken and Hernes 2003; Wimmer 2004) also for **organizations** as a specific type of social system, in contrast to interaction systems and society as the comprehensive social system. Accordingly, the specific operation for organizational reproduction is understood as **communication of decisions** (e.g. decisions on the organizational purpose, on values a given organization pursues, or on changes in its infrastructures and resources, or on solving any specific problems). "The autopoiesis of an organization thus becomes an autopoiesis of decisions – one decision generates endless decision-making ...." (Moeller 2006, pp. 31–32). Furthermore, organizations condition their decision-making processes by three kinds of structural **premises**: decision programs (either of the type of conditional programs or goal oriented programs), pathways of communication and regulations for deployment (Seidl and Becker 2006). The consequence of this theory for **controlling** organizations by their management subsystems (or from outside) as well as for **altering** organizations is that changes, in order to be effective and sustainable, have to be enacted by the everyday decisions of the members of the organization itself. Therefore any intervention coming from outside needs to address and to relate to the way an organization takes decisions. To be sustainable, it best has to be represented/integrated in the organization's structural premises.

Last but not least, we are building up on considerations from the fields of **quality philosophy** and management which have in the last decades become very influential for the management of health care organizations, especially hospitals. Quality, in general, can be understood as the sum of characteristics of an object, system or process. Within quality management, it is defined as "conformance to requirements" (Crosby 1979). In the quality model by Donabedian (1966), which was developed in the context of health care, quality can and has to be observed and measured not only on an outcome level, but also on the level of organizational structures and processes. Donabedian assumes that the quality of outcomes is determined by the quality of structures and processes, which, therefore, have to be addressed by interventions. We will argue later that, in our perception, the characteristics "health promoting" and "salutogenic" can best be understood as specific desired qualities of an organization.

This kind of systems and quality-theory based approach to organizations seems especially apt for defining an organization as salutogenic or health promoting and also for understanding (possibilities and limitations for) management and organizational change.

What Can Be Understood by a Health Promoting or Salutogenic Organization or Hospital?

What Can Be Understood by a Health Promoting or Salutogenic Organization?

Following our use of the terms "salutogenic" and "health promoting", salutogenic or health promoting organizations are organizations that take responsibility for supporting people's maintenance or improvement of their health. Therefore, we need a better understanding on how people reproduce their health, for defining these kinds of organizations in more detail. Using autopoietic systems theory combined with the model of salutogenesis and quality philosophy as introduced in the last chapter, we understand the somato-psycho-social **health and wellbeing** of people as an **outcome** of the **autopoietic (re)production** of **living systems** or organisms in interaction with their relevant environments. The specific **outcome** of a certain health status is based both on supportive or salutogenic, as well as risky or pathogenic **structures** and **processes** of the human living system itself (e.g. processes of metabolism), and of the relevant environments that provide conditions or inputs (e.g. specific qualities of nutrition, water, air) the system needs for its healthy reproduction.

Health therefore is conditioned by the combination of (structural and processual) qualities of the living system and its relevant environments. Following the concept of Antonovsky's salutogenesis, humans can, to a certain degree, compensate risky factors in their environments by their salutogenic capacity, i.e. by a favorable sense of coherence or orientation to life. In this perception, the predominance of supportive over risky factors in the living system's environments, and of salutogenesis over pathogenesis within the living system's reproduction, would be indispensable preconditions for its sustained viability and quality of life.

Organizations, as far as they are relevant environments of people in their specific roles, e.g. as health care professionals or patients, therefore can support the maintenance or improvement of people's health by offering material and social conditions that are, as far as possible, free from direct risk or stress factors to people's health, and furthermore provide infrastructures and resources that allow people to better cope with unavoidable risk and stress factors. Following the concept of the autopoietic organization, these organizational conditions have to be reproduced by organizational decisions within the framework of the organizational decision premises.

In this sense, any organization has (unintended) impacts on the health of the individuals it affects. If the organization intends to deliberately strive for salutogenic or health promoting effects, it needs at least to observe the health status of people affected and the salutogenic or health promoting qualities of its structures and processes. But why should an organization invest in this direction? First, there is some evidence that healthy people are better able to fulfill the role expectations with regard to organizational performance (e.g. work performance of workers, academic achievement of students). Second, there is some evidence that organizations can have an impact on the health of their members, and by that also on the performance of these. In this sense, investment in organizational health interventions can be expected to produce valuable return on investment (Riedel et al. 2001; Kramer et al. 2009). Another, more public health oriented reason for organizations to invest in the health of their staff (and clients) is there adherence to concepts of sustainability and corporate social responsibility. This type of investment, too, can have some (indirect) effects on the better survival of the organization, e.g. by increasing its reputation.

For motivations of this kind to become concrete and legitimate, evidence and tools have to be made available and accessible to organizations.

Summing up, a healthy or salutogenic organization can be defined as one that, following the social systems theory concept of autopoiesis, has integrated a consideration of its potential effects on the health of its target groups into its decision programs and actual decision-making so that structures and processes of reproduction and production, as well as its outcomes, can be characterized as health promoting or salutogenic.

What Can Be Understood by a Health Promoting Hospital?

In how far can or has the hospital to be regarded as a specific type of organization? Organizational systems theory sensu Luhmann paid only limited attention to specifying particular types of organizations, including the hospital (an exception is Baecker 2008). But approaches of other organization theorists, who did focus a.o. on hospitals, can be integrated into a systemic understanding of organizations. Using their concepts, hospitals can best be understood as people-changing and partly people-processing and -sustaining organizations (Hasenfeld 1983) or professional bureaucracies (Mintzberg 1979), which means that specific **services**, in contrast to the production of goods, are conducted on people by professionals in a rather bureaucratic context. The performance of these services requires a high level of skills, since the task of health care is complex and science based and stately regulated. Furthermore patients differ with regard to their biological and mental parameters. Therefore, the **quality** of the services hospitals provide can only partly be standardized and regulated by local management, while it highly depends on the (continuous) qualification of healthcare professionals by adequate education and training and peer control. These characteristics pose specific challenges to the management of professional organizations, and to interventions aimed at the deliberate change of professional performance.

The more specific challenge with regard to the hospital's health promoting or salutogenic orientation results from its people-changing purpose and the healthcare-related tasks of the hospital's core business. The purpose is to manage illness – i.e. to eliminate or at least mitigate (severe episodes of) – disease. Thus, in hospitals, at least for patients and clients, **health effects** are not only a side effect, so as in production facilities whose staff may never even see the purchasers whose health may be affected by their products, **but a result of the core business**. Therefore, while health promotion or salutogenesis as an organizational concept is, in production companies, usually mostly associated with occupational health, client health too needs to be considered in people-processing organizations like hospitals. And, with regard to the latter, the disease-oriented approach of the hospital needs to be broadened towards a comprehensive and positive concept of health which challenges the traditional professional identity of healthcare staff.

Again following the concept of autopoiesis with regard to people's health, hospital staff cannot directly produce health in their clients but need to work with them, which puts focus on the quality concept of co-production. In hospitals, it is not only necessary that staff with different professional backgrounds, belonging to different departments and levels of hierarchy work together, but they also need to involve their clients since they need to support healthcare e.g. by providing information about their condition, or by complying to prescribed treatment regimes. There is a wealth of studies demonstrating that the active involvement of patients as co-producers in this sense increases chances for better health outcomes (Scheibler and Pfaff 2003; Groene and Garcia-Barbero 2005).

Furthermore, since healthcare can be quite risky for **patients** (e.g. medical errors, nosocomial infections, stress, hospitalism), hospital-based health promotion or salutogenic orientation should in any case also aim at reducing these risks e.g. by hygiene and risk management.

Last but not least, since health as a product is usually not "ready" when the patient leaves the hospital but is further (co-)produced by the patient after discharge partly in collaboration with other health and social services or providers of care (including the patients' family), hospitals, in order to sustain their health outcome, need to have professional discharge management and interface management with healthcare organizations throughout the healthcare chain.

For **staff,** hospitals are one of the most risky work environments as they accumulate a multitude of potential physical and mental strains as well as exposures to nuclear, biological and chemical substances (Parent-Thirion et al. 2007; Pelikan et al. 2010). Therefore, they represent an important setting for workplace health promotion especially in times where human resources for healthcare institutions become scarce.

Furthermore, hospitals can have considerable negative health effects on their wider **environments** (including also vegetal and faunal systems), as they produce problematic waste, emissions and wastewater, and a lot of traffic (patient transports, visitors, staff). A focus on these wider effects in the sense of corporate social responsibility is only slowly gaining momentum, as e.g. supported by NGOs like the Global Green and Healthy Hospitals network or by Healthcare without Harm (Weisz et al. 2011).

In light of these different potential effects or impacts of hospitals on the health and disease of their clients, staff and bystanders, the HPH concept (Pelikan et al. 2005) summarizes 18 core strategies to improve the health effects of the hospital. These comprise nine strategies that can be incorporated into the routine quality of hospitals, and nine strategies that describe additional health promotion interventions that can either be performed by hospitals themselves or by other organizations they cooperate with (Table 9.1).

Summing up, a health promoting hospital is actively attempting to integrate health promotion criteria into its decision premises and processes, and, consequently, taking comprehensive and continuous action to promote the health of its patients, staff, and the population in the community it is located in (Pelikan et al. 2001).

How Can Hospitals (Still) Be Developed Towards Health Promoting or Salutogenic Organizations?

Organizations and even hospitals are usually not oriented towards health promotion or salutogenesis. These concepts have been developed and propagated by health policy and health sciences who want organizations to take them up and to invest in

Table 9.1 Eighteen HPH core strategies (Pelikan et al. 2005)

	Target group		
Strategy	Patients	Staff	Community
Empowerment of stakeholders for health promoting self reproduction/ self management	Developing health promoting living conditions for patients in the hospital	Developing health promoting work life for staff	Developing health promoting access to the hospital for citizens
	PAT-1	**STA-1**	**COM-1**
Empowerment of stakeholders for health promoting coproduction	Encouraging patients' participation, cooperation and co-production in treatment and care	Encouraging health promoting work processes	Developing health promoting cooperation with services in the region
	PAT-2	**STA-2**	**COM-2**
Health promoting & empowering hospital setting for stakeholders	Developing a health promoting hospital setting for patients	Developing a health promoting workplace setting for staff	Developing the hospital as a health promoting environment for the community
	PAT-3	**STA-3**	**COM-3**
Empowering illness management (patient education) for stakeholders	Encouraging patients' health promoting self-management of specific diseases	Encouraging staff's health promoting illness management	Participate in alliances to encourage citizens for a health promoting self-management of specific diseases
	PAT-4	**STA-4**	**COM-4**
Empowering lifestyle development (health education) for stakeholders	Encouraging patients to lead a health promoting lifestyle	Encouraging staff to lead a health promoting lifestyle	Participate in alliances to encourage citizens to lead a health promoting lifestyle
	PAT-5	**STA-5**	**COM-5**
Participation in health promoting & empowering community development for stakeholders	Developing health promoting living conditions for patients after leaving the hospital	Developing a health promoting community setting for staff	Participate in alliances to develop health promoting community settings
	PAT-6	**STA-6**	**COM-6**

organizational change interventions. Following our theoretical perspective on organizational autopoiesis, quality and people-changing professional bureaucracies, this is not an easy and trivial task.

From the **concept of autopoietic organizations** follows that every change has to be intended and enacted by the organization itself. Accordingly, systematic, comprehensive and sustainable change needs to be based on changes of the organization's decision premises and decision-making processes. As already outlined above, the organizational system needs some reason for changing its decision premises and decision-making. This can either be an understanding of health promotion or salutogenesis as a solution to organizational problems in the sense of conditional programs (for example, they may perceive occupational health promotion as a means to reduce staff turnover; or they may perceive health promotion for a specific group of patients as a means to increase medical outcomes and to increase customer satisfaction). Or organizations see a need to adapt to observed changes in their relevant environments, such as legal requirements, funding mechanisms or public expectations, in the sense of goal orientation programs. Both types of programs have to be oriented at the seven health promotion criteria by Rootman (2001): empowering, participatory, holistic, intersectoral, equitable, sustainable, and multistrategy.

Thus, from the perspective of (external) advocates of a salutogenic or health promoting orientation, both good arguments and evidence for effective and efficient problem solution by these concepts, and supportive external environments, are needed.

Since especially the pursuit of goal oriented programs needs to be based on a continuous process (e.g. oriented at the Deming cycle), deliberate, comprehensive and sustainable change needs specific supportive capacities (infra structures and resources) within the organization. These can either be integrated into already existing capacities like **quality management structures** which today exist in most hospitals, or take the form of a specific organizational support system for health promotion or salutogenesis.

But change in core processes of **professional bureaucracies** (Mintzberg 1979) cannot be solely brought about by local quality management, since professional decisions in the daily routines of hospitals depend to a large degree on the professional qualification and the standards of professional peers which can only to a small degree be developed or changed locally. One example within healthcare are standards and guidelines based on evidence-based medicine and nursing which are developed by professional associations and societies (such as the Cochrane Collaboration). Thus, changes have to go on within and outside organizations. Specifically for professional bureaucracies, it makes sense to motivate professional societies to develop specific recommendations also with regard to health promotion and salutogenesis.

In which way were these approaches towards organizational change pursued in the international network of Health Promoting Hospitals (HPH)? Despite the skepticism towards deliberate change that results from the concepts introduced so far, we have been supporting initiatives to develop hospitals towards health promotion or salutogenesis since 1988 when first attempts to develop HPH concepts were started. Already the first model project "Health and hospital" in the hospital Rudolfstiftung in Vienna, Austria (1989–1997), demonstrated that change can, if not be brought about from the outside, be initiated and supported by external actors under certain conditions. In the Rudolfstiftung, organizational autopoiesis was considered by introducing health promotion as an organizational learning process, structured by health promotion projects to solve specific organizational problems (in the sense of conditional programs) and supported by organizational consultation. The project was continuously externally evaluated to assure and develop the quality of the project. A similar approach was taken in the European Pilot Hospital Project (1993–1997) that involved 20 hospitals from 11 European countries in a soft benchmarking process that marked a next step in taking up quality concepts in HPH (Pelikan et al. 1998).

In order to enable growth and continuity of HPH after the pilot hospital projects, national and regional HPH networks were established as specific capacity structures to support hospitals in taking up and implementing the concept (Dietscher 2012). Another tool for capacity-building in HPH are annual conferences (since 1993), specific media (a newsletter, a scientific journal, websites) and specific training offers.

In a reaction to the rising importance of quality management within hospitals, explicit quality management instruments, i.e. the 18 HPH core strategies, seven implementation strategies (Pelikan et al. 2005; Pelikan 2007), and the five standards (Groene 2006) were developed later on. These tools cannot only be integrated into the local quality management structures of individual hospitals, but are also used by HPH task forces to adapt them for specific types of healthcare organizations (e.g. psychiatric health services), to address specific target groups (e.g. migrants and cultural minorities) and health topics (e.g. tobacco-free hospitals). Furthermore, they can also support the cooperation with relevant external environments of hospitals such as national quality agencies and professional associations who can use them for integration into their standards and guidelines.

How Can Interventions to Achieve HPH Be Researched?

In relation to the routine functioning of hospitals, change attempts to implement health promotion (or any other type of reform) in these organizations can be considered as a meta-activity, and the research of these attempts, consequently, is a meta-meta activity. As such, research has to follow the logic of the meta-activity change (intervention) which in turn has to follow, or adapt to, the logic of the functioning activities of the reproduction and production of the intervened (organizational) system.

Independently of these considerations, two types of research need to be distinguished from each other, i.e. basic research, which aims at identifying the principle mechanisms of organizational change (intervention research), and evaluation research to observe the feasibility and effects of a given specific (and already tested) intervention within a specific (organizational) environment with regard to specific defined criteria. In health promotion, especially in relation to the settings approach, these two research perspectives are often intertwined, since it is hardly possible to do laboratory research, or randomized controlled trials, on organizational interventions because of the high complexity of these. Furthermore, change interventions that are subject to research are often not tested but applied in practice for the first time, based on merely theoretical or pragmatic considerations.

Thus, organizational research in health promotion sees itself confronted with the (contradicting) expectations to identify effective change mechanisms in organizations, to test the principle effectiveness of new interventions in real life, and to evaluate the specific feasibility and effectiveness of interventions in concrete organizational contexts. Suggestions on how best to juggle these conflicting demands have filled many textbooks (including Pawson and Tilly 1997; Rootman 2001; McQueen and Jones 2007) and pose specific challenges to researchers – the first of which is to be very explicit about the purpose of research, and on how this research purpose translates into research design and methodology.

Taking a health promotion, quality and systems theory perspective on change interventions brings about additional considerations for research.

From our **health promotion perspective** follows that research as a meta-intervention, too, needs to follow basic principles of health promotion. Thus, in order to be health promoting, research needs to be participative and empowering, oriented at a holistic concept of health, equitable (both by involving different stakeholder perspectives in the research, and by focusing on the involvement of, and intervention outcomes for, different target groups), multi strategy (triangulating research methods), intersectoral and sustainable in so far as applicable (compare Rootman 2001).

From the **quality perspective** follows that research needs to define criteria and use indicators for measurement not only with regard to desired outcomes of interventions (Nutbeam 1998), but also for the structures and processes that are expected to bring about these outcomes (compare Pelikan 2007).

From a **systems theory perspective** follows that research (which is usually conducted in form of projects and thus takes the form of a temporary organization), too, can be considered as a social system that reproduces itself on the basis of specific decision premises. Thus, it is important to consider whose perspectives are represented in these decision premises, and what perspectives on the researched subject (in light of theories applied, research traditions followed, and stakeholders involved) they are likely to produce. And, by studying interventions from a systems theory perspective, research needs to focus on how interventions irritate the routine functioning of organizations and thus raise the likelihood of sustainable change in decision premises and decision-taking in organizations. In this perspective, research also needs to focus on relevant environments of intervened organizations, following the system-environment distinction. Especially for **professional bureaucracies**, training institutions and professional associations are relevant environments that should be considered.

We will try to illustrate how these considerations can be combined in a concrete research project, using the example of the "Project on a Retrospective Internationally Comparative Evaluation Study on HPH – PRICES-HPH" (Pelikan et al. 2011, 2012; Dietscher 2012).

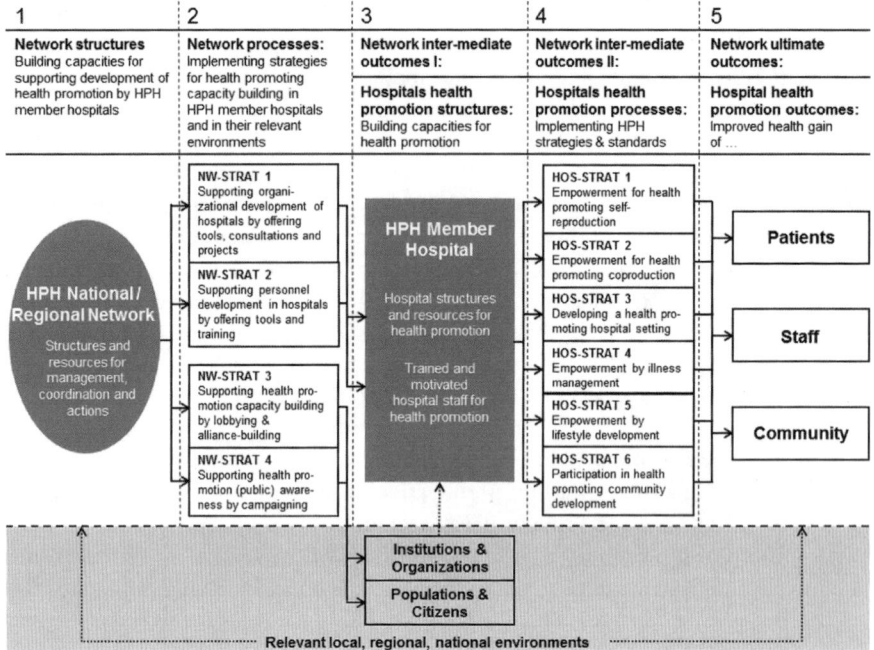

Fig. 9.1 The PRICES-HPH evaluation framework (Pelikan et al. 2011)

PRICES-HPH was conducted from 2008 to 2012, coordinated by the WHO Collaborating Centre for Health Promotion in Hospitals and Healthcare, Vienna. In light of criticism towards HPH for being under-researched, the project aimed at collecting and analyzing data on 2 levels: (1) Structures developed and strategies applied by HPH networks as specific capacities to support the implementation of health promotion in hospital organizations (N=28), which resembles a return rate of 80 %, and (2) Health promotion structures and interventions implemented in member hospitals of these networks (N=180, which resembles a return rate of 34 %).

The study followed a **quality approach**, defining network structures and processes as relevant contexts for the implementation of health promotion structures in hospital organizations (which were defined as a first type of intermediate network outcome). These structures, then, were understood as a relevant context of hospital health promotion processes, as the second type of intermediate network outcome (compare Fig. 9.1 above). In this perspective, individual health – as the ultimate outcome– was understood as resulting from a complex chain.

Health promotion principles were met in several ways in PRICES-HPH. For example, a holistic perspective on health was represented in the definition of criteria and indicators. Participation was a key principle in tool development: there were sounding boards on hospital and network level supporting the development of research questions, and providing feedback on draft versions of the survey tools. Empowerment of networks and member hospitals was pursued via workshops and discussions on findings at international conferences, as well as via publication strategies.

A **systems theory perspective**, finally, was taken by understanding HPH networks and HPH member hospitals as autopoietic systems that need to reproduce themselves following the concept of autopoiesis. In addition, networks were understood as relevant environments of their member hospital organizations that try to irritate, i.e. intervene into, the reproduction of these hospitals by a number of strategies. These include attempting to raise the general relevance of health promotion (a.o. through advocacy, alliance-building and lobbying activities), as well as supporting organizational and personnel development towards health promotion (Pelikan et al. 2011; Dietscher 2012). Furthermore, following the concept of supportive environments, the existence of legal regulations and funding mechanisms for health promotion was also researched, so as cooperation with professional associations, following the perspective or **professional bureaucracies**.

Conclusions

From our considerations follows that it is unlikely and there is no guarantee that even well-planned deliberate organizational health interventions will directly result in the desired effects. An orientation at the autopoiesis of systems rather leads to more modest expectations towards the effects of interventions by a more realistic understanding of the intervened systems and of the intervention as an autopoietic system itself. Both can be understood as structurally coupled systems which are relevant environments for each other that develop and adapt in a co-evolutionary way. Thus, change takes the form of a reflexive process based on continuous observation, feedback and learning.

References

Antonovsky, A. (1979). *Health, stress, and coping: New perspectives on mental and physical well-being*. San Francisco: Jossey-Bass.

Antonovsky, A. (1987). *Unraveling the mystery of health. How people manage stress and stay well*. San Francisco: Jossey-Bass.

Antonovsky, A. (1996). The salutogenic model as a theory to guide health promotion. *Health Promotion International, 11*(1), 11–18.

Baecker, D. (2008). Zur Krankenbehandlung ins Krankenhaus. In I. Saake & W. Vogd (Eds.), *Moderne Mythen der Medizin. Studien zur organisierten Krankenbehandlung*. Wiesbaden: VS Verlag für Sozialwissenschaften.

Bakken, T., & Hernes, T. (Eds.). (2003). *Autopoietic organization theory: Drawing on Niklas Luhmann's social systems perspective*. Frederiksberg: Copenhagen Business School Press.

Crosby, P. B. (1979). *Quality is free: The art of making quality certain*. New York: McGraw-Hill.

Dietscher, C. (2012). *Interorganziational networks in the setting approach of health promotion – The case of the international network of health promoting hospitals and health services (HPH)*. Dissertation, Universität Wien, Wien.

Donabedian, A. (1966). Evaluating the quality of medical care. *The Milbank Memorial Fund Quarterly, 44*, 166–206.

Groene, O. (Ed.). (2006). *Implementing health promotion in hospitals: Manual and self-assessment forms.* Copenhagen: World Health Organization.

Groene, O., & Garcia-Barbero, M. (Eds.). (2005). *Health promotion in hospitals: Evidence and quality management.* Copenhagen: World Health Organization Regional Office for Europa.

Hasenfeld, Y. (1983). *Human service organizations.* Englewood Cliffs: Prentice-Hall.

Kramer, I., Sockoll, I., & Bödeker, W. (2009). Die Evidenzbasis für betriebliche Gesundheitsförderung und Prävention – Eine Synopse des wissenschaftlichen Kenntnisstandes. In *Fehlzeiten-Report 2008* (pp. 65–76). Berlin/Heidelberg: Springer.

Luhmann, N. (1984). *Soziale Systeme. Grundriß einer allgemeinen Theorie.* Frankfurt am Main: Suhrkamp. (English translation available: Social Systems. Stanford: Stanford University Press, 1996)

Luhmann, N. (1997). *Die Gesellschaft der Gesellschaft* (6th ed.). Frankfurt am Main: Suhrkamp.

Luhmann, N. (2000). *Organisation und Entscheidung.* Opladen: Westdeutscher Verlag.

Maturana, H. R., & Varela, F. J. (1980). *Autopoiesis and cognition: The realization of the living.* Dordrecht: Reidel.

McQueen, D., & Jones, C. (Eds.). (2007). *Global perspectives on health promotion effectiveness.* New York: Springer.

Mintzberg, H. (1979). *The structuring of organizations: A synthesis of the research.* Englewood Cliffs: Prentice-Hall.

Moeller, H.-G. (2006). *Luhmann explained: From souls to systems.* Chicago/La Salle: Open Court Pub Co.

Moeller, H.-G. (2012). *The radical Luhmann.* New York: Columbia University Press.

Nutbeam, D. (1998). Evaluating health promotion: Progress, problems and solutions. *Health Promotion International, 13*, 27–44.

Parent-Thirion, A., Macías, E. F., Hurley, J., & Vermeylen, G. (2007). *Fourth European working conditions survey.* Luxembourg: European Foundation for the Improvement of Living and Working Conditions.

Pawson, R., & Tilly, N. (1997). *Realistic evaluation.* London: Sage.

Pelikan, J. M. (2007). Health promoting hospitals- assessing developments in the network. *Italian Journal of Public Health, 4*(4), 261–270.

Pelikan, J. M., Garcia-Barbero, M., Lobnig, H., & Krajic, K. (1998). *Pathways to a health promoting hospital: Experiences from the European pilot hospital project 1993–1997.* Gamburg: Health Promotion Publications.

Pelikan, J. M., Krajic, K., & Dietscher, C. (2001). The health promoting hospital (HPH): Concept and development. *Patient Education and Counseling, 45*(4), 239–243.

Pelikan, J. M., Dietscher, C., Krajic, K., & Nowak, P. (2005). Eighteen core strategies for health promoting hospitals. In O. Groene & M. Garcia-Barbero (Eds.), *Health promotion in hospitals: Evidence and quality management* (pp. 48–67). Copenhagen: World Health Organization.

Pelikan, J. M., Schmied, H., & Dietscher, C. (2010). Prävention und Gesundheitsförderung im Krankenhaus. In K. Hurrelmann, T. Klotz, & J. Haisch (Eds.), *Lehrbuch Prävention und Gesundheitsförderung* (3., vollst. überarb. u. erw. Aufl. 2010 ed., pp. 290–301). Bern: Hans Huber.

Pelikan, J. M., Dietscher, C., Schmied, H., & Röthlin, F. (2011). A model and selected results from an evaluation study on the International HPH Network (PRICES-HPH). *Clinical Health Promotion, 1*, 9–15.

Pelikan, J. M., Schmied, H., & Dietscher, C. (2012). Improving organizational health: The case of health promoting hospitals. In G. F. Bauer & O. Hämmig (Eds.), *Bridging occupational, organizational and public health.* New York: Springer.

Riedel, J. E., Lynch, W., Baase, C., Hymel, P., & Peterson, K. W. (2001, January/February). The effect of disease prevention and health promotion on workplace productivity: A literature review. *American Journal of Health Promotion, 15*(3), 167–190.

Rootman, I. (2001). Introduction. In I. Rootman, M. Goodstadt, B. Hyndman, D. McQueen, L. Potvin, J. Springett, & E. Ziglio (Eds.), *Evaluation in health promotion: Principles and perspectives* (pp. 3–6). Copenhagen: World Health Organization.

Scheibler, F., & Pfaff, H. (Eds.). (2003). *Shared decision-making: Der Patient als Partner im menschlichen Entscheidungsprozess*. Weinheim: Juventa.

Seidl, D., & Becker, K. H. (2006). Organizations as distinction generating and processing systems: Niklas Luhmann's contribution to organization studies. *Organization: The Critical Journal on Organization, Theory and Society, 13*(1), 9–35.

Varela, F., Maturana, H., & Uribe, G. (1974). Autopoiesis: The organization of living systems, its characterization and a model. *Biosystems, 5*, 187–196.

Weisz, U., Haas, W., Pelikan, J. M., & Schmied, H. (2011). Sustainable hospitals: A socio-ecological approach. *Gaia, 20*, 191–198.

Wimmer, R. (2004). *Organisation und Beratung. Systemtheoretische Perspektiven für die Praxis*. Heidelberg: Carl Auer.

World Health Organization. (1948). *Constitution of the World Health Organization* (Basic documents, 45th ed., Supplement, October 2006). Geneva: World Health Organization. Retrieved from http://www.who.int/governance/eb/who_constitution_en.pdf

World Health Organization. (1986). *Ottawa Charter for Health Promotion* (WHO/HPR/HEP/95.1). Geneva: World Health Organization. Retrieved from http://www.who.int/hpr/NPH/docs/ottawa_charter_hp.pdf

Chapter 10
The Limits of Control: A Systemic, Model-Based Approach to Changing Organisations Towards Better Health

Gregor J. Jenny and Georg F. Bauer

Abstract In this chapter, we combine a generic health development model, developed by researchers, with a management model, developed for company leaders, blending the logics of research and practice. The emerging Organisational Health Development (OHD) model is devised as a frame of reference for organisations, consultants and intervention researchers collaborating on targeted health-optimisation projects. This model serves as a common mindmap used to generate visibility of health development, enable all stakeholders to speak the same language, develop compatible perspectives and facilitate mutual action and the cross-linking and monitoring of targeted measures. It is also thought to support systemic thinking, i.e. enable the system's members to see their blind spots, formulate hypotheses on work and health and raise awareness for the circularity of and the interactions between processes, organisations and employees. In applying this model, our intention is to also facilitate the generation of acceptable evidence for the research community. So far, our experience has shown that companies are interested in using mindmaps to facilitate discourse and action on health optimisation. Our approach is especially attractive to larger companies that already implement many optimisation measures, but that want to ameliorate their corresponding strategic efforts, i.e. companies that want to reduce complexity, enhance strategic visibility and necessity and optimise operative planning and spending on the multiple optimisation processes they use to target health and performance.

Keywords Organisational health development • Systems theory • Capacity building

G.J. Jenny (✉) • G.F. Bauer
Division of Public and Organizational Health, Institute of Social and Preventive Medicine,
University of Zurich, Hirschengraben 84, 8001 Zurich, Switzerland
e-mail: gjenny@ifspm.uzh.ch; gfbauer@ifspm.uzh.ch

G.F. Bauer and G.J. Jenny (eds.), *Salutogenic Organizations and Change:*
The Concepts Behind Organizational Health Intervention Research,
DOI 10.1007/978-94-007-6470-5_10, © Springer Science+Business Media Dordrecht 2013

Conceptual Background of Health Development in Organisations

Work and Health in the Context of Organisations

For more than a decade, occupational health psychologists have urged for the design, creation and maintenance of healthy work environments (Adkins 1999; Quick 1999). Most of the research in this field has studied how individual health is created and maintained within the working environment from both a detrimental perspective (stressors and strain) and a progressively positive perspective (resources and well-being). Antecedents of individual health at individual and organisational levels have been discussed, such as *personal resources* (coping skills, self-efficacy), *job demands and resources* (time pressure, overload, support, appreciation) or *organisational factors* (team climate, physical environment) (e.g. Zapf and Semmer 2004). Further, the interaction between these levels has been elaborated, for example moderating effects of personal resources on the job demands–strain relationship, and reciprocal mechanisms have been identified, such as gain and loss spirals regarding (un)healthy individuals and their resources (e.g. Hakanen et al. 2008).

Individual health has been similarly established as broad concept with physical, mental and social facets, assessed positively and negatively, and from an emotional and functional perspective (Hofmann and Tetrick 2003; Tetrick 2002; Seligman 2008; Keyes 2007; Hart and Cooper 2001; Pelikan 2009; Bauer et al. 2006; Quick et al. 2009). In addition, there is an on-going debate on the "health" of the organisation itself, conceptualised as vitality, viability, adaptivity, sustainability, productivity, etc., and how these factors relate to individual health and to individual and organisational facets (Bennett et al. 2002; MacIntosh et al. 2007; Shoaf et al. 2004). Labels and models have evolved to grasp this interdependent, multi-valued and multi-dimensional issue of work and health, stressing both positive and organisational dimensions of health (DeJoy and Wilson 2003; Quick et al. 2007; Cotton and Hart 2003; Hart and Cooper 2001; NHS Institute for Innovation and Improvement 2009; Peiro and Rodriguez 2008; Bauer and Jenny 2012; Corbett 2004; Danna and Griffin 1999; Dür et al. 2010).

Targeted Improvement of Health in Organisations

Based on these bodies of theory and evidence, a range of approaches and practices have emerged that target the work environment and aim at altering it towards more 'healthiness'. In German-speaking countries, the prevailing approach is called 'corporate health management', emphasising the role of management in developing health promoting organisational settings and replacing traditional, individual-oriented approaches of workplace health promotion and expert-oriented occupational health approaches (e.g. Badura 2001; see also DeJoy and

Wilson 2003). For reasons that will become clear in this chapter (see also Bauer and Jenny 2012), we expanded this approach to 'Organisational Health Development' (OHD), defined as follows:

> Organisational Health Development is both the *on-going* reproduction and the *targeted* improvement of health in organisations as social systems, based on the interaction (process dimensions) of individual and organisational capacities (structural dimensions) (Bauer and Jenny 2012, p. 135).

This approach comprehends health development as an on-going interaction between people and social systems, where latter play a key role as actors in the targeted improvement of health. It is grounded in a systemic viewpoint; in recent years a number of (occupational) health researchers have pondered connecting the settings approach, health development and health promotion to the overarching concept of systems theory (Bennett et al. 2002; Best et al. 2003; Paton et al. 2005; Pelikan 2007; MacIntosh et al. 2007; Shoaf et al. 2004; Ureda and Yates 2005; Bauer and Jenny 2012; Dür et al. 2010; NHS Institute for Innovation and Improvement 2009). Here, organisations are seen as complex social systems, over which intervening agents have limited control.

Taking a Systemic Viewpoint on Organisational Change

In complex social systems, system elements interact non-linearly and non-trivially: Intervening will change (pre-)conditions of the system, causing similar but subsequent interventions to produce dissimilar effects (Rüegg-Stürm 2003b). This complexity not only complicates the prediction of an intervention's outcome but also leads to unexpected side effects and the emergence of new elements that are unforeseeable based on the characteristics of present elements. Yet, complex social systems develop order through repetition and routine. According to the concept of constructivism, social systems monitor themselves and their environment, reducing the range of possibilities and potential outcomes, transforming ambiguous information to a degree of unambiguousness allowing secure functioning (Weick 1995).

Systems' Self-Referential Logic

Essentially, organisations can be understood as self-monitoring systems of routinised processes that reproduce themselves over time, where the system becomes the producer and product of itself (Luhmann 1984, 2006; Rüegg-Stürm 2003b). This kind of genesis creates self-referentiality, where processes attach to processes within the system's own logic and self-created order. A circular relationship between processes and structure is underlined, where structures channel processes and are simultaneously shaped by these processes – like a river and its riverbed (Giddens 1984; Haken and Schiepek 2006; Rüegg-Stürm 2003b). Lastly, social systems develop within an environment, construct borders through distinction and mark the "inside" from the "outside" (Spencer Brown 1969), focussing on aspects that are relevant for the system's self-preservation and reproduction.

Altering the System

Change agents who see organisations as self-referential systems usually consider alternative ways to destabilise ('unfreezing') the system and achieve change ("moving" in the terminology of Lewin's stage model of organisational change; for fundamental discussions see e.g. Armenakis and Harris 2009; Pettigrew et al. 2001; Van de Ven and Poole 1995; Weick and Quinn 1999). Systemic approaches to change and development acknowledge the self-referential logic and the limitations in controlling social systems. They reject a delusional sense of feasibility with regard to steering social systems and the notion that consultants are great architects (MacIntosh et al. 2007). Social systems theory stresses the notion of "irritating systems". Intervening agents develop hypotheses on how their irritation will uncover blind spots, affect routines, what side effects may occur, and how self-organisation and self-monitoring will be enhanced. Systemic interventions are thus neither intrusions aimed at linear change of outcomes nor are they pure hits by chance: Rather, they aim to connect to the system's logic and develop system-adequate hypotheses of change (Königswieser 2006).

Developing new processes or modifying existing ones demands information on the organisational order that channels these processes. Change begins with the change of order, as processes 'happen' or 'flow' and cannot be changed directly (Rüegg-Stürm 2003b). Organisational order is constituted by the structure, strategy and culture of an organisation (Rüegg-Stürm 2003a), and it is argued that change in organisational structure and strategy is easier to achieve than change in an organisation's culture (Pelikan 2007).

Connecting to the System's Logic

Building on this viewpoint, we claim that researchers and intervention experts need to connect to the self-referential logic of the system targeted, i.e. to the existing structures, strategies, culture(s) and processes (Bauer and Jenny 2007, 2012). Connecting to the logic of the system, first and above all, should enhance the chance to *win* companies for a targeted OHD process. Second, once the companies recognise the external expert as relevant for its reproduction and formalize this relationship, the approach enhances the chance that the intervention will develop the right form of 'fit' needed to alter ('irritate') the system, which will trigger self-reflection and change.

As intervention researchers in the fields of occupational health psychology, health promotion and public health, we follow our own self-referential logic: We reproduce ourselves through generating and publishing knowledge on (successful) health-oriented change in organisations. For this, we stick to intervention research protocols, which – to some extent – misfit the logics of our study object. To overcome this misfit, we chose to combine a generic health development model (European Community Health Promotion Indicator Development Model, 'EUHPID Model') developed by researchers with a management model (New Management Model of St. Gallen) developed for company leaders. These models both reflect our systemic view on social systems and health development within these systems, as outlined and defined above. The emerging OHD model serves as a frame of reference for organisations, consultants and intervention researchers collaborating in OHD projects. It serves as common mindmap to produce *visibility* of health and OHD, enable all stakeholders to speak the same *language*, develop compatible *perspectives* on OHD, and facilitate *mutual action* and the *cross-linking* and *monitoring* of measures. This, so our intention, will also facilitate generating evidence for the research community.

Merging the Logics of Health Development and Management: The OHD Model

Underlying Health and Management Models

Combining Luhmann (1984, 1997) and Donabedian (1966), Pelikan (2007, 2009) stated that health is an outcome of both individual constitution and a history of interaction with relevant environments, i.e. other systems' structures and processes (see also Udris 2006). This conception is the basis of the generic '**Health Development Model**' developed for the EUHPID project and shows how the health of individuals is reproduced in interaction with their socio-ecological environment (Bauer et al. 2006). In this process of health reproduction, ideally, individuals are health literate and motivated, while the system enables and encourages them, providing health development opportunities. A second important aspect is the analysis of this dynamic health development process not only from a pathogenic perspective but also from a salutogenic point of view as a mirror perspective, asking the question: What keeps people healthy, despite all the detrimental physical, mental and social risk factors? (Antonovsky 1979; Bauer et al. 2006). This perspective reinforces the notion of positive health as distinct from ill or negative health (Bauer and Jenny 2012; see below, 'Key foci of OHD'; Brauchli et al. 2012). The **New Management Model of St. Gallen** (Rüegg-Stürm 2003a), is committed to systems theory and proposes dimensions for designing, guiding and developing – i.e. 'managing' (Ulrich 1984) – purpose-built socio-technical organisations. The New Management Model of St. Gallen also integrates organisational ethics, depicting organisations as (inter)acting in an environment with selected relevant stakeholders (including the members of the organisations). In this history of interaction, the organisation has developed order (structure, strategy, culture), which channels

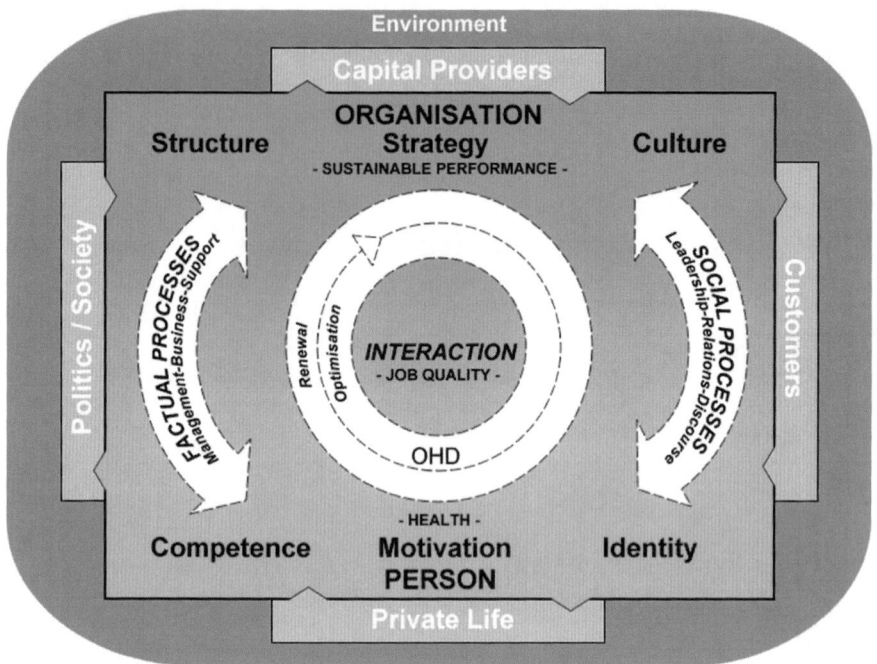

Fig. 10.1 Organisational Health Development (OHD) model

processes and simultaneously is shaped by them (Giddens 1984). Processes comprise management, business and supporting processes, as well as optimisation and profound renewal processes. From these two models, the OHD model emerged.

Organisational Health Development (OHD) Model

The OHD model depicts the organisational system as organisational structure, strategy and culture in interaction with its members' individual competence, motivation and identity, contributing to individual health, job quality and sustainable organisational performance as key foci of OHD (Fig. 10.1). Customers, capital providers, society/politics and private life are depicted as relevant environmental stakeholders of the organisation.

Central to the model is the interaction between individuals as members of the organisation and the organisation itself. This interaction 'comes to life' and is experienced in factual *(job related)* and social *(people related)* processes. As defined above, this reflects the process-based view of organisations and **OHD as on-going reproduction of health**: Through processes health is created and maintained; referring to Weick's (1995) notion of organis-*ing,* these processes are 'an inter-act-*ing*'.

Assuming circular causality, processes are channelled by and simultaneously form the organisation and individuals: This is reflected in the depicted model by dashed lines around the process arrows.

On the other hand, **OHD as targeted improvement of health** is conducted by the organisation itself as part of its general optimisation and renewal processes but focussed on improving health-relevant and especially salutogenic interactions between individuals and the organisation (i.e. the on-going health reproduction within the system).

Finally, the thick black line around the organisational system symbolises the system's self-referentiality, i.e. its self-defined boundaries and own logic generated through its genesis and selective, self-preserving focus on relevant stakeholders in the environment.

Following the aim of merging perspectives of management and health development, the following sections describe the model's dimensions from both perspectives and points to implications for OHD as on-going reproduction *(on-going OHD)* and targeted improvement of health *(targeted OHD)*. The model shows that OHD needs to build on personal, organisational and environmental dimensions ('order' resp. capacities, see below) to trigger change in the organisation's processes, and such – in the long run – alter the key foci of OHD, i.e. individual health and sustainable organisational performance.

Organisational Structure, Strategy and Culture

The OHD model distinguishes three dimensions of organisational order: structure, strategy and culture. The organisation's order – together with individuals' constitution – is the riverbed in which daily labour flows. Organisational order constitutes the strategic division and sequencing of labour leading to a product or service that has guaranteed business success resp. reproduction up to the present.

Organisational Structure

Organisational structure is differentiated into frames and chains (Rüegg-Stürm 2003a). *Frames* are organisational units such as departments, divisions and teams, i.e. subsystems within the system. *Chains* are defined as formalized process sequences, i.e. 'who does what with whom when and where'. Of relevance for both on-going and targeted OHD are the formalized latitude of roles in these frames and chains, the working schedules and contracts (e.g. shift-work, short-time contracts, etc.) or structural opportunities for social exchange, teamwork and problem-solving (Bond et al. 2006; Zapf and Semmer 2004). Further, the number and heterogeneity of units should be considered, as this indicates how targeted OHD can be disseminated and structured within the organisation. Equally, for long-term integration of targeted OHD and initial adaptation to the system, present facilities for OHD interventions are of importance.

Organisational Strategy

Strategy can be defined as a balanced consideration of capacities, range of products and the needs of stakeholders such as customers or members of the organisation. It combines market-based with resource-based views as well as normative-ethical and strategic perspectives (Rüegg-Stürm 2003a). Regarding both on-going and targeted OHD, the degree to which the organisations' goals are transparent to the employees, and how compatible they are to employees' own goals, is relevant. Further, we need to know if the organisation is conscious of its health impact and if it has explicitly integrated health development into its strategy for both ethical and strategic reasons (Bauer and Jenny 2010).

Organisational Culture

From a systemic-constructivist perspective, meaning and relevance are produced in an on-going, discursive and self-monitoring manner: 'Local theories' are created as cultures of stringent collective cognitions (values, norms, attitudes, expectancies), which are reflected in manifest socio-cultural artefacts (e.g. symbols, logos, architecture) (Rüegg-Stürm 2003a; Baumgartner 2006). Regarding both on-going and targeted OHD, a culture of 'employee orientation' is of relevance, represented through perceived trust, fairness or justice (Badura et al. 2008). Further, organisational consciousness of individual health as well as cultures of communication, participation and change need to be taken into account.

Personal Competence, Motivation and Identity

On the individual level, the OHD model distinguishes personal competence, motivation and identity, in reference to Faltermaier's integrative model of salutogenesis (Faltermaier 2005; Antonovsky 1979). These individual dimensions heuristically mirror the three organisational dimensions of the OHD model: *Competence* mirrors *structure*, *motivation* mirrors *strategy*, and *identity* mirrors *culture* (see also the next section below). This connects loosely to person-environment-fit theories, where abilities and needs, and demands and supplies should fit on different levels and dimensions (Edwards and Shipp 2007).

From a general health perspective, health related *competencies* are understood as personal resources that support successful health development and enhance positive health (Faltermaier 2005; Antonovsky 1979); they include personal-mental, social-interpersonal, physical-constitutional and socio-cultural capacities of the individual, including specific health knowledge. *Identity* covers health awareness and health beliefs (Faltermaier 2005). *Motivation* refers to the vast body of models and research on health behaviour and behaviour change (Faltermaier 2005; Glanz 2008) – here, we concentrate on the motivational aspect of readiness to change (Weiner 2009; Weiner et al. 2009).

Regarding on-going OHD, competencies and skills such as work-related self-efficacy (Rigotti et al. 2008), job crafting (Tims and Bakker 2010), coping skills (Carver 1997), psychological capital (Luthans et al. 2008) or leadership qualities (Dellve et al. 2007) are of relevance: These are individual capacities that inhibit the emergence of job demands, enable coping with demands, facilitate recovery from demands, and such diminish negative health effects. Further, these capacities trigger the emergence of job resources, boost their motivational potential, and such increase positive health effects. Further, competence and motivation to engage in organisational change processes and individual behaviour change, and essentially to engage in targeted OHD activities seems particularly important (Weiner 2009). In regard to identity, values and attitudes towards health and health development at work, leadership style or team orientation could be of relevance (see below too).

Processes as Interaction Between Person and Organisation

Fundamental to our understanding of organisations is that impact is generated and experienced in *processes*. Here, the system's (inter-)action patterns become visible: Analysing processes produces information on how the order of the organisation and the constitution of its members emerge into interaction (Rüegg-Stürm 2007). We distinguish factual *(job related)* and social *(people related)* processes. In reference to the New Management Model of St. Gallen (Rüegg-Stürm 2003a), factual processes are grouped into management processes, business processes and supporting processes. Social processes refer to social interactions of members of the organisation, which are grouped into leadership processes, relationship processes and discursive processes.

At this stage, we do not hypothesize how, for example, organisational culture (such as employee orientation or trust) interacts with individual identity (values and attitudes such as leadership style or team orientation), or how individual motivation (such as readiness for change) interacts with organisational strategy (such as health, safety and environment strategies). For an overview on transactional, person-environment and process-oriented views on occupational stress we refer among others to Hart and Cooper (2001), Cotton and Hart (2003), and Edwards and Shipp (2007).

Factual Processes

Management processes are differentiated into normative, strategic and operative management processes. *Normative management processes* deal with the legitimisation of the business model in relation to the organisation's environment. Regarding both on-going and targeted OHD, ethical and responsible acting towards fair working conditions, health and respecting human rights and integrity are relevant issues. *Strategic management processes* deal with building competitive advantages, i.e. producing superior benefit for customers and being more cost-effective than rival organisations. Possible issues relevant for on-going OHD are building good customer relationships through enhancing employee satisfaction or reducing sick leave and fluctuation through strategic employee support. *Operative management processes* deal with guiding and monitoring of daily business processes, financial controlling, quality management, and leadership processes. Leadership processes are particularly health relevant (see below).

Business processes are 'where things happen', where the organisation performs its core activities and what most employees experience and describe as daily labour: dealing with customers and their needs, producing goods and services, manufacturing, supplying and all processes of innovation and research (Rüegg-Stürm 2003a). As business processes are perceived as key element of working conditions, they are one of the prime research issues in work and organisational psychology; studies assess working conditions from the individual's perspective, who experiences control over his job, high work load, time pressure, clear roles, etc. (Zapf and Semmer 2004).

Supporting processes deal with human resource development and qualification, supplying and maintenance of infrastructure, processing of business data, evaluation of risks, legal compliance and communication building (Rüegg-Stürm 2003a). Relevant for on-going OHD are processes of rewarding and qualifying the organisation's members; failure to do so often results (e.g.) in perceived effort-reward imbalance (Siegrist et al. 2004). Generally speaking, supporting processes deal with the flow of resources, which are not only supportive for daily business processes and health development but also for sustained innovation development (Hazy 2008).

Social Processes

Leadership processes are the daily guidance of employees by superiors (Rüegg-Stürm 2003a), which also gives us insight on how problems are handled and solutions created. Leadership processes are central to research in occupational health psychology: A multitude of studies have shown how leadership behaviour, appreciation, trust, participation, information, change involvement and support by superiors influence employee motivation, well-being and health (e.g. Dellve et al. 2007). Leadership processes also include the active process of transforming multiple, contradictive perspectives into a coherent worldview (Kofman 2006) and thus reducing ambiguousness (Weick 1995).

Relationship processes are the daily contacts among the organisation's members and their mutual support. Overall, social support and fairness among colleagues are important issues in health research and relevant for on-going OHD as well as for jointly developing a trusting organisational culture (Badura et al. 2008). Simultaneously, borders are (re-)constructed between subsystems of the organisation just as well as interfaces are routinised. Finally, the quality of relationship processes is another aspect proposed to enhance the development of innovation in an organisation (Hazy 2008).

Discursive processes are the daily monitoring and interpretation of organisational (inter-)action within the system. People focus and select events from the on-going stream of action in their organisation, building individual identity (Keupp 2006), discursively constructing a common and coherent worldview (Rüegg-Stürm 2003a) and validating them consensually (Weick 1995). Planned or unplanned, targeted OHD will introduce and establish a new focus of attention on personal and organisational health issues, influencing this permanent discursive process.

Relevant Environment

Business organisations are purpose-built and competition-driven (Rüegg-Stürm 2003a). They focus on aspects of their environment that are relevant for reproduction, and they monitor and react to development trends. Considering both on-going and targeted OHD, we name four stakeholders in the environment that we regard to be relevant. For this, we refer to the logic of the Balanced Scorecard, which addresses four perspectives that a successful business company needs to consider within its strategic management (Kaplan and Norton 1996): (human) resources, customers, processes and finances (see also Hart and Cooper 2001).

Capital providers are relevant to guarantee a solid financial base for optimisation processes, including targeted OHD. *Customers* are the main target of business organisations, and good customer relations enhance profits and employee satisfaction. *Private life*, i.e. family and friends, is relevant as a resource for the members of the organisation with regard to a meaningful life, job performance and health: Work-life balance as one aspect of interaction between organisation members and their private life has been shown to be an important determinant of health (Jones et al. 2006). *Politics and society* define and enforce rules and regulations affecting business processes as well as workers' safety and health and human rights.

Key Foci of OHD

The model focuses on three key foci of both on-going and targeted OHD: individual health, job quality and sustainable organisational performance. As described above, *individual health* is (re-)produced in permanent interaction between persons and organisation, and within the persons themselves. We refer to Faltermaier's (2005) 3×3-matrix of health, where physical, mental and social facets of health are cross-tabulated with the dimensions of well-being, functionality and disorders. Many combinations are possible: A person might be mentally well and socially fully functioning in spite of physical disorders. We also refer to Keyes' (2007) distinction of emotional and functional dimensions of (mental) health, and stress the notion of positive and negative health (Hofmann and Tetrick 2003; Tetrick 2002; Seligman 2008; Hart and Cooper 2001; Pelikan 2009; Bauer et al. 2006; Quick et al. 2009). As such, we conceptualize health having a positive and negative axis, both of which are distinguished into an emotional and functional dimension (e.g. joy vs. anxiety, fitness vs. handicap), which can further be analysed in regard to physical, mental and social facets (e.g. being able to fulfil social roles and feeling embedded in harmonious social relationships) (Bauer and Jenny 2012; Brauchli et al. 2012).

Job quality is a work-related outcome of the quality of interaction between organisation and person. All members of the organisation permanently (re-)negotiate and adapt their terms of interaction, according to their identity, motivation and competence. Successful negotiation of interaction terms will enhance the chance that the interaction is perceived positively as 'job quality'. Job quality can be operationalised as work-related sense of coherence, or 'Work-SoC' (Bauer and Jenny 2007; in reference to Antonovsky 1979): Members will experience meaning in their daily work, and it will be manageable and comprehensible. This also relates to what is considered a contemporary, individualised search for meaning, where traditional meta-narrations are replaced by individual and daily identity formation (Keupp 2006). As a focus of a system's self-monitoring, Work-SoC could figure as landmark for an active process of creation and negotiation of meaning between organisations and individuals (Vogt et al. 2012).

On the organisational level, as stated above, many concepts are offered as indicators of a 'healthy organisation' (Bennett et al. 2002; MacIntosh et al. 2007; Shoaf et al. 2004). We favour *sustainable performance*, as an expression of an organisation fulfilling economic, ecological and social goals. Regarding on-going OHD, healthy employees and salutogenic working processes are the most relevant social performance goals, contributing to society's well-being and ultimately to the environment in which the organisation "lives". Additionally, OHD could enhance aspects that lead to the emergence of innovation, as noted above. Innovation is considered to be a vital element of organisational self-preservation and reproduction (Hazy 2008). It is also supposed that openness to monitoring processes and active handling of generated, critical information will support the organisation's learning abilities (Baitsch 2008) and thus its innovativeness. Finally, studies have shown that employee health and productivity are related (Grawitch et al. 2006), which points to the role that OHD plays in reaching economic performance goals.

Targeted OHD as an Organisation-Driven Optimisation/Renewal Process

OHD is integral to the organisational system and is depicted as a targeted process of (self-)optimisation or renewal, i.e. as a process of incremental or radical change. In most cases, targeted OHD can be considered more evolutionary than revolutionary, i.e. a continuous optimisation of routinised processes that is part of the general optimisation and renewal processes. If an organisation does not yet have a focus on health and OHD or, on the other hand, if it is already in a phase of routine, external expertise will be less desired or needed. Usually, OHD experts are contracted by organisations that have already developed (for whatever reasons) at least a minimum level of health awareness and health strategy and these organisations view the consultant as a relevant environmental stakeholder. Thus, according to the key role that the organisation assigns itself in our model, this encourages the notion that external consultants support targeted OHD by the organisation, but they cannot 'do' OHD for the organisation.

Applying the OHD Model for Theory-Driven Interventions

Capacity Building for Targeted OHD: A Configurational Intervention Approach

At the beginning of this chapter, we defined OHD as both the *on-going reproduction* and the *targeted improvement* of health in organisations as social systems [...] (Bauer and Jenny 2012, p. 135). Based on the information that was presented above, we summarise the following key points:

- **On-going OHD** relates to factual and social processes within the organisation that have a salutogenic or pathogenic impact on individual health and sustainable performance.
- **Targeted OHD** relates to (self-)optimisation processes within the organisation that are aimed at improving the on-going reproduction of individual health and sustainable performance.

As argued, targeted OHD is often supported by external consultants or, in our case, by intervention researchers. The spectrum of support ranges from single optimisation actions (such as offering a course on relaxation skills to the organisation's members) and systematic 'one-cycle' projects (such as offering a participatory problem-solving-cycle, most commonly in a pilot unit), to systemic approaches, where the consultant offers the system a capacity-building project and tools for self-optimisation.

Most declarations on (workplace) health promotion and health development push for such systemic, empowering and sustainable approaches (European Network for Workplace Health Promotion 1997; World Health Organization 1986). We refer to 'capacity building' as a configurational approach used to enhance a system's health-oriented self-optimisation, i.e. its targeted OHD (Hoffmann et al. 2013; Bauer and Jenny in this volume).

Implementation of Capacity Building

We refer to Bauer et al. (2013) for details on both the conceptualisation and realisation of the capacity-building approach. In brief, based on the system's present configuration (organisational structure, strategy, culture and individual competence, motivation, identity), consultants devise and propose an *intervention architecture* (see Fig. 10.2) to implement the capacity-building approach. The intervention architecture consists of three *intervention phases* (initiation, optimisation and integration)

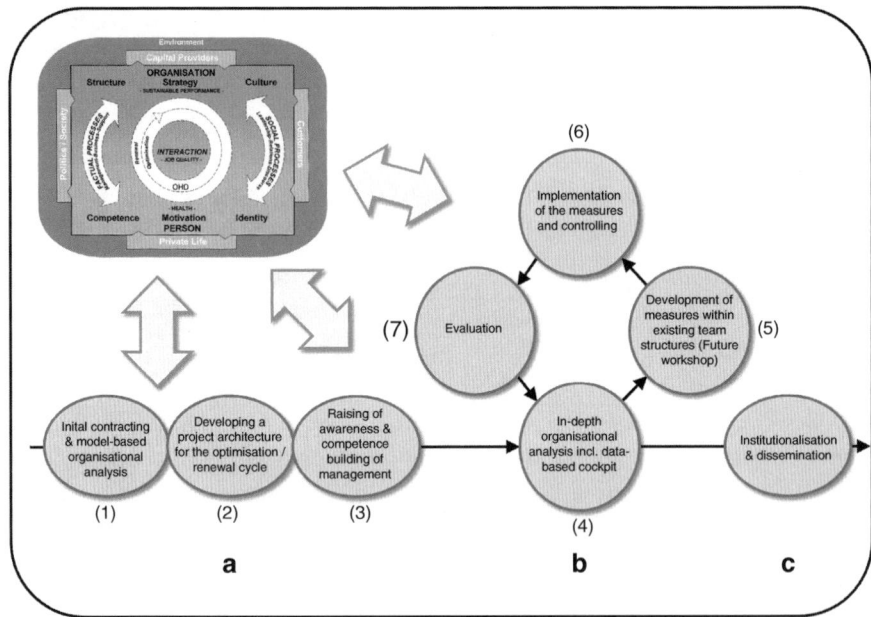

Fig. 10.2 Building capacities for health-oriented self-optimisation, informed and guided by the logic of the OHD model. (**a**) Initiation phase. (**b**) Optimisation/renewal cycle. (**c**) Integration (see Bauer et al. 2013)

and eight *intervention elements* (e.g. the competence building of management, participatory development of measures, etc.).

The consultants offer a workshop to line managers who learn to see and talk about OHD from their perspective and within the logic of the current system. As such, they learn to recognise the salutogenic and pathogenic qualities of factual and social processes and they are empowered to work with their team on OHD. In the team workshops (labelled 'future workshop'), team leaders and employees engage in a discussion – guided by the OHD model – about both the organisation's demands and resources and about how to reduce first and strengthen latter. As is common with such participatory project elements, participants in these workshops create lists of measures that are targeted at the individual, leader, team or organisational levels. In refresher sessions, the implementation progress is controlled and the participants reflect upon their experiences.

Key Role of the OHD Model

A schematic version of the OHD model (see Fig. 10.3) is integral to this process. It serves as both a frame of reference and a mental model. As previously stated, it serves as common mindmap to generate visibility of health development, enabling the stakeholders to speak the same language, develop compatible perspectives and facilitate

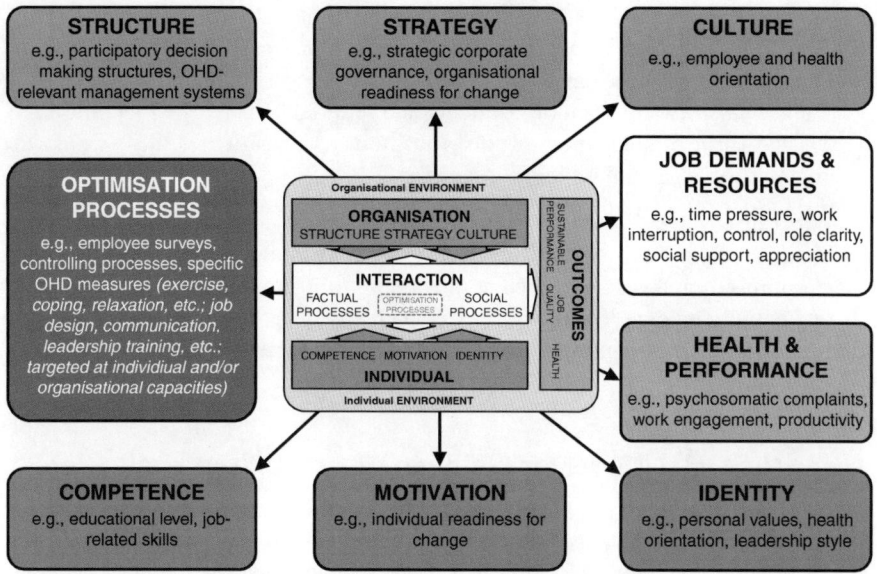

Fig. 10.3 Schematic version of the OHD model with examples for each box relevant to OHD (see Bauer et al. 2013)

mutual action and the cross-linking and monitoring of measures. It is also thought to support systemic thinking, i.e. enable the system's members to see their blind spots, formulate hypotheses on work and health and raise awareness about the circularity of and the interactions between the processes, the organisation and employees. For example, during the initiation phase, the model is used to sensitise management to the dynamics and multiple levels of organisational health development and the implications for targeted OHD interventions. Later, during the optimisation phase, the model is used, for example, to map the targets of the developed measures, i.e. in regard to the organisation or individual, and in regard to work or social processes. In the schematic version of the OHD model, each box can be filled with indicators from qualitative and quantitative sources gathered at any step and time, with respect to the project cycle.

Intermediary Outcome: Capacities for Targeted OHD

One *intermediary outcome* of such a model-based OHD cycle is the organisation's and the individuals' *capacities for targeted OHD*; for example:

- The *individual team members'* verbal and mental competence and their motivation to engage actively in the problem-solving processes related to working processes and health.
- The *team leaders'* competence to actively guide workshops on participatory, health-oriented optimisational issues in a transparent and fair way.

- The *team's* structural, strategic and cultural capacities for optimisation, e.g. clearly defined roles in regard to the optimisation steps and consensus on the importance of the issue as well as open communication in regard to it.
- The *organisation's* structural, strategic and cultural capacities for optimisation, e.g. the early establishment of the workshops as a routine element within the organisation's general optimisation processes.

With such capacities for targeted OHD, the system is supposed to be able to maintain a health-oriented (self-)optimisation process, i.e. to successfully implement optimisation measures aimed at the organisational and individual dimensions that potentially emerge into salutogenic or pathogenic processes and finally lead to individual health and organisational performance outcomes.

Using the OHD Model for Guiding Theory-Driven Evaluation

The presented systemic, model-based approach to OHD has been developed in close collaboration with consultants in the field (see acknowledgements). The model itself has been applied as an evaluation framework in a large-scale stress management intervention project (see Fig. 10.4) to structure and condense data from

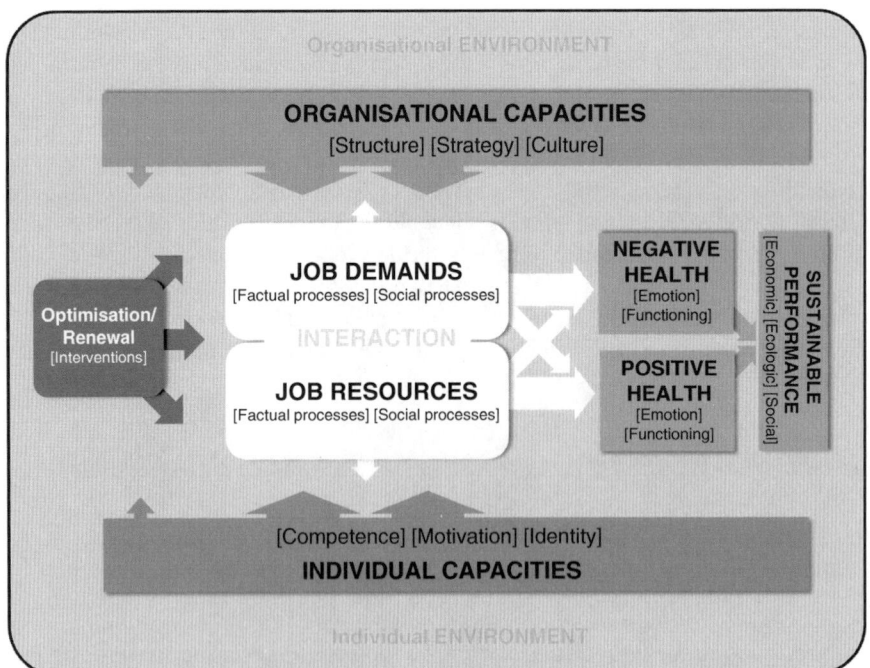

Fig. 10.4 Research version of the OHD model (see Bauer and Jenny 2012; Jenny et al. 2011)

multiple quantitative and qualitative sources (Jenny et al. 2011). It was also used to build a causal narration for the final evaluation report as well as for structural equation modelling in regard to the core of the model (Brauchli et al. 2012), where factual and social processes are distinguished in regard to their demanding or resourceful quality (Bakker and Demerouti 2007).

So far, our experience has shown that companies are interested in using mindmaps to facilitate discourse and action on OHD. Our approach is especially attractive to larger companies that already implement many OHD-related optimisation measures, but that want to ameliorate their corresponding strategic efforts, i.e. companies that want to reduce complexity, enhance strategic visibility and necessity and optimise operative planning and spending on the multiple optimisation processes they use to target health and performance. Such management processes evade experimental research paradigms. Yet, to study the immediate outcomes of capacity building for targeted OHD, as described above, we focus on smaller units of analysis and change, i.e. the teams and their team leaders. Obviously, this limits our research design to companies that feature such subsystems (e.g. as opposed to matrix organisations). The results of this research endeavour will be due for presentation in 2 years.

Acknowledgements We thank our consulting professionals: Anita Blum-Rüegg, Alice Inauen and Anja Barizzi. We also thank our former consulting professionals: Katharina Lehmann, Silvia Deplazes and Anita Emch. We thank our research team: Rebecca Brauchli, Désirée Füllemann, Annemarie Fridrich, Katharina Vogt, Romualdo Ramos, Andrea Huber and Ariane Wepfer.

References

Adkins, J. A. (1999). Promoting organizational health: The evolving practice of occupational health psychology. *Professional Psychology: Research and Practice, 30*(2), 129–137.

Antonovsky, A. (1979). *Health, stress, and coping.* San Francisco: Jossey-Bass.

Armenakis, A. A., & Harris, S. G. (2009). Reflections: Our journey in organizational change research and practice. *Journal of Change Management, 9*(2), 127–142. doi:10.1080/14697010902879079.

Badura, B. (2001). Betriebliches Gesundheitsmanagement: Was ist das, und wie lässt es sich erfolgreich praktizieren? [Corporate health management: What is it, and how can it be practiced successfully?]. *Bundesgesundheitsblatt, Gesundheitsforschung, Gesundheitsschutz, 44*, 780–787.

Badura, B., Greiner, W., Rixgens, P., Ueberle, M., & Behr, M. (2008). *Sozialkapital: Grundlagen von Gesundheit und Unternehmenserfolg* [Social capital: Basis for health and business success]. Berlin: Springer.

Baitsch, C. W. R. (2008). Organisationale Lernfähigkeit gestalten. Ein Instrumentenvorschlag zur Analyse und Bewertung einer zentralen Unternehmensressource [Developing organisational learning aptitude: Proposing a method for analysis and appraisal of a pivotal business resource] [Journal Article (10)]. *OrganisationsEntwicklung, 27*(2), 79–86.

Bakker, A. B., & Demerouti, E. (2007). The job demands-resources model: State of the art. *Journal of Managerial Psychology, 22*, 309–328.

Bauer, G. F., & Jenny, G. J. (2007). Development, implementation and dissemination of occupational health management (OHM): Putting salutogenesis into practice. In S. McIntyre & J. Houdmondt (Eds.), *Occupational health psychology. European perspectives on research, education and practice* (pp. 219–250). Castelo da Maia: ISMAI.

Bauer, G. F., & Jenny, G. J. (2010). Anspruch und Wirklichkeit: Zum aktuellen Stand der betrieblichen Gesundheitsförderung [Aspiration and reality: On the present state of workplace health promotion]. In G. Faller (Ed.), *Lehrbuch Betriebliche Gesundheitsförderung* (pp. 48–56). Bern: Hans Huber, Hogrefe AG.

Bauer, G. F., & Jenny, G. J. (2012). Moving towards positive organisational health: Challenges and a proposal for a research model of organisational health development. In J. Houdmont, S. Leka, & R. Sinclair (Eds.), *Occupational health psychology: European perspectives on research, education and practice* (pp. 126–145). Oxford: Wiley-Blackwell.

Bauer, G. F., Davies, J. K., & Pelikan, J. (2006). The EUHPID health development model for the classification of public health indicators. *Health Promotion International, 21*(2), 153–159. doi:10.1093/heapro/dak002.

Bauer, G. F., Lehmann, K., Blum-Rüegg, A., & Jenny, G. J. (2013). Systemic consulting for organizational health development: Theory and practice. In G. F. Bauer & O. Hämmig (Eds.), *Bridging occupational, organizational and public health*. Dordrecht: Springer (in press).

Baumgartner, M. (2006). *Gestaltung einer gemeinsamen Organisationswirklichkeit: Systemische Strukturaufstellungen und Mitarbeiterbefragungen zur Diagnose von Organisationskultur* [Forming common reality in organisations: Systemic structural constellation and employee surveys for analysis of organisational culture]. Heidelberg: Carl-Auer.

Bennett, J. B., Cook, R. F., & Pelletier, K. R. (2002). Toward an integrated framework for comprehensive organizational wellness: Concepts, practices, and research in workplace health promotion. In J. C. Quick & L. E. Tetrick (Eds.), *Handbook of occupational health psychology*. Washington, DC: American Psychological Association.

Best, A., Moor, G., Holmes, B., Clark, P. I., Bruce, T., Leischow, S., et al. (2003). Health promotion dissemination and systems thinking: Towards an integrative model. *American Journal of Health Behavior, 27*, 206–216.

Bond, F. W., Flaxman, P. E., & Loivette, S. (2006). *A business case for the management standards of stress* (HSE Research Report 431). Sudbury: HSE Books.

Brauchli, R., Jenny, G. J., Füllemann, D., & Bauer, G. F. (2012). *Developing an expanded job demands-resources model predicting negative and positive health*. Manuscript in progress.

Carver, C. S. (1997). You want to measure coping but your protocol's too long: Consider the brief COPE. *International Journal of Behavioral Medicine, 4*, 92–100.

Corbett, D. (2004). Excellence in Canada: Healthy organizations – Achieve results by acting responsibly. *Journal of Business Ethics, 55*(2), 125–133.

Cotton, P., & Hart, P. M. (2003). Occupational wellbeing and performance: A review of organisational health research. *Australian Psychologist, 38*(2), 118–127.

Danna, K., & Griffin, R. W. (1999). Health and well-being in the workplace: A review and synthesis of the literature. *Journal of Management, 25*(3), 357–384.

DeJoy, D. M., & Wilson, M. G. (2003). Organizational health promotion: Broadening the horizon of workplace health promotion. *American Journal of Health Promotion, 17*(5), 337–341.

Dellve, L., Skagert, K., & Vilhelmsson, R. (2007). Leadership in workplace health promotion projects: 1- and 2-year effects on long-term work attendance. *European Journal of Public Health, 17*(5), 471–476.

Donabedian, A. (1966). Evaluating the quality of medical care. *The Milbank Memorial Fund Quarterly, 44*(3, Suppl), 166–206.

Dür, W., Pelikan, J., & Waldherr, K. (2010). *Dealing with complexity in health and health promotion in settings: The Vienna organizational health impact and health promotion intervention model*. Vienna: Ludwig Boltzmann Institute Health Promotion Research.

Edwards, J. R., & Shipp, A. J. (2007). The relationship between person-environment-fit and outcomes: An integrative theoretical framework. In C. Ostroff & T. A. Judge (Eds.), *Perspectives on organizational fit* (pp. 209–258). San Francisco: Jossey-Bass.

European Network for Workplace Health Promotion. (1997). *The Luxembourg Declaration on Workplace Health Promotion in the European Union*. Available at: http://www.enwhp.org/fileadmin/rs-dokumente/dateien/Luxembourg_Declaration.pdf. 12 Dec 2012.

Faltermaier, T. (2005). *Gesundheitspsychologie* [Health psychology]. Stuttgart: Kohlhammer Urban.

Giddens, A. (1984). *The constitution of society: Outline of the theory of structuration*. Cambridge: Polity Press.

Glanz, K. (2008). *Health behavior and health education theory, research, and practice* (4th ed.). San Francisco: Jossey-Bass.

Grawitch, M. J., Gottschalk, M., & Munz, D. C. (2006). The path to a healthy workplace: A critical review linking healthy workplace practices, employee well-being, and organizational improvements. *Consulting Psychology Journal: Practice and Research, 58*(3), 129–147. doi:10.1037/1065-9293.58.3.129.

Hakanen, J. J., Perhoniemi, R., & Toppinen-Tanner, S. (2008). Positive gain spirals at work: From job resources to work engagement, personal initiative and work-unit innovativeness. *Journal of Vocational Behavior, 73*(1), 78–91. doi:10.1016/j.jvb.2008.01.003.

Haken, H., & Schiepek, G. (2006). *Synergetik in der Psychologie. Selbstorganisation verstehen und gestalten* [Synergetics in psychology. Understanding and developing self-organisation]. Göttingen: Hogrefe.

Hart, P. M., & Cooper, C. L. (2001). Occupational stress: Toward a more integrated framework. In D. S. N. Anderson, H. K. S. Ones, & C. Viswesvaran (Eds.), *Handbook of industrial, work and organizational psychology* (Vol. 2, pp. 93–114). London: Sage.

Hazy, J. (2008). *Complex systems leadership theory: How complexity science is changing management*. Paper presented at the 3rd Augsburger conference "Leading in complexity", University of Augsburg, Germany, 7 Oct 2008.

Hoffmann, S., Jenny, G. J., & Bauer, G. F. (2013). Capacity building as a key mechanism of organizational health development. In G. F. Bauer & O. Hämmig (Eds.), *Bridging occupational, organizational and public health*. Dordrecht: Springer (in press).

Hofmann, D. A., & Tetrick, L. E. (2003). The etiology of the concept of health: Implications for "organizing" individual and organizational health. In D. A. Hofmann & L. E. Tetrick (Eds.), *Health and safety in organizations: A multilevel perspective* (pp. 1–26). San Francisco: Jossey-Bass.

Jenny, G. J., Inauen, A., Brauchli, R., Füllemann, D., Müller, F., & Bauer, G. (2011). *Project SWiNG – Final report of the evaluation*. Available at: http://www.gesundheitsfoerderung.ch/swing/. 12 Dec 2012.

Jones, F., Burke, R. J., & Westman, M. (Eds.). (2006). *Work-life balance. A psychological perspective*. Hove: Psychology Press.

Kaplan, R. S., & Norton, D. P. (1996). Using the balanced scorecard as a strategic management system [Article]. *Harvard Business Review, 74*(1), 75–85.

Keupp, J. (2006). Gesundheitsförderung als Identitätsarbeit [Health promotion: An issue of active identity formation]. *Zeitschrift für qualitative Bildungs-, Beratungs- und Sozialforschung, 2*, 217–238.

Keyes, C. L. M. (2007). Promoting and protecting mental health as flourishing: A complementary strategy for improving national mental health. *The American Psychologist, 62*(2), 95–108. doi:10.1037/0003-066x.62.2.95.

Kofman, F. (2006). *Conscious business: How to build value through values*. Boulder: Sounds True.

Königswieser, R. (2006). Zur Interventionsarchitektur von Beratungsprojekten. [Intervention architecture of consulting projects]. In M. Hillebrand, E. Sonuç, & R. Königswieser (Eds.), *Essenzen der systemischen Organisationsberatung: Konzepte, Kontexte und Kommentare* [Essentials of systemic consulting of organisations: Concepts, contexts and comments] (pp. 80–99). Heidelberg: Carl-Auer.

Luhmann, N. (1984). *Soziale Systeme. Grundriss einer allgemeinen Theorie* [Social systems]. Frankfurt: Suhrkamp.

Luhmann, N. (1997). *Die Gesellschaft der Gesellschaft* [The society of society]. Frankfurt: Suhrkamp.

Luhmann, N. (2006). *Organisation und Entscheidung* [Organisation and decision] (2nd ed.). Wiesbaden: VS Verlag für Sozialwissenschaften.

Luthans, F., Norman, S. M., Avolio, B. J., & Avey, J. B. (2008). The mediating role of psychological capital in the supportive organizational climate: Employee performance relationship. *Journal of Organizational Behavior, 29*(2), 219–238. doi:10.1002/job.507.

MacIntosh, R., MacLean, D., & Burns, H. (2007). Health in organization: Towards a process-based view [Article]. *Journal of Management Studies, 44*(2), 206–221. doi:10.1111/j.1467-6486. 2007.00685.x.

NHS Institute for Innovation and Improvement. (2009). *Organisational health: A new perspective on performance improvement?* Coventry: NHS Institute for Innovation and Improvement.

Paton, K., Sengupta, S., & Hassan, L. (2005). Settings, systems and organization development: The healthy living and working model. *Health Promotion International, 20*(1), 81–89. doi:10.1093/Heapro/Dah510.

Peiro, J. M., & Rodriguez, I. (2008). Work stress, leadership and organizational health. *Papeles del Psicologo, 29*(1), 68–82.

Pelikan, J. M. (2007). Gesundheitsförderung durch Organisationsentwicklung: Ein systemtheoretischer Lösungszugang [Health promotion through organisational development: An approach by systems theory]. *Prävention und Gesundheitsförderung, 2*, 74–81.

Pelikan, J. M. (2009). Ausdifferenzierung von spezifischen Funktionssystemen für Krankenbehandlung und Gesundheitsförderung oder: Leben wir in der "Gesundheitsgesellschaft"? [Differentiation of specific functional systems for disease treatment and health promotion, or: Do we live in a "health society"?]. *Österreichische Zeitschrift für Soziologie, 34*(2), 28–47.

Pettigrew, A. M., Woodman, R. W., & Cameron, K. S. (2001). Studying organizational change and development: Challenges for future research. *The Academy of Management Journal, 44*(4), 697–713.

Quick, J. C. (1999). Occupational health psychology: The convergence of health and clinical psychology with public health and preventive medicine in an organizational context. *Professional Psychology: Research and Practice, 30*, 123–128.

Quick, J. C., Macik-Frey, M., & Cooper, C. L. (2007). Managerial dimensions of organizational health: The healthy leader at work. *Journal of Management Studies, 44*(2), 189–205.

Quick, J. C., Little, L. M., & Nelson, D. L. (2009). Positive emotions, attitudes, and health: Motivated, engaged, focused. In S. Cartwright & C. L. Cooper (Eds.), *The Oxford handbook of organizational well being* (pp. 214–235). New York: Oxford University Press.

Rigotti, T., Schyns, B., & Mohr, G. (2008). A short version of the occupational self-efficacy scale: Structural and construct validity across five countries. *Journal of Career Assessment, 16*(2), 238–255. doi:10.1177/1069072707305763.

Rüegg-Stürm, J. (2003a). *Das Neue St. Galler Management-Modell: Grundkategorien einer integrierten Managementlehre. Der HSG-Ansatz* [The new management model of St. Gallen: Basic dimensions for integrated management studies. The HSG-approach] (2nd ed.). Bern: Paul Haupt.

Rüegg-Stürm, J. (2003b). *Organisation und organisationaler Wandel. Eine theoretische Erkundung aus konstruktivistischer Sicht* [Organisations and organisational change. A theoretical investigation from a constructivistic perspective] (2nd ed.). Wiesbaden: Westdeutscher Verlag.

Rüegg-Stürm, J. (2007). Management – der blinde Fleck der Managementlehre? [Management – The blind spot of management studies?]. In *2. Berliner Biennale für Management und Beratung im System: X-Organisationen,* Berlin, Germany.

Seligman, M. E. P. (2008). Positive health. *Applied Psychology, 57*, 3–18. doi:10.1111/j.1464-0597. 2008.00351.x.

Shoaf, C., Genaidy, A., Karwowski, W., & Huang, S. H. (2004). Improving performance and quality of working life: A model for organizational health assessment in emerging enterprises. *Human Factors and Ergonomics in Manufacturing & Service Industries, 14*(1), 81–95. doi:10.1002/hfm.10053.

Siegrist, J., Starke, D., Chandola, T., Godin, I., Marmot, M., Niedhammer, I., et al. (2004). The measurement of effort-reward imbalance at work: European comparisons. *Social Science & Medicine, 58*, 1483–1499.

Spencer Brown, G. (1969). *Laws of form.* New York: Dutton.

Tetrick, L. E. (2002). Individual and organizational health. In *Research in occupational stress and well-being* (Vol. 2, pp. 117–141). Bingley, UK: Emerald Group Publishing Limited.

Tims, M., & Bakker, A. (2010). Job crafting: Towards a new model of individual job redesign. *SA Journal of Industrial Psychology, 36*(2), 9 p. doi:10.4102/sajip.v36i2.841.

Udris, I. (2006). Salutogenese in der Arbeit: ein Paradigmenwechsel? [Salutogenesis at work: A change in paradigms?]. *Wirtschaftspsychologie, Sonderheft zur Salutogenese in der Arbeit, 8*(2/3), 4–13.

Ulrich, H. (1984). *Management*. Bern: Paul Haupt.

Ureda, J., & Yates, S. (2005). A systems view of health promotion. *Journal of Health and Human Services Administration, 28*(1), 5–38.

Van de Ven, A. H., & Poole, M. S. (1995). Explaining development and change in organizations. *The Academy of Management Review, 20*(3), 510–540.

Vogt, K., Jenny, G. J., & Bauer, G. F. (2012). Work-related sense of coherence as a measure of health promoting work situations. Manuscript in progress.

Weick, K. E. (1995). *Der Prozess des Organisierens* [Original work published 1969: The social psychology of organizing] (G. Haucke, Trans.). Frankfurt: Suhrkamp.

Weick, K. E., & Quinn, R. E. (1999). Organizational change and development. *Annual Review of Psychology, 50*(1), 361–386. doi:10.1146/annurev.psych.50.1.361.

Weiner, B. J. (2009). A theory of organizational readiness for change. *Implementation Science, 4*(1), 67.

Weiner, B. J., Lewis, M. A., & Linnan, L. A. (2009). Using organization theory to understand the determinants of effective implementation of worksite health promotion programs. *Health Education Research, 24*, 292–305. doi:10.1093/her/cyn019.

World Health Organization. (1986). *The Ottawa charter for health promotion*. Available at: http://www.who.int/healthpromotion/conferences/previous/ottawa/en/index.html. 12 Dec 2012.

Zapf, D., & Semmer, N. K. (2004). Stress und Gesundheit in Organisationen [Stress and health in organisations]. In H. Schuler (Ed.), *Organisationspsychologie – Grundlagen und Personalpsychologie* (Vol. 3, pp. 1007–1112). Göttingen: Hogrefe.

Part III
Concepts of Organizational Health Interventions and Change

Chapter 11
Policy Level Interventions for Organizational Health: Development and Evolution of the UK Management Standards

Colin Mackay and David Palferman

> *Work is the grand cure of all the maladies and miseries that ever beset mankind*
>
> Thomas Carlyle (1795–1881) Scottish Philosopher

Abstract In 2000, the UK Health and Safety Commission (HSC), the body at the time responsible for health and safety matters in the UK, set targets for the overall reduction in the burden of occupational health (including that of the contribution from work-related stress). As a result, a 10-year priority programme was devised to meet these targets. A key part of the intervention programme was the development of the concept of a series of 'Management Standards' together with a suite of associated resources that would allow organizations to both gauge their performance and to facilitate continuous improvement in both individual and organizational key performance indicators. We recognize that health is a multidimensional concept, that the most effective strategy is to tackle health inequalities at a population level and that individual and organizational health is inextricably linked albeit sometimes in complex ways. The Management Standards themselves consist of both a desirable 'state to be achieved' for individual psychosocial work characteristics ('what to do and what it should look like') and a process by which organizations can assess and manage their exposure to such factors ('how to do it') and implement interventions. In the context of the current book such interventions are designed to help organizations move from a less 'healthy' state to a more 'healthy' one even though the rationale behind the targets was to lessen the likelihood of individual ill-health

C. Mackay (✉) • D. Palferman
Economic and Social Analysis Unit (ESAU), Corporate Science Engineering
and Analysis Division (CSEAD), Health and Safety Executive, Bootle, Merseyside, UK
e-mail: colin.mackay@hse.gsi.gov.uk; david.palferman@hse.gsi.gov.uk

G.F. Bauer and G.J. Jenny (eds.), *Salutogenic Organizations and Change:*
The Concepts Behind Organizational Health Intervention Research,
DOI 10.1007/978-94-007-6470-5_11, © Springer Science+Business Media Dordrecht 2013

using a risk based paradigm. But this can equally well be seen within a salutogenic model for promoting health. Although there are weaknesses as well as strengths in the current approach (which we discuss) we think the Management Standards approach provides a useful model for the improvement of organizational health. We describe a series of developments that have been designed to improve usability of the methodology and widen the scope of the Management Standards.

Keywords Policy level interventions • UK Management Standards

Introduction

The aim of this chapter is to document learning from the implementation of the Management Standards and the associated tool-kit and to provide other stakeholders with a number of key points to consider when planning future organizational and policy interventions. The discussions within the paper will not examine the UK Health and Safety Executive (HSE) policy making processes behind the intervention programme, as these are discussed elsewhere (Mackay et al. 2012) rather we concentrate on the core concepts that underpin the approach and will focus on learning from the specific aspects of the Management Standards approach, the intervention delivery process and reflect on important outcomes. Previous research commissioned by the HSE (Tyers et al. 2009; Broughton et al. 2009) has documented the implementation programme; these studies were limited in scope and were not intended to cover all the technical aspects of the implementation programme.

The learning points highlighted here are those based on reflection of the experience of the authors in delivering the Management Standards implementation programme. The materials used in compiling this paper include internal HSE documents, diary notes, flip charts from workshops but most importantly the experience and anecdotal evidence gathered from interacting with representatives from over 1,000 organizations.

Population Approach to Organizational Health

The targets set by the UK Health and Safety Commission (HSC) specified a reduction in the incidence of work-related ill-health (in this case 'stress' and 'stress ascribed conditions') of 20 % and a reduction in associated sickness absence of 30 % over a 10-year period (2000–2010). To achieve these targets we opted for a population approach that emphasised the arbitrariness of defining individual 'cases' of work-related ill-health (although they are required for 'counting' purposes); rather emphasising the fact that for many common conditions, such as stress and musculoskeletal disorders that make up the vast bulk of work-related morbidity, their severity is continuously distributed in the population. In this approach what is therefore needed is a positive shift in the underlying distributions of contributory risk factors to bring about subsequent improvements in health outcomes. For 'stress' these outcomes range from cardiovascular disease, mental-ill health and mood disorders amongst others – in other words a very wide range of potential 'health' issues. Particularly in the context of 'stress' a simple 'disease' model is no longer sufficient and 'health' must be regarded as multidimensional. Work is a social determinant of these dimensions of health. It is seen that the workforce seem able to cope with large burden of illness and disease issues without that impinging greatly upon functionality or leading necessarily to sickness (absence) – even those with considerable morbidity describe their 'health' as good or very good. So 'health' should be regarded as an asset or resource for the individual not just an outcome. This observation is important in the organizational context. It means minimising risks but maximising opportunities to be exposed to situations, interactions and environments that are now known to be beneficial for health protection and promotion but recognizing that contextual factors are very important. An understanding of what these factors and the extent to which they positively effect health are increasingly known even if we do not fully understand the mechanisms by which this is accomplished or, the specificity in the relationship between factors and health and perhaps importantly how they interact with one another. Even if an additive rather than multiplicative model is used implementing improvements in the range of psychosocial context and content even small shifts in these work characteristics would have large positive effects in the working population. We discuss some of these issues below.

Public Policy Interventions for Health and Well-Being at Work

So the *health* of the workforce and particularly their 'mental health', is an issue of critical national importance (Black 2008). The links between employment and population health at the macroeconomic level have been known for many years (Brenner 1973) and thus a case can be made such that intervening in organizational health such that it should have a positive impact at national level. And from a historical perspective health has not been just about diagnosis and treatment but the struggle for healthiness and how to maintain it – in the sense of a proactive discipline promulgating health maintenance and promotion (Bergdolt 2008). In the UK a Foresight Report on mental capital and well being by Cooper (2008) confirms that the presence of wellbeing strategies and work life balance strategies have a significant effect on reporting of work-related stress. Cooper (2008) states the promotion of health and wellbeing makes good business sense and argues that organization find the dual approach risk assessment and health and wellbeing promotion as a logical approach. Foresight also concluded that the investment of capital into health and wellbeing strategies produces significant financial return on investment.

In the UK the National Institute of Clinical Evidence Public Health Advisory Committee produced guidance on mental health promotion in work place in 2009. The guidance specifically recommended that the use of the Management Standards approach in tackling work-related stress and the promotion of mental health and wellbeing. The Public Health Advisory Committee produced a model that emphasises how there are different vectors influence mental health promotion and wellbeing. One of the key vectors was the psychosocial environment in which organizations work. The Management Standards approach that we describe later is specifically concerned with reducing psychosocial risk and encouraging better management of people. To summarise we can say that work is better than lack of work but that in the working population as a whole there is a gradient in the quality of jobs and that this gradient impacts upon individual health and well-being. Work is a social determinant of health. Promoting healthier workplaces is not just a matter of more effective health promotion. Employers and other stakeholders must address the root causes of ill-health in the workplace. It is increasingly recognised that psychosocial factors that are present in all work environments are health protective and health promoting. Some of these factors are features of the individual and thus not easily and permanently amenable to change but some are features of the external environment. These can equally well be thought of as 'salutogenic'.

Thinking About 'Health' in Organizational Settings

Traditionally occupational medicine has been concerned with the eradication of illness and disease by reducing exposure to toxic agents (Mackay and Lucas 1986). Here health and disease are placed on the same axis but are diametrically opposed to each other and even sometimes treated dichotomously as 'cases' and 'normals' (see below). Also, in studies of public health and morbidity different concepts of ill-health are often seen to be interchangeable. In fact there seem to two 'triads' – the first containing 'illness, 'disease and 'sickness' and second containing 'disability', 'impairment' and 'handicap' (Susser 1990). Here we wish to concentrate on the first of these triads in a way that helps us conceptualise how 'health' is distributed in organizations. **Disease** is defined as a condition that is diagnosed by a physician or other medical expert. It is reserved for objective physiological or mental disorder at the organic level (operating at the individual level) typically having specific biomarkers and tests. Generally speaking common diseases have well established causal factors and treatments. In the occupational context they may be caused or made worse by work. **Illness** on the other hand is reserved for a subjective state, based on the perception of bodily state and thus self-reported mental and physical symptoms (and mood). Illness may range from short term minor fluctuations in perceived bodily state to much more profound and long-lasting conditions. As with disease, illness operates at the level of the individual but may be seen as rather wider conceptually. In the occupational context many common health problems are in the illness category and again may be caused or made worse by work or interfere with day-to-day functioning. **Sickness** refers to a state of social dysfunction; a social role assumed by the individual that is variously specified according to the expectations of the individual and the society in which they are embedded, and particularly, within the current context, the organizational milieu in which they work. One common measure of organizational health is 'sickness absence' (or more properly 'absence attributed to sickness'). The main point in the current context is that poorly managed psychosocial work characteristics increase the likelihood of causing the onset of stress-related disease and illness and also by making existing conditions worse. Conversely where psychosocial work characteristics are well-managed they will lessen the possibility of existing illness and disease impacting on work performance and sickness behaviour.

The Population Strategy to Organizational Level Stress Management

The Management Standards were launched in November 2004. The approach is preventative and is underpinned by the rationale that 'collective protective measures should be given priority over individual protective measures' (Mackay et al. 2004: 101). Taking what is known as a 'population strategy' (Rose 1992) the approach is intended to be applied to populations rather than to those individuals identified as 'high risk', or conspicuously 'ill' – in other words 'stress cases'. The population approach also applies to the **distribution of risk factors** in an environment as well as the distributions of disease and illness within it. Rose was primarily concerned to improve individual health using a population approach but noted that it could have a collective effect by improving population health (and, presumably, in a sector or an individual organization). The population strategy attempts to control the determinants of incidence of disease, to lower the mean level of risk factors and to shift the whole population in a favourable direction (from a less desirable to a more desirable state). Hence '*the states to be achieved*' as incorporated into the standards. The idea is predicated on the fact that a large number of people exposed to a small risk may generate a greater population burden than a small number exposed to a conspicuous risk, and, conversely, if large populations are exposed, a small change in a risk factor may bring about substantial improvements in the health of the working population. This thinking has implications for the types of organizational interventions that may be appropriate – strength, coverage, cost, implement ability etc.

Based on these concepts it was hypothesised that making small changes to address the risk factors associated with work-related stress could bring substantial improvement to the health of the working population (Mackay et al. 2004: 107). Small changes may include alterations in job content, redesign of work, changes in manager or co-worker behaviour and gradual changes in organizational culture. In some sense the idea is forerunner to the more recently published concept of 'nudging' and how this may be used to improve population health (Marteau et al. 2011). Of course, this strategy carries with it the risk that it will bring little obvious benefit (or indeed *awareness* of ongoing organizational changes) in the majority of individuals who would not have developed work-related stress symptoms anyway.

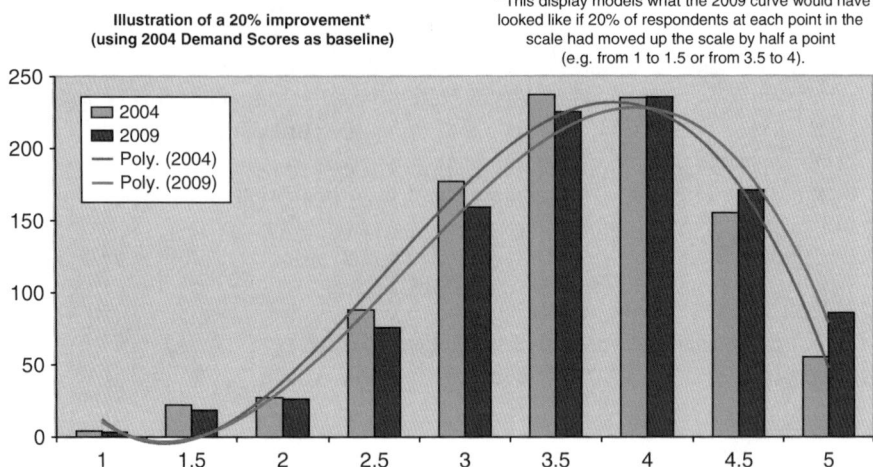

Fig. 11.1 An illustration of what a 20 % improvement in work characteristics (***demand***) would look like – on the x-axis, 1 represents poor management of ***demand***, 5 represents good management of ***demand***

The approach to reducing the number of cases of work-related stress was to attempt to shift the entire distribution of exposure to the risk in a favourable direction. For a discussion about the application of this approach to mental health see Anderson et al. (1993) and Rose (1988).

Using, as an example, the Management Standard for Demand, Fig. 11.1 shows schematically and for illustrative purposes what a 20 % positive shift (using the HSE indicator tool questions) between the years 2004 (pre launch) and 2009 would look like. Our modelling shows that such a shift would bring about a concomitant improvement in the number of psychological symptoms of distress in the population. The population approach to prevention does rely on one critical assumption when applied in this context. Adams and White (2005) showed that if the association between exposure and harm is non-linear, then the strategy may be harmful to some individuals. Evidence from the Whitehall II study, presented in Rydstedt et al. (2006), shows a linear association between work stressors and health, supporting the argument that it was reasonable to apply the population approach to tackling workplace health problems.

The Management Standards Approach

In this section we briefly review the inception of the Management Standards as a risk based assessment approach, describe the implementation and delivery mechanisms and then conclude with a brief review of their impact at organizational and population level.

The Legal Basis

The legal starting point for the development of the Management Standards approach to work-related stress, in UK and European law, is that there is a duty of care on organizations as the generators of the risk (Health and Safety at Work Act 1974, Management of Health and Safety at Work Regulations 1999, European Framework Directive on Health & Safety). Employers are responsible for conducting suitable and sufficient risk assessments for the relevant hazards (to health, as well as safety) and intervening to take appropriate control measures for mitigating any possible stress-related effects on employee safety and health (HSE 2001). The emphasis in doing so is on primary prevention through the design and management of work, work systems and the organization, referred to in terms of *psychosocial* or *work and organizational* factors (e.g. Cox 1993). Nevertheless it is recognised that there will be individual concerns that may need to be addressed by other methods.

Aim of the Management Standards Approach

The Management Standards approach was developed by the Health & Safety Executive (HSE) to reduce the levels of work-related stress reported/experienced by working people in Britain (http://www.hse.gov.uk/stress/standards). The overall aim was to bring about, using the population approach described above, a reduction in the incidence and prevalence of cases and the associated number of employees who are absent from work due to stress-related sickness or who cannot perform well at work because of their experience of stress. The Management Standards approach was developed to provide managers with the information, procedures and tools needed to achieve this. It was intended to demonstrate good practice in the management of health at work through evidence-based, joint problem solving (managers and other employees) through the application of a risk management methodology (Cousins et al. 2004; Mackay et al. 2004). The report "Reducing risks, protecting people" (2001) sets out the philosophy underpinning HSE's approach to managing risks to work-related health.

Key Psychosocial Work Characteristics as Indicators of a Healthy Organization

It would be inappropriate and invidious of us to try to distil the very considerable literature on this topic in both scholarly work and that found in self-help books for senior managers so we will confine our remarks to first, our long experiences of being participants in many kinds of organizations over the years and second, our work in helping organizations diagnose, analyse and intervene in workplace issues.

It goes without saying that these are very largely 'people issues' and that they revolve around the behaviours of individuals, teams and departments. Successful organizations have the characteristic of people interacting effectively – such interactions are possible and do-able. Behaviour is not immutable. Some of the things we think are important are the following. We have confined our discussion to intrinsic factors rather than remuneration and grading issues. In highly functioning organizations (healthy ones) the structure and function (which are inextricably linked) are highly focussed upon to short-term and long term-goals. These are shared and understood by all members of the organization. Problem solving is highly pragmatic – where members work together informally 'leaders' are frequently challenged in a non-confrontational environment. Decision making is driven by ability, sense of responsibility and availability of information – meaning that such organizations must be information rich and this information is analysed and acted upon rather than just collected passively. Organizational members have a proper sense of voice such that their concerns will be heard and issues acted upon. Identical procedures are adopted identically across the organization. These factors are to do with justice, fairness and equity. Communication is continuous, two way and requires active participation. Learning is a powerful tool to individual and organizational development where appropriately positive feedback is given – active participation and engagement is thereby encouraged. The culture is one of mutual support where relationships are open and honest and not driven by self interest. Progress is very much derived from collaboration. Especially in risky or crisis situations a high degree of trust between members promulgates good outcomes and where subsequent organizational learning can take place. There is no punishment of 'mistake makers' who are proximal to an event. Organizational structures, policies and procedures are not bureaucratic, hierarchically rigid and 'traditional' ('we've always done it this way'). Change, appropriately managed is regarded as positive – a necessity for adapting to future environments where innovation, opportunities and the possibility to be creative can thrive. Leadership is open and outward – it chimes with active workforce participation ("top led – bottom fed"). The foregoing reads somewhat like a list and one could analyse organizations as to the presence or absence of the properties so described – this would be a mistake because most organizations would find themselves on a spectrum on each of these desirable attributes – typically somewhere in the middle. The important issue is to convince leaders in organizations that these factors are very critical for performance and that interventions can be done to improve matters. Using these concepts it is possible to facilitate the growth of healthy organizations that thrive, are resilient and high on 'survivability'. These ideas might well be known but are not widely practised. What is increasingly demonstrated and accepted is these psychosocial factors are critical in protecting and promoting individual health and well-being and that investing in appropriate interventions is cost-beneficial even though the epidemiological evidence linking work characteristics to health is, at the time of writing, not yet as good as one would hope. The Management Standards approach has two fundamentals aspects: an assessment model and a risk management methodology. Together they try to encapsulate the critical factors and cultural determinants of organizational health described above.

The assessment model takes the form of a taxonomy that describes the key psycho-social work characteristics in terms of *six* domains or dimensions (Cousins et al. 2004; Mackay et al. 2004). These are:

- **Demands** (workload, skills, abilities)
- **Control** (over pace of work, development opportunities, work patterns)
- **Support** (feedback and support from line managers and co-workers, awareness of support and how to access it)
- **Relationships** (promotion of positive behaviours, avoiding conflict and dealing with unacceptable behaviour)
- **Role** (clear and compatible requirements and responsibilities)
- **Change** (timely consultation and support during organizational change)

This six factor model has been translated into a set of standards described in terms of desirable 'states to be achieved' through the risk management process. It has been argued that the standards can provide a benchmark for organizations against which to measure their current performance and to assess subsequent improvements. In addition to the performance statements that go to make up each of the standards each of the six specifies that '*systems should be in place to deal with individual concerns*'. However little guidance was given as to how this requirement should be discharged in the event of cases of individual distress.

Assessment Model and Its Implementation

The Management Standards approach is a key component of the HSE's 'stress tool-box'. The recommended HSE risk assessment for managing stress is based on five steps that would be expected to be followed by organizations. Securing senior management commitment to support the approach and to provide sufficient resources for its development is seen as a key preliminary. Setting up an active stress steering group, or similar entity, to coordinate the different phases of the initiative is also crucial. Thus, initial organizational preparation is critical to a successful conclusion of the overall process. Then, briefly, the five steps are as follows:

Step 1 of the risk assessment requires organizations to get an understanding of the psychosocial risk factors. Each Standard is defined essentially by a desirable state to achieve to mitigate stress risks. For instance, regarding *organizational change*, the *Standard* is that the employees indicate that the organization engages them frequently when undergoing an organizational change, and systems are in place locally to respond to any individual concerns. The *states to be achieved* are that the organization provides employees with timely information to enable them to understand the reasons for proposed changes; employees have access to relevant support during changes, etc. **Step 2** is about deciding who might be harmed and gathering data. To compare the desirable conditions with their actual work environment, organizations can use the HSE 'Indicator Tool', which is a 35-item survey questionnaire, measuring the six job characteristics (Cousins et al. 2004). The data collected enable a score to be calculated for each of the six Standards, which can inform employers about which areas to prioritise within their organization. This tool has robust psychometric properties (e.g. Edwards et al. 2008; Kerr et al. 2009) which have been demonstrated in recent empirical studies (e.g. Bartram et al. 2009). The use of other data such as sickness absence, staff satisfaction surveys, staff turnover, occupational health referrals and return to work data is also strongly recommended to fully and reliably identify problem areas. *Step 3* concerns the evaluation of risks, exploring issues and developing solutions. Whilst data from Step 2 is informative, it may not be sufficient to understand local and specific issues. Therefore the guidance suggests the holding of focus groups with employees to discuss survey results, unravel specific local issues and suggest practical solutions. *Step 4* involves taking the suggestions from the previous step and developing prioritized interventions and an agreed action plan. Finally, *Step 5* is concerned with reviewing action plan(s) and assessing effectiveness of interventions. A period of 12–18 months is suggested for re-assessment of the workforce but this can vary according to factors such as the type of interventions (quick wins or longer term solutions) being put in place and the size of organizations taking part.

During implementation of the Management Standards the key drivers in the change journey included the following:

- Securing engagement from organizations in target sectors who fully support the implementation of the Management Standards approach (especially in the pilot phase – Sector Implementation Plan 1 – see below)
- Where possible the help and involvement of partner agencies to develop and provide training, support and guidance for participating organizations in specific sectors and increased awareness of solutions and business benefits
- Achieving 'buy-in' from board level senior management (and equivalents) to support the adoption of the Management Standards (especially resourcing adequately)
- Management and workforce working collaboratively to collect data, identify potential stressors, discuss implications.
- Management and workforce then working together to discuss practical ways to address problems and identify and implement interventions (control measures)
- Monitor the extent to which interventions have been properly implemented and have led to improvements and benefits in key performance indicators. The latter can be seen a form of organizational learning.

Dissemination Across Sectors and Industries

To implement the change pathway the overall strategy was rolled-out in three parts – two targeted at five sectors known as Sector Implementation Plans 1 and 2 (SIP1 and SIP2) and a Wider Implementation Plan (WIP) to cover all the remaining sectors and industries in the UK. It was envisaged that they would run consecutively so that learning from each stage could be incorporated into the subsequent steps. Details of this programme can be found in Mackay et al. (2012).

Sector Implementation Plan 1 (SIP1)

This phase of the programme aimed to support up to 100 'willing' organizations in the 5 priority sectors to implement the Management Standards approach to tackling the causes of work-related stress. The five primary sectors are those sectors that, based on HSE data, have the highest incidence and prevalence of work-related stress, they are: health and social care, central government, local government, education and finance. The purpose of SIP1 was to allow the Management Standards approach to be evaluated and refined to inform future work, and, in particular to generate learning for SIP2.

Organizations were recruited via a targeted invitation from the HSE to the CEO or chair explaining the purpose of the programme and the value of participating. The prospective organizations were invited to sign up to the programme by attending a conference held at HSE offices in London. Each volunteer organization, accepted into the programme, was provided with a 'Stress Partner' – an HSE inspector trained for this role, who provided advice and support to the organization without the threat of enforcement action (on stress only). Participating organizations were also given access to free additional resource if required.

Sector Implementation Plan 2 (SIP2)

This was designed to be the main delivery phase for the programme of implementation in the 5 target sectors. In response to feedback from stakeholders it was decided to try and improve knowledge and awareness of the Management Standards approach within organizations in our target sectors – the aim was to help them understand the process and to improve their skills and confidence to take it forward. Organizations, in the 5 target sectors, that collectively employed 80 % of the employees in that particular sector were targeted and were subject to a programme of high level stakeholder engagement and then invited to attend workshops.

There was an expectation that organizations who attended the workshops would then go back to their respective organizations and implement the MS or an equivalent approach. During the 06/07 financial year HSE ran 67 workshops followed by further 'master classes' during 07/08. This represented a significant resource investment and in order to maintain momentum and capitalise on this investment, a programme of follow up inspection work was developed. Approximately 141 HSE inspectors and 100 Local Authority (LA) inspectors were trained to do this work. Note, LA inspector enforce the finance sector while HSE inspectors are responsible for enforcing the remaining four primary sectors. To further support these inspectors an inspection tool was developed to help assess and record duty holders progress with risk assessment and control both in terms of rate of progress and also the quality of their implementation. The follow up inspections began in April 07 and continued until the end of the 09/10 financial year. This inspection tool is available on our website www.hse.gov.uk/stress. Because of changed priorities in the last part of the decade in which the programme was running the third component of the roll-out – the Wider Implementation Plan (WIP) was not done.

Evaluation of the Management Standards Approach

To evaluate the impact of SIP1 and SIP2 several extramurally funded projects were commissioned by HSE (Tyers et al. 2009; Broughton et al. 2009; Cox et al. 2009) together with a number of internal data gathering exercises, such as the inspections, as part of SIP2, described above, carried out by HSE staff. To monitor the impact of the programme at the population level national statistics are routinely collected to assess trends and impacts in psychosocial work characteristics and on health data (www.hse.gov.uk/statistics/stress).

Results of Process Evaluation at the Organizational Level

The success of the overall stress priority programme was predicated at action being taken at organizational level in order to bring about fewer incident cases. It is clear, taking into account the various evaluation studies that took place, that assumptions about how organizations would respond to efforts to implement the Management Standards process were, if not incorrect, optimistic especially as regards resources and timescales. Here we make some general comments about factors that either enabled or impeded progress with implementation.

- Organizations were often committed to taking part in SIP1 but found it difficult to integrate into work plans that had been agreed for example in the previous financial year – this was very difficult to reconcile with HSE's timing. Senior management (or equivalent depending on sector) commitment was absolutely vital – preparatory work to help with questions (Typically, 'What's in it for us?') raised by the board was found helpful here.
- Some organizations (or levels within them) were uncomfortable with language drawn from the health and safety world (e.g. 'risk assessment').
- Additionally, our work on stress (particularly during the workshops where it was found that messages that are framed **positively** – playing more to the business case – are likely to be more powerful determinants of decisions to take action and more persuasive than those based solely on harm reduction) has drawn attention to the contribution of management behaviour and culture on psychological ill-health and more recent work has indicated that other aspects of management, leadership and climate can have, separate, but positive effects on well-being.

Specifically, the drivers for action in organizations are concerns with impacts on individual and organizational performance.

- Many large organizations were found to have initiatives in place that replicated some features of the Management Standards process – it was found that these could be recruited without starting the whole process '*de novo*'. On the other hand some of these were part of annual staff surveys and there was often the issue of 'survey fatigue'. There is also the issue of fitting new projects into existing planning cycles that was sometimes problematic.

- Some organizations found that (even with HSE support) they had difficulty in adapting the generic guidance material to their specific needs (the analogy that was often used was of 'flat-pack' furniture that needed self-assembly rather than being custom made for a particular sector or organization).

- In an earlier piece of research done for HSE (Jordan et al. 2003) it was demonstrated that where key corporate units (Human Resources, Occupational Health, Health and Safety) cooperated in tackling occupational health issues then outcomes tended to be better – in other words they worked together as a team with an integrated approach. Conversely, where activity was uncoordinated then the reverse was the case – where the approach was piecemeal and departments were sometimes at odds with each other. Of particular note was the difficulty some organizations had in collecting, analysing and interpreting data (and, sometimes, sharing or knowing that organizationally relevant data existed!), all of which are critical to the Management Standards process. In fact as a post workshop activity special data handling seminars ('*Masterclasses*') were held for those participating organizations that were struggling with this key step. The critical learning point is that a key individual or group needs to take 'ownership' of the project and inject sufficient resource.

- The successful completion of the process is critically dependant on workforce engagement – the guidance recommends the use of (facilitated) focus groups to complete this step. Some participants who had historically found active worker participation in decision making difficult found this critical step hard to complete with the result that action planning and decisions on what interventions were appropriate was not done properly. Linked to this was a perceived need by some organizations that they needed a 'recipe book' that would assist them in choosing appropriate interventions. This is perhaps a reflection of not trusting the workforce to be able to specify what would make real improvements to their jobs or management concern about what the outcome might be in terms of resource commitment. In reality most of the interventions that were implemented proved to be low cost.

- A generic issue that became apparent in many organizations was the issue of line manager competency to address work-related stress issues at both an individual (cf. each of the six Management Standards specifies '*systems should be in place to deal with individual concerns*') and team level. This seems to be a reflection of the training that managers are given, that, in many organizations, reflects the technical requirements of their post rather than the ability to address how they interact appropriately with their staff. To an extent this has been addressed by the work HSE has co-funded on line manger competency (see below).

• Finally, and perhaps most disappointingly at an organizational level, the Management Standards themselves – that is *the states to be achieved* – to guide progress in developing specific interventions – appear to be used only occasionally – perhaps reflecting an overemphasis on the risk assessment process. Further discussion of these, and other, barriers and enablers can be found in Mellor et al. (2011)

Evaluation of Impact at the UK Population Level

The overall thrust of this programme we have described was to both reduce the incidence and prevalence of work-related stress (and associated sickness absence) and, in so doing, achieve country (UK) level targets using the population approach (see above). This approach has been to take a public health model of prevention and apply it to a workplace health issue – using data from epidemiological studies but also with various untestable assumptions that were made about the extent to which this could be successful – given the constraints of the overall programme. From the outset it was recognised that the targets were both ambitious, and, to some extent, arbitrarily specified. In the event the 10 year targets for an overall reduction in incidence and prevalence of 20 % was met. There were considerable reductions in sickness absence attributed to work-related stress and by 2009 the overall 30 % target was met. In subsequent years however there has been an upswing in overall population sickness absence. We used the 35 item indicator tool (see above) on an annual basis starting in 2004 until 2011 using a representative sample of the UK workforce to test the idea that population shifts in the six psychosocial work characteristics could be demonstrated (as in Fig. 11.1). Over the period there were non-significant improvements in **demand**, **role** and **relationships** and significant improvements in **support** and **change**. Disappointingly, given its criticality in models of health and work, **control** showed a significant worsening over the period. All these data can be accessed at www.hse.gov.uk/statistics/stress. We have discussed some of the reasons why the data look as they do and their implications elsewhere (Mackay et al. 2012).

Evolving the Management Standards

To address some of the theoretical, practical and usability (and other) issues raised by the evaluation results (some of which are described above) a number of development activities were begun – mainly as a form of continuous improvement and enhancement of the Management Standards tool-box. This developmental work should be seen within an evolving policy context that shifted from a risk based approach to one that emphasised the positive and protective effects of work on health – with two key messages. First, that work offers an opportunity to promote individual health and well-being and second, that work should be recognised by all as important and beneficial and access to, and retention of, work promotes and improves the overall health of the population. On the downside poor working conditions can impair health and well-being and long-term sickness absence is a strong predictor of mortality. As well as a fundamental re-design of the stress web-site to reflect this more positive approach that was re-launched in 2009 the following initiatives were begun.

The Concept of 'Equivalence'

The Management Standards only represent 'guidance' in UK law although they are underpinned by a European based regulatory architecture. Organizations are required, under these regulations, to make a 'suitable and sufficient' risk assessment, and depending upon what this assessment reveals to then undertake to implement 'reasonably practicable' control measures. The Management Standards were envisaged as one method by which these duties could be discharged. But it was clear from the outset that there would be many other ways that an organization could fulfil its basic obligations especially by relying or adapting existing initiatives – for example many organizations had programmes on improving well-being. We began work on the idea of 'equivalence' so that organizations could be flexible in their approach to addressing health issues and were not constrained by using a particular (e.g. HSE) approach (or, indeed, parts of it). In other words what features of a system should be seen to be 'equivalent' to the Management Standards approach? We were very much helped in the work by The Division of Occupational Psychology of The British Psychological Society who undertook with their members a consultation on equivalence (Division of Occupational Psychology, BPS 2006; report available from the authors). We deemed the key features that one would expect to see in an approach that was 'equivalent' to include the following:

- That is based on organizational approaches rather than identifying and treating 'high-risk' individuals
- That it is concerned with primary rather than secondary or tertiary prevention
- That the interventions chosen reflect these two requirements
- There is demonstrable senior management commitment – the later to include the provision of adequate resource
- There is a process that is evidence based
- There is active participation of a justifiable percentage of the workforce to ensure that the outcomes are valid and reliable
- The process is not linear – rather it is cyclical so that organizational (double-loop) learning can be done. For a useful, recent summary see Karanika-Murray et al. (2012).

Other Uses of the Management Standards

Since the launch of the management standards it has become apparent that they are not being used solely as an organizational tool for the prevention of work related stress. At the outset it was never made clear how organizations could comply with the platform statement in each of the six standards that **'systems shall be in place to deal with individual concerns'** nor indeed what those concerns might be although there is now guidance on our website.

It is our belief that other uses for the Management Standards approach may include the following:

- As a framework for dealing with 'individual concerns'
- As an adjunct to annual appraisals
- For *a priori* assessment of risks in particular types of work
- As a way of task analysis
- As part of competency frameworks and for developing a training needs analysis
- For career planning and monitoring

A Management Competency Framework

As well as the above it recognized early on that the Management Standards framework was relevant in the context of how managers interact with staff regarding job content. This is for a number of reasons. First, it is widely recognised that that managers are in a position to have a positive impact upon most, if not all, aspects of work design. Managers are typically 'gate-keepers' to work-redesign initiatives and development/change initiatives more generally (Lewis et al. 2012) both from supporting and resourcing such initiatives. Second, mangers may be in a position to detect distress in individuals and its concomitant pressures and demands. Third, there is an increasing body of literature causally linking manager behaviour to health such that manager behaviour can be a source of support and resilience, but conversely may adversely impact on employee health and well-being. Fourth, manager behaviour is also likely to impact on the likelihood of psychosocial factors impinging on the employee for good or bad – for example by the degree of control they are willing to cede to an individual worker. Thus line managers have a vital role to play in determining the psychosocial environment (and thus health) in which their reportees and teams operate.

As recognition of the criticality of line manager behaviour a further development of the Management Standards approach has been the development of a Management Competency Framework for work related stress. Work by Donaldson-Fielder et al. (2009), Yarker et al. (2007, 2008) examines the application of the Management Standards to Competency Frameworks on management and leadership. Out the outset of a three phase research project they established that previous competency frameworks for management did not cover all the six areas of the Management Standards for work-related stress. They concluded that there was a need for a competency framework which addressed specifically the appropriate competencies and behaviours necessary for a manager to manage work related stress. After the launch of the Management Standard in 2004, the Health and Safety Executive (HSE) was asked by employers to define what areas of line management and management in general were important in helping to manage work related stress. The HSE and the Chartered Institute of Personal Development (CIPD), and latterly with Investors in People (IiP), set up together in a collaborative research programme to develop a set of competencies and behaviours perceived as being the most relevant and appropriate for helping managers to be better at manage work related stress.

The Management Competency Framework has four overarching competencies with an additional 12 sub competencies. Each competency has associated behaviours, both positive and negative which allow organizations to identify areas of management strengths and development needs around the skills necessary for tackling work related stress. The four competencies are as follows:

- Respectful and responsible – managing ones emotions and having integrity
- Managing and communicating existing and future work
- Reasoning/managing situations
- Managing the individual within the team

It can be seen at once how these factors map across to the Management Standards themselves. The unique aspect of this research is that the Management Competency Framework has been developed in consultation throughout with representatives of employees and employers. Specifically employees have identified the key types of behaviours which they believe are present in line managers who are acknowledged to managing work related stress within their organization. Additionally a 360 feedback tool has been developed to assist managers and employees in identifying strengths and weaknesses. Feedback from managers has been positive and employees feel that the Competency Framework has been a useful way of helping to identify good managers. The research that led up to the development of the competencies and the tools themselves may be accessed on our website.

Embedding the HSE Indicator Tool

The Indicator Tool was named as such because it provides a **broad indication** of an organization's performance against the six psychosocial risk factors contained within the Management Standards. In an organizational context it was never intended to be a 'stand-alone' assessment methodology. It was strongly recommended that the analysis of data collected from the completed questionnaires should be combined with the analysis of other data available within the organization (sickness absence, turnover, key performance indicators etc.) to provide a more holistic diagnosis of the issues to be discussed with employees. In practice, there have been some common errors made in the use of the indicator tool and the subsequent data analysis, including, but not limited to the following. First, the results of an employee survey using the indicator tool questionnaire are used as the only data, qualitative or quantitative, within the risk assessment process. Second, the indicator tool questionnaire is seen as the risk assessment process rather than just a part thereof and in this instance there is a danger that data are used to give legitimacy to what is already known. Third, over-interpretation of the analysis of completed questionnaires leading to 'paralysis by analysis', and fourth lack of engagement with employees prior to the survey resulting in poor response rates.

However there have been some positive developments with the demonstrating aspects of the reliability and validity of the tool. A paper by Guidi et al. (2012) showed that the indicator tool subscales are negatively associated with psychological distress as measured by a short form of the General Health Questionnaire (GHQ) and positively associated with a measure of workability (The Work Ability Index, WAI). There is considerable international activity underway to produce country specific versions of the indicator tool (especially non-English versions; e.g. Guidi et al. 2012; Kumar and Madhu 2012; Magnavita 2012) and to develop short forms with fewer items than the original 35 question version (Edwards and Webster 2012).

Co-morbidity

In 2005 HSE commissioned a series of surveys of workers, as part of the evaluation of its strategic programme to reduce work-related ill-health in GB. A survey of 6,500 households done in 2006 included a small number of questions about workplace ill-health that respondents had experienced in the previous 3 months. Four symptoms relating to musculoskeletal disorders and five to mental health were combined to form two dichotomous variables indicating the presence or absence of illness. The results demonstrated a strong association between symptoms of musculoskeletal disorders (MSD's) and 'stress'. More people reported co-morbid symptoms (23 %), than stress alone (16 %) or MSD symptoms alone (19 %). Forty-three percent of those surveyed reported no symptoms. Amongst those who did report symptoms 39 % report both MSD's and 'stress' simultaneously. Respondents with co-morbid symptoms reported having taken more time off from work in the last 3 months than those with stress and MSD symptoms only. Other work has shown that such co-morbidity exists and that the psychosocial risk characteristics inherent in the Management Standards may predict or co-vary with other common health problems (particularly) MSD's as well as 'stress' (see e.g. Deeney and O'Sullivan 2009). This partly led on to a further development that is described next.

Need for Further Adaptations Identified by Occupational Health Experts

Five years after the launch of the Management Standards research for HSE by Cox et al. (2009) used a Delphi methodology to consult with a range of experts in occupational health about their views on the Management Standards approach. The study reiterated some of the findings from the SIP evaluations, for example identifying the importance of staff involvement and of the competencies of managers to implement the approach successfully. The experts were mindful of the difficulty of assessing cause and effect since organizational changes are likely to have a delayed impact. Of particular concern to the experts was their recognition of a discrepancy between assessment and action because many felt that although the Management Standards approach enables organizations to identify areas of weakness in performance, it doesn't necessarily facilitate the development of strategies for improvement in these areas. The Delphi panel were concerned that there is a distinct lack of a sound evidence base about what makes a good intervention for preventing work-related stress. They suggested that a more prescriptive approach regarding how to address the problems identified in a risk assessment would be useful and could involve the provision of sector or organization specific examples or case studies.

First, it suggested the incorporation of higher level organizational factors (as in our discussion earlier – see above) in the assessment model and Indicator Tool. It was widely felt that the assessment model was too focussed at the level of the workplace and design and management of work. There is a widely perceived need to incorporate higher order organizational factors in the model and in the Indicator Tool. Issues relating to organizational structure, function and strategy as well as culture were mentioned. Attention might be paid to management style and practice and to issues relating to the psychological contract between the organization and its employees.

Second, modify the risk model to allow for the "balancing out" of positive and negative drivers of employee health. There is a need to develop what would be perceived as a more positive approach to risk management. This could be done by modifying the risk model to allow for the balancing out of positive (salutogenic) and negative (risk) drivers of employee health in the assessment and intervention stages of the Management Standards approach. This is made possible by the bipolar nature of many work and organizational factors and the way that they are known to interact.

Third, provide further evidence of the validity and reliability of the Indicator Tool and risk management process. The HSE should continue to encourage and support research into the reliability and validity of the Indicator Tool (and equivalent assessment instruments and procedures) and the usefulness of the overall risk management approach. It should also encourage the harvesting and dissemination of the findings from this research. This research may include the nature of the assessment model (and the Management Standards), the associated norms, the psychometric properties of the Indicator Tool, and evidence for the effectiveness of the Management Standards approach in relation to employee health and performance. The HSE should make better and wider spread use of the existing evidence for the reliability, validity and usefulness of the Management Standards approach. In fact work both to improve the psychometric properties of the Indicator Tool (see above) and the usability of the Analysis Tool are currently in progress.

Conclusion

In this chapter we have briefly described a national programme aimed at reducing the burden of work-related stress at both a national and organizational level, and, based on subsequent developments and learning, how the evolution of concepts and methods is taking place. We have attempted to draw some general lessons for those who may wish to repeat such an exercise. The overall conclusion must be that such programmes are 'doable' but consume large resources in terms of time and effort. Such commitment is easy to underestimate both nationally and organizationally. The overall thrust of this programme we have described was to both reduce the prevalence of work-related stress (and associated sickness absence) and, in so doing, achieve country (UK) level targets. The approach has been to take a public health model of prevention and apply it to a rather complex workplace health issue – various untestable assumptions were made about the extent to which this could be successful given the constraints of the overall programme (even though the underlying science was known to be sound and that individual (key) components of the model had previously been tested and validated). From the outset it was recognised that the targets were both ambitious, and, to some extent, arbitrarily specified. In retrospect it perhaps should have been better to do some preliminary tasting of the power of the Management Standards approach to bring about sustained improvements over a specified time period – but under the constraints of the overall policy requirements and associated timescale such testing was not possible. At the outset a considerable amount of front loading of engagement of key stakeholders was done so that the chosen sectors were primed and that awareness of the launch of the programme was assured. Although considerable effort was expended in this launch and post-launch activity it is clear from extensive surveys done on HSE's behalf that *awareness* and eventual *uptake* (key parts of the ILM) were patchy. In retrospect in seems that assumptions about how quickly this *diffusion* would happen across the target sectors was very considerable overestimated. This lead to the SIP phases of the programme to be 'squeezed' such that the full learning from SIP1 participating organizations could not be incorporated into the content of the SIP2 workshops. One can also speculate that the wrong sectors were chosen for the initial implementation work and that, perhaps, those where incidence of cases was low (indicating where some activity had already taken place) or where existing management systems were more conducive to Management Standards implementation might have provided a better test bed. The second part of the implementation plan was based around workshops ('*Managing sickness absence and work-related stress*'). It may be that the linking of these two issues was not the right approach – that delegates became, on their return to their organizations, focussed on sickness absence management rather than more fundamental commitment to job design and organizational change. Also, in retrospect the design of the content of the workshop, could have been improved. The focus was very much (because of time constraints) upon the early stages of the Management Standards process – very little of the material covered action planning and the choice of interventions; monitoring and review and organizational learning aspects was only touched upon. Perhaps the overall lesson here is that organizations became more comfortable and proficient at sickness absence **management** but were less convinced about the importance of **primary prevention** approaches. Structural changes in job content (towards 'good jobs') would seem to need much more time to be achieved as evidenced from data in changes in work characteristics. More detailed analysis, that is currently ongoing, should help us to disentangle the drivers towards improvement. The UK national level approach was also predicated very much upon a partnership approach between key stakeholders and other Government agencies and whilst there were some very good examples of how this worked effectively greater planning and time would have allowed these collaborations to work more synergistically.

A better approach focusing more widely on improving the quality of working life for employees by seeking to enhance their well-being is likely to have a positive impact on other common health conditions beyond work-related stress and might be easier to implement. The experts in Cox et al.'s Delphi study (2009) were in favour of making the Management Standards approach broader to address well-being issues and the findings from the some case studies certainly highlighted the similarity between enablers and barriers for well-being programmes and for organizational stress interventions. On the other hand, the uncertainty about the relationship between stress and well-being is also a case for keeping them as separate issues.

On the positive side there is now plenty of evidence about why and how the Management Standards have been implemented from the abundance of case studies and anecdotal examples of good practice, however there is much less evidence about whether the approach has been successful at the micro and macro levels because it is difficult to attribute positive outcomes to the implementation of the Management Standards approach. A need for further long-term data collection, both qualitative and quantitative, has been identified by numerous commentators including Cox et al. (2007), Jordan et al. (2003), and LaMontagne et al. (2007). This would improve the generalisability of the findings and enable us to better understand the impact of the approach upon end user organizations. A carefully controlled matched comparison study could provide an estimate of the counterfactual where, for example, within one organization the Management Standards approach is adopted in certain parts of the organization (test group) but not others (control group) so that before and after data could be compared for each. However such an approach would still only be providing evidence about the impact of the approach in a single organization and because the approach is intended to be flexible and tailored to suit the needs of different organizations, the findings would not necessarily be comparable between or generalizable across different organizations. There are a number of other issues with this type of research including ethical issues, – it would mean that some parts of the organization would be receiving a potentially beneficial treatment whilst others were not and it may be difficult to find an organization that is sufficiently homogenous so that its different parts would be directly comparable.

Because robust evaluations and research studies of organizational interventions (such as the case control design discussed above) are likely to continue to prove difficult to achieve for reasons such as organizations being unable or unwilling to commit to long term evaluation studies and not having the resources or capabilities to conduct their own robust studies, it might be useful to consider how we can make the best use of existing evidence sources. It would be much harder to meet the requirements of rigorous evaluation at the macro societal level therefore it is unlikely that we will be able to say what the impact of the approach has been on levels of work-related stress in wider society. It is difficult to address the issue of causality at the societal level because it is not possible to evaluate the counterfactual, or what would have happened anyway. However, the Psychosocial Working Conditions Survey focuses specifically upon the stressor areas covered in the Management Standards and the baseline from before the launch of approach is very valuable because it provides that much sought after counterfactual. Although so far the survey has found some significant changes relating to psychosocial working conditions since the launch of the Management Standards, evidence suggests that tangible changes to working conditions following implementation of organizational interventions may require a longer gestation period than originally anticipated so it will be interesting to continue monitoring the results from the survey in the long term if possible.

Our own case study work suggests that such interventions do not have lengthy, costly or complex to have the desired effects. This links to the population approach that emphasises that small changes in large populations can bring about large shifts in population. In many instances as with the line managers and those aspects of the management standards 'states to be achieved' the interventions will be behavioural – they will be about roles, relationships and support – but in other domains not thus far covered. We think the population approach will be increasingly relevant in dealing with the burden of work-related common health problems. In this context we must consider the question 'what is the role of the organization (and actors within it)'. It must be several fold but first the organization must be convinced that it is in their interest to address these issues with the diligence and the resources that are needed to take action and to make significant improvements. We know that legal and morale arguments go so far but, certainly in the current economic climate, it is important to demonstrate hard business benefits for action to happen. Experience is accumulating on what factors are drivers and barriers to effective action (Mellor et al. 2011).

Good evidence exists to show that there is a shared set of causal factors for the main work-related common health problems. These 'psychosocial' factors largely relate to aspects of the design and management of work, work systems, work organizations and culture. They are well enough established to have been incorporated into aetiological theories for both musculoskeletal disorders and work-related stress.

There is evidence for co-morbidity in relation to the two main common health problems at work: those reporting musculoskeletal disorders also frequently report experiencing stress in relation to work although only some of those who report experiencing such stress report musculoskeletal disorders. The available evidence regarding a shared causation and co-morbidity supports the possibility of a single (unified) approach to the management of the two main common health problems at work: they share important causal factors and there is some co-morbidity. Two things follow: first, such a unified approach may also be appropriate for other common health problems at work if they also share causal factors and demonstrate co-morbidity, and, second, any such unified approach must be flexible enough to allow for tailoring to particular circumstance.

In response to some of the above, a changing policy environment and to user needs on specific limitations of the existing Management Standards approach we have described a number of developments in both evolve and make the process more integrated. The Nottingham Delphi exercise made a number of specific recommendations to further develop the approach. One was rather than focussing on minimising psychosocial hazards development should aim to achieve a more business focussed approach by being more positively framed and by seeking to improve and maintain employee health and well being and organizational performance rather than just reducing harm. Another was to develop the Management Standards approach so that they could be used as a tool for the management of common health problems – not just usual for prevention of 'stress' outcomes and not just prevention. The first steps in any such integration involve establishing the core concepts and common models, developing a framework model to facilitate integration and then populating that model with the necessary foundation data. At the time of writing HSE has commissioned work into the development of a Common Health Management Tool (CHMT) to take forward some of the recommendations made in the Delphi exercise. It will be an adjunct to the existing Management Standards approach. Its focus will be on helping those with existing health issues to be accommodated within working environments by the use of targeted tools and support.

References

Adams, J., & White, M. (2005). When the population approach puts the health of individuals at risk. *International Journal of Epidemiology, 34*, 40–43.

Anderson, J., Huppert, F., & Rose, G. (1993). Normality, deviance and psychiatric morbidity in the community: A population-based approach to General Health Questionnaire data in the Health and Lifestyle Survey. *Psychological Medicine, 23*, 475–485.

Bartram, D., Yadegarfar, G., & Baldwin, G. (2009). Psychosocial working conditions and work-related stress among UK veterinary surgeons. *Occupational Medicine, 59*, 334–341.

Bergdolt, K. (2008). *Wellbeing: A cultural history of healthy living* (English Translation by J. Dewhurst). Malden: Polity Press.

Black, C. (2008). *Review of the health of Britain's working age population: Working for a healthier tomorrow*. London: TSO.

Brenner, H. M. (1973). *Mental illness and the economy*. Cambridge, MA: Harvard University Press.

Broughton, A., Tyers, C., Denvir, A., et al. (2009). *Managing stress and sickness absence: Progress of the sector implementation plan – Phase 2* (HSE RR694). Sudbury: Health and Safety Executive.

Cooper, C. L. (2008). *Foresight project on mental capital and wellbeing* http://www.foresight.gov.uk/OurWork/ActiveProjects/mental%20capital/Welcome.asp. Last accessed June 2010.

Cousins, R., MacKay, C. J., Clarke, S. D., Kelly, C., Kelly, P. J., & McCaig, R. H. (2004). 'Management standards' and work related stress in the UK: Practical development. *Work and Stress, 18*, 113–136.

Cox, T. (1993). *Stress research and stress management: Putting theory to work* (HSE RR61). [Online]. Last accessed 18 July 2010.

Cox, T., Karaninki, M., Mellor, N., et al. (2007). *Implementation of the management standards for work-related stress: Process evaluation SIP1 technical report* (T/6267). Institute of Work, Health and Organizations, University of Nottingham.

Cox, T., Karanika-Murray, M., Griffiths, A., et al. (2009). *Developing the management standards approach within the context of common health problems in the workplace: A Delphi study* (Health and Safety Executive, Contract Research Report 687). Sudbury: HSE Books.

Deeney, S., & O'Sullivan, L. (2009). Work related psychosocial risks and musculoskeletal disorders: Potential risk factors, causation and evaluation methods. *Work: A Journal of Prevention, Assessment and Rehabilitation, 34*(2), 239–248.

Donaldson-Fielder, E. J., Lewis, R., & Yarker, J. (2009). *Preventing stress: Promoting positive manager behaviour.* CIPD Insight Report. London: CIPD Publications.

Edwards, J., & Webster, S. (2012). Psychosocial risk assessment: Measurement invariance of the UK Health and Safety Executive's Management Standards Indicator Tool across public and private sector organizations. *Work and Stress, 26*, 130–142.

Edwards, J., Webster, S., van Laar, D., et al. (2008). Psychometric analysis of the UK Health and Safety Executive's Management Standards work-related stress indicator tool. *Work and Stress, 22*, 96–107.

Guidi, S., Bagnara, S., & Fichera, G. (2012). The HSE Indicator Tool, psychosocial stress and work ability. *Occupational Medicine, 62*, 203–209.

HSE. (2001). *Tackling work-related stress: A managers guide to improving and maintaining employee health and well-being* (HS(G)218). Sudbury: HSE Books.

Jordan, J., Gurr, E., Tinline, G., Giga, G., Faragher, B., & Cooper, C. (2003). *Beacons of excellence in stress prevention.* Sudbury: HSE Books.

Karanika-Murray, M., Biron, C., & Cooper, C. L. (2012). Distilling the elements of successful organizational intervention implementation. In C. Biron, M. Karanika-Murray, & C. L. Cooper (Eds.), *Organizational stress and well-being interventions: Addressing process and context* (pp. 353–361). London: Routledge.

Kerr, R., et al. (2009). HSE management standards and stress related work outcomes. *Journal of Occupational Medicine, 59*, 574–579.

Kumar, K., & Madhu, G. (2012). An analysis of work-related stress factors in selected industries in Kerala, India. *International Journal of Engineering Research and Development, 1*, 31–36.

LaMontagne, A., Keegel, T., Louie, A. M., & Landsbergis, A. P. (2007). A systematic review of the job-stress intervention evaluation literature 1990–2005. *International Journal of Occupational and Environmental Medicine, 13*(3), 268–280.

Lewis, R., Yarker, J., & Donaldson–Feilder, E. (2012). The vital role of line managers in managing psychosocial risks. In C. Biron, M. Karanika-Murray, & C. Cooper (Eds.), *Managing psychosocial risks in the workplace: The role of process issues.* London: Routledge.

Mackay, C. J., & Lucas, E. G. (1986). Occupational aspects of whole person health care. In M. J. Christie & P. G. Mellett (Eds.), *The psychosomatic approach: Contemporary practice of whole person care.* Chichester: Wiley.

Mackay, C. J., Cousins, R., Kelly, P. J., Lee, S., & McCaig, R. H. (2004). Management standards' and work related stress in the UK: Policy background and science. *Work and Stress, 18*, 91–112.

Mackay, C. J., Palferman, D. J., Saul, H., Webster, S., & Packham, C. (2012). Implementation of the Management Standards for work-related stress in Great Britain. In C. Biron, M. Karanika-Murray, & C. Cooper (Eds.), *Managing psychosocial risks in the workplace: The role of process issues.* London: Routledge.

Magnavita, N. (2012). Validation of the Italian version of the HSE Indicator Tool. *Occupational Medicine, 62*, 288–294.

Marteau, T. M., Ogilvie, D., Roland, M., Suhrcke, M., & Kelly, M. P. (2011). Judging nudging: Can nudging improve population health? *British Medical Journal, 342*, d228.

Mellor, N., Mackay, C., Packham, C., Jones, R., Palferman, D., Webster, S., & Kelly, P. (2011). 'Management Standards' and work-related stress in Great Britain: Progress on their implementation. *Safety Science, 49*(7), 1040–1046. doi:10.1016/j.ssci.2011.01.010.

Rose, G. (1988). The mental health of populations. In P. Williams, G. Wilkinson, & K. Rawnsley (Eds.), *The scope of epidemiological psychiatry: Essays in honour of Micheal Shepherd* (pp. 77–85). Routledge: London.

Rose, G. (1992). *The strategy of preventive medicine*. Oxford: Oxford University Press.

Rydstedt, L., Ferrie, J., & Head, J. (2006). Is there support for curvilinear relationships between psychosocial work characteristics and mental well-being? Cross-sectional and long-term data from the Whitehall II study. *Work and Stress, 20*, 6–20.

Susser, M. (1990). Disease, illness, sickness; impairment, disability and handicap (editorial). *Psychological Medicine, 20*, 471–473.

Tyers, C., Broughton, A., Denvir, A., et al. (2009). *Organizational responses to the HSE management standards for work related stress: Progress of the sector implementation plan – Phase 1* (RR693). Health and Safety Executive.

Yarker, J., Donaldson–Fielder, E., Lewis, R., & Flaxman, P. E. (2007). *Management competencies for preventing and reducing stress at work: Identifying and developing the management behaviours necessary to implement the HSE Management Standards*. Sudbury: HSE Books.

Yarker, J., Donaldson–Fielder, E., Lewis, R., & Flaxman, P. E. (2008). *Management competencies for preventing and reducing stress at work: Identifying and developing the management behaviours necessary to implement the HSE Management Standards: Phase 2*. Sudbury: HSE Books.

Chapter 12
An Automated and Systematic Web-Based Intervention for Stress Management and Organizational Health Promotion

Dan Hasson and Karin Villaume

Abstract Healthy organizations are proactive and focus systematically on interventions for health promotion and a sustainable work environment. They have concrete tools for employees, managers and management to proactively and reactively promote and monitor a good psychosocial and physical work environment. The workplace should be adaptive to the needs of the employees and vice versa. It is also important to plan for today and tomorrow and prioritize long-term benefits and sustainable solutions. This chapter presents the theoretical framework and practical experiences of using the HealthWatch tool for systematic organizational health promotion. It describes an automated web-based intervention for organizational health promotion and provides important lessons learned when developing and implementing such web-based tools. The chapter also outlines an approach for how to strive for a healthy organization through proactive and reactive efforts and by systematic focus on interventions for health promotion and a sustainable work environment. It discusses strategies for assessing the psychosocial work-environment and health related factors. It also describes how to implement real-time/regular monitoring with early warning systems in order to proactively counteract ill health and dysfunctional group patterns at an early stage. The importance of implementing standardized/tailored action plans directed to all levels of the organization; employees, managers and management is emphasized. It is concluded that organizational health promotion

D. Hasson (✉)
Department of Learning, Informatics, Management and Ethics,
Medical Management Centre, Karolinska Institutet, Stockholm, Sweden

Stress Research Institute, Stockholm University, Stockholm, Sweden
e-mail: dan.hasson@ki.se

K. Villaume
Department of Learning, Informatics, Management and Ethics,
Medical Management Centre, Karolinska Institutet, Stockholm, Sweden
e-mail: karin.villaume@ki.se

G.F. Bauer and G.J. Jenny (eds.), *Salutogenic Organizations and Change:*
The Concepts Behind Organizational Health Intervention Research,
DOI 10.1007/978-94-007-6470-5_12, © Springer Science+Business Media Dordrecht 2013

may increase organizational profits, wellbeing and reduce absenteeism and thereby making it possible to endure in the competitive economy of today and tomorrow.

Keywords Stress management • Organizational health development • Health promotion • Work environment • Intervention • Web • Internet

Background

This chapter presents the theoretical framework and practical experiences of using the HealthWatch tool for systematic organizational health promotion. Following a brief research overview on traditional organizational health promotion, an innovative approach will be introduced. It discusses strategies for assessing the psychosocial work-environment and health related factors as well as how to achieve a healthy organization. The chapter entails important lessons learned when developing and implementing such web-based tools.

Workplace-Based Interventions for Health Promotion

There is a multitude of successful workplace health promotion interventions directed at the individual level (Goetzel and Pronk 2010; Goetzel et al. 2007; Lindberg and Vingård 2012; Zimolong and Elke 2009). To mention a few examples, there have been successful interventions for stress management (Hasson et al. 2005; Kawakami et al. 2006), increasing physical activity (Spittaels et al. 2007), improving eating habits (Oenema et al. 2001), smoking cessation (Strecher et al. 2008) and decreasing alcohol consumption (Kypri et al. 2004). Even though beneficial effects of single interventions in workplace settings (directed at the individual level) have been reported, scientific reviews advocate multimodal approaches (Goetzel and Pronk 2010; Goetzel et al. 2007; Lindberg and Vingård 2012; Zimolong and Elke 2009). It seems as if combining interventions is the most effective strategy for promoting healthy organizations. Multimodal health promotion interventions are often integrated as a part of the organization's ordinary operations and strategies. They address individual, environmental, cultural and policy factors and target several health issues simultaneously. Health screenings are implemented as well as tailored programs to meet specific needs of individuals and groups. These organizations are also characterized by effective ways of communication, high participation rates, collaborations with networks and healthcare providers as well as evaluations and continuous improvement (Zimolong and Elke 2009). Thus, organizations utilizing multimodal interventions seem to have integrated health promotion as part of their core values and strategy to achieve success and growth. Single interventions may indeed yield beneficial effects, but continuity and sustainability seem to be dependent on a more comprehensive approach.

In order to promote good practice in occupational health promotion, the European network for workplace health promotion (ENWHP) has constituted a declaration (European Network for Workplace Health Promotion (ENWHP) 2007). They define workplace health promotion as the combined efforts of employers, employees and society to improve the health and well-being of people at work. It is further declared that it can be achieved through a combination of: (a) improving organizational factors and the work environment, (b) promoting active participation and (c) encouraging personal development.

Even though there are numerous studies on workplace health promotion interventions, it is problematic to draw general conclusions concerning best practices. Most studies differ in methodologies and ways of assessment and results are therefore difficult to compare and generalize. Consequently, there is a need to establish golden standards for how effective and beneficial interventions should be conducted and evaluated. Future studies should emanate from generally agreed upon sets of questions or questionnaires to evaluate different dimensions of interest. International collaboration of this kind is well needed and would make studies more comparable and conclusions more generalizable.

Healthy Organizations

The concept of 'healthy organizations' has gained more and more attention during the past decades. This is contrasting the more customary approach of occupational health research where focus has been on prevention, treatment and elimination of causes and risk factors for work-related ill health. This more 'positive' salutogenic focus is similar to developments emerging within the fields of psychology and medicine. For instance, there is a substantial increase of research publications on positive psychology and biological correlates of longevity, resiliency, wellbeing and recovery. However, a challenge to the concept of healthy organizations is that there is no consensus on how to define a healthy organization or a healthy work environment (Lindberg and Vingård 2012). Wilson and colleagues (2004) define it as follows:

> "A healthy organization is one characterized by intentional, systematic, and collaborative efforts to maximize employee well-being and productivity by providing well-designed and meaningful jobs, a supportive social–organizational environment, and accessible and equitable opportunities for career and work–life enhancement".

According to our similar view, healthy organizations are proactive and focus systematically on interventions for health promotion and sustainable work environments. They should have concrete tools for employees, managers and management to proactively and reactively promote and monitor good psychosocial and physical work environments. The workplace should be adaptive to the needs of the employees and vice versa. It is also important to plan for today and tomorrow and prioritize long-term benefits and sustainable solutions. We also believe that healthy organizations should have a high level of awareness. There is a visionary leadership where goals are achieved by conscious, systematic efforts. An optimal level of job satisfaction, fairness and job security prevails. There is a well-established plan for salutogenic interventions and it is adaptive and flexible to the needs and dynamics of the organization. Before major activities are implemented, risk and consequence analyses are customary. These should include potentially positive and negative short- and/or long-term consequences for all organizational levels. Sainfort et al. (2001) and Wilson et al. (2004) additionally mention that a healthy organization is characterized by both financial success and a healthy workforce. A more holistic view includes an interaction between organizational factors (e.g. productivity, profitability) and employee well-being. Most previous interventions however have focused only on enhancing one or a few of these dimensions.

In this chapter, we will describe our approach to organizational health promotion, which includes not only multilevel interventions, but also a well-formulated implementation process.

New Approach of Organizational Health Promotion

After more than a decade of experience in working with systematic, automated web-based interventions for stress management and health promotion we now present our approach. It emanates from the fact that the implementation procedures are crucial for achieving optimal success of the intervention. Naturally, the intervention itself needs to be of high quality and easy to use. The main idea behind our approach is that a healthy organization focuses systematically and continuously on interventions for health promotion and a sustainable work environment. It emanates from continuous data collections and dialogue with the employees rather than acting upon preconceptions. Real-time or regular monitoring with early warning systems is utilized to proactively counteract ill health and dysfunctional group patterns at an early stage. Standardized and tailored action plans are used and directed to all levels of the organization; employees, managers and management. These interventions should include education, self-help and personal empowerment features.

From Theory to Practice: HealthWatch – A Web-Based Tool for Organizational Health Promotion

HealthWatch is an interactive web-based system aimed at providing tools for all levels in an organization; the individuals, managers and management. The aim is to maintain and promote health, wellbeing and performance as well as to prevent ill-health – thus creating a healthy organization. The system provides continuous real-time monitoring with instant feedback on the individual, group and organizational levels. Tailored self-help, self-education tools and action plans are offered to all levels. For employees, there are also automated features for referral to the occupational healthcare provider. Figure 12.1 describes an overview of the content and features of HealthWatch.

Individual level (employees and managers)	Group and organizational level

Assessments

Brief survey
15 seconds, real-time monitoring of wellbeing, health, stress and work conditions; responded to regularly – from daily up to every second week.

Extensive survey
15 minutes screening of the most common public health disorders and psychosocial work environment. Conducted 1 – 4 times annually (frequency decided by the organization).

Interventions

1. **Instant feedback and monitoring over time**
a) Own ratings on the *brief survey*. Graphs illustrate current ratings and comparisons with same socioeconomic group and the whole database, development over time. Optional to add other health-related variables such as weight, blood pressure, blood sugar, steps (pedometer), etc.
b) Own ratings on the *extensive survey*. Tailored, written feedback and a referral to the occupational healthcare provider if needed.

2. **Self-help exercises.** Health promotion and stress management (scientifically proven) exercises with elements of cognitive behavioral therapy, classical and innovative relaxation techniques, structured problem solving, conflict management, skills training, body awareness, etc.

3. **Diary** for notes and expressive writing used with optional frequency.

4. **News and information** about stress, health and wellbeing.

1. Regular, real-time **feedback on workgroup's and organization's wellbeing**, health, stress and psychosocial work environment (from the *brief survey*).

2. Real-time feedback (group and organizational level) on the **psychosocial work environment and health indicators** (from the *extensive survey*).

3. **Self-and organizational development and education.** Exercises and tools to improve leadership skills and endorse organizational health promotion and systematic psychosocial work environment improvement.

Fig. 12.1 An overview of the content in HealthWatch at the individual, group and organizational level

A Brief Historical Background and Current State

The precursor of HealthWatch started as an intervention targeting only the individual level in six organizations. It was evaluated in the so called Health-IT study, using a prospective randomized, controlled research trial. The study was conducted in 2002 and targeted companies from the information technology and media sector (Hasson et al. 2005). It aimed at developing a brief web-based screening tool for the psychosocial work environment and health variables with possibilities for unlimited assessments and instant feedback and monitoring. In addition, the intervention group was also provided with interactive exercises for health promotion and stress management. Several beneficial effects were found in the intervention group compared to the controls, e.g. improved perceived stress management ability, improved sleep quality, increased mental energy and concentration ability. Furthermore, significant improvements in stress- and recovery related biomarkers were found at the end of the 6-month intervention (Hasson et al. 2005).

Since the Health-IT study, HealthWatch (and its predecessor www.pql.se) has been publically available free of charge for individuals and for smaller groups (≤25). It is currently utilized by approximately 20,000 persons. A fundamental principle behind HealthWatch is that it should be continuously developed and improved. This is achieved for instance through feedback from users, research studies and technological advancements. One such improvement was to make the tool available for company use and it is currently used by approximately 40 national and international companies.

The company users have also identified a need for practical interventions that helps managers to promote health, wellbeing and performance in their work groups. Consequently, HealthWatch also includes interactive self-learning tools for managers to conduct interventions for improving the psychosocial work environment and for developing their leadership skills.

After years of interaction with companies of various sizes, a general need for guidance on how to efficiently implement the system in organizational settings has emerged. Concequently, a recently terminated project assessed' the implementation procedures and some preliminary results and recommendations will be described below.

Overview of the Content in HealthWatch

HealthWatch currently consists of surveys for assessment of the psychosocial work environment and occupational health interventions that can be used at the individual, group and organizational levels. The content is briefly described in Fig. 12.1 and more thoroughly below.

Features for the Individual (Employee)

Each employee is offered the opportunity to create a personal account through an encrypted link distributed via e-mail at the introduction seminar (described further below). HealthWatch contains a 15-second survey consisting of 11 global questions concerning health, sleep, concentration, energy, control, social life, stress, work efficiency, work load, job satisfaction and job atmosphere. Instant feedback is provided with the indicators green (healthy level), yellow (improvement needed) and red (unhealthy level). The feedback bars are clickable for an interpretation and recommendation of self-help exercises in the system. The exercises are categorized according to areas such as "Breathing, Relaxing and Sleep", "Cognitive restructuring" and "Emotional control and Body awareness" for instance. All exercises are tagged with a time-estimation and are available in different formats (PDF, plain text and FLASH) in order to suit different learning styles and preferences. There is a diary for expressive writing and a function for adding own measurements such as biomarkers (e.g. blood pressure, blood sugar etc.) and physical activity (e.g. Nordic walking/running distance and pace etc.). These functions were added at request from the users. The results from the 15-second survey can also be monitored retrospectively, both by viewing results from specific dates, but also in the form of trend curves showing their development from start.

The *brief survey* (15 s) can be filled in as often as the individual wishes and reminders are set in their own account. If the reminder is set for example every Monday at 10 AM, one receives an e-mail at that time including an encrypted link. When clicking the link, one is automatically directed to the 15-second survey. There is also a mobile application for smart phones that can be used to access the system.

The individual level tool aims at increasing awareness and empowerment of one's own health, wellbeing, stress and work situation. It also provides concrete resources for stress management and health promotion.

The *extensive survey* provides an overview of health-related variables and the psychosocial work environment. It takes approximately 15 min and is usually distributed one to four times a year. The frequency is decided by the companies and/or workgroups. Individuals receive instant and tailored feedback on some of their health-related responses after filling in the survey. They can also receive an automated referral to the occupational healthcare provider if the results indicate a need for it. This is the case if one for instance displays symptoms of long-term stress or musculoskeletal pain problems. Each company decides if and to what extent the occupational healthcare provider should be involved.

Features for the Manager

The managers use the same functions (described above) as all employees. In addition, they have access to an account where they can monitor the survey results and statistics for their own group. Two prerequisites for group level feedback are that there is at least 50 % response rate and a minimum of ten individuals, otherwise no feedback is given. The feedback information can be accessed and retrieved at any time. The results of the extensive survey are presented at group level to the group leader via an automatic structured display of results. This is the usual way managers receive feedback from work environment, health and risk assessment surveys – they face a long list of graphs. These are not always easy to interpret and understand. Indeed, it can be a stressful task to describe the results for employees and to form action plans, which is often expected or mandatory. In order to reduce this, for many managers, stressful task we have created "The 5-minute report". The idea is that a manager within 5 min should know the strengths of his/her group/s and what kinds of improvements are needed. It includes a brief summary of positive health- and work-related outcomes and three to four improvement/focus areas that should be prioritized. These reports are compiled by a work environment expert from the occupational healthcare provider, a person from the HR-department or an external consultant. Preferably they should be compiled in-house and it is of essence to educate staff from the HR department in how these brief reports are composed.

Another main function in this account is the toolkit for managerial support, self-help and education (called 'exercises'). The exercises cover a broad range of issues relating to leadership, work and health, conflict management, work climate, employee development, crisis management and problem solving. It also includes education on goal setting, communication and information, recruitment, monitoring and feedback, strategies for change work, time management, the work environment act, rehabilitation and stress management. These managerial exercises are based on the concept "From quick fix to fundamental change, and something in between". This means that there are exercises that are quick and concise for the manager who only has a few minutes to spare, and more complex time-demanding exercises for the managers who wish to engage in developing their leadership styles and competencies over time. The exercises are primarily based on organizational behavioral analysis which is an application of learning theories (applied behavior analysis) on the organizational level (Wilder et al. 2009). The dual aim of the exercises is to promote work engagement and wellbeing as well as organizational productivity and health development using positive reinforcement strategies. All exercises are accessible at any time.

Features for the Management and Human Resources (HR) – Completing the Circle

The top-level management, HR department or an external consultant (e.g. occupational healthcare provider) can monitor the whole organization as well as all subgroups. This means that they can offer support to managers proactively if they need or desire. They also have access to the managerial exercises as described above. In practice, it is commonly applied as follows.

A dedicated person monitors all groups/departments in the organization. If this person finds some risk trends or results (e.g. worsened sleep, wellbeing and efficiency) from the assessment he/she ideally contacts the manager to inquire if they need assistance. Sometimes a manager simply states that the problem is temporary and will be resolved by itself. Another scenario is that a manager has a difficult situation to handle. In those cases, the dedicated person should offer help and support. We would like to emphasize that similar to the managers, feedback is only given if the response rate is higher than 50 % and there are at least ten individuals in the group. No one has access to the account of a single user other than the user him- or herself.

In summary, this approach provides tools for all levels in an organization and thus becomes an integrated part in the proactive and systematic work for creating a healthy organization. By targeting interventions at all levels of the organization, and by working in a systematic way, health and the psychosocial work environment become natural aspects of the organizational agenda.

The Underlying Principles of the HealthWatch System

The development of HealthWatch has always been guided by five principles, i.e. to be time efficient, primarily offer systematic and proactive, but also reactive solutions, be a user-driven and tailored system, monitor trends rather than capturing snapshots and provide multilevel self-help and educational exercises. These principles are briefly described in the following section.

Time Efficiency

Our main presupposition is that stress management and health promotion programs need to be time efficient in order to be utilized. The initial idea was that stressed individuals avoid spending time on stress management and stress management should not be stressful. However, our hypothesis was that even highly stressed individuals have the time to take their medicine. The time to pour up a glass of water and swallow a pill was estimated to take 30–40 s, and that was the time frame that the intervention was built upon. Knowledge about neural plasticity (Martin 2010), has also been influential. It means that frequent repetition of a behavior is more sustainable for introducing habits than less frequently repeated behaviors. Consequently, it is more favorable to spend 30–60 s per day to become aware of health, stress and wellbeing rather than 1 h monthly or more seldom. This is the foundation for the brief survey in which the individual is also "rewarded" with instant feedback. The interventions, e.g. exercises, also need to be time efficient and a time frame is displayed for all exercises (at the individual level and the managerial levels). This offers an additional sense of control as users can select exercises according to the time available. The time it takes to conduct an exercise ranges from a few seconds to an hour or more, with others taking 15 min to learn but then only a few seconds to apply later on. This gives the user flexibility both in learning and applying the acquired skills.

Offer Systematic and Proactive, but Also Reactive Solutions

Health promotion initiatives often concern risk prevention rather than more proactive strategies. Instead of focusing only on risk prevention, the main idea is to use the HealthWatch system for systematic maintenance, promotion and improvement of health and wellbeing. This is in line with recent suggestions from Nielsen and Randall (2012) who state that more research is needed to test and describe interventions that include positive aspects of work and employee development. In our approach, this is achieved by encouraging ongoing, systematic assessments and monitoring of the psychosocial work conditions and employee health. This is a part of a continuous improvement effort. The frequent assessments also allow for monitoring progress of different interventions and encourage striving towards goals.

The brief and extensive surveys also fill other functions. They can be seen as an early warning system so that potential risks can be managed at an early stage. Although this apparently is prevention rather than promotion, it differentiates from many traditional risk assessments by the instant feedback and regularity of the measurements. These features facilitate early detection, as managers and HR representatives can monitor the development of departments in real time. If there are negative trends, managers and HR can become aware at an early stage and take action. If there is a positive trend, this could function as positive reinforcement for the group. Thus, collaborative problem solving is encouraged between the HR-department and managers, where the managers can both ask for and be offered support.

The tool also identifies individuals with signs of ill health and automatically offers them to be contacted by the occupational healthcare provider. If a person responds positively to the offer, she/he should be contacted within 24 h. The request to the occupational healthcare provider (which can be customized for each organization) is e-mailed by the individual via the system.

User-Driven and Tailored System

Another guiding principle is that the system should be user-driven and adaptive to the needs of individuals, groups, and organizations. This is addressed in several ways. For example, continuous modifications, such as new functions and exercises, are made based on the needs and preferences of the users. Each organization can edit the extensive survey by adding and omitting questions. For instance, a work group with specific problems or goals can be offered additional questions for evaluation purposes. The importance of adaptive tools that take different needs of the workgroups into consideration has also been highlighted elsewhere (Brisson et al. 2006). Previous research of web-based health promotion interventions indicates that tailoring messages for individuals or for work groups is more effective than presenting generic information. Tailoring seems to be beneficial in terms of engaging individuals, building their self-efficacy and improving health behaviors (Lustria et al. 2009).

Monitoring Trends Rather than Relying on Snapshots

Our approach emphasizes the importance of following trends over time instead of only measuring and reacting on cross-sectional results. This is important since it has been found that the current state when filling out a questionnaire will most probably influence retrospective ratings of for instance the last month (Gorin and Stone 2001;

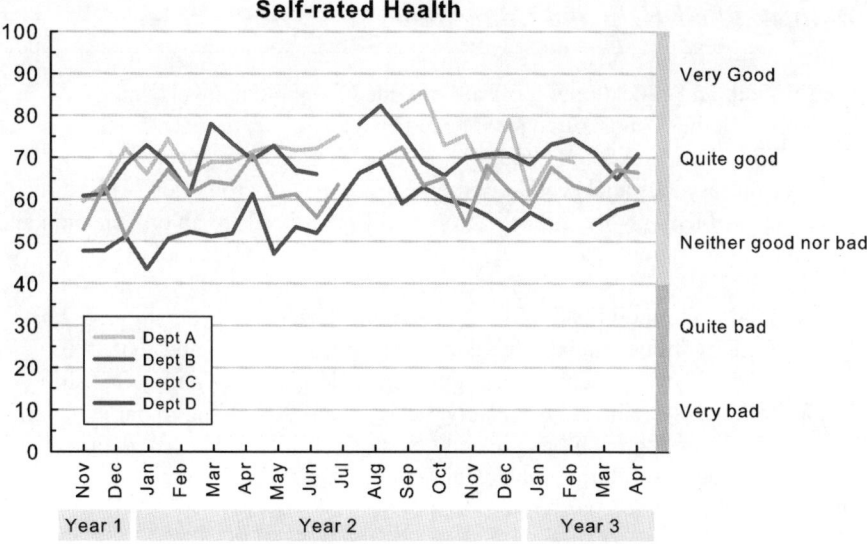

Fig. 12.2 Mean values of self-rated health for employees at four departments during 18 months. It is evident that there is a large variation over time. Self-rated health is usually better during summer and after vacations and worse in November/December for instance. Department D in the figure had initial problems with the leadership and in January the manager was replaced, yielding a more beneficial trend. Monitoring trends makes it possible to intervene only when there is a true need rather than a temporary shift

Hasson 2005; Holte et al. 2003). According to our experience, measurements of occupational health and wellbeing such as questionnaires, are like snapshots with a camera. They capture the moment, which in turn is determined by the mood and the situation a person experiences. The outcomes of a survey will depend on the weather for instance, yielding better results when it is sunny and worse if it rains or snows. With regards to this, monitoring trends can give a more accurate picture of the situation since our health and wellbeing is dynamic.

An example is illustrated in Fig. 12.2, which shows the trends for self-rated health in four departments in a company that have used HealthWatch regularly for 18 months. Self-rated health is a simple, yet powerful measure that is a strong predictor of future morbidity and mortality (Bailis et al. 2003; Idler and Benyamini 1997) as well as functional decline, disability and utilization of healthcare (Bailis et al. 2003; Farmer and Ferraro 1997; Goldman et al. 2004). Lower levels are therefore an important (early) warning for increased risk of ill health. From Fig. 12.2 it becomes clear that there are fluctuations in self-rated health over time. A cross-sectional survey, therefore, is highly vulnerable to timing. Monitoring trends makes it possible to intervene only when there is a true need rather than a temporary shift. This means that repeated assessments make it possible to use resources in a more efficient and cost-effective way and to make sure that the interventions are relevant to treat an existing problem. However, this also means that the survey needs to be quick and easy to complete.

Multilevel Self-Help and Education

The self-help and educational tools are provided for the employees, managers and for the management (most often represented by the HR department). The idea is that all levels in the organization should be able to work continuously with improvements of the psychosocial work environment and health promotion. This strategy makes it possible to involve all key actors in different levels of an organization and to enable collaboration. It also offers an opportunity to tailor the tool to the needs of these key actors. In the light of this, a combination of multilevel level interventions, including both the individual and organizational levels has been suggested as an optimal strategy for beneficial intervention outcomes (Lamontagne et al. 2007).

In sum, these five principles have guided the development and composition of the HealthWatch system, and ultimately the approach. According to our experience and research, this approach has yielded beneficial results. However, in order for a method to be successful, the implementation procedures are essential. The following section will describe our implementation process.

The Implementation Process

One of the most important factors in the approach to obtain beneficial outcomes is the implementation process. According to our experience, a properly performed implementation provides high participation rates (85 % in average), commitment, motivation and engagement. The process involves the whole organization; the management, managers and the employees, addressed in that order. The importance lies in a commitment of all organizational levels to the intervention. All parties need to understand how and why it is significant as a way of promoting health, wellbeing and improving the psychosocial work environment (Fig. 12.3).

The *first step* in the implementation is aimed at providing top-management and HR representatives with information on how this approach works and how it may be of use for them. They are invited to a seminar held by a trained person with profound knowledge and insight in the approach. The scientific background is presented, the tool and its features are demonstrated and the approach as a whole is thoroughly described. The aim is to achieve acceptance of the approach and at these seminars there is room for questions and comments. This is also an opportunity for negotiation procedures in the sense that adaptations can be made to fit the needs of the organization and employees. If there is a positive attitude towards adopting the approach, step two in the implementation process is initiated.

The *second step* involves presenting the same information to managers, with the same opportunity to ask questions and to negotiate. They are informed about their role in the approach and about practical implications. At the end of the seminar, a time-plan for the rest of the implementation process is formulated and contact with the occupational healthcare provider is established in order to educate them about their role in the approach.

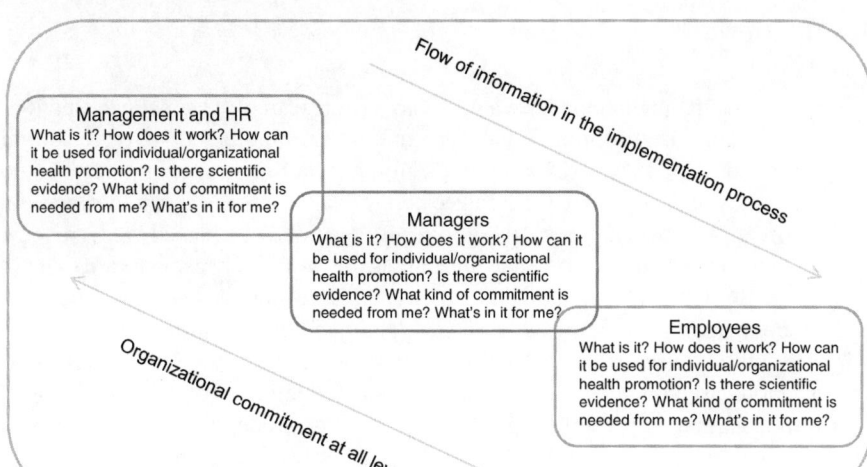

Fig. 12.3 The implementation process involves providing all levels of the organization with information in a structured way. The approach is thoroughly described along with the scientific background, previous experiences and the tools and features are demonstrated

The *third step* in the process involves the whole organization. Employees are invited to one/several introduction seminar(s) depending on the size of the organization. It is highly recommended that a HR representative, the involved managers and a person from the top management are present at the seminar as well. The top management person should introduce the seminar by emphasizing the importance of active participation and that there is a full commitment from the management. After that, an inspirational presentation is held about the psychosocial work environment, health and stress and the beneficial scientific results found in previous studies. Then the tool is described and demonstrated and there is room for questions. The aim of the seminar is to increase the motivation to participate and to provide the information needed in order to commit fully to the approach. After the seminar, all the staff is informed that an encrypted link has been sent to their e-mail address. They are invited to create their accounts and fill in the initial extensive survey adjacent to the seminar. Some groups reassemble for a brief session of comments and questions after the surveys have been completed.

The *fourth step* is maintenance and adherence, which is obtained in several ways. One of the most crucial success factors for adherence is that the group's feedback from the brief survey is presented regularly, at least once a month. This constitutes a basis for continuous dialogue about work environment and health within the work group, i.e. a form of maintenance. The results from the extensive surveys should be presented as soon as possible after the introduction seminar, preferably within 3 weeks. The 5-minute report (described above) suggests areas for improvement so that actions can be applied immediately. When the system is used in this way, the employees often feel that their participation yields tangible outcomes, which promotes adherence.

Evaluation

In order to ensure quality and have a good basis for research, systematic evaluations of organizational health promotion interventions are important. There are several ways of conducting these evaluations. According to our view, interventions should be assessed using prospective randomized controlled trials assessing both short- and long-term effects whenever methodologically justified. Repeated and frequent assessments are important to better understand for instance seasonal variations in responses. Preferably, a combination of quantitative approaches (e.g. questionnaires, biomarkers, physiological variables) and qualitative approaches (e.g. interviews) should be used for a broader understanding of outcomes. When web-based interventions are conducted, it is important to automatically (or manually) log as much information as possible, e.g. number of logins or adherence, which features are used and how often, etcetera. This enables a better analysis and understanding of usage patterns and user behaviors. Consequently it can indicate if some parts of the intervention need to be clarified, simplified or removed for instance. It can also help distinguish patterns between users with different levels of motivation, participation, health and wellbeing.

Implementation processes (process evaluations) should be studied in order to distinguish between the effect of for instance a charismatic researcher or excellent implementation procedures and actual effects of the intervention. An excellent implementation of a poor method may still yield beneficial results and vice versa. These analyses can also indicate if there are components in the intervention that are superfluous or of particular importance and therefore need to be removed or emphasized. It is a true advantage if data is collected so that both qualitative and quantitative analyses can be conducted.

Profitability and Cost Effectiveness of Organizational Health Promotion Interventions

Since it is easier to promote and motivate organizations to use salutogenic programs that have been documented to be profitable, cost-benefit analyses should be conducted. This can be a complicated task since there are several ways of making these calculations and analyses. It is also ethically important that interventions have a favorable financial impact as costly solutions can influence the profits of the company negatively. In a worst case scenario, poor investments of any kind can jeopardize the survival of the company or lead to downsizing. It might not be very realistic that a salutogenic intervention in itself would have these dramatic effects. However, from an organizational and scientific perspective it is essential to know whether salutogenic interventions are cost effective or not. Some studies and reviews about cost effectiveness have been conducted (Aldana 2001; Aldana et al. 2005; Chapman 2005). They conclude that there is strong evidence for reductions in healthcare costs, absenteeism and sick leave after multicomponent health promotion interventions. The authors of one review stressed however that there is no consensus on how to measure the cost effectiveness of these interventions (Chapman 2005). Thus, there seems to be some support for the cost-effectiveness and return of investments of worksite health promotion interventions. However, it is currently difficult to draw general conclusions, partly since measures of cost effectiveness vary.

The effect on productivity is also a variable that should be calculated and re-calculated into monetary equivalents. This is truly a difficult task as several methods can be utilized for this purpose and there is no golden standard. Previous studies on this topic have used different approaches (Aldana 2001; Brooks et al. 2010; Proper et al. 2004; Riedel et al. 2001; Schwartz and Riedel 2010; von Thiele Schwarz and Hasson 2011), each with strengths and weaknesses. For instance, some studies seem to presuppose that an employee can be 100 % productive all the time. A more rea-sonable approach according to our view would be that optimal productivity would be around 70 %. This figure is of course dependent on the kind of profession and work environment that is studied and optimal productivity needs to be calculated accordingly. Furthermore, in productivity assessments, the focus is often on costs for ill health and absenteeism rather than (benefits of) health. In sum, calculating return of investment and productivity is a challenging but important task.

Importance of Novel Thinking and Appropriate Strategies for Data Analyses

When it comes to data-analytic approaches there is a clear need for more research. Data analyses should include pattern recognition techniques – patterns are more important than single risk indicators. Pattern analyses (e.g. Bayesian statistics and causal analyses) have the advantage of taking more variables into account when reaching conclusions. For instance, theoretically, poor sleep may not be a risk factor for ill health if other variables such as self-rated health and concentration ability are in a good status. However, if both sleep and concentration ability is poor, it may constitute a risk in spite of other variables indicating a healthy status. Using single risk indicators will not allow for this kind of depth in the analyses and may conse-quently also yield incorrect conclusions.

Another aspect with regards to patterns is that they may change over time. Therefore, the pattern analyses need to be conducted both cross-sectionally and longitudinally using repeated assessments. In the HealthWatch system there may be several assessments during a year – a person may answer daily yielding over 300 measurement points. Even if employees in an organization respond weekly to the brief questionnaire, there will still be approximately 50 measurement points. It can be challenging to analyze these kinds of data in a meaningful way and there is no consensus as to which statistical methods to use. All methods have their advantages and disadvantages and presuppositions that may skew the results and conclusions. Irrespectively, these methods (e.g. time series analyses, machine learning techniques, etcetera) need to take multiple variables or patterns of them into acount. Adjustments or stratifications for seasonal variations, age and sex for instance should be included in the analyses.

Understanding patterns better needs to be complemented by valid risk scores and cut-offs. A proper cut-off will indicate the urgency of a problem and give a clear, easy-to-understand indication to managers and management to act upon. A manager could for instance be presented with the fact that his/her department has a 95 % probability of decreasing health and productivity with 40 % within 6 months. This will provide a substantial foundation to act upon and also information that can be used to have interventions sanctioned from the management. The same scenario is also applicable for the management, and with clear indications in the example above it will be easier to assess other important values than the purely financial. Extrapolating on this thought, ideally it could become an important variable when assessing the success or value of a company.

Since the results from the assessments form the basis of the action plans, proper calculations and conclusions are crucial. This is easier said than done and future research needs to establish valid cut-offs as well as pattern recognition indications and predictive models for signs of health and ill health.

Lessons Learned

After more than a decade of research and development, the approach described in the present chapter is still evolving. Needless to say, creating and maintaining healthy organizations is not always easy, but the opposite, i.e. handling ill health is probably even more difficult and surely detrimental. This final section will describe some of the lessons learned.

According to our experience there are some key factors that promote successful implementation and adherence. One of the most important factors is the engagement of the manager. In our recently terminated study, the adherence is by far better in groups or departments where the manager is active and engaged. A manager who displays the results of the brief survey to his/her department at least once monthly or more seems to have higher participation rates. There are examples of groups with 100 % adherence, compared to the average of 85 % participation rate. Conversely, in groups with low managerial engagement, the adherence is substantially lower. It is equally important that the intervention is strongly sanctioned and advocated by the management. Ideally, the CEO or any other top-level manager participates in all the seminars and emphasizes the importance of a healthy staff.

User-friendliness is another key factor. If the intervention features are not intuitive and easy-to-use, this will negatively impact utilization of the system. Therefore, the user-driven approach described above is of essence. To our experience, user-friendliness is particularly important in automated web-based interventions since people seem to have less patience with computer-based systems. We have examples of individuals refraining from participation due to lack of time. They claim that even

15–30 s for the brief questionnaire is too time consuming for them. Thus it is difficult to meet all the needs of some users. Also, the internet as a medium may not be suitable for all. Consequently, implementing the system in workplaces with low utilization of computers can be problematic, especially if the employees lack e-mail addresses.

Personal integrity and internet security also constitutes central points of discussion in seminars and meetings. The HealthWatch system has therefore multiple solutions for this. First of all, the system adheres to the standard of secure payments in banks, including encrypted surfing (SSL) and there are also other features to protect the integrity of single individuals. For instance, an employee can change the corporate e-mail address to his/her private one without the company knowing. In the administrative system the corporate e-mail address is still displayed, but all the e-mails and correspondence is sent to the private address. The individual can always access their own results but managers and management can only view group level outcomes. The 'ethical blockage' restricts feedback on groups smaller than ten individuals and in groups with lower response rates than 50 %. The issue of integrity and internet security is always discussed at all levels since it is vital for usage according to our experience.

There are other examples of factors that promote successful implementation and adherence. Some of them may seem simple, but should not be underestimated. For instance, sometimes measurement tapes are distributed to measure waist-hip ratio (as one variable in the calculation of type 2 diabetes risk score in the extensive survey). These gifts with some logotypes and information stimulate discussions and acts as reminders for the users. In follow-up meetings, the measurement tapes are often mentioned as a popular gimmick.

Finally, the tailored individual and group feedback on the brief and extensive surveys is also rewarding and may promote adherence. Lack of feedback often results in questionnaire fatigue among the employees. Indeed, when HealthWatch is first introduced to an organization, questionnaire fatigue is commonly mentioned as a main opposing argument. However, to our experience it is often the employees who request follow up assessments. The reason for this is most probably the instant or fast feedback and action plans on a group level. When employees notice that their questionnaire responses yield tangible improvements the motivation to maintain the intervention seems to increase. This constitutes the bottom-up effect. At the same time the implementation process emanates from a top-down approach. When these two are combined there is a higher motivation and commitment in the whole organization. According to our experience, this fruitful combination of bottom-up and top-down is often achieved when implementing the HealthWatch system. We believe that the features described in this chapter, including structured intervention processes, user-friendliness, built-in rewards, etcetera, may play an important role.

The take home messages from this chapter are based on our experiences from several workplace interventions. These are that:

(A) *Proactive organizational health promotion activities need to be systematic and continuous, but also reactive.* In order to achieve sustainable outcomes, regular assessments preferably with instant feedback and tailored interventions are desirable. When a manager or HR (human resource) person can monitor development over time for various groups/departments, signs of ill health and dysfunctional group processes can be halted at early stages. Sometimes however, unhealthy patterns have already occurred on an individual or group level. In those circumstances there needs to be a readiness for reactive measures.

(B) *Teach the organizations how to fish – build the competence within the organization instead of becoming dependent on external consultants.* Long-term sustainable results are more easily accomplished when the competence of health promotion and how to achieve a healthy work environment increases. All levels in an organization need to be educated so that employees, managers and management will know how to contribute to the organizational health development by themselves and together.

(C) *Intelligent interactive system yields self-help and human interactions on demand – sustainability and scalability.* In this chapter an intelligent, interactive tool with interventions on the individual, group and organizational level is presented. A major advantage with web-based interactive self-help educative measures is *scalability*. The interventions can target large groups of individuals at reasonable costs and the responsibility of using and acting upon the tools is decentralized. A major increase in users will only increase the costs and efforts marginally even if administrative procedures can temporarily increase initially. The *sustainability* is derived from the fact that the individuals are not only provided with self-help and educational measures but also human interactions on demand. When there are signs of ill health or if it has occurred already, the system should include automated and simple ways for employees and managers to be contacted by the occupational healthcare provider (OHP) or HR for instance. If such a request is sent, a contact should be established within 24 h preferably. Another form of human interaction is that the survey results can be utilized for a continuous dialogue about health and the work environment. This dialogue could consist of problem analyses and focus on constructive solutions. It should be held between the managers and employees as well as between management and managers since the problem solving should be a joint effort.

Concluding Remarks

Our approach to organizational health promotion presented in this chapter largely corresponds to statements made by the ENWHP (European Network for Workplace Health Promotion (ENWHP) 2007, 2010) about evidence based strategies for successful workplace health promotion. Similar to our conclusions, they declare that sustainable occupational health promotion is based on multimodal approaches and beneficial outcomes require full commitment from all involved parties. All the staff and all levels in the organization need to be involved and preferably the occupational health promotion aspects should be integrated in all important decisions. They further ascertain that all measures and interventions should be part of a problem-solving cycle that includes needs analysis, setting priorities, planning, implementation and continuous control and evaluation (European Network for Workplace Health Promotion (ENWHP) 2007).

The systematic, sustainable and scalable approach described in the present chapter is a practical application of these principles. Several challenges are present in modern work environments, including increased complexity, globalization, downsizing, rapid changes, high demands and an ageing workforce to mention some. The organizations of today and tomorrow are thus dependent on healthy employees that can perform and be innovative and flexible under these potentially stressful conditions. As the age of retirement will most probably increase in the future, people will stay in the workforce longer, increasing the need to provide sustainable and healthy workplaces. Consequently, it will be more important to integrate organizational health promotion activities as inherent features of working life. It can help employees and organizations to maintain and improve their health, wellbeing and performance. In combination with the documented effects of lowering absenteeism, organizational health promotion may increase organizational profits and thereby making it possible to endure in the competitive economy of today and tomorrow.

Acknowledgements Our deepest gratitude is directed to Jens Pettersson, our outstanding system architect and developer. Thanks to your kind, meticulous and creative efforts together with your immense skills, this system is unique and constantly improving. We would also like to express our deepest and warmest gratitude to our funding bodies throughout the years: Alecta, AFA Försäkring, the European Social Fund and Bliwastiftelsen. Finally, we would like to thank all the users as well as participants and organizations in our studies and projects throughout the years for your commitment, engagement and help in improving the system.

Competing Interests Dan Hasson has commercialized HealthWatch and is owner of the company supplying it together with Jens Pettersson.

References

Aldana, S. G. (2001). Financial impact of health promotion programs: A comprehensive review of the literature [Review]. *American Journal of Health Promotion (AJHP), 15*(5), 296–320.

Aldana, S. G., Merrill, R. M., Price, K., Hardy, A., & Hager, R. (2005). Financial impact of a comprehensive multisite workplace health promotion program [Comparative study]. *Preventive Medicine, 40*(2), 131–137. doi:10.1016/j.ypmed.2004.05.008.

Bailis, D. S., Segall, A., & Chipperfield, J. G. (2003). Two views of self-rated general health status. *Social Science & Medicine. Part A, 56*(2), 203–217.

Brisson, C., Cantin, V., Larocque, B., Vézina, M., Vinet, A., Trudel, L., et al. (2006). Intervention research on work organization and health: Research design and preliminary results on mental health. *Canadian Journal of Community Mental Health (Revue canadienne de santé mentale communautaire), 25*(2), 241–259.

Brooks, A., Hagen, S. E., Sathyanarayanan, S., Schultz, A. B., & Edington, D. W. (2010). Presenteeism: Critical issues [Review]. *Journal of Occupational and Environmental Medicine, 52*(11), 1055–1067. doi:10.1097/JOM.0b013e3181f475cc.

Chapman, L. S. (2005). Meta-evaluation of worksite health promotion economic return studies: 2005 update. *American Journal of Health Promotion (AJHP), 19*(6), 1–11.

European Network for Workplace Health Promotion (ENWHP). (2007). *Luxembourg Declaration on Workplace Health Promotion*. http://www.enwhp.org/fileadmin/rs-dokumente/dateien/Luxembourg_Declaration.pdf

European Network for Workplace Health Promotion (ENWHP). (2010). *The Edinburgh Declaration on the Promotion of Workplace Mental Health and Wellbeing*. http://www.enwhp.org/fileadmin/downloads/8th_Initiative/Edinburgh_Declaration.pdf

Farmer, M. M., & Ferraro, K. F. (1997). Distress and perceived health: Mechanisms of health decline. *Journal of Health and Social Behavior, 38*(3), 298–311.

Goetzel, R. Z., & Pronk, N. P. (2010). Worksite health promotion how much do we really know about what works? *American Journal of Preventive Medicine, 38*(2 Suppl), S223–S225. doi:10.1016/j.amepre.2009.10.032.

Goetzel, R. Z., Shechter, D., Ozminkowski, R. J., Marmet, P. F., Tabrizi, M. J., & Roemer, E. C. (2007). Promising practices in employer health and productivity management efforts: Findings from a benchmarking study [Research Support, U.S. Gov't, P.H.S. Review]. *Journal of Occupational and Environmental Medicine, 49*(2), 111–130. doi:10.1097/JOM.0b013e31802ec6a3.

Goldman, N., Glei, D. A., & Chang, M. C. (2004). The role of clinical risk factors in understanding self-rated health. *Annals of Epidemiology, 14*(1), 49–57.

Gorin, A. A., & Stone, A. A. (2001). Recall biases and cognitive errors in retrospective selfreports: A call for momentary assessments. In A. Baum (Ed.), *Handbook of health psychology* (pp. 405–413). Mahwah/London: Lawrence Erlbaum Associates.

Hasson, D. (2005). *Stress management interventions and predictors of long-term health: Prospectively controlled studies on long-term pain patients and a healthy sample from IT- and media companies* (Digital Comprehensive Summaries of Uppsala dissertations from the Faculty of Medicine). Uppsala: Acta Universitatis Upsaliensis : Univ.-bibl [distributör].

Hasson, D., Anderberg, U. M., Theorell, T., & Arnetz, B. B. (2005). Psychophysiological effects of a web-based stress management system: A prospective, randomized controlled intervention study of IT and media workers [ISRCTN54254861] [Randomized Controlled Trial Research Support, Non-U.S. Gov't]. *BMC Public Health, 5*, 78. doi:10.1186/1471-2458-5-78.

Holte, K. A., Vasseljen, O., & Westgaard, R. H. (2003). Exploring perceived tension as a response to psychosocial work stress. *Scandinavian Journal of Work, Environment & Health, 29*(2), 124–133.

Idler, E. L., & Benyamini, Y. (1997). Self-rated health and mortality: A review of twenty-seven community studies. *Journal of Health and Social Behavior, 38*(1), 21–37.

Kawakami, N., Takao, S., Kobayashi, Y., & Tsutsumi, A. (2006). Effects of web-based supervisor training on job stressors and psychological distress among workers: A workplace-based randomized controlled trial [Randomized Controlled Trial Research Support, Non-U.S. Gov't]. *Journal of Occupational Health, 48*(1), 28–34.

Kypri, K., Saunders, J. B., Williams, S. M., McGee, R. O., Langley, J. D., Cashell-Smith, M. L., et al. (2004). Web-based screening and brief intervention for hazardous drinking: A double-blind randomized controlled trial. *Addiction, 99*(11), 1410–1417. doi:10.1111/j.1360-0443.2004.00847.x.

Lamontagne, A. D., Keegel, T., Louie, A. M., Ostry, A., & Landsbergis, P. A. (2007). A systematic review of the job-stress intervention evaluation literature, 1990–2005. *International Journal of Occupational and Environmental Health, 13*(3), 268–280.

Lindberg, P., & Vingård, E. (2012). Indicators of healthy work environments – A systematic review. *Work: A Journal of Prevention, Assessment and Rehabilitation, 41*, 3032–3038. doi:10.3233/wor-2012-0560-3032.

Lustria, M. L., Cortese, J., Noar, S. M., & Glueckauf, R. L. (2009). Computer-tailored health interventions delivered over the Web: Review and analysis of key components [Review]. *Patient Education and Counseling, 74*(2), 156–173. doi:10.1016/j.pec.2008.08.023.

Martin, E. A. (2010). Concise medical dictionary. New York: Oxford University Press.

Nielsen, K., & Randall, R. (2012). Opening the black box: Presenting a model for evaluating organizational-level interventions. *European Journal of Work and Organizational Psychology*, 1–17.

Oenema, A., Brug, J., & Lechner, L. (2001). Web-based tailored nutrition education: Results of a randomized controlled trial [Clinical Trial Randomized Controlled Trial Research Support, Non-U.S. Gov't]. *Health Education Research, 16*(6), 647–660.

Proper, K. I., de Bruyne, M. C., Hildebrandt, V. H., van der Beek, A. J., Meerding, W. J., & van Mechelen, W. (2004). Costs, benefits and effectiveness of worksite physical activity counseling from the employer's perspective [Clinical Trial Randomized Controlled Trial]. *Scandinavian Journal of Work, Environment & Health, 30*(1), 36–46.

Riedel, J. E., Lynch, W., Baase, C., Hymel, P., & Peterson, K. W. (2001). The effect of disease prevention and health promotion on workplace productivity: A literature review [Review]. *American Journal of Health Promotion (AJHP), 15*(3), 167–191.

Sainfort, F., Karsh, B. T., Booske, B. C., & Smith, M. J. (2001). Applying quality improvement principles to achieve healthy work organizations [Review]. *The Joint Commission Journal on Quality Improvement, 27*(9), 469–483.

Schwartz, S. M., & Riedel, J. (2010). Productivity and health: Best practices for better measures of productivity. *Journal of Occupational and Environmental Medicine, 52*(9), 865–871. doi:10.1097/JOM.0b013e3181ed8686.

Spittaels, H., De Bourdeaudhuij, I., & Vandelanotte, C. (2007). Evaluation of a website-delivered computer-tailored intervention for increasing physical activity in the general population [Controlled Clinical Trial Research Support, Non-U.S. Gov't]. *Preventive Medicine, 44*(3), 209–217. doi:10.1016/j.ypmed.2006.11.010.

Strecher, V. J., McClure, J. B., Alexander, G. L., Chakraborty, B., Nair, V. N., Konkel, J. M., et al. (2008). Web-based smoking-cessation programs: Results of a randomized trial [Randomized Controlled Trial Research Support, N.I.H., Extramural]. *American Journal of Preventive Medicine, 34*(5), 373–381. doi:10.1016/j.amepre.2007.12.024.

von Thiele Schwarz, U., & Hasson, H. (2011). Employee self-rated productivity and objective organizational production levels: Effects of worksite health interventions involving reduced work hours and physical exercise [Randomized Controlled Trial Research Support, Non-U.S. Gov't]. *Journal of Occupational and Environmental Medicine, 53*(8), 838–844. doi:10.1097/JOM.0b013e31822589c2.

Wilder, D. A., Austin, J., & Casella, S. (2009). Applying behavior analysis in organizations: Organizational behavior management. *Psychological Services, 6*(3), 202.

Wilson, M. G., Dejoy, D. M., Vandenberg, R. J., Richardson, H. A., & McGrath, A. L. (2004). Work characteristics and employee health and well-being: Test of a model of healthy work organization. *Journal of Occupational and Organizational Psychology, 77*(4), 565–588. doi:10.1348/0963179042596522.

Zimolong, B., & Elke, G. (2009). Management of work site health-promotion programs: A review. In B.-T. Karsh (Ed.), *Ergonomics and health aspects of work with computers* (Lecture notes in computer science, Vol. 5624, pp. 131–140). Berlin/Heidelberg: Springer.

Chapter 13
The Nature of Change in Organizational Health Interventions: Some Observations and Propositions

Maria Karanika-Murray and Caroline Biron

Abstract Despite an accumulation of knowledge on organizational health interventions, theoretical integration and progress in the area still seems to be slow. This chapter is premised on the need to understand the nature and mechanisms of change in organizational health interventions, which can offer predictions on when change interventions will succeed or fail. To proactively manage change it is important to understand its properties and mechanisms. Indeed, latest research points to the pivotal role of process issues, or the 'how' and 'why' that need to be taken into account when implementing interventions. Here, we expand on this line of work by harvesting current knowledge and harnessing possible properties of change. Specifically, we examine the nature of change in organizational health interventions and the forces, at the fundamental level of the individual, that can facilitate the transition between before and after an intervention, and make some propositions on the possible mechanisms of change in organizational health interventions (i.e. relating to the dimensions, direction, levels, stakeholders, psychosocial mechanisms, and temporal patterns of change). In terms of mechanisms, we suggest a few (including diffusing, sharing, identifying, comparing, influencing, learning), based on well-established psychological theory. Summarizing and building on this knowledge, we offer six propositions on the nature of change in organizational health interventions. As such, we hope to stir discussion and theoretical progress in the area of organizational health interventions.

Keywords Organizational interventions • Health and well-being • Change • Mechanisms • Process evaluation

M. Karanika-Murray (✉)
Division of Psychology, Nottingham Trent University, Nottingham, UK
e-mail: maria.karanika-murray@ntu.ac.uk

C. Biron
Department of Management, Laval University, Quebec City, Canada
e-mail: caroline.biron@fsa.ulaval.ca

G.F. Bauer and G.J. Jenny (eds.), *Salutogenic Organizations and Change: The Concepts Behind Organizational Health Intervention Research*, DOI 10.1007/978-94-007-6470-5_13, © Springer Science+Business Media Dordrecht 2013

Introduction

The Need to Understand Change in Organizational Health Interventions

In the last few years there has been an increasing interest in understanding why and when organizational health interventions fail or succeed, when evaluating such interventions (Biron et al. 2012a; Nielsen et al. 2010). This is understandable, given the large amounts of resources that such interventions absorb, as well as the impact on both individuals' and organizations' health and effectiveness. We wish to add some observations on the nature of change in such interventions. We start with the observation that although this body of work and our understanding of organizational health interventions is growing fast, our knowledge seems to be lacking an understanding of the underlying forces of change; a utilitarian theory of change in organizational health interventions has not been achieved yet. What are the principles that govern how change occurs and what factors can facilitate or inhibit it? What are the possible mechanisms that link causes and effects in organizational health interventions, beyond the content of the intervention? How can an intervention impact change at the multiple levels of individuals, work practices, and organizational structures? Although the context of organizations and the focus of interventions (psychosocial risks, work, individuals, health and well-being) are in a constant process of change, which can make any intervention difficult to implement and outcomes difficult to predict, organizational health intervention theory has typically focused on stability and planned movement between fixed states and almost entirely ignored the issue of how transformations happen and how they persist. Understanding change is part of understanding why and how interventions produce or fail to produce their effects. Such knowledge can bolster the value and possibility of planning, and help to proactively influence the direction and impact of organizational health interventions.

Theories of (Individual, Social and Organizational) Change

There is a distinction between models of organizational intervention (interventions for specific health issues) and theories of change (how individual behavior, for example, changes over time and can be changed) (Connell 1998). A theory of change describes how and why an initiative works (Weiss 1995). Change is the alteration of patterns of behavior, practices, culture, or structure over time. In organizational health interventions, change invariably involves the complex interaction of psychosocial elements (including objective procedures and subjective experiences), job/work design, systems and policies, structure, and the organizational external environment. To understand change we need to ask questions about how change happens and how causes and effects are linked. Essentially, how can changes in psychosocial work characteristics, structures and behaviors (the content of an intervention) impact on employee outcomes (the intended change targets)?

Change is a theme in a range of related fields in the social sciences. At the organizational level, change explains how organizations and their structures undergo large scale transformations. So far, the knowledge from the organizational change literature has rarely been applied to the development and implementation of organizational stress literature because of paradigmatic clashes between the school of thoughts (Heaney 2003; Dawson 1994). Heaney (2003) notes that intervention developers and researchers would benefit from considering organizational change theories when conducting interventions. The reverse is also true – we know for example that in contexts of organizational change, individuals are sensitive to new conditions brought by the change and that negative events produce stronger and longer lasting effects than positive ones (Baumeister et al. 2001). Further, social change is concerned with changes in the structures of social groups or even societies. Unlike behavior change theory (e.g., Prochaska and DiClemente 1986), organizational change theory (e.g., Armenakis and Bedeian 1999; Armenakis and Harris 2009), or social change theory (Vago 1999), organizational health intervention theory has so far failed to explain how change actually happens and the conditions for the impact of an intervention on the desired outcome.

Both organizational and social change, however, have the individual at their core. After all, it is individuals who enact environment, structures and events into existence and action (Weick 1988). At the individual level, change explains the psychosocial mechanisms involved in the uptake and maintenance of attitudes and behaviors (e.g., Prochaska and DiClemente 1986). Beyond that, the concept of enactment provides a direct link between individual processes and the environment (Fiske and Taylor 1991).

Intervention researchers have used insights from psychology to understand the success or failure of interventions. For example, Randall et al. (2009) have suggested that employees' appraisals of an intervention are a key determinant of uptake. Similarly, the concepts of resistance and readiness for change (Holt et al. 2007) evoke the extent of individuals' commitment to the change. Change at the individual level is about individuals making choices such that "the real engine for change in social programs which is the process of differently resourced subjects making choices about the opportunities provided" (Pawson and Tilley 1997, p. 46). In other words, after Weick (1988), change, be it at the individual, organizational or societal levels, is about individuals making sense of and assigning meaning to the events and their environment.

Aim of This Chapter

In this chapter, we attempt to identify specific forces and mechanisms of change and make some propositions towards developing our understanding of change in organizational health interventions. We do not offer a comprehensive theory and do not wish to be prescriptive in our suggestions or exhaustive in our discussion. Rather, we wish to offer some pointers that will hopefully stir discussion and theoretical progress in the area and provide impetus for understanding change in organizational health interventions. We draw from psychology and behavior change and organizational studies but refrain from discussing organizational change; other researchers have successfully done that (Tetrick et al. 2012; Tvedt and Saksvik 2012). After briefly discussing what change is in organizational health interventions, we present some observations and outline some principles about the nature of such change and its possible mechanisms, and discuss what these propositions may mean for intervention research and practice.

Understanding the Nature of Change in Organizational Health Interventions

Organizational Change vs. Organizational Health Interventions

The aim of an organizational health intervention is to impact change in a state by affecting individuals, work systems/practices, and relationships. It is to introduce X in order to impart a change in Y, where X is evaluated by comparing pre- and post-Y. Organizational change and organizational health interventions differ in many respects, primarily in scale and scope. Regardless of the scale at which organizational interventions can be deployed (e.g., introduction new policies across the organization, or changes in job characteristics in one work group) and the target and scope of intervention, they necessarily imply some sort of change. However, in our view, the topic of organizational change is much broader than organizational health interventions; interventions aimed at improving employee health and well-being are a particular type of change. Organizational health interventions necessary imply change (Tvedt et al. 2008, 2009), but not all organizational change actions are aimed at improving employee health or well-being. Yet, as Tetrick et al. (2012) and Tvedt and Saksvik (2012) have shown, organizational change theory can help us to extract principles that can then be applied to developing organizational interventions focusing on specific health issues. Organizational health interventions are paradoxical because they are developed out of a need for change, and by definition imply a group of at-risk employees. If they were not, they would be equivalent to delivering smoking cessation programs to non-smokers (Semmer 2006). Furthermore, because individual and organizational health are interdependent (Quick et al. 1997), organizational health interventions often exert their effects at multiple levels (individual, group, organizational, community) and are experienced by multiple stakeholders (the decision makers as well as those affected by change). Therefore, there is potential for cross-over of effects and unintended consequences at different levels. In addition, organizational health interventions are always planned and intentional, whereas organizational change can also be accidental, developmental, or emergent. Not only that, but because organizations are complex adaptive systems (Schneider and Somers 2006; Karanika-Murray and Cox 2010), attempts to reconfigure work practices or structures for improving individual and organizational health can be difficult and interventions can often have unplanned, diffused, and unintended effects (Baril-Gingras et al. 2012; Tvedt and Saksvik 2012; Biron et al. 2010). Possible unintended consequences or 'side-effects' ought to be understood and taken into account for interventions to succeed. These unintended consequences can be the result of inadequate evidence about causes and effects, unexpected outcomes of intervention implementation, or simply the fact that other initiatives in the organization's life cycle can compete with resources and affect the success of a health intervention (for an example see, Biron et al. 2010). Furthermore, those who make the decisions about resource allocation are typically not those who are affected by these decisions or who are in need of the changes in their work methods or stress and well-being levels. This is nowhere more pronounced than in organizational health interventions, making intervention implementation more challenging. Finally, the two types of change differ in priority. Contrary to other organizational change initiatives, organizational health interventions are rarely the main concern of top management, although this would be highly desirable. They are often ad hoc projects, carried alongside regular business and other organizational initiatives (e.g., restructuring, implementing new production systems) which tend to be considered by top management as a priority, well resourced, and often better planned.

Proximal and Distal Change and Sustainability

Understanding at what level change happens (proximal or distal to the content and target outcome/s) can help to predict how sustainable change is.[1] As highlighted by Biron et al. (2010), organizational interventions are often evaluated in terms of their success in changing health (proximal) outcomes, or performance (distal) outcomes. However, success lies in the eyes of the beholder, in that Biron et al. (2010) reported an implementation failure, whereas the company in which the study was conducted took pride in achieving a 15 % implementation rate, as described in their corporate social responsibility report. Biron et al. (2013, forthcoming) suggest that researchers evaluate proximal changes, instead of only distant criteria. Proximal change could for example consist of increasing levels of readiness for change and participants' perceptions regarding the intervention, or increasing the engagement of stakeholders towards the change process. These early changes could predict the future success of the change process and sustainability of its effects over time, but have rarely been addressed in the intervention literature.

---

[1]We should note that although sustainability should be considered as a criterion for successful change and an important issue for organizational health interventions, sustainability is rarely addressed in research.

Elements of Change in Organizational Health Interventions

Organizational health interventions consider change in individuals' health (broadly defined as physical and psychosocial health and well-being) brought by changes in behaviors, relationships, work configurations, and organizational policies, procedures and structures. To understand how change occurs we harvest knowledge on change from multiple perspectives and discuss six elements of change in organizational health interventions: dimensions of change, levels of change, stakeholders of change, mechanisms of change, and temporal patterns of change.

Dimensions of Change

There are four dimensions that can help to understand change in organizational health interventions. These concern the content (the substance of the intervention), criterion (the outcome of the intervention, what is intended to change), context (internal and external needs, regulations and boundaries) and process (resources and opportunities, the actual implementation) of an intervention. These four dimensions are corroborated by two large and established bodies of work: organizational change and program evaluation theory, albeit in different guises. Specifically, organizational change theory discusses change under context, content and process (Pettigrew 1987; Barnett and Carroll 1995; Armenakis and Bedeian 1999). Equally, program evaluation theory talks about the importance of context, input, process, and product for the success of an intervention (Mertens and Wilson 2012; Stufflebeam 2007). Table 13.1 summarizes these four dimensions and provides definitions adapted to

Table 13.1 Dimensions of change in organizational health interventions

Content of change	The actual substance of the intervention
	Concerning e.g. knowledge and skills, communication, work environment/work design, work schedules, organizational structures
Context of change	The internal and external socio-economic conditions in an organization's environment; the system within which change/interventions operate
	Outer context: the political, economic, social, technological, regulatory and competitive environment; Inner context: organizational culture, structure, policies and processes, political context and power (Pettigrew 1987)
Criterion of change	The outcome/s that an intervention is designed and intended to change
	Invariably, employee health, well-being and productivity
Process of change	The working mechanisms of change/interventions; these focus on how an intervention is implemented and the actions taken to optimize this implementation
	Planned intervention; intentionally implemented

the field from Armenakis and Bedeian (1999), Biron et al. (2012a), Mertens and Wilson (2012), and Pettigrew (1987).

Considering change under these headings provides a clear distinction between 'process' and 'variance' models (Mohr 1982). Process models focus on patterns in events, activities and choice, whereas variance models focus on explanations in terms of relationships among dependent and independent variables (Mohr 1982). Clearly, the former are of use for managing change and for developing sustainable interventions. Unfortunately, variance models have dominated research in the social sciences such that true process theories are rare (Gilbert 1995).

The area of organizational health interventions, however, is only beginning to report such elements and evidence regarding process and contextual issues (Egan et al. 2009; Murta et al. 2007). Conventional intervention theory mainly focuses on content and criterion, but recent developments show that there is much to gain by linking process, context, criterion and content in our research and practice (see Biron et al. 2012a). Because process distinguishes between what changes and how it changes (Pettigrew 1987), the focus on process in organizational health interventions is something of a turning point in the field. Rather than simply comparing the intervention target before and after the intervention, the focus here is on understanding the actual mechanisms that caused the change. This could allow the intervention to be replicated more confidently, adjusted to a different organization, and open the 'black box' of interventions (Nielsen and Randall 2012).

Organizational health intervention theory is currently developing along these four dimensions, and the field is clearly moving towards developing true process models that explain the mechanisms of interventions.

Levels of Change

To a great extent, employee health is related to or reliant on the healthiness of the work group and the organization, in the same way as organizational health relies on the healthiness of the employees and work groups that compose it (Quick et al. 1997). It is the organization's psychosocial environment, which is governed by individuals and their collective, that greatly influences traditional indicators of organizational health such as absenteeism, grievances, and financial viability (Hofmann and Tetrick 2003). As people perceive themselves to be in an organization where their well-being is taken into account, they also report less exposure to psychosocial constraints (Dollard and Bakker 2010). Similarly, "individual action [...] does not occur in a vacuum, nor is it random" (Morgeson and Hofmann 1999, p. 251). Rather, individual action takes place in a broader organizational context which provides the boundaries and opportunities to individuals' attitudes and behaviors (Cappelli and Sherer 1991; Johns 2006). Because of this interdependency between individual and organizational health (Quick et al. 1997), inevitably, a change targeted at one level, may inevitably infer change at another level. It makes sense to take such possible unintended consequences in any planning when developing organizational health interventions.

The fact that organizational health interventions aim to impact change on individual (e.g. well-being) and organizational outcomes (e.g. absence) by implementing organization-focused activities adds an additional complexity. As such, a model of change that explains what changes and how at both the individual and the organizational levels, i.e. a model that works across levels (see Hitt et al. 2007) and explains employees' socially constructed work places and experiences would be useful. Regardless of the starting point, change can have upward or downward effects. For example, changes in management practices and policies will inevitably impact on employees' attitudes and behaviors. Similarly, changes in job specifications across the workgroup can also impact on the workplace climate and work structures.

Effects further afield are also possible. Work organizations are seen as valuable conduits for promoting public health (Egan et al. 2009; Waddell and Burton 2006), such that the effects of organizational health interventions can permeate to fields beyond the organization. As Karanika-Murray and Weyman (2013) note, "we might also speculate a ripple effect, whereby employee behavior change achieved via the workplace may percolate to impact on the health orientations and behaviors of family and kinship members beyond the organization. The workplace thus affords a potentially valuable focus for propagating the realization of key lifestyle public health objectives (Black 2008). However, it offers the opportunity for more than this".

Not only that, but there is evidence that organizational level change will be more likely to succeed if it is supplemented by individual level change (LaMontagne et al. 2007). LaMontagne et al. (2012) highlight the disproportionate emphasis on individual change and the need for organizational-level interventions in order to effectively manage workplace psychosocial health. Interventions to manage employee health should combine actions targeting the individual or worker with actions directed at the organization or work (LaMontagne et al. 2012). Others have also supported a comprehensive or systems approach as being the most effective at protecting and promoting individual and organizational health (also see Mellor et al. 2012). Brun et al. (2008) provide a good example of how an intervention incurred change simultaneously at various levels of the organization, also illustrating that more comprehensive approaches have more chances of success (LaMontagne et al. 2007).

Based on this work, we make the following two propositions:

Proposition 1 *Change at one level (individual or organizational) will inevitably be transmitted to another level*

Proposition 2 *Change at the individual level should be supplemented by change at the organizational level and vice versa*

Stakeholders of Change

Organizational health interventions are typically voluntary, in that they are driven by purposeful and planned efforts by top management to improve employee health, well-being and performance. They can be driven by external factors such as legislation and the enforcement of legal requirements, are often driven by corporate social responsibility, or sometimes instigated as a result of work attitude surveys. Typically, the initiator of change in organizational health interventions is the senior management and its architect the occupational health/well-being team. Each of these actors has different powers and influences which can determine the success or failure of change efforts. These powers are unequally distributed, however, such that senior management involvement has been suggested as a crucial first achievement towards a successful intervention (Cox et al. 2007; Dollard and Bakker 2010; Karanika-Murray et al. 2012b; LaMontagne et al. 2012).

Beyond that first achievement, a change agent that understands the theory and practice of organizational health interventions is essential for overseeing intervention implementation (Cox et al. 2007). Nevertheless, the question remains as to whether organizational health intervention professionals have the power and ability to negotiate the health agenda and the need for change with senior management (Karanika-Murray and Weyman 2013). The capacity of intervention professionals to make a strong case for and demonstrate the value of organizational health interventions can be mitigated by training and guidance on available tools, enabling access to essential resources, and strengthening their role in informing strategic thinking on health priorities (Karanika-Murray and Weyman 2013).

It has also been frequently emphasized that the organizational health interventions, as all change initiatives, require the participation of all employees (Rosskam 2009; Karanika-Murray et al. 2012b). Indeed, participatory approaches are essential for ensuring buy-in or compliance with the intervention, ownership of the new values beliefs and behaviors, and sustainability of an intervention in the long term. Participation has the added advantage of building awareness and teaching skills that can support behavior and attitude change. Here, notions of resistance and readiness for change (Armenakis et al. 2007; Randall et al. 2009; Armenakis and Harris 2009) are important preparatory steps before the actual implementation of an intervention.

Furthermore, the politics of change is one of the three groups of determinants used by Dawson (1994) to explain the process of organizational change. The politics of change refers to all the stakeholders, be they directly involved or remotely influencing the change process. In terms of the politics of change and the roles of various stakeholders, Biron et al. (2012b) highlight the importance of external resources and line managers are triggers by which the intervention has an effect on outcomes. Using realistic evaluation theory (Pawson and Tilley 1997), they suggest that during an intervention research, the context provided by the research offers an opportunity for managers to develop and implement interventions while being supported by the researchers, the external consultant, and senior management. This opportunity involves resources which would not be otherwise available. In this context, the support given by the external consultants and the researchers acted as a mechanism which increased the level of ownership of line managers and employee regarding the intervention. Interventions are not just magic recipes that can be replicated from one context to another (Pawson and Tilley 1997). Interventions sometimes provide opportunities and resources to participants who then have the choice of using them or not.

Ultimately, as mentioned earlier, in organizational settings often the agents who take the decisions are different to the actors who are affected by these changes. The implementers and the recipients of organizational interventions are often different groups of stakeholders (Schrader-Frechette 1998). Although they rarely make the decisions about intervention strategy and allocation of resources, employees are expected to implement the change. They are therefore active actors rather than passive recipients of change. Although employee participation is important for the success of the intervention, in organizational settings it is the senior management that has the ultimate power to control resources and make decisions on the allocation of these resources and on intervention priorities (Cox et al. 2007).

On the basis of this literature, we make the following proposition:

Proposition 3 *All stakeholders, including those targeted by an organizational health intervention, should be actively involved in decisions regarding and implementation of the intervention*

Psychosocial Mechanisms of Change

A good change theory must specify plausible mechanisms that explain the way that the intervention content exerts its impact, account for the difference before and after intervention implementation, and essentially explain and establish causation. Because individual behavior is the most elementary unit of analysis in any social system (Parsons 1951; Frese and Zapf 1994) and in organizational health intervention, the mechanisms described below have the individual as their focus; they describe change at the attitudinal and behavioral rather than the structural and organizational levels. Because organizational health interventions concern individuals, change here is about attitudes, values, and behaviors, regardless of the ultimate target outcome of the intervention. In other words, whether interventions aim to modify individuals' attitudes and behaviors (i.e. secondary or tertiary prevention) or eliminate exposure to risks by modifying work-related aspects (i.e. primary prevention), change involves individuals who make decisions, who participate and engage in the change process, and who are affected by it. In organizational settings, because individuals are nested within work groups (Bamberger 2008), it is also necessary to explain the mechanisms of transmission of change among individuals or work groups.

Here we briefly discuss six psychosocial mechanisms that can explain how an intervention can exert its impact on individuals and workgroups: diffusing, sharing, identifying, comparing, influencing, and learning.

Diffusion, Contagion, Spillover Effects

A group of mechanisms of diffusion, contagion and spillover have been clearly articulated in the work-life balance literature. Diffusion of 'memes', the mental analogue of a gene to describe ideas and beliefs, and also emotional states and behaviors is not uncommon in workplaces where individuals interact and communicate on a daily basis. Diffusion or cross-over can be facilitated via several conditions, including the frequency of interactions, empathy, susceptibility to contagion, and similarity (Bakker and Demerouti 2009).

Also important is the more specific concept of emotional contagion. To an extent, individuals' emotions are determined by the emotions of those with whom they interact (Parkinson 1995). What is transmitted is poor affective well-being (Daniels and Guppy 1997) but also positive motivational states. The process of emotional contagion is influenced by the valence of the emotion and the energy by which the emotion is expressed (Barsade 2002).

In the context of organizational health interventions, these mechanisms should be an essential part of developing interventions to take into account of possible diffusion, contagion, or spillover of the effects of an intervention. This can include intended diffusion of positive effects from one work group to another, or even unintended spillover of effects from the intervention to the control group if there is communication between the two. It may be necessary, for example, to select the agents of change very carefully, as those individuals who, through their strong connections in the workgroup, can facilitate diffusion of intervention effects among colleagues.

Shared Meaning

Over time, and via interactions among individuals, the workplace and organizational culture help to convey a sense of identity and a sense of shared meaning among individuals (Deal and Kennedy 1982). Shared meaning is essentially the common thread that captures Pettigrew's (1979) conceptualization of organizational culture as a "family of concepts" (symbols, language, ideologies, beliefs, rituals, and myths) (Harris and Ogbonna 1999). It is through shared meanings that organizational culture originates, and specifically via individuals' interaction, negotiation and learning that help to develop shared norms, values and beliefs (Schein 2004). Indeed, the symbolic-interpretative perspective of organizational culture suggests that through shared symbols and interaction, individuals create meaning and define the organizational reality within which they react (Schultz 1995). It is these meanings that give shape and direction to individuals' experiences (Pettigrew 1979).

In the context of organizational health interventions, it may be possible or needed to create, through rhetoric and action, shared meaning and therefore a drive for change (Dutta-Bergman 2003). Such a mechanism of change can bolster the benefits of participatory approaches and generate ownership of the change among employees whose working lives are impacted by the intervention and among managers who are often responsible for implementing the interventions within their teams or departments (Biron et al. 2010).

Social Identity

The strength of one's identification with their work group (Ashforth and Mael 1989) can determine the degree to which they internalize the group's values and goals. Social identity theory offers two concepts to organizational health interventions: social groups are important to individuals and help them define their personal identity (self-categorization), and people tend to categorize others such that within group differences are minimized and between group differences maximized (social identification) (Bartunek et al. 1992; Fiske and Taylor 1991; Tajfel 1982). Social identity provides an intrinsic motivational component that can influence individuals to act in line with group membership and to actively engage in the group's activities. It is therefore likely that the degree to which an individual accepts and participated in an intervention will depend on the strength of their identification with their workgroup (the group that is affected by the intervention): the change itself and the way it is implemented can be strongly influenced by group membership and social identity (Karanika-Murray et al. 2012a).

In practice and in the context of organizational health interventions, a number of possible prerequisites for successful interventions can be proposed, including designing interventions in accordance with the group's identity, goals and values; recruiting influential individuals within the group as intervention champions; strengthening identification with the leader or perceptions of the leader as congruent with the group's identity; or adapting an intervention as it is being implemented to assimilate changes in group differences and social identification.

Social Comparison Processes

Another mechanism that could potentially explain the effects of organizational health interventions is provided by social comparison theory. Social comparison theory proposes that individuals compare themselves to others, and in this case, others' psychological well-being (Buunk and Hoorens 1992). Comparisons to others with better well-being act as role models, whereas comparisons to others with poorer well-being can help to boost the individual's self-esteem. As such, the referent serves to consolidate the individual's views and attitudes and even motivation to act, in this way possibly helping to boost participation in an intervention.

Based on the notion of comparison is equity theory (Adams 1965), but in this case comparison arises from a process of investment or exchange of resources. Equity theory suggests that individuals seek reciprocity in social relationships; they expect their investments and gains from a relationship should be proportional to the investments and gains of the other party in the relationship, or that their gains should be proportional to their investments (Pritchard 1969). The notion of equity has been referred to as social exchange, organizational justice (Cropanzano et al. 2001), effort-reward imbalance (Siegrist 1996), which essentially describe the same construct (Petrou et al. 2011). Perceptions of inequity have been associated with negative outcomes including burnout, health complaints and sickness absence (Buunk and Schaufeli 1993; Taris et al. 2002), reduced commitment (Taris et al. 2004), turnover intentions (Geurts et al. 1999) and counterproductive work behavior (Skarlicki and Folger 1997).

In relation to interventions, an example of applying equity theory relates to situations where, for example, a control group exists of which participants in the intervention group area aware of. Social comparison processes could be intentionally used to boost participation and ownership of an intervention, essential elements for success. It may also be possible for the intervention implementers to raise awareness of the organization's commitment and investment in employee welfare in order to bolster comparison and reciprocity and therefore participation in the intervention.

Interpersonal Influence

One of the main characteristics of individuals working together is communication, interaction, and work group interdependence which can increase the number of connections between individuals (Wageman 2001). Interpersonal influence here is an important mechanism by which intervention effects can be transmitted and maintained. Social or intra-organizational influence mechanisms (Kipnis et al. 1980) convey meaning, such that people who work together in the same workplace more than often share the same experiences, views, attitudes, and even behaviors. These shared or collective experiences provide a type of context and can be as influential as individuals' personal experiences. Where the product of interpersonal influence is shared among individuals working together, interpersonal influence can also shape organizational culture.

Intervention researchers could find a fertile field in the laws of interpersonal influence and dimensions of intra-organizational influence (Cialdini 2001; Kipnis et al. 1980) for developing interventions, not least to mention the roles of change agents and intervention stakeholders.

Social Learning Theory

Social learning theory describes the process of human learning and behavior change as a function of personal (e.g., instincts, drives, traits) and environmental factors (e.g., situational influences) (Bandura 1986; Pajares 1996). Learning and behavior change depend on a number of variables which include an individual's self-efficacy, outcome expectations relating to the consequences of a behavior, self-control, ability for emotional coping, behavioral reinforcements, and potential for observational learning. In addition, one's self-efficacy or beliefs concerning their competence in a specific behavior, are critical for their choice of behavior, course of action, performance and persistence in actions relating to this behavior (Anderson and Betz 2001), as well as their emotional reactions to these actions (Pajares 1996).

Self-efficacy beliefs are strongly linked to an individual's engagement in a specific action or intervention, specifically where the intervention concerns changing individuals' behaviors and attitudes, for example participation and compliance with new work procedures.

Intervention success is governed by the mechanics of change concerning behavioral, attitudinal and social-relational elements. Diffusion, sharing, identification, comparison, influence, and learning are only a few possible psychosocial mechanisms by which change in organizational health interventions, at the fundamental level of the individual, can take place. They can explain change in individuals, but also within and across work groups, and upward in the organization. They can potentially help to develop a common language among workgroups, commitment and ownership of the intervention, transmitting effects within and between teams, and facilitating mutual learning. Implicitly more than explicitly, such mechanisms are taken into account in the practice of intervention design and implementation. More explicitly though, they can be viewed as frames of reference that allow intervention theory to link causes and effects. Based on the above, we make the following proposition:

Proposition 4   *Understanding how and why things change involves an understanding of the psychosocial mechanisms of change within individuals and workgroups*

Maturity for and Temporal Patterns of Change

Interventions are about change and understanding change is also about the dynamic process of moving from one configuration to another. Here, considering time is about understanding not only when the most fertile time is to initiate change, but also the temporal patterns of change.

With regards to timing the introduction of an intervention, many researchers have stressed that often simultaneous interventions may compete for resources and therefore jeopardize the success of the intervention (e.g. Cox et al. 2007). Saksvik et al. (2007) note that the healthiness of the change process includes a level of maturity of the organization and its culture. Organizational maturity is as important here as is individuals' readiness for change. A certain level of organizational maturity is essential not only for implementing interventions but also for integrating interventions into normal business practice (European Agency for Safety & Health at Work 2010; Karanika-Murray et al. 2012b). Such maturity requires the ability to detect obstacles early, to initiate and implement corrective action and review, to redefine the way things work, and to learn from failure. Biron et al. (2010) reflects how managers were not feeling the need for change, as the qualitative data in that intervention suggested. Indeed, most participants perceived no need for a stress risk assessment tool, and most thought that stress was only a managerial problem, not an employee one. They did not perceive the need to conduct a risk assessment, therefore no intervention was implemented following the risk assessment that some conducted.

Proposition 5 *Organizational maturity can affect intervention implementation*

It is also important to understand the temporal pattern of change, in order to manage its course, inject resources and, in general, to know when to act and when to let things take their course. For example, behavior change models such as Prochaska and DiClemente's (1986) suggest that change is cyclical rather than linear, such that relapses or failures to convert to the desired behavior are taken into account. The implementation of organizational health interventions ends with an evaluation of whether the desired outcome that the intervention intended to change was achieved. Often, it may be necessary to reinforce change with repetition and awareness-raising in order to achieve sustainable outcomes.

Furthermore, as the organizational change literature suggests, change in organizational health interventions can be gradual or sudden, evolutionary or revolutionary, transactional or transformational. Where change concerns shifts in the organization's structure, processes, or environmental conditions, it can be sudden and discontinuous (Kimberly and Bouchikhi 1995) rather than incremental and continuous (Weick and Quinn 1999). Such tipping points describe situations where small incremental changes can lead to sudden and unexpected change at a grander level (Gladwell 1996). Through the mechanisms of diffusion, emotional contagion and interpersonal influence, this principle can be used successfully when implementing interventions to 'spread' change from the small to a larger scale.

Furthermore, for health to be truly integrated into normal business practice and its effects ingrained and therefore sustained, it is important that change has both a transformational and a transactional hue. As such, transformational change concerns alterations that "demand entirely new sets of behavior patterns from organizational members" (e.g. mission and strategy, leadership, and organizational culture) (Burke and Litwin 1992). On the contrary, transactional change is about change in organizational factors (structure, management practices, systems, work unit climate, task and individual skills, motivation, individual needs and values; Dutta-Bergman 2003). In the context of organizational change interventions, change is determined by the predominance of transformational over transactional factors and relates to how deeply ingrained change needs to be. For an intervention to have deep and lasting effects, change ought to be primarily transformational but supported by transactional elements.

Conclusions

Organizational health intervention theory should be predictive as well as pragmatic and utilitarian. Being able to explain how and why things change can allow us to better predict and manage both the implementation and outcomes of organizational health interventions, rather than rely on post-hoc analyses of unexpected outcomes and failed interventions (e.g., Aust et al. 2010; Biron et al. 2010; Dahl-Jørgensen and Saksvik 2005; Mikkelsen and Saksvik 1998). Understanding the conditions for successful and sustainable change can help to channel human, time, and monetary resources where they can make the most impact to individual and organizational health and well-being. We hope that researchers and practitioners will find ways to incorporate these observations and propositions into the design and implementation of organizational health interventions.

References

Adams, J. S. (1965). Inequity in social exchange. In L. Berkowitz (Ed.), *Advances in experimental social psychology* (Vol. 2, pp. 267–299). New York: Academic.

Anderson, S. L., & Betz, N. E. (2001). Sources of social self-efficacy expectations: Their measurement and relation to career development. *Journal of Vocational Behavior, 58*(1), 98–117.

Armenakis, A. A., & Bedeian, A. G. (1999). Organizational change: A review of theory and research in the 1990s. *Journal of Management, 25*(3), 293–315.

Armenakis, A. A., & Harris, S. G. (2009). Reflections: Our journey in organizational change research and practice. *Journal of Change Management, 9*(2), 127–142. doi:10.1080/14697010902879079.

Armenakis, A. A., Bernerth, J. B., Pitts, J. P., & Walker, H. J. (2007). Organizational change recipients' beliefs scale: Development of an assessment instrument. *The Journal of Applied Behavioral Science, 43*(4), 481–505. doi:10.1177/0021886307303654.

Ashforth, B. E., & Mael, F. (1989). Social identity theory and the organization. *Academy of Management Review, 14*(1), 20–39. http://www.jstor.org/stable/258189

Aust, B., Rugulies, R., Finken, A., & Jensen, C. (2010). When workplace interventions lead to negative effects: Leaning from failures. *Scandinavian Journal of Public Health, 38*, 106–119.

Bakker, A. B., & Demerouti, E. (2009). The crossover of work engagement between working couples: A closer look at the role of empathy. *Journal of Managerial Psychology, 24*, 220–236.

Bamberger, P. (2008). Beyond contextualization: Using context theories to narrow the micro-macro gap in management research. *Academy of Management Journal, 51*, 839–846.

Bandura, A. (1986). *Social foundations of thought and action: A social cognitive theory.* Englewood Cliffs: Prentice-Hall.

Baril-Gingras, G., Bellemare, M., & Brisson, C. (2012). How can qualitative studies help explain the role of context and process of interventions on occupational safety and health and on mental health at work? In C. Biron, M. Karanika-Murray, & C. L. Cooper (Eds.), *Organizational stress and well-being interventions: Addressing process and context* (pp. 135–162). London: Routledge.

Barnett, W. P., & Carroll, G. R. (1995). Modeling internal organizational-change. *Annual Review of Sociology, 21*, 217–236.

Barsade, S. G. (2002). The ripple effect: Emotional contagion and its influence on group behavior. *Administrative Science Quarterly, 47*(4), 644–675.

Bartunek, J. M., Lacey, C. A., & Wood, D. R. (1992). Social cognition in organizational change: An insider-outsider approach. *The Journal of Applied Behavioral Science, 28*(2), 204–233.

Baumeister, R. F., Bratslavsky, E., Finkenauer, C., & Vohs, K. D. (2001). Bad is stronger than good. *Review of General Psychology, 5*(4), 323–370.

Biron, C., Gatrell, C., & Cooper, C. L. (2010). Autopsy of a failure: Evaluating process and contextual issues in an organizational-level work stress intervention. *International Journal of Stress Management, 17*(2), 135–158.

Biron, C., Karanika-Murray, M., & Cooper, C. L. (Eds.). (2012a). *Improving organizational interventions for stress and well-being: Addressing process and context*. London: Routledge.

Biron, C., Karanika-Murray, M., & Cooper, C. L. (2012b). What works, for whom, in which context? Researching organizational interventions on psychosocial risks using realistic evaluation principles. In C. Biron, M. Karanika-Murray, & C. L. Cooper (Eds.), *Improving organizational interventions for stress and well-being: Addressing process and context* (pp. 163–183). London: Routledge.

Biron, C., & Karanika-Murray, M. (2013, forthcoming). Process evaluation for organizational stress and well-being interventions: Implications for theory, method, and practice. *International Journal of Stress Management* (Special issue).

Black, C. (2008). *Working for a healthier tomorrow*. London: TSO.

Brun, J. -P., Biron, C., & Ivers, H. (2008). *Strategic approach to preventing occupational stress* (R-577). Québec: Institut de recherche Robert-Sauvé en santé et en sécurité du travail.

Burke, W. W., & Litwin, G. H. (1992). A causal model of organizational performance and change. *Journal of Management, 18*(3), 523–545.

Buunk, B. P., & Hoorens, V. (1992). Social support and stress: The role of social comparison and social exchange processes. *British Journal of Clinical Psychology, 31*, 445–457.

Buunk, B. P., & Schaufeli, W. B. (1993). Burnout: A perspective from social comparison theory. In W. B. Schaufeli, C. Maslach, & T. Marek (Eds.), *Professional burnout: Recent developments in theory and research* (pp. 53–69). London: Taylor & Francis.

Cappelli, P., & Sherer, P. D. (1991). The missing role of context in OB: The need for a meso-level approach. *Research in Organizational Behavior, 13*, 55–110.

Cialdini, R. B. (2001). The science of persuasion. *Scientific American, 284*, 76–81.

Connell, R. (1998). Interpreting historical change: Comments on Toews and Zolberg. *Theory and Society, 27*(4), 597–598.

Cox, T., Karanika, M., Griffiths, A., & Houdmont, J. (2007). Evaluating organisational-level work stress interventions: Beyond traditional methods. *Work and Stress, 21*(4), 348–362. doi:10.1080/02678370701760757.

Cropanzano, R., Rupp, D. E., Mohler, C. J., & Schminke, M. (2001). Three roads to organizational justice. In G. Ferris (Ed.), *Research in personnel and human resources management* (Vol. 20, pp. 1–113). Greenwich: JAI Press.

Dahl-Jørgensen, C., & Saksvik, P. Ø. (2005). The impact of two organizational interventions on the health of service sector workers. *International Journal of Health Services, 35*(3), 529–549.

Daniels, K., & Guppy, A. (1997). Stressors, locus of control, and social support as consequences of affective psychological well-being. *Journal of Occupational Health Psychology, 2*(2), 156–174.

Dawson, P. (1994). *Organizational change: A processual approach*. London: Paul Chapman/Sage.

Deal, T. E., & Kennedy, A. A. (1982). *Corporate cultures the rites and rituals of corporate life*. Reading: Addison-Wesley.

Dollard, M. F., & Bakker, A. B. (2010). Psychosocial safety climate as a precursor to conducive work environments, psychological health problems, and employee engagement. *Journal of Occupational and Organizational Psychology, 83*(3), 579–599. doi:10.1348/096317909x470690.

Dutta-Bergman, M. (2003). The linear interaction model of personality effects in health communication. *Health Communication, 15*, 101–115.

Egan, M., Bambra, C., Petticrew, M., & Whitehead, M. (2009). Reviewing evidence on complex social interventions: Appraising implementation in systematic reviews of the health effects of organisational-level workplace interventions. *Journal of Epidemiology and Community Health, 63*(1), 4–11. doi:10.1136/jech.2007.071233.

European Agency for Safety & Health at Work. (2010). *Mainstreaming occupational safety and health into business management*. Luxembourg: Office for Official Publications of the European Communities.

Fiske, S. T., & Taylor, S. E. (1991). *Social cognition* (2nd ed.). New York: McGraw-Hill.

Frese, M., & Zapf, D. (1994). Action as the core of work psychology: A German approach. In H. C. Triandis, M. D. Dunnette, & L. M. Hough (Eds.), *Handbook of industrial and organizational psychology* (Vol. 4, pp. 271–340). Palo Alto: Consulting Psychologists Press.

Geurts, S. A., Schaufeli, W. B., & Rutte, C. G. (1999). Absenteeism, turnover intention and inequity in the employment relationship. *Work and Stress, 13*(3), 253–267.

Gilbert, M. (1995). *Technological change as a knowledge transfer process*. Ph.D. thesis, Cranfield University.

Gladwell, M. (1996, June 3). The tipping point. *The New Yorker*, pp. 32–38.

Harris, L. C., & Ogbonna, E. (1999). Developing a market oriented culture: A critical evaluation. *Journal of Management Studies, 36*(2), 177–196.

Heaney, C. A. (2003). Worksite health interventions: Targets for change and strategies for attaining them. In J. C. Quick & L. E. Tetris (Eds.), *Handbook of occupational health psychology*. Washington, DC: American Psychological Association.

Hitt, M. A., Beamish, P. W., Jackson, S. E., & Mathieu, J. E. (2007). Building theoretical and empirical bridges across levels: Multilevel research in management. *Academy of Management Journal, 50*(6), 1385–1399.

Hofmann, D. A., & Tetrick, L. E. (2003). The etiology of the concept of health: Implications for "organizing" individual and organizational health. In D. A. Hofmann & L. E. Tetrick (Eds.), *Health and safety in organizations: A multilevel perspective* (pp. 1–26). San Francisco: Jossey-Bass.

Holt, D. T., Armenakis, A. A., Feild, H. S., & Harris, S. G. (2007). Readiness for organizational change: The systematic development of a scale. *The Journal of Applied Behavioral Science, 43*(2), 232–255.

Johns, G. (2006). The essential impact of context on organizational behavior. *Academy of Management Review, 31*, 386–408.

Karanika-Murray, M., & Cox, T. (2010). The use of artificial neural networks and multiple linear regression in modeling work-health relationships: Translating theory into analytical practice. *European Journal of Work & Organisational Psychology, 19*(4), 461–486. doi:10.1080/13594320902995916.

Karanika-Murray, M., Biron, C., & Randall, R. (2012a, June). *When change interventions succeed: A social identification perspective*. Paper presented at the 3rd Institute of Work Psychology conference, Sheffield, UK.

Karanika-Murray, M., Biron, C., & Cooper, C. L. (2012b). Distilling the elements of successful organizational intervention implementation. In C. Biron, M. Karanika-Murray, & C. L. Cooper (Eds.), *Organizational stress and well-being interventions: Addressing process and context* (pp. 353–361). London: Routledge.

Karanika-Murray, M., & Weyman, A. (2013). Optimising workplace interventions for health and wellbeing: A commentary on the limitations of the public health perspective within the workplace health arena. *International Journal of Workplace Health Management, 6*(2), 104–117.

Kimberly, J. R., & Bouchikhi, H. (1995). The dynamics of organizational development and change: How the past shapes the present and constrains the future. *Organization Science, 6*(1), 9–18.

Kipnis, D., Schmidt, S. M., & Wilkinson, I. (1980). Intraorganisational influence tactics: Explorations in getting ones way. *Journal of Applied Psychology, 65*, 440–452.

LaMontagne, A. D., Keegel, T., Louie, A. M., Ostry, A., & Landbergis, P. A. (2007). A systematic review of the job-stress intervention evaluation literature, 1990–2005. *International Journal of Occupational and Environmental Health, 13*, 268–280.

LaMontagne, A. D., Noblet, A. J., & Landsbergis, P. A. (2012). Intervention development and implementation: Understanding and addressing barriers to organisational-level interventions. In C. Biron, M. Karanika-Murray, & C. L. Cooper (Eds.), *Improving organizational interventions for stress and well-being: Addressing process and context* (pp. 21–38). London: Routledge.

Mellor, N., Karanika-Murray, M., & Waite, E. (2012). Taking a multi-faceted, multi-level, and integrated perspective for addressing psychosocial issues at the workplace. In C. Biron, M. Karanika-Murray, & C. L. Cooper (Eds.), *Improving organizational interventions for stress and well-being: Addressing process and context* (pp. 39–58). London: Routledge.

Mertens, D. M., & Wilson, A. T. (2012). *Program evaluation theory and practice: A comprehensive guide*. New York: The Guilford Press.

Mikkelsen, A., & Saksvik, P. Ø. (1998). Learning from parallel organizational development efforts in two public sector settings. *Review of Public Personnel Administration, 2,* 5–22.

Mohr, M. (1982). *Explaining organizational behavior*. San Francisco: Jossey-Bass.

Morgeson, F. P., & Hofmann, D. A. (1999). The structure and function of collective constructs: Implications for multilevel research and theory development. *Academy of Management Review, 24*(2), 249–265.

Murta, S. G., Sanderson, K., & Oldenburgh, B. (2007). Process evaluation in occupational stress management programs: A systematic review. *American Journal of Health Promotion, 21*(4), 248–254.

Nielsen, K., & Randall, R. (2012). Opening the black box: A framework for evaluating organizational-level occupational health interventions. *European Journal of Work & Organizational Psychology*. doi:10.1080/1359432X.2012.690556.

Nielsen, K., Taris, T. W., & Cox, T. (2010). The future of organizational interventions: Addressing the challenges of today's organizations. *Work and Stress, 24*(3), 219–233.

Pajares, F. (1996). Self-efficacy beliefs in academic settings. *Review of Educational Research, 66*(4), 543–578.

Parkinson, B. (1995). *Ideas and realities of emotion*. London: Routledge.

Parsons, T. (1951). *The social system*. New York: Free Press.

Pawson, R., & Tilley, N. (1997). *Realistic evaluation*. London: Sage.

Petrou, P., Kouvonen, A., & Karanika-Murray, M. (2011). Social exchange at work and emotional exhaustion: The role of personality. *Journal of Applied Social Psychology, 41*(9), 2165–2199.

Pettigrew, A. M. (1979). On studying organizational cultures. *Administrative Science Quarterly, 24,* 570–581.

Pettigrew, A. M. (1987). Context and action in the transformation of the firm. *Journal of Management Studies, 24*(6), 649–670.

Pritchard, R. D. (1969). Equity theory: A review and critique. *Organizational Behaviour and Human Performance, 4,* 176–211.

Prochaska, J. Q., & DiClemente, C. C. (1986). Toward a comprehensive model of change. In W. R. Miller & N. Heather (Eds.), *Treating addictive behaviors: Processes of change* (pp. 3–27). New York: Plenum Press.

Quick, J. C., Quick, J. D., Nelson, D. L., & Hurrell, J. J., Jr. (1997). *Preventive stress management in organizations*. Washington, DC: American Psychological Association.

Randall, R., Nielsen, K., & Tvedt, S. D. (2009). The development of five scales to measure employees' appraisals of organizational-level stress management interventions. *Work and Stress, 23*(1), 1.

Rosskam, E. (2009). Using participatory actin research methodology to improve worker health. In P. Schnall, M. Dobson, & E. Rosskam (Eds.), *Unhealthy work: Causes, consequences, cures* (pp. 211–229). Amityville: Baywood.

Saksvik, P. O., Tvedt, S. D., Nytro, K., Andersen, G. R., Andersen, T. K., Buvik, M. P., & Torvatn, H. (2007). Developing criteria for healthy organizational change. *Work and Stress, 21*(3), 243–263.

Schein, E. H. (2004). *Organizational culture and leadership*. New York: Wiley.

Schneider, M., & Somers, M. (2006). Organizations as complex adaptive systems: Implications of complexity theory for leadership research. *The Leadership Quarterly, 17*(4), 351–365.

Schultz, M. (1995). *On studying organizational cultures*. Berlin: Walter de Gruyter.

Schrader-Frechette, K. S. (1998). *Risk and rationality: Philosophical foundations for populist reforms*. Berkeley: University of California Press.

Semmer, N. K. (2006). Job stress interventions and the organization of work. *Scandinavian Journal of Work and Environmental Health, 32*(6, special issue), 515–527.

Siegrist, J. (1996). Adverse health effects of high-effort/low-reward conditions. *Journal of Occupational Health Psychology, 1*(1), 27–41.

Skarlicki, D. P., & Folger, R. (1997). Retaliation in the workplace: The roles of distributive, procedural, and interactional justice. *Journal of Applied Psychology, 82*(3), 434–443.

Stufflebeam, D. L. (2007). *Strategies for institutionalizing evaluation: Revisited* (Occasional paper series #18). Kalamazoo: Western Michigan.

Tajfel, H. (1982). Social psychology of intergroup relations. *Annual Review of Psychology, 33*, 1–39. doi:10.1146/annurev.ps.33.020182.000245.

Taris, T. W., Kalimo, R., & Schaufeli, W. B. (2002). Inequity at work: Its measurement and association with worker health. *Work and Stress, 16*(4), 287–301.

Taris, T. W., Van Horn, J. E., Schaufeli, W. B., & Schreurs, P. J. G. (2004). Inequity, burnout and psychological withdrawal among teachers: A dynamic exchange model. *Anxiety, Stress, and Coping, 17*(1), 103–122.

Tetrick, L. E., Quick, J. C., & Gilmore, P. L. (2012). Research in organizational interventions to improve well-being: Perspectives on organizational change and development. In C. Biron, M. Karanika-Murray, & C. L. Cooper (Eds.), *Organizational stress and well-being interventions: Addressing process and context* (pp. 59–76). London: Routledge.

Tvedt, S. D., & Saksvik, P. Ø. (2012). Perspectives on the intervention process as a special case of organizational change. In C. Biron, M. Karanika-Murray, & C. L. Cooper (Eds.), *Organizational stress and well-being interventions: Addressing process and context* (pp. 102–119). London: Psychology Press/Taylor & Francis Group.

Tvedt, S. D., Saksvik, P. Ø., & Nytrø, K. (2008). *Organizational change and employee health.* Paper presented at the 7th APA-NIOSH-SOHP international conference on occupational stress and health, Washington, DC.

Tvedt, S. D., Saksvik, P. Ø., & Nytrø, K. (2009). Does change process healthiness reduce the negative effects of organizational change on the psychosocial work environment? *Work and Stress, 23*, 80–98.

Vago, S. (1999). Strategies of change. In *Social change* (4th ed., pp. 332–372). Englewood Cliffs: Prentice Hall.

Waddell, G., & Burton, A. K. (2006). *Is work good for your health and well-being?* London: TSO.

Wageman, R. (2001). How leaders foster self-managing team effectiveness: Design choices versus hands-on coaching. *Organization Science, 12*(5), 559–577.

Weick, K. E. (1988). Enacted sensemaking in crisis situations. *Journal of Management Studies, 25*(4), 305–317.

Weick, K. E., & Quinn, R. E. (1999). Organizational change and development. *Annual Review of Psychology, 50*, 361–386.

Weiss, C. H. (1995). Nothing as practical as good theory: Exploring theory-based evaluation for comprehensive community initiatives for children and families. In J. P. Connell, A. C. Kubisch, L. B. Schorr, & C. H. Weiss (Eds.), *New approaches to evaluating community initiatives: Concepts, methods, and contexts* (pp. 65–92). Washington, DC: Aspen Institute.

Chapter 14
Process Monitoring in Intervention Research: A 'Dashboard' with Six Dimensions

Raymond Randall

Abstract The increased interest in process evaluation as part of intervention research is leading to a much stronger understanding of the reasons behind inconsistent intervention outcomes. Variables such as employee participation, line manager attitudes and actions, pre-intervention working conditions and the quality of pre-intervention risk assessment are among the many factors that have been identified as being linked to intervention outcomes. In this research, process and context evaluation data are usually collected at the same time as intervention outcome data. Those delivering and receiving interventions in organizations may also benefit from access to this information about the quality of intervention processes and the impact of contexts *before* and *during* intervention activities. Such information could then be used to anticipate and manage implementation problems or to shape modifications to the intervention activities to protect and enhance their impact. In this chapter, the feasibility of measuring process and context concurrent to intervention activities will be examined. I will discuss how the assessment of some potentially important process and contextual factors can be better utilized as formative evaluation data (i.e. a 'dashboard') to monitor intervention activities and shape adaptive interventions. The type of data collection required (and its timing and frequency) and the ways in which process monitoring data could be used to manage intervention activities are also discussed.

Keywords Intervention • Monitoring process • Context evaluation

R. Randall (✉)
School of Business and Economics, Loughborough University, Loughborough, UK
e-mail: R.Randall@lboro.ac.uk

G.F. Bauer and G.J. Jenny (eds.), *Salutogenic Organizations and Change:*
The Concepts Behind Organizational Health Intervention Research,
DOI 10.1007/978-94-007-6470-5_14, © Springer Science+Business Media Dordrecht 2013

Introduction: The Nature of Organizational Interventions

The recent rapid growth in process and context evaluation has highlighted the wide range of issues that need to be considered when evaluating the outcomes and effectiveness of organizational-level interventions. These interventions are usually delivered as changes to the design, organization and management of work. Implementing these changes is a process that includes several stages of activity, many of which can include various forms of employee participation. To begin with, some form of problem-analysis is often completed before intervention planning activities begin. The implementation of the resulting plans tends to involve multiple stakeholders (e.g. managers, consultants, individual employees) in numerous different specific intervention activities that take place over a long period. These processes can also take place across different organizational contexts (e.g. in different worksites or different work teams). Currently, there are few comprehensive and integrative models of intervention processes and contexts that identify these factors, but some preliminary frameworks do exist (Murta et al. 2007; Nielsen and Randall 2012b; Tvedt et al. 2009). These frameworks commonly include factors such: as management attitudes to the intervention; the actions line managers take during implementation; the management of diversity and conflicts during the intervention process; and the impact of various contextual events (such as concurrent organizational change) on intervention activities.

As discussed elsewhere in this volume, there is now some good quality new evidence about the links between many of these factors and interventions outcomes. Process, context and outcome evaluation have been successfully integrated in the evaluation of a number of interventions. There is now stronger evidence that specific significant concurrent events damage intervention effectiveness (Landsbergis and Vivona-Vaughan 1995); management training and support can underpin the success of teamwork interventions (Nielsen and Randall 2009); individual differences can be linked to the outcomes of participatory work re-design interventions (Bond et al. 2008); and that employee perceptions of intervention quality being linked to their uptake intervention activities (Nielsen et al. 2007). These and other findings have led some to make suggestions about how intervention effects can be maximized and some of the risks of failure can be reduced (Egan et al. 2009; LaMontagne et al. 2007; Nytrø et al. 2000; Semmer 2006).

To date, intervention research has been characterized by ad hoc (i.e. post-intervention) analysis of the links between intervention processes and outcomes. Often this is done in an effort to better understand disappointing or unexpected intervention outcomes. This approach reflects a research agenda that has stimulated much of the published intervention work. This has, understandably, been focused on developing a valid and generalizable 'list' of process and context factors that need to be included in ad hoc evaluation analysis to provide a more realistic evaluation of intervention effects when interventions are complex and contexts are far from benign, predictable and controllable. In this chapter I will argue that process and context evaluation data can be used during intervention activities in ways that can increase the chances of interventions success.

The Limitations of Intervention Research

Many intervention studies include controlled intervention plans, executed with an underlying ethos that intervention activities need to be protected from buffeting by the context and implemented in a way that is faithful to outcomes of pre-intervention planning activities (often referred to as intervention fidelity). Contextual and process factors tend to conceptualized as 'threats' to intervention plans. After the intervention activities have been in place for some time, this approach allows us to estimate the damage to intervention effectiveness attributable to low fidelity and contextual influences. This linear 'compare before-with-after' approach to evaluation is a product of the perceived 'gold-standard' of good quasi-experimental design. In the best traditions of academic research this can push forward theory and provide important lessons for other researchers (see Bambra et al. 2007).

This emphasis on researching the generalizable effects of interventions raises the risk of a number of unfortunate, albeit unintended, consequences for intervention participants. The first problem is that in effort to properly test the in intervention it remains fixed once it has been formulated through the planning process (i.e. efforts are made to ensure that the intervention follows a pre-determined plan). This can crystallize and 'lock-in' problems with intervention design. Furthermore, if the organizational context changes, the intervention may no longer fit the problem that it was designed to tackle (indeed the problem may no longer exist). The second problem is that if attempts to protect the intervention activities fail (e.g. because of a turbulent or difficult context), any 'damage' to the intervention is logged and documented but not repaired as this could change the nature of the intervention (thus potentially altering its active ingredients or theoretical justification). Third, it results on a focus on managing the intervention activities in a milieu of 'unmanageable' context influences. This means that little consideration is given to the manipulation of context as a way of protecting of enhancing intervention effectiveness. It may be that this could be seen to damage the purity and simplicity of the intervention package that is the experimental manipulation (and hence lower its external validity).

Unfortunately, and importantly, for those employees involved in the failed intervention, knowing that the researchers maintained the scientific rigor of the quasi-experimental method is likely to be of little comfort. Process and context evaluation can make the autopsy of failure (Biron et al. 2010) more thorough and accurate (or indeed the reasons for success more apparent). However, to extend the medical analogy, it is too late to save the patient. In other words, integrating process, context and effect data *only* after the intervention can waste potentially useful information.

The aims of this chapter can be summarized by extending the medical analogy a little further. I will look at how process and context data may be used to monitor the proper delivery and 'dosage' of the treatment while treatment is taking place. It may even lead to changes to the patient's treatment and the environment in which they are cared for with the aim of increasing the chances of a good outcome. In the chapter I draw upon the relatively new and small body of process evaluation research to achieve these aims. Therefore, my suggestions are not definitive but are designed to stimulate researchers and practitioners to think about how the effectiveness of interventions can be enhanced through the more creative use of process and context data.

The Potential Offered by Adapting Interventions

The current dominant approach to process evaluation reflects linear quasi-experimental thinking: process variables are hypothesized to predict changes in outcome variables. In contrast, transactional theories of work stress indicate that a more systemic description of intervention activities is likely to be more accurate. In other words, intervention processes and outcomes can be linked in reciprocal transactions with intervention outcomes influencing intervention processes in complex systems. For example, if intervention activities lead to increased demands and poor well-being, workers may withdraw from intervention activities thus reducing their exposure. This type of erosion cycle could provide a possible explanation for disappointing results in a number of research studies. By the same token, gain cycles may be established when positive intervention outcomes encourage workers to seek out additional exposure to intervention activities.

Re-thinking interventions in this way opens up the possibility of *adapting interventions* while they are being delivered (in other words, intervening within the intervention process). Such adaptive interventions may require adjustments to numerous variables in response to comprehensive and timely monitoring data. Efforts can be made to increase exposure to the active ingredients of planned interventions, changes can be made to exposure workers to different and potentially more effective active ingredients, intervention contexts can be modified, important employee resources developed and so on.

This systems-approach to interventions is not consistent with controlled quasi-experimental research. It entails collecting concurrent formative evaluation data about the intervention that can then be used to shape its subsequent delivery and thus the likelihood of success. This principle is well-established in health promotion intervention (see Freimuth et al. 2001). The concurrent use of data about the intervention turns the output of process and context measures into 'dashboard data'. I will argue that these dashboard data can be useful in intervention research. This is in much the same way as it is useful for a driver to know what speed a car is travelling at any given time rather than to just find out the average speed they drove the car *after* the journey had been completed: to extend the analogy further the process evaluation data are no longer just post-hoc 'telemetry'. This continuous monitoring approach involves using much of what is known about the nature and measurement of intervention processes and context. It extends it by examining how it can be applied to provide on-going information about the execution and effects of intervention activities.

Such an approach can be seen in the mechanisms used in the early stages of many organizational-level changes. Participatory problem-solving groups often lead to fast feedback from stakeholders about the feasibility of plans and may lead to some piloting of intervention activities with feedback being used to re-shape plans (Heaney et al. 1993). Risk assessment activities can also include a consideration of intervention contexts that shapes intervention planning (Nielsen et al. 2010b). After these intervention planning and piloting activities there is very little evidence that on-going adjustment of interventions occur. This may be because of the imperative to protect the purity of the intervention implement to disrupt (in a positive way) baseline organizational practices. It may also be because the data collection processes and feedback mechanisms needed to support adaptive interventions *(interventions within interventions)* have not been fully considered.

The Process and Context Monitoring 'Dashboard'

In this section I present a brief justification for the monitoring of a number of elements of intervention processes and contexts (I examine *what* needs to be monitored and *why* it needs to be monitored). I also discuss *how and when* process and context assessment methods can be used to provide the necessary process dashboard data. The key dimensions of the dashboard are summary Table 14.1.

The dashboard includes two clusters of dimensions: process elements and context elements. Process dimensions are associated with how the intervention activities are delivered, perceived and experienced. Context elements are associated with the various organizational systems in which the intervention occurs (e.g. worker's circumstances, the work group context, the organizational context or even the national economic context). These are dimensions of intervention fit, indicating: how well the intervention fitted given the resources available within the organization; the individual workers' psychological resources (e.g. self-efficacy); and facilitating/obstructing aspects of the design, organization and management of work (i.e. those not targeted directly by the intervention but that had some impact on its effects). In existing intervention research there is evidence that all six dimensions are inter-related: they are considered separately here in order to provide clarity of definition.

Table 14.1 Key components of the process and context monitoring dashboard

Process dimensions

Participation in intervention decisions

Stakeholder appraisals of intervention plans and activities

Observable and perceived exposure to intervention activities

Context dimensions

Organizational resources

Psychological resources

Facilitating and obstructing elements of the design, organization
   and management of work

Participation in Intervention Decisions (Depth and Distribution)

It is well-established that participatory approaches to intervention can activate a number of important processes that are linked to positive intervention outcomes (e.g. employee perceptions of autonomy and control and better fit of the intervention to the context). This is likely to be particularly important at the pre-intervention planning stage. Theories of work stress would indicate that both activities designed to increase participation should be logged and employee perceptions of participation be monitored: this is because activities aimed at increasing participation may not always be perceived as such (Nielsen and Randall 2012a).

To collect data, employees could be asked to indicate their perceived level of participation in specific intervention design activities as well as in work decisions in general. These data can then be used to assess whether an optimum level of participation has been achieved for the intervention to be effective. This optimum level is likely to be determined by the working mechanism of the participation process. If participation was intended to result in shaping of the intervention to context then participation levels would only need to be high in the steering group/problem-solving group. If participation itself is as an important active ingredient of intervention exposure, high levels of perceived participation would need to be evident across the workers targeted for intervention. The opportunity to allow employees to participate and the depth of that participation may also be linked to the nature of the intervention and its urgency. Simple interventions which tend to be effective (e.g. workload reduction) may require little in the way of employee input into the design process as they work through straightforward psychological mechanisms. The urgency of intervention may also mean that high participation is not desirable.

Relatively simple questionnaire measures of perceived participation in intervention design activities could be used to gather such data (Randall et al. 2009). If perceived participation appears too shallow (e.g. employees report little control over the design or delivery of the intervention) or insufficiently widespread given the type of participation envisaged, the existing research would suggest that efforts be made to correct both problems at an early stage of intervention planning.

Stakeholder Appraisals of Intervention Plans and Activities

Very few researchers have asked intervention participants to directly appraise the intervention activities that are planned for them. This is surprising given the importance of perception and appraisal in the majority of theoretical models linking experiences of the work environment and employee well-being, satisfaction and performance. While participatory approaches increase the chance that intervention activities will be viewed favorably by their recipients, this cannot be guaranteed (e.g. when it is employee representatives who are involved in the intervention design process). Negative employee perceptions of the intervention can reduce uptake and reduce its impact for those who take part. Therefore, relatively simple questionnaire measures to capture data on perceived intervention quality and sustainability can be used to monitor likely employee expectations (see Nielsen et al. 2007). Simple questionnaire measures of intervention readiness also provide insight into employees' pre-intervention views of the plan. It may be, of course, that the intervention has a proven track record of success in other settings but that employee perceptions of it are not favorable. Therefore, it is also important to gather data on how much information employees have received about the intervention as a lack of information can lead to suspicion and negative expectations. In such circumstances, honest, timely and accurate information about the intervention can be provided before intervention activities begin (Nielsen et al. 2010b). However, in the face of negative employee appraisals of the intervention, these could be fed back into the intervention planning process and re-design considered. This, in itself, may be a very efficient way of increasing employee participation.

Similar steps can also be taken when the intervention activities are taking place. Gathering on-going data about employees' perceptions of intervention activities may not always be practicable, but methods such as short questionnaires, brief interviews and experience sampling methodologies could be useful in this respect. Using this information to adjust the delivery of intervention activities is generally not discussed in published intervention studies. The links between post-intervention appraisals of intervention activities and intervention outcomes indicate that this could be a useful way of maximizing the impact of intervention activities.

Observable and Perceived Exposure to Intervention Activities

This is perhaps the most fundamental of all monitoring data. Employees are unlikely to benefit from an intervention unless they are exposed to its active ingredients (Lipsey and Cordray 2000). Exposure can be evaluated in several different ways. The delivery of many intervention activities is observable. If these activities are recorded then reliable assessments of whether key intervention events are taking place (e.g. staff meetings, introduction of new equipment, changes to work schedules, reductions to workload) can be made and action can be taken to address any deviations from the plan. This means that having procedures in place to record such events should be an important part of process monitoring. Research has shown that employee perceptions of these events are also important. Observable intervention activities are not always noticed by their intended recipients (Randall et al. 2005), and if they are then the perceived impact may be quantitatively and qualitatively different than planned (Randall et al. 2007). Because of subtle differences in work demands, some participants may report that a change had a large perceived impact, others that it was more modest. Changes intended to enhance one aspect of work (e.g. employee control) may be instead perceived as enhancing another (e.g. co-worker support: see Randall et al. 2007). These direct data on intervention mechanisms are especially important as it is now well-established that perceived changes in working conditions mediate the effects of exposure to intervention activities on employee well-being (Bond et al. 2008). At the very least, information on the size (from none through to a great deal) and valence (very negative to very positive) of perceived impact can be collected in relation to key intervention activities. Information about the diversity of working conditions affected by a single intervention could be collected through brief interviews or open-ended questionnaire items.

These exposure data can be used to identify and address problems with intervention delivery mechanisms (i.e. if the intervention is appropriate and just not 'getting through' to the target audience). If the intervention is being noticed but perceived as having a large negative impact then it is likely that more fundamental intervention design issues may need to be addressed. The remedial steps needed when low levels of exposure are identified may differ according to the type of intervention being delivered. Some interventions require proactive behavior on the part of the employee (i.e. the employee makes a decision to avail themselves of the intervention activities). In this instance the intervention may remain the same, but it may be promoted or communicated in a different way. If the intervention is more passive (i.e. there is a mechanism for delivering it to the employee) then low reported exposure should result in scrutiny of the intervention delivery mechanisms. This may be the result of simple 'human error' in the execution of the plan or a symptom of more fundamental problems with the intervention design that need to be revisited. There is another potential positive side-effect of using these data. If employees are informed that their views have been used to adjust intervention activities, perceived participation can be injected in to the later stages of intervention activity.

Organizational Resources

Most intervention researchers now include discussion of how interventions were impacted by various contexts. Often this information is used to develop plausible explanations for unexpected intervention results. Another way of using this information is to look at the context as a source of barriers and facilitators to the intervention before and during its delivery. This can result in the adjustment of intervention plans (usually achieved through participatory processes) in order to adapt the intervention to fit the context. It may also be possible to adjust intervention contexts. This second possibility has received relatively little attention but as many interventions make demands on organizational resources it merits further attention when interventions are being planned and managed. Important discrete contextual factors that need to be monitored are likely to include staffing/vacancy levels, changes to important aspects of workforce diversity (e.g. skills, tenure and seniority) and concurrent significant workplace changes (e.g. down-sizing and mergers). Other, more subjective, on-going contextual factors should also be monitored: these include senior management support and the availability of specialist expertise to guide the intervention process.

If context is found to have a significant impact on the likelihood of intervention success, then steps may need to be taken to ensure that any significant contextual problems are remedied and/or resources mustered in order to support intervention activities. This can include addressing problems with staffing levels, changing the timing of concurrent interventions (by bringing these forward to better prepare the group for intervention, or by delaying them to prevent disruption to intervention activities), securing external expertise, publicizing senior management commitment, and ensuring that employees have the resources needed to benefit from intervention activities. It may also be that the intervention can be adjusted to provide a better fit with the prevailing context. Such changes can be made at the intervention planning stage. This is facilitated by a comprehensive risk assessment that considers the organizational constraints on, and resources available to, the change process.

Stakeholders' Psychological Resources

Organizational-level interventions in themselves can place additional demands on employees, as can the changes they bring about (Tvedt et al. 2009). Naturally, many effective interventions are designed to increase employees' resources (e.g. job control). However some interventions require employees to have pre-existing resources in order for them to achieve maximum benefit. This may include situation-specific self-efficacy (the confidence to work in new ways or to participate fully in the change process) and the psychological flexibility required to focus on the contingencies of the change process. Poor psychological well-being, negative mood or low levels of work engagement may leave employees with too little energy or desire to engage fully with the change process. Assessments of well-being are often carried out as part of pre-intervention planning: these are often used to assess the need for intervention but rarely to examine employee readiness for the demands the change process might bring. Several recent studies have shown lower levels of voluntary involvement in interventions among those with poor well-being (e.g. Nielsen and Randall 2009, 2012a). These circumstances can, if left unchecked, result in an *intervention paradox* in which those who need the intervention the most are least likely to be in a position to benefit from it.

All of the aforementioned psychological states can reliably be measured through relatively short self-report questionnaires. Logically these data should be collected at the same time as other pre-intervention measures. Since situation-specific psychological states are being measured (e.g. efficacy about making the most of intervention activities) it may be appropriate to also capture these data once employees are aware of the nature of the planned interventions. This would also facilitate an assessment of the likely demands on employees of the planned intervention activities, and therefore the importance of developing appropriate resources prior to (or in combination with) the main intervention activities should be assessed. This may include the use of some individual-level interventions, several of which are relatively straightforward and can be delivered to groups of employees. Recent research shows that psychological capital (hope, optimism, efficacy and resilience) can be developed through short courses in which participants are encouraged to reflect on their success in a range of tasks (Luthans et al. 2008). Effective interventions to increase psychological flexibility can also be delivered with little disruption (Bond et al. 2008). It is also well-established that lack of skill and competence can be a source of threat appraisals when working conditions are evaluated. Therefore, if intervention activities require employees to use persistence, confidence, planning and specific skills then employees' perceptions of their competencies can be used to design and deliver supplementary training as required. As yet there is a dearth of research into the use individual-level resource building interventions as a pre-cursor or bolster to organizational-level interventions. The growing body of research highlighting the linkages between individual differences and the impact of organizational-level interventions indicates that the need for the proactive development of employee resources should be considered during the intervention process.

Organizational-level interventions often place significant additional demands on line managers, not all of whom may have the resources required to meet these demands with subsequent loss of intervention effectiveness. Given the nature of some of the most effective interventions (such as the release of additional control/autonomy to employees), particularly important factors appear to be levels of transformational leadership behavior, general managerial support (Nielsen and Randall 2009) and the management of conflicts (Tvedt et al. 2009). Transformational leadership can be developed through training interventions (Nielsen et al. 2010a). It would seem prudent to make an assessment of typical levels of transformational leadership pre- and during-interventions (and the diversity of managerial behavior within the group) and to offer additional support/development for managers tasked with implementing particularly complex interventions.

Facilitating and Obstructing Elements of the Design, Organization and Management of Work

Many organizational-level interventions are targeted at specific problems with work design. These problems are likely to interact with other aspects of the working environment e.g. a lack of perceived control at work may be linked to poor or malfunctioning management communication structures. This means that other working conditions may have to be adjusted to provide the conditions for the intervention to be implemented and maintained. For example, pre-intervention levels of social support might predict workers' exposure to a teamwork intervention: those settings where support networks were already well-established could well-placed to carry out the tasks associated with the teamwork intervention. Indeed, if many problems exist then there may be need for the sequencing of multiple interventions, with each intervention leading to progressively more benign conditions for the implementation of the next intervention. Many interventions place additional quantitative demands on employees and raise the potential for conflict (Tvedt et al. 2009). Therefore, levels of perceived workload can be monitored to prompt any restrictions in employees' exposure to other discretionary demands, thus allowing them to focus on intervention activities. An assessment of the various working conditions linked to the delivery of the intervention is needed (not just those working conditions identified as indicators of intervention impact). Where these may be barriers to intervention success, plans can be made to address these within a package of intervention activities.

Cautions and Caveats

In writing the preceding section, the intention was to point to the positive potential of process monitoring. The use of process and context data to intervene within the intervention is largely untested but I hope that this Chapter has alerted readers to the possibilities that it may offer for strengthening organizational-level interventions. Naturally, it is also important to consider some of the drawbacks and potential dangers of this approach.

There is growing evidence of the links between intervention processes, contexts and intervention outcomes but this body of research is new and characterized by a diversity of measurement and data analysis approaches. Moreover, with such a small body of research, few consistent and clear conclusions can be identified. This means that a cautious approach to using dashboard data to prompt modifications to processes and context is needed until more research findings are published and some consistent patterns begin to emerge. That said, modifications to increase exposure to interventions that have succeeded in various contexts (e.g. worker autonomy and other enhancements to resources) and participation appears likely to strengthen intervention outcomes.

Tests of the impact of making available intervention dashboard data are needed to examine whether the use of 'interventions within interventions' enhance the effects of change. Research designs that compare outcomes for intervention groups who have access to these data to those that do not would provide a good test of the added value afforded by process and context monitoring.

Dashboard data are indicators of problems that may be suppressing intervention effects. These indicators may be driven by a number of different potential root causes (just as the failure of a car engine to start on a cold day could be the result of a number of different electrical or mechanical faults combined with the effect of poor weather conditions). Therefore, it is likely that some expert diagnosis will be needed to identify the root cause of malfunctioning intervention processes. An appropriately knowledgeable and skilled group of stakeholders from within the organization (i.e. a steering group) may be needed to interpret dashboard data and identify what needs to be done in response. This raises the possibility of over-intervention i.e. that monitoring data will stimulate excessive adjustments that will prevent the planned intervention activities from maturing and becoming effective.

The optimal level of adjustment needed in response to some common patterns of monitoring data is likely to emerge as intervention study designs begin to include more consideration of process and context.

The collection of dashboard data can be efficient and need not be disruptive. But placing frequent demands on participants to provide information about their experiences may increase participant attrition and add significantly to the demands of the intervention process. To avoid this problem, expert judgments will also need to be made about the priority issues to be monitored (this is likely to vary according to the nature of the intervention and its delivery mechanisms) so that these can be the focus of data collection. Informing participants of how their data are being used to adjust the intervention may also enhance retention.

Process monitoring could also stimulate the use of more complex intervention mechanisms and intervention exposure patterns. This is not very compatible with the methodological constraints of quasi-experimental research designs (Noblet and LaMontagne 2009). It could be argued that the frequent collection of process evaluation data is an intervention in itself (e.g. a type of Hawthorne effect whereby the additional attention paid to the participants itself becomes an active ingredient in the intervention process). These concerns need to be balanced against the ethical issues associated with limiting participants' exposure to an effective intervention experience. For example, if process evaluation data indicated low levels of exposure to an intervention that had a proven high success rate, then it would be ethical to make the modifications needed to allow more participants to access its active ingredients. Making available dashboard data can help to focus intervention activities onto the needs of those delivering and receiving the intervention. It may also be that linear quasi-experimental approaches to evaluation are not entirely well-suited with the evaluation of changes that are complex interventions taking place in complex functioning social systems.

Concluding Remarks

The recent developments in process and context evaluation have produced a great deal of information about what can be done to make interventions more effective. It seems wasteful to wait to make use of these data until intervention activities have been completed. A number of well-researched process and contextual factors can be monitored at various stages of intervention activity. This monitoring can stimulate well-informed adjustments to intervention activities that give interventions a better chance of producing the desired outcomes.

References

Bambra, C., Egan, M., Thomas, S., Petticrew, M., & Whitehead, M. (2007). The psychosocial and health effects of workplace reorganisation. 2. A systemic review of task restructuring interventions. *Journal of Epidemiology and Community Health, 61*, 1028–1037.

Biron, C., Gatrell, K., & Cooper, C. (2010). Autopsy of a failure: Evaluating process and contextual issues in an organizational-level work stress intervention. *International Journal of Stress Management, 17*, 135–158.

Bond, F. W., Flaxman, P. E., & Bunce, D. (2008). The influence of psychological flexibility on work redesign: Mediated moderation of a work reorganization intervention. *Journal of Applied Psychology, 93*, 645–654.

Egan, M., Bambra, C., Petticrew, M., & Whitehead, M. (2009). Reviewing evidence on complex social interventions: Appraising implementation in systemic reviews of the health effects of organisational-level workplace interventions. *Journal of Epidemiology and Community Health, 63*, 4–11.

Freimuth, V., Cole, G., & Kirby, S. D. (2001). Issues in evaluating mass-media health communication campaigns. In I. Rootman et al. (Eds.), *Evaluation in health promotion: Principles and perspectives* (pp. 475–492). Denmark: WHO.

Heaney, C., Israel, B., Schurman, S., Baker, E., House, J., & Hugentobler, M. (1993). Industrial relations, worksite stress reduction, and employee well-being: A participatory action research investigation. *Journal of Organizational Behavior, 14*, 495–510.

LaMontagne, A. D., Keegel, T., Louie, A. M., Ostry, A., & Landsbergis, P. A. (2007). A systematic review of the job-stress intervention evaluation literature, 1990–2005. *International Journal of Occupational and Environmental Medicine, 13*, 268–280.

Landsbergis, P., & Vivona-Vaughan, E. (1995). Evaluation of an occupational stress intervention in a public agency. *Journal of Organizational Behavior, 16*, 29–48.

Lipsey, M., & Cordray, D. (2000). Evaluation methods for social intervention. *Annual Review of Psychology, 51*, 345–375.

Luthans, F., Avey, J. B., & Patera, J. L. (2008). Experimental analysis of a web-based training intervention to develop positive psychological capital. *The Academy of Management Learning and Education, 7*, 209–221.

Murta, S. G., Sanderson, K., & Oldenburg, B. (2007). Process evaluation in occupational stress management programs: A systematic review. *American Journal of Health Promotion, 21*, 248–254.

Nielsen, K., & Randall, R. (2009). Managers' active support when implementing teams: The impact on employee well-being. *Applied Psychology: Health and Well-Being, 1*, 374–390.

Nielsen, K., & Randall, R. (2012a). The importance of employee participation and perceptions of changes in procedures in a teamworking intervention. *Work and Stress, 26*, 91–111.

Nielsen, K., & Randall, R. (2012b). Opening the black box: Presenting a model for evaluating organizational-level interventions. *European Journal of Work and Organizational Psychology*. doi:10.1080/1359432X.2012.690556.

Nielsen, K., Randall, R., & Albertsen, K. (2007). Participants' appraisals of process issues and the effects of stress management interventions. *Journal of Organizational Behavior, 28*, 793–810.

Nielsen, K., Randall, R., Holten, A. L., & Rial González, E. (2010a). Conducting organizational-level occupational health interventions: What works? *Work and Stress, 24*, 234–259.

Nielsen, K., Randall, R., & Christensen, K. B. (2010b). Does training managers enhance the effects of implementing teamworking? A longitudinal, mixed methods field study. *Human Relations, 63*, 1719–1742.

Noblet, A. J., & LaMontagne, A. D. (2009). The challenges of developing, implementing, and evaluating interventions. In S. Cartwright & C. L. Cooper (Eds.), *The Oxford handbook of organizational well-being* (1st ed., pp. 466–496). Oxford: Oxford University Press.

Nytrø, K., Saksvik, P. Ø., Mikkelsen, A., Bohle, P., & Quinlan, M. (2000). An appraisal of key factors in the implementation of occupational stress interventions. *Work and Stress, 14*, 213–225.

Randall, R., Griffiths, A., & Cox, T. (2005). Evaluating organizational stress-management interventions using adapted study designs. *European Journal of Work and Organizational Psychology, 14*, 23–41.

Randall, R., Cox, T., & Griffiths, A. (2007). Participants' accounts of a stress management intervention. *Human Relations, 60*, 1181–1209.

Randall, R., Nielsen, K., & Tvedt, S. D. (2009). The development of 5 scales to measure participants' appraisal of organizational-level stress management interventions. *Work and Stress, 23*, 1–23.

Semmer, N. K. (2006). Job stress interventions and the organization of work. *Scandinavian Journal of Work and Environmental Health, 32*, 515–527.

Tvedt, S., Saksvik, P. Ø., & Nytrø, K. (2009). Does change process healthiness reduce the negative effects of organizational change on the psychosocial work environment? *Work and Stress, 23*, 80–98.

Part IV
Intervention and Change Concepts Guiding Theory-Driven Interventions

Chapter 15
Integrated Safety Management as a Starting Point for Changing the Working Environment

Louise Møller Pedersen and Kent Jacob Nielsen

Abstract The effective management of organizational change involves understanding and appreciating the complex interactions of technology, people, organizations, economical factors, legislation, and aspects of cultural, physical, and psychological context. The behavior based and culture based approaches to safety are two seemingly incompatible approaches to creating organizational change in safety performance. However, combined, the two approaches may provide a new perspective on conducting effective and healthy organizational changes. DeJoy has proposed an integrative approach to safety management based on a combination of a behavior-based 'problem-solving process' and a 'culture change process'. The participatory problem-solving process and the culture change process require involvement and commitment from management and workers. The 'problem-solving process' and the 'culture change process' work in parallel, and strives towards a self-regulatory system where the right messages reach the right people, enabling these to solve the right problems with the right solutions. The problem solving process leads to visible and focused activities, which can be diffused and disseminated throughout the organization and thereby potentially create cultural change. Communication and mutual trust between managers and workers are essential for the process to succeed. The integrated approach to safety management can be operationalized by aiming interventions towards the safety committee, middle managers, and workers using individual and group based coaching, and group workshops. The approach has been tested at 18 small and medium sized Danish enterprises and the chapter will include examples from this study.

L.M. Pedersen (✉)
Department of Sociology and Social Work, University of Aalborg, Aalborg, Denmark
e-mail: Lmpd@socsci.aau.dk

K.J. Nielsen, Ph.D.
Department of Occupational Medicine, Danish Ramazzini Centre, Herning Regional Hospital, Herning, Denmark
e-mail: kent.nielsen@vest.rm.dk

G.F. Bauer and G.J. Jenny (eds.), *Salutogenic Organizations and Change:*
The Concepts Behind Organizational Health Intervention Research,
DOI 10.1007/978-94-007-6470-5_15, © Springer Science+Business Media Dordrecht 2013

Keywords Integrated safety management • Small and medium enterprises (SME) • Coaching • Workshops • Intervention • Safety culture

Introduction

The effective management of workplace health and safety involves understanding and appreciating the complex interactions of technology, people, organizations, economical factors, legislation, and aspects of cultural, physical, and psychological context (Aagaard Nielsen and Svensson 2006; Dahl-Jørgensen and Saksvik 2005; Egan et al. 2009; Nielsen and Randall 2012; Saksvik et al. 2002). A narrow focus on any individual component usually falls short of producing sustained levels of high health and safety performance – both on an individual and group level. Not only must all of these components be considered, but particular attention must also be given to how they interact and impact on each other. This thinking has fostered attention to organizational, cultural, and leadership factors within the health and safety literature during the last two to three decades. Concepts such as transformational leadership and organizational culture help us to understand how people, technology, and organizations interact. Ultimately they help us to adopt a more integrative perspective on managing health and safety. Much of what we have learned from this work tells us about what good health and safety performance is. However, little is known about how this health and safety performance is achieved, and how to optimize the effect of leadership efforts and health and safety training. As the primary focus of this book is on health and no other chapters relates to safety, this chapter begins with a brief general introduction, where salutogenesis and healthy organizations are related to safety. This is followed by an introduction to DeJoy's (2005) theory of integrated safety management and how this can be applied in occupational health and safety interventions.

Safety and Salutogenesis

Occupational injuries continue to be one of the major work environment challenges facing legislators, organizations and workers worldwide. The direct and indirect consequences of fatal and non-fatal injuries for victims, organizations and society as a whole have been well documented, e.g. loss of life, lost working years, compensation costs, lost productivity, medical and rehabilitation treatment etc. Based on data from 2003, Hamalainen et al. (2009) estimate that 1,000 workers are killed and nearly 960,000 workers are injured globally in occupational accidents – every day. In spite of an increased cross-national, national, organizational, and research focus, the global rate of lost-time injuries has generally been stable from 1993 to 2008 (Hamalainen et al. 2009; International Labour Office (ILO) 1993–2008). Thus the reduction of occupational injuries is one of the major health challenges facing European organizations. A multitude of intervention strategies aimed at reducing occupational injuries have been proposed and tested with varying success (Guastello 1993; Lund and Aaro 2004; Robson et al. 2007; Tompa et al. 2009). Moreover, even though many studies emphasize worker involvement in safety programs, only few studies include this aspect (Hasle et al. 2012). Hence, new approaches to safety interventions are needed.

Salutogenesis describes an approach focusing on factors that *support* human health and well-being, rather than on factors that *cause* disease. Within safety science this is paralleled by newer approaches to safety management that focus on safe operations and safe processes instead of the occurrence of accidents and injuries. Thus, in safety terms salutogenesis can be seen as the focus on proactive leading indicators and how to be safe, instead of reactive lagging indicators focusing on the occurrence of accidents and injuries (Dyreborg 2009). This can be seen as part of a historical development towards a more proactive approach to safety – at least among larger enterprises. One such proactive leading indicator is safety culture, and safety wise a healthy organization would be characterized as having a good safety culture, proactively working with leading indicators to continuously reduce the risk of injuries. Like salutogenesis, safety culture is a dynamic concept, influenced by context that can be used as a strategic management tool.

Behavior and Culture Based Approaches to Safety Management

Two of the major approaches to safety management are the behavior-based and the culture-based approach (DeJoy 2005). These two approaches use very different methods, but both have culture change as the ultimate endpoint.

The Behavior-Based Approach

The behavior-based perspective is a "bottom up"-approach focusing on the workers' behavior. It is based on behaviorism, which has been successful in creating behavior-change within a lot of areas, including safety (DeJoy 2005; Guastello 1993). The behavior based approach understands injuries as a consequence of individual behavior and human error (Reason 1997). Behavior is seen as directly linked to injuries and losses. Hence, the focus of preventive efforts is on identification and modification of critical safety behavior, typically at the worker level. Safety management is mainly seen as a matter of providing contingent feedback and reinforcement (punishment and rewards). The process is driven by data analysis and communication about results in an effort to create lasting change in objectively defined behavior, e.g. the workers' use of personal protection equipment. The method involves systematic observation of individual worker behavior and subsequent feedback, during a set number of weeks resulting in a prolonged period with a behavior change effort. However, the behavior-based approach has faced some empirical and theoretical challenges regarding the limited scope of the change effort, which is isolated to the specific observed behavior, and the problem of maintaining changes after the intervention ends. However, behavior change proponents argue that successful behavior change programs will lead to 'spill-over'-effects and thus spread throughout the organization and produce sustained safety culture changes (DeJoy 2005).

The Culture-Based Approach

The culture-based approach works "top down" and focuses on the organizational structures, values and priorities. It focuses on creating change at the *organizational level* and identifies the indirect causes of accidents and injuries in the safety culture. Culture is defined as the organizations core values, which are shown through artifacts, values, norms and politics. The approach is more anthropological in nature and is rooted in management and organizational literature. According to the culture-based approach the organizational culture affects the member's behavior and expectations on both the individual and group level. This means that the organizations' core values and approaches to health and safety influence the health and safety initiatives, the effort to implement these and the way health and safety issues are handled (DeJoy 2005). Based on the perception of these processes, the workers form their opinion of the true prioritizing of health and safety in the organization, including the importance of complying with health and safety practices, reporting health and safety incidences etc. Culture change involves understanding and changing an organizations core values and practices. Hence, culture based interventions will almost always addresses enterprise management which is seen as essential in deciding, implementing and maintaining change (DeJoy 2005; Hale et al. 2010; Hildebrandt and Brandi 2006; Nielsen et al. 2008; Zohar 2010). The strength of the approach is the focus on organizational change and the broad approach to safety management. The weakness is the generally 'fuzzy' nature of the culture concept, which is difficult to operationalize and use in practice. Culture-change is difficult, slow and unpredictable and measures of culture will often be indirect and ill-suited to establish causal connections. Furthermore, culture-based interventions are often not related to specific safety behaviors (DeJoy 2005). Though the approach emphasizes workers involvement in intervention processes, in practice this is often limited. The principles behind the behavior- and the culture-based approach are presented in Table 15.1 (see below).

Theory of Integrative Safety Management

As presented in Table 15.1, the behavior based and culture-based approaches to safety differ regarding their scientific background, key elements and implementation strategies. A culture-based intervention will involve a comprehensive and long term focus on role-behaviors and attitudes, often at management level. This process will ideally lead to a self-sustaining process (DeJoy 2005). On the other hand, a

Table 15.1 The behavior-based and culture-based approaches to organizational change

Characteristics	Behavior-based approach	Culture-based approach
Background	Operant psychology/behavior modification	Organizational theory and anthropology
Key aspects	"Bottom up" approach	"Top down" approach
	Analytic/data-driven	Intuitive/ethnographic
	Setting specific	Setting specific
	Continuous process	Self-sustaining
Typical implementation	Identify and define critical behaviors	Assess aspects of culture (values, beliefs, assumptions, etc.)
	Set performance goals	
	Observe/sample behavior	Devise alternative vision
	Provide contingent feedback/ reinforcement	Work with leadership (and employees) to implement change
Principal strengths	Specific technology	Emphasizes organizational change
	Objective/empirical	Focuses on basic causes
	Focus on "objective" effects	Comprehensive
	Participatory (usually)	Participatory (often)
	Shop floor focus	
Principal weaknesses	Victim-blaming	Diffuse technology
	Minimizes environment	Subjective/intuitive
	Focus on immediate causes	Indirect causes
		(From DeJoy 2005, p. 109)

behavior-based intervention will be based on numerous quantitative measures of the workers' safety behavior, observed through a short or long period of time, and feedback on these. The observations are easy to conduct, but the effect can be limited to the observed behavior.

However, the two approaches also have important similarities. Both approaches use a systematic or strategic focus on safety to improve safety outcomes and identify behaviors, attitudes and cultures as important in this process. Moreover, even though the culture-based approach operate on the management level and the behavior-based approach on the worker level, both approaches see safety as a continuous process (DeJoy 2005). Both approaches see management commitment and willingness to invest time and resources in a systematic effort as pre-conditions for the process, and emphasize some level of worker involvement. Feedback on intervention effects is crucial, especially positive feedback, as this gives motivation to maintain the process or to further changes. Furthermore, both approaches see cultural change as possible and are inspired by an organizational learning perspective in their approach to long term change. The process is seen as context specific which is relevant for the intervention design and for generalizing the results.

Based on these similarities, David DeJoy argues that the culture and behavior-based approach to safety management are largely complementary, where the data-driven bottom-up approach from behavior-based safety can be integrated with the intuitive top-down approach from the culture change tradition (DeJoy 2005). He proposes a theory of 'integrated safety management' based on a combination of the behavior-based 'problem-solving process' and a 'culture change process' with safety culture change as the outcome (DeJoy 2005). This is interesting, as the behavior-based and culture-based approach to safety have, individually, been shown to be among the most effective in attaining injury reduction (Guastello 1993; Lund and Aaro 2004), and current evidence points to the combination of different injury prevention approaches as the most effective strategy (Hale et al. 2010). However, the two approaches have not been combined before, and until recently (Kines et al. 2013; Nielsen et al. under review; Pedersen under review) the effect of integrating the two approaches has not been systematically evaluated.

There are two critical tasks that need to be implemented, if the culture- and behavior-based approaches are to be integrated successfully. First of all a comprehensive multi-level participatory problem-solving process needs to be configured. This process needs to be able to continuously identify, remedy and monitor safety issues on all organizational levels. This is basically the data-driven approach to safety management from behavior-based safety that is combined with the comprehensive focus of the culture-based approach. Secondly, the culture change process needs to be specified and 'demystified'. The culture change process has to become more concrete and measureable in the form of different steps or phases that can be verified and used to measure progress. Thus, the culture change process is based on a combination of the broad culture change approach with the concrete and specific technology from the behavior-based approach. The problem-solving process and the culture change process work in parallel, and strive towards a self-regulatory system where the right messages reach the right people, enabling them to solve the right problems with the right solutions.

Approach to Change

Based on this, DeJoy puts forth an integrative approach to safety management change (Fig. 15.1). At the centre of this approach there is a multilevel problem-solving process based on management support and employee involvement. The data for this process stem from the organizational culture (the key features being politics and practices), the management system (priorities and rewards) and the exposures that are in the organization (the behavior of workers and the general working conditions). These organizational factors are influenced on the macro level by exogenous factors such as societal and economic trends.

The problem-solving process leads to visible and focused safety activities which give tangible outcomes as they are implemented. As the activities are developed in a participatory process, they are (relatively) easily diffused and disseminated throughout the enterprise, which over time is expected to lead to culture change (DeJoy 2005).

Key indicators of the culture change process are improved worker perceptions related to trust and affective commitment to the organization, which are built and fostered through the comprehensive and participatory problem-solving process. This process also has the potential to create more balanced attributions when

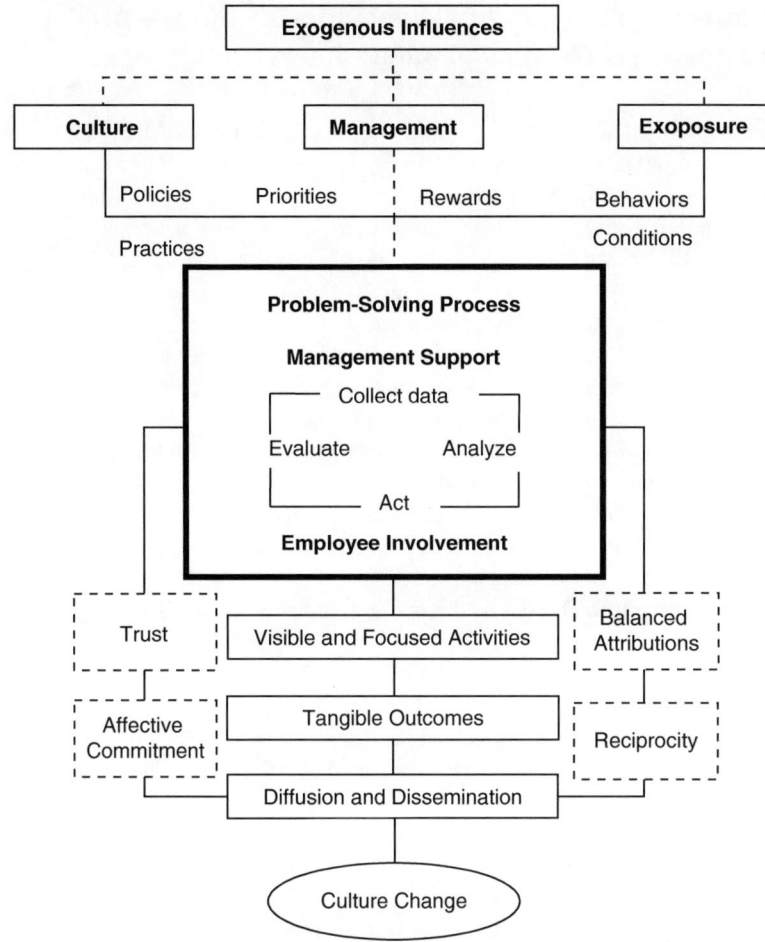

Fig. 15.1 DeJoys integrated approach to safety management (From Dejoy 2005, p. 119)

drawing inference of cause and effect in the realm of safety, as managers and workers have similar information regarding the nature, level, decisions and results of the safety efforts. Finally, a higher level of reciprocity (mutual safety obligations, psychological contracts) is also to be expected as part of the culture change, as managers and workers both participate in the problem-solving process and perceives that the other part takes safety seriously and puts forth its best effort (DeJoy 2005; Nielsen et al. under review). The level of affective commitment (Christian et al. 2009; Kuvaas 2006; Pedersen and Kines 2011), balanced attributions (DeJoy 2005), mutual trust (Conchie et al. 2006; Kath et al. 2010; Luria 2010) and reciprocity (DeJoy 2005) between manager(s) and workers have each proven important for the process and results of occupational change processes. However, the four mechanisms have not previously been included in the same study.

Operationalization and Implementation of DeJoy's Model to Occupational Health and Safety Interventions

This section will show an example of how we have translated DeJoys model into practice in an attempt to work proactively with safety culture during a 6 months period in a project involving 18 small enterprises. The study included 14 manufacturing enterprises with 10–19 employees and 4 enterprises with around 35 employees. Eight of the smallest enterprises and two of the medium-sized served as controls. The key features of the integrative approach to safety management are a comprehensive multilevel data-based and participatory problem-solving process combined with an explicit culture change process. The basis for these parallel processes is knowledge about factors related to culture, management and exposures. A baseline mapping was performed in all enterprises to uncover these factors. This consisted of a questionnaire to all workers, interviews with selected workers and managers and observations of behavior and working conditions. Through these mappings, knowledge on culture, management and exposures was collected that was subsequently used to fuel the problem-solving process in the intervention enterprises.

Although the ultimate goal of the integrative approach to safety management is culture change, the current project did not focus on this as an effect measure. The reason for this was that culture change is not easily verified, and presumably would take longer than allowed in a study focusing on small and medium-sized enterprises, which often have a relatively short time horizon. Instead, the effect measure was defined as change in the safety level of the enterprises. Change in the safety level was understood as a stepping stone for culture change, and operationalized through behavioral, cultural and structural indicators. The behavioral indicator looked at how safe the day-to-day work performed by workers was. This was measured with a questionnaire scale on 'safety behavior'. The cultural indicators tried to uncover the priority and status of safety in the enterprises among both management and workers. This was assessed through the interviews and by three scales in the questionnaire covering 'safety leadership', 'safety knowledge' and worker 'safety involvement'. The structural indicators measured how safe the working conditions were and how well-functioning the safety organization was. This was discussed in the interviews and measured with a questionnaire scale covering the 'safety representative's commitment' to safety.

Implementation of the Problem-Solving Process

The problem-solving process was initiated at workshops attended by management and workers. In the smallest enterprises the entire workforce participated in the same 1-hour workshop chaired by the manager (often the owner), while three 2-hour workshops with 10–15 workers each were held in the two medium-sized intervention enterprises. The three workshops in the medium-sized enterprises were organized around the normal work groups in the enterprises, which is believed to increase the relevance of the problems discussed and the workers' commitment to the process and the results. The workshops were centred on the problem-solving process and focused on discussion and analyses of data collected at the baseline mapping. Through this agreements on specific activities were reached. The processes aimed at a high degree of worker involvement by having them formulate and discuss health and safety issues that they found important. At the same time management also participated in the workshop, and thus could show support for the process and participate in the discussion on health and safety problems and solutions. Thus, the purposes of the workshops were to increase safety communication between management and workers and increase commitment to and prioritization of safety. During the workshops, lists of activities to be carried out were formulated, e.g. buy new gloves or safety goggles. For each activity a deadline was set and one or more responsible persons were appointed, who could be both managers and/or workers. The whole group was responsible for checking up on all activities and communicating the results within the group. The managers were responsible for stimulating culture change by communicating the group results to the whole department, e.g. at a department meeting. Moreover, the top manager was continually informed about the results and encouraged to follow up on the process. So, the end product of the workshops was lists of activities to be implemented and thus lead to tangible outcomes. In the six smallest intervention enterprises 3–4 workshops were held during the intervention period, while the workshops were only held once in the two medium-sized enterprises. In the latter, an equivalent workshop was held with the safety committee (according to Danish law enterprises with less than ten employees are not obliged to have safety committees).

Implementation of the Culture-Change Process

The culture-change process occurred parallel to and integrated with the problem-solving process. The main activity in this was individual coaching sessions with managers once a month during the intervention period, which has previously been shown to be effective in creating health and safety change (Kines et al. 2010; Reinhard 2007). In the smallest enterprises it was the owner that participated in the coaching sessions. The aim was to get him/her to set realistic and manageable goals for safety performance. The first session focused on results from the baseline mapping, while the following sessions focused on how to give feedback and show recognition for good safety performance, overcome barriers and resistance, and formulate new activities. In the two medium-sized enterprises, a short workshop about safety and leadership was held for all managers before the individual coaching sessions began. Apart from this, the culture change process was identical, with a focus on the manager's behavior and safety leadership skills in the coaching sessions. The coaching sessions were performed by researchers from the project, who

Table 15.2 Putting the integrative approach into practice

What	How	Focus	Results
Collect data	Baseline mapping of culture, management and exposure	Politics, practice, priorities, rewards, behavior and conditions	Data to be used in the problem-solving and culture-change process.
Problem-solving process	Workshops with workers and managers	Worker involvement	List of activities to implement
	Workshop with safety committee	Management support Safety committee performance	List of activities to implement
Culture-change process	Individual coaching sessions with managers	Role-behavior Safety leadership	List of activities to implement

had attended a 2-day training course in coaching. Each coaching session ended with a list of focused and visible activities that the managers had to perform before the next session, e.g. talk about safety at a forthcoming staff-meeting.

One of the subjects discussed during the first coaching session was the manager's role at the problem-solving workshops. To integrate the culture-change and problem-solving process, it was important that the managers were aware of their role during the workshops and tried to get workers involved by conducting them in a participatory manner, while also sending clear messages about the prioritization of safety (Table 15.2).

Results from the Application of the Integrative Safety Management Approach

When evaluating the interventions, it is important to both look at process and effect evaluation measures. In this study, the number of implemented activities from workshops and coaching sessions were used as process measures of the degree of implementation. In the small enterprises 85 % of the workshop activities were implemented at follow-up (Table 15.3) while 79 % of the activities from coaching were implemented from session to session. Looking at the two medium-sized intervention enterprises, the results differ between them. While 80 % of the work-shop activities and 84 % of the coaching activities were implemented in the first intervention enterprise (I1), the same was only the case for 48 and 59 % of the activities in the second intervention company (I2) (Table 15.3). The same picture was seen for the activities from the safety committee workshop, where 82 % compared to 20 % of the activities were implemented. Thus, the intervention process resulted in more visible activities in the first intervention enterprise than in the second, and a higher percentage of the activities were also successfully imple-mented in the first enterprise.

Table 15.3 Implementation of activities from workshops and coaching

Enterprise	Small (n=6)	Medium I1	Medium I2
No of workshop activities	**48**	**71**	**21**
Not implemented (%)	2	10	29
In progress (%)	13	10	24
Implemented (%)	85	80	48
No of coaching activities	**29**	**34**	**32**
Not implemented (%)	10	6	19
In progress (%)	10	21	22
Implemented (%)	79	74	59

I1 Intervention enterprise no 1

I2 Intervention enterprise no 2

The theoretical goal of the integrative approach to safety management is culture change, but it is difficult to verify such a change. Instead, the effect measures in the current study were based on questionnaire-based indicators of possible culture change. In the six small intervention enterprises the questionnaire data showed improvements in 'safety knowledge', 'safety involvement' of workers, 'safety leadership' and the 'commitment of the safety representative'. This is understood as changes in the general approach to safety in the enterprises, and as such an indicator of culture change. No such improvements were seen in the control enterprises. 'Affective commitment', 'safety participation', 'trust', balanced attributions to safety and reciprocity between management and employees are seen as key indicators of the culture-change process (Fig. 15.1). In all six small intervention companies and one of the medium sized intervention companies questionnaire data documented changes in trust and safety participation. Finally, interviews with managers and workers generally indicated an increased affective commitment to safety and a higher level of balanced attributions to safety and reciprocity between managers and workers. In the control companies no changes were seen.

In the two medium-sized intervention enterprises, differences were also evident in the effect evaluation measures. While there were improvements in all effect measures in the first intervention enterprise (I1), no changes were seen in the second (I2). Furthermore, there was a decrease in 'trust' and 'affective commitment' which DeJoy considers to be key indicators of the culture-change process, in the second intervention enterprise.

Taken together, the results indicate a successful implementation of the integrative approach to safety management in the six small enterprises and one of the medium-sized enterprises (I1). In these enterprises many focused and visible activities were formulated on the basis of the problem-solving and culture-change process. A high percentage of these activities were subsequently implemented, which led to tangible outcomes that could be diffused and disseminated throughout the enterprises. In the end, this led to improvements in the culture change indicators. This is in accordance with the integrative safety management model (see Fig. 15.1). However, the intervention process failed in the second medium-sized enterprise. Although the problem-solving process did result in focused activities, a lower level of implementation was seen in the second intervention enterprise. Qualitative data from the interviews can expand a bit on the reasons behind this, as employees reported a perceived low level of commitment to safety from management and a lack of trust and reciprocity towards managements' handling of project activities. An employee stated:

> The activities we were responsible for have been implemented… but only because we did it ourselves. Management has not done much. (…) The little things, that are important to us, are not acted upon. If management cannot even remedy such small things, how should they be able to deal with bigger issues? (Follow-up interview, employee, Intervention enterprise no 2).

The data from workshop activities somewhat support this, as 13 of the 20 (65 %) activities that workers were responsible for were implemented, while only 33 % (2 of 6) of the activities, where supervisors were responsible, were implemented (Nielsen et al. under review). As management support, trust and reciprocity are important features of the integrative approach to safety management it is not surprising that the implementation failed, when these factors were not present. Further details on the results of this project can be found elsewhere (Kines et al. 2013; Nielsen et al. under review).

Strengths of the Integrated Approach to Organizational Changes

There is a lack of development, systematic implementation and evaluation of health and safety management systems for enterprises with less than 50 workers (Hasle and Limborg 2006). In the US and the EU-27 over 95 % of enterprises have less than 20 employees (Eurostat 2011; U. S. Census Bureau 2011), and employment and economic growth to a large extent depend on these enterprises. Small enterprises pose a special challenge in this regard, as they have limited resources, and lack formalization of working environment issues (Hasle and Limborg 2006). Furthermore, health and safety issues are often dealt with on an ad hoc and informal basis, without any written safety policies or procedures (Hasle 2009). There is often a tendency for small enterprises to ignore or downplay the contributing causes to injuries, and therefore a failure to follow up with safety initiatives. It is critical that health and safety initiatives targeted towards small enterprises are straightforward, short, clear, related to tangible tasks, and easily adaptable to existing organizational structures. DeJoy's theory of integrated safety management fills this gap in current work environment research and practice by providing new intervention approaches for health and safety changes involving both managers and workers. The completed study at 18 Danish enterprises with less than 50 employees documents the models potential to create culture changes at both manager and worker level. Table 15.4 summarizes the identified potentials of the theory of integrated safety management.

Table 15.4 Potentials and barriers for health and safety changes identified in the integrative approach to safety management

Potentials	Barriers
All company levels are actively involved	Other competing agendas including production pressure
The participants identify and solve specific health and safety problems based on a comprehensive mapping of these	Power relations between the participants
The process creates involvement and ownership among the participants	Different interests among the participants
Well-functioning health and safety organization	Power relations between the enterprise and those who conduct the intervention

All the identified potentials do not need to be present in order to apply the theory of integrated safety management, but will support the implementation of the interventions. Especially the direct participation of all company levels and a well-functioning safety organization are seen as important in order to create culture change. Likewise the four barriers can be of varying importance depending on the intervention.

Limitations of the Integrated Approach to Organizational Changes

The theory of integrated safety management has some limitations which must be addressed. So far the theory has only been tested on Danish small and medium sized enterprises. Denmark is characterized by a strong political focus on the working environment, e.g. a mandatory safety committee and a safety representative in all enterprises with more than ten workers (Beskæftigelsesministeriet (The Danish Department of Labour) 2010). Furthermore, Denmark has a relatively low power distance between workers and management and a long-standing tradition for open exchanges. The workshops were all based on workers and managers engaging in open and constructive dialogue, and as such the ability to do this was a prerequisite for the intervention. Therefore, this type of intervention might not be successful in more authoritative countries or in enterprises with bad relations between workers and management.

Hence, more research within different national contexts, under stable as well as disruptive organizational conditions, supportive and competing, is needed. Likewise, further research with a longer time perspective is needed, to tie the model to lasting culture change. The results from the above study also show that it is crucial to ensure management support throughout the implementation process, which is a challenge in any change process.

Conclusion

Within safety science, salutogenesis can be understood as working with proactive leading safety indicators focused on how to be safe, instead of reactive, lagging indicators such as the occurrence of accidents and injuries. One such leading indicator is safety culture, and the theory of integrated safety management is a new theoretical approach for creating safety culture change. The model is based on an integration of a participatory problem-solving process and an open culture-change process with the involvement of both management and workers. In this chapter we have given an example of how the theory of integrated safety management can be operationalized into a coaching intervention aimed at managers and workshops for the workers, facilitated by the manager or an external person. This approach was tested in 18 small and medium sized enterprises, where numerous safety problems were identified and solved through the interventions. Moreover, the direct and meaningful involvement of all company levels and the simple follow-up system of the interventions ensured organizational changes.

The theory of integrated safety management has been shown to be a straight forward and effective way to work with safety at all levels of the organization. However, mutual trust between managers and workers and the manager's commitment are important for the intervention process and results. The theory of integrated safety management fills the gap in current work environment research and practice by providing new theoretical and practical approaches for health and safety management. However, more evidence is needed about the models ability to create long term changes.

Acknowledgements The project was funded by the Danish Working Environment Research Fund, project 28-2007-09 and involved another study which was also based on DeJoy's theory of integrated safety management. The methods developed in the study were subsequently adapted into an easy to use 'Safety toolbox' for use by companies and working environment professionals (Nielsen et al. 2011). The authors would like to thank the other members of the research group: MSc Dorte R. Andersen, PhD Pete Kines, PhD Lars Peter Andersen, and PhD Kurt Rasmussen for fruitful discussions of the intervention design and results.

References

Aagaard Nielsen, K., & Svensson, L. (Eds.). (2006). *Action and interactive research. Beyond practice and theory*. Maastricht: Shaker Publishing.

Bekendtgørelse Af Lov Om Arbejdsmiljø Nr. 1072 Af 7. (2010, September). [Law for Working Environmental Issues Number 1072, September 7th. 2010] (in Danish).

Christian, M. S., Bradley, J. C., Wallace, J. C., & Burke, M. J. (2009). Workplace safety: A meta-analysis of the roles of person and situation factors. *Journal of Applied Psychology, 94*(5), 1103–1127. doi:10.1037/a0016172.

Conchie, S. M., Donald, I. J., & Taylor, P. J. (2006). Trust: Missing piece(s) in the safety puzzle. *Risk Analysis, 26*(5), 1097–1104. doi:10.1111/j.1539-6924.2006.00818.x.

Dahl-Jørgensen, C., & Saksvik, P. Ø. (2005). The impact of two organizational interventions on the health of service sector workers. *International Journal of Health Services, 35*(3), 529–549.

DeJoy, D. M. (2005). Behavior change versus culture change: Divergent approaches to managing workplace safety. *Safety Science, 43*(2), 105–129. doi:10.1016/j.ssci.2005.02.001.

Dyreborg, J. (2009). The causal relation between lead and lag indicators. *Safety Science, 47*(4), 474–475. http://dx.doi.org/10.1016/j.ssci.2008.07.015

Egan, M., Bambra, C., Petticrew, M., & Whitehead, M. (2009). Reviewing evidence on complex social interventions: Appraising implementation in systematic reviews of the health effects of organisational-level workplace interventions. *Journal of Epidemiology and Community Health, 63*(1), 4–11. doi:10.1136/jech.2007.071233.

Eurostat. (2011). *Key figures on European business: With a special feature on SMEs* – 2011 edition. http://epp.eurostat.ec.europa.eu/cache/ITY_OFFPUB/KS-ET-11-001/EN/KS-ET-11-001-EN. PDF. Accessed 12 Sept 2012.

Guastello, S. J. (1993). Do we really know-how well our occupational accident prevention programs work. *Safety Science, 16*(3–4), 445–463. http://dx.doi.org/10.1016/0925-7535(93)90064-K

Hale, A. R., Guldenmund, F. W., van Loenhout, P. L. C. H., & Oh, J. I. H. (2010). Evaluating safety management and culture interventions to improve safety: Effective intervention strategies. *Safety Science, 48*, 1026–1035. http://dx.doi.org/10.1016/j.ssci.2009.05.006

Hamalainen, P., Saarela, K. L., & Takala, J. (2009). Global trend according to estimated number of occupational accidents and fatal work-related diseases at region and country level. *Journal of Safety Research, 40*(2), 125–139. http://dx.doi.org/10.1016/j.jsr.2008.12.010

Hasle, P., & Limborg, H. J. (2006). A review of the literature on preventive occupational health and safety activities in small enterprises. *Industrial Health, 44*(1), 6–12.

Hasle, P., Kines, P., & Andersen, L. P. (2009). Small enterprise owners' accident causation attribution and prevention. *Safety Science, 47*(1), 9–19. http://dx.doi.org/10.1016/j.ssci.2007.12.005

Hasle, P., Limborg, H. J., Kallehave, T., Klitgaard, C., & Andersen, T. R. (2012). The working environment in small firms: Responses from owner-managers. *International Small Business Journal, 1*, 1–18. doi:10.1177/0266242610391323.

Hildebrandt, S., & Brandi, S. (2006). *Forandringsledelse* [Change management]. Copenhagen: Børsens Forlag (in Danish).

International Labour Office (ILO). (1993–2008). *ILO database "occupational injuries" (annual)*. http://laborsta.ilo.org/. Accessed 12 Sept 2012.

Kath, L. M., Magley, V. J., & Marmet, M. (2010). The role of organizational trust in safety climate's influence on organizational outcomes. *Accident Analysis and Prevention, 42*(5), 1488–1497. http://dx.doi.org/10.1016/j.aap.2009.11.010

Kines, P., Andersen, L. P. S., Spangenberg, S., Mikkelsen, K. L., Dyreborg, J., & Zohar, D. (2010). Improving construction site safety through leader-based verbal safety communication. *Journal of Safety Research, 41*(5), 399–406. http://dx.doi.org/10.1016/j.jsr.2010.06.005

Kines, P., Andersen, D. R., Andersen, L. P. S., Nielsen, K. J., & Pedersen, L. M. (2013). Improving safety in small enterprises through an integrated safety management intervention. *Journal of Safety Research, 44*(1), 87–95. http://dx.doi.org/10.1016/j.jsr.2012.08.022

Kuvaas, B. (2006). Work performance, affective commitment, and work motivation: The roles of pay administration and pay level. *Journal of Organizational Behavior, 27*(3), 365–385. doi:10.1002/job.377.

Lund, J., & Aaro, L. E. (2004). Accident prevention. presentation of a model placing emphasis on human, structural and cultural factors. *Safety Science, 42*(4), 271–324. http://dx.doi.org/10.1016/ S0925-7535(03)00045-6

Luria, G. (2010). The social aspects of safety management: Trust and safety climate. *Accident Analysis and Prevention, 42*(4), 1288–1295. http://dx.doi.org/10.1016/j.aap.2010.02.006

Nielsen, K., & Randall, R. (2012). Opening the black box: Presenting a model for evaluating organizational-level interventions. *European Journal of Work and Organizational Psychology* (Open access), 1–17. http://www.Tandfonline.com/doi/pdf/10.1080/1359432X. 2012.690556

Nielsen, K. J., Rasmussen, K., Carstensen, O., & Glasscock, D. (2008). *Forandring som vilkår. om udvikling og ledelse af arbejdsmiljø* [To manage and advance working environment under organizational changes]. Copenhagen: Børsen (in Danish).

Nielsen, K. J., Pedersen, L. M., Andersen, L., & Kines, P. (2011). *Sikkerhedskassen* [Safety tool box]. http://www.amkherning.dk/dk/videnomarbejdsmilj/arbejdsulykker/sikkerhedskassen. Accessed 16 Feb 2012 (in Danish).

Nielsen, K. J., Kines, P., Pedersen, L. M., Andersen, L. P. S., & Andersen, D. R. (under review). A multi-case study of the implementation of an integrated approach to safety in medium-sized enterprises.

Pedersen, L. M. (under review). Applying a realistic evaluation model to occupational safety interventions.

Pedersen, L. M., & Kines, P. (2011). Why do workers work safely? Development of safety motivation questionnaire scales. *Safety Science Monitor, 15*(1), Article 10. http://ssmon.chb.kth.se/vol15/10_Pedersen-Kines.pdf

Reason, J. (1997). *Managing the risks of organizational accidents* (3rd ed.). Cornwall: MPG Books Ltd.

Reinhard, S. (2007). Coaching: A process of personal and social meaning making. *International Coaching Psychology Review, 2*(2), 191–216.

Robson, L. S., Clarke, J. A., Cullen, K., Bielecky, A., Severin, C., Bigelow, P. L., et al. (2007). The effectiveness of occupational health and safety management system interventions: A systematic review. *Safety Science, 45*(3), 329–353. http://dx.doi.org/10.1016/j.ssci.2006.07.003

Saksvik, P. O., Nytro, K., Dahl-Jorgensen, C., & Mikkelsen, A. (2002). A process evaluation of individual and organizational occupational stress and health interventions. *Work and Stress, 16*(1), 37–57. doi:10.1080/02678370110118744.

Tompa, E., Dolinschi, R., de Oliveira, C., & Irvin, E. (2009). A systematic review of occupational health and safety interventions with economic analyses. *Journal of Occupational and Environmental Medicine, 51*(9), 1004–1023. doi:10.1097/JOM.0b013e3181b34f60.

U.S. Census Bureau. (2011). *Statistics about business size (including small business from the U.S.)*. Available at: http://www.census.gov/econ/smallbus.html. Accessed 12 Sept 2012.

Zohar, D. (2010). Thirty years of safety climate research: Reflections and future directions. *Accident Analysis & Prevention, 41*, 1517. http://dx.doi.org/10.1016/j.aap.2009.12.019

Chapter 16
Building Healthy Organizations Through Music and Culture Interventions

Vibeke Milch, Jonas Rennemo Vaag, Fay Giæver, and Per Øystein Saksvik

Abstract Interventions at work are often directed towards solving specific problems in the work environment. They are typically located on one of three levels: primary, secondary and tertiary. However, little research has been done on countervailing interventions, that is, proactive and health promoting interventions that focus on facilitating the positive aspects of the work situation and through this counteract the effects of negative situations and events. The intervention project "The sound of well-being" was a culturally based intervention to stimulate well-being for employees in the public sector. It was utilized to spread joy, increase motivation and unity, and to encourage work engagement and well-being in general. The project involved the forming of local choirs, rehearsals with and without professional musicians, mini concerts, choir battles, musical arrangements, sing back and ultimately a grand finale. In this chapter we investigate the utilization of countervailing interventions that take on a pro-active approach, aimed at promoting health and well-being in the workplace without being introduced as a response to an existing problem in the organization. It is our aim that this chapter will highlight the need for new ways of thinking concerning interventions, and explore new ways of developing cost efficient, yet effective interventions to promote employee health and well-being.

Keywords Well-being • Workplace interventions • Positive psychology • Countervailing interventions • Arts and health

V. Milch (✉) • J.R. Vaag • F. Giæver • P.Ø. Saksvik
Department of Psychology, Norwegian University of Science and Technology,
Trondheim, Norway
e-mail: vibeke.milch@svt.ntnu.no; jonas.vaag@svt.ntnu.no; fay.giaver@svt.ntnu.no;
per.saksvik@svt.ntnu.no

G.F. Bauer and G.J. Jenny (eds.), *Salutogenic Organizations and Change:*   291
The Concepts Behind Organizational Health Intervention Research,
DOI 10.1007/978-94-007-6470-5_16, © Springer Science+Business Media Dordrecht 2013

Introduction

The objective of this chapter is to illuminate the need to further explore the use of new forms of intervention. There has been a pathological and a preventative focus in extant literature, something which represents a negative bias. In line with the growing interest in health promotion and the building of healthy organizations, we argue for the importance of researching and exploring interventions that are not only directed towards solving problems, but also interventions directed towards enhancing positive aspects of the work environment and positive experiences and emotions. This is important in order to develop the field of health promotion and further our understanding of how to build healthy organizations.

We start off with an exploration of the concept of "healthy organization" and introduce our understanding of the term. We further focus our attention on the current trends in intervention research and positive psychology. Further, we discuss the concept of countervailing interventions as proposed by Kelloway et al. (2008). An example of a countervailing intervention is presented, and finally, implications and effect of this form of intervention is discussed.

A Pro-active Approach Towards Building Healthy Organizations

The constantly changing work life has led to many challenges. With globalized enterprises, technological advances and increasing competition, organizational change has become commonplace and employees are faced with greater workloads, increased job demands and job insecurity, which has been associated with higher levels of occupational stress and stress related diseases (Christensen 2012). Parallel to this trend there has been a growing interest in health promotion, and the development of healthy organizations.

According to the American Psychological Association, psychologically healthy workplaces are defined in terms of incorporating health promoting activities, treating employees fairly, providing flexible working conditions, offering employee development programs, prioritizing health and safety and prevention of work stress (APA 1999).

Our understanding of the concept "healthy organization" is partly influenced by the challenges we face in Norwegian work life, particularly in the public sector. The public sector has been subject to extensive reorganization over the recent years. A reorganization that is historically related to the increased focus on New Public Management which has led to increased job demands and more job insecurity for employees (Saksvik and Gustafsson 2004). In Norway, developing and promoting healthy workplaces has been a key objective both politically and in research. In fact, it is embedded as a part of Norwegian legislation. The Revised Working Environment Act (Norway 2006) states that work should be organized in a way that does not put physical or psychological strain on the employee, and that the working environment should provide a basis for a healthy and meaningful work situation.

We argue that managing and dealing with change in a healthy way therefore constitutes an important part of creating healthy organizations in the public sector. In our research we have studied healthy change processes, and have identified factors related to managing change in a healthy way. In a study of middle managers in the public sector (Saksvik and Tvedt 2009) we investigated what made them successful in terms of managing healthy change. Our frame of interest was how they were able to lead their co-workers through a change process avoiding health constraints and deterioration in the work environment. The main finding was that the middle managers were pro-active and very involved in the process. They committed to the change process, embraced the people involved, and made sure the co-workers mastered the change as a collective.

We define a healthy organization as a pro-active organization in terms of dealing with change in a healthy way, and being pro-active in constantly working towards promoting and cultivating employee health and well-being.

Organizational Health Intervention Research – Need for a Different Approach?

Primary, Secondary and Tertiary Stress Prevention

In intervention literature, workplace interventions are often classified in to three different categories; primary, secondary and tertiary interventions (Reynolds 1997; Richardson and Rothstein 2008). Primary interventions are aimed at directly reducing or removing stressors in the working environment, for instance redesigning badly designed jobs. Secondary interventions involve changing how the individual perceives and reacts to stressors. Lastly, tertiary interventions are focused on the outcome of a stress process, and involve treating individuals who have had a stress reaction, thereby reducing the impact on the individual.

Primary interventions are in most situations considered to be the best and most efficient approach, because they involve directly dealing with the source of the problem, but since they are costly and wide-ranging, secondary and tertiary interventions are often preferred by managers (Hurrell and Murphy 1998). Consequently, research has primarily been focused on the latter two categories, resulting in few studies on primary interventions. Saksvik et al. (2002) note that research on primary health and stress interventions generally has yielded inconclusive results with regard to evaluating effectiveness, and that there have been few studies that have reported fully positive results.

The three categories of intervention all share a common denominator; they are typically implemented to correct anomalies and solve specific problems that have already occurred; improving the work environment, reducing sickness absence, or reducing sources to or consequences of occupational stress. In this sense, they often represent a recuperative and ameliorating approach. In considering interventions in terms of a pro-active approach to building healthy organizations, one can argue that primary interventions should be preferred over secondary and tertiary interventions, considering that they are aimed directly towards the source of the problem. However, they are still typically implemented subsequent to the identification of a problem and therefore represent a preventative approach to building healthy organizations. We argue that a pro-active approach also involves promoting positive resources in the work environment.

It is essential to underline that the existing intervention research has been of great importance, and that the main focus when building healthy organizations should be to identify and eliminate stressors in the work environment that might have a negative effect on employees. However, in addition to this, it is crucial to investigate the effects of interventions aimed at enhancing the positive aspect of the work environment. Turner et al. (2002) underline the importance of exploring positive aspects in the work environment, and argue that neglecting these facets is inappropriate and hinder us in fully comprehending the meaning and effects of working. To be able to meet the challenges we face in today's work life, identifying and promoting positive factors that enable employees to handle increased demands and organizational change represents a crucial objective. Arguably, we should broaden our view on the use of interventions, and explore other options in addition to the traditional triad.

Countervailing Interventions to Promote Positive Aspects at Work

Kelloway et al. (2008) assert that the focus in the intervention literature has been too narrow, and propose the concept of countervailing interventions as a counterpart. The concept refers to interventions aimed at enhancing the positive experience of work, as opposed to decreasing the negative aspects. The idea is that interventions directed towards promoting and developing the positive aspects of the work environment may have a countervailing function, and thus counteract effects of negative situations in the work place.

There is a growing body of literature that supports this notion. In the recent years, the field of positive psychology has emerged, bringing about a focal shift. Positive psychology is described as the science of positive subjective experiences, positive individual traits and positive institutions (Seligman and Csikszentmihalyi 2000). One of the main purposes of positive psychology is to even out the bias in the psychological literature towards negative psychological states. Bakker and Derks (2010) address this at the negativity bias in the field of psychology by example of the clinical psychologists traditional focus on diagnosis and treatment of pathology; social psychologist focus on errors of the human being; evolutionary psychologists emphasis on human selfishness in order to survive etc. We also recognize this negative bias in occupational psychology, where one could say that there has been a tradition in focusing on negative aspects such as what creates stress and absenteeism. Instead of focusing on the weaknesses and problems that may prevent an organization from being healthy, in positive psychology, there is an emphasis on strengths, resources and psychological capacities (Luthans 2002). An important line of argument is that in order to create and sustain a positive work environment it is not sufficient to solely reduce the negative factors that function as stressors, but it is also important to foster and develop the positive aspects – the resources that help employees handle stressors (Christensen 2012).

Positive Emotions as Key Mechanism

Several studies have shown that positive emotions are associated with increased openness (Fredrickson and Branigan 2005), creativity (Isen et al. 1987) and prosocial and helping behavior (George and Brief 1992). Furthermore several theorists have pointed out that positive emotions facilitate approach behavior or continued action due to the inherent need to maintain positive emotional experiences, something in which ensures enduring positive effects of positive emotions over time (e.g. Carver and Scheier 1990). Based on this idea Fredrickson (2001) developed the "broaden-and-build" theory which postulated that although positive affect is transient and potentially only associated with short term behavioral effects, positive emotions have the capacity to expand peoples' thought-action repertoires, and thus build and accumulate resources over time that can be drawn upon as resources in the future. Similarly, positive emotional experiences have been found to build individual resilience, and enhance engagement and well-being both in an individual and a collective level (Fredrickson and Losada 2005; Fredrickson et al. 2003). In addition, positive experiences have also been found to function as a buffer for high demands (Hakanen et al. 2005) and to be positively correlated with individual resilience and negatively correlated with turnover intentions (Allen and Meyer 1997). These studies indicate that positive emotions and experiences may represent resources that enable employees to handle high demands and stressors in the work environment. Accordingly, countervailing interventions that involve a positive-psychological perspective are interesting and might provide a cost-efficient and innovative way to promote healthy organizations.

The Example of Music and Culture Interventions

In the following section we will present an example of a countervailing intervention that focuses specifically on the role that music and culture can play to spur on positive emotional experiences among employees with possible short term as well as long term effects on their individual well-being and their work environment.

Previous Research on Arts and Health

The use of arts in health may be regarded as a field with roots back to ancient times (Prior 2010). In recent history, arts and health programs have been in existence for over 20 years, and attention has been focused on how the arts can contribute to health, well-being, social inclusion and healthcare practice across a range of settings (Clift et al. 2009). In recent years, we have seen the emergence of two international journals within the field of arts and health. In 2009, the journal *Arts & Health: An International Journal of Research, Policy and Practice* was established. A year later, in 2010, the *Journal of Applied Arts and Health* followed. Both journals emphasize the interdisciplinary nature of arts and health, thus providing space for a multidisciplinary approach to research on this topic, with regard to both theoretical and methodological perspectives. From the viewpoint of occupational health psychology, we have gained interest in how arts-based interventions may influence and promote health in organizations. In doing so, we see the need to combine knowledge from the field of arts and health with the growing field of occupational health psychology.

Choir singing can contribute to creating a positive environment and social cohesion, both at work as well as in the community (Clift and Hancox 2001; Purcell and Kagan 2007). Studies indicate that choir singing has a positive impact on well-being and quality of life in general (Grape et al. 2002) and even strengthens the immune system. Saliva tests show that singing stimulates immunity markers like immunoglobulin A (S-IgA), as well as reduce the level of stress cortisol (Kuhn 2002; Theorell 2009; Kreutz et al. 2004). Several Scandinavian studies indicate that participation in cultural activities in general is important for maintaining and strengthening good health; both for the individual and in a societal perspective (Kjeøy 2009 – referencing the HUNT-studies; Bygren et al. 1996, 2009a, b). There is reason to assume that cultural participation could be an important condition for individual and collective development, meaning, coping and the feeling of coherence in a lifetime aspect. Better quality of life and improved self-experienced health repeatedly surface in the evaluation reports from "The culture and health projects" from Scandinavia in the 1990s, which strengthen the assumption that participation in meaningful cultural activities can be a contributing factor for achieving improved health and quality of life (Ruud and Stige 1994). A review article of a selection of Norwegian and Swedish research studies concerning cultural participation and health (published; 1995–2009) point in the same direction (Cuypers et al. 2011), although the authors underline the need for more research, especially on the long term effects.

Implementation of the Pilot Project "Sound of Well-Being"

We have recently evaluated a project termed "The sound of well-being" (Vaag et al. 2012). The project was initiated by Nord-Trøndelag Health Trust in collaboration with Rock City, and was also later implemented in Namsos Municipality. Our involvement in the project started when we were asked to undertake an evaluation of the project. This was in the initial face in Nord Trøndelag Health Trust. The project was a culturally based intervention implemented to encourage engagement, motivation and well-being among employees in the public sector through music and choir singing. The initiative was, in contrast to numerous other interventions, not implemented to solve an existing problem, but instead employed to promote well-being and stimulate the work-environment. In this way SOW is in line with the concept of countervailing interventions, and can be said to represent a different approach than what has been common in intervention research.

Participation in "SOW" was offered to every employee in the two organizations, and information in addition to invitations to participate was sent out by e-mail to each employee and to the managers 2 weeks before the project commencement. In Nord-Trøndelag Health Trust, the intervention lasted from March to November 2011, with a break for summer vacation from June to August. In Namsos Municipality, on the other hand, the intervention period was shorter, lasting from February to May, 2012. Beside this, the intervention program was identical in the two organizations. The core of the intervention involved the establishment of local choirs based on department structure. Three professional musicians instructed and facilitated the choirs and accompanied them with guitar, piano and vocals. The repertoire consisted of five well-known pop and rock songs chosen by the musicians, three of which were Norwegian and rooted in Namsos. The choirs participated in choir rehearsals, mini-concerts, "choir battles" and ultimately a "grand finale". In addition, a conductor, a choreographer, students from the media department of the local college and suppliers of sound, lighting and film were made available to the artists and choirs. Choir rehearsals took place after work hours. In addition to the rehearsals, various activities were initiated, including the making of a music video and four concerts that were open to the general public. All concerts were sold out and the project was subject to considerable attention in both national and local media.

Evaluation of the Pilot Project "Sound of Well-Being"

Our objective was to find what differentiated the participants from the non-participants on several well-being and health indicators. In this way we hoped to identify important factors for participating in this form of interventions, and at the same time describe the participants and non-participants' own perception of change during the project. The results from the study showed that those who had participated in SOW reported greater organizational commitment and a higher level of engagement compared with non-participants. In addition we found a self-reported positive change with regard to psychosocial work environment and global health in participants compared to non-participants. With regard to personality differences, participants described themselves as more extroverted than did the non-participants (Vaag et al. 2012).

Because of our late involvement in the SOW-project, we did not have the opportunity to use a pre-post design in our study in Nord Trøndelag Health Trust. The cross-sectional nature of our study and the use of one-off measures may be regarded as a limitation considering that we had little opportunity to study casual relationships, something in which has restrained our ability to evaluate the effectiveness of the intervention. Nonetheless, the findings from our study resulted in useful descriptions of participants and non-participants, something which may guide the development of new questions and hypotheses. We have recently started a new study where we are evaluating the effectiveness of the intervention in Namsos Municipality, using a pre-post-design and in-depth interview data. The objective of this study is directed towards subjective health and well-being effects as a result of the intervention. We are still processing the results.

Future Research on Countervailing Interventions

Understanding the Mechanisms and Plausible Outcomes

The SOW-project makes an example of a countervailing intervention aimed at promoting employee well-being and health, and at the same time promotes positive aspects in the work environment. The idea is that this form of intervention may counteract potentially negative effects of stressors through strengthening positive resources. In addition, there is an underlying assumption that the intervention, through strengthening positive resources, will also influence health outcomes and ability of individuals to handle stress and change. An important question is whether this form of intervention actually does influence well-being and health outcomes in a positive way, and function as a counteractive force against negative effects of stressors through the focus on positive aspects in the working environment.

The findings from our study are interesting, and suggest that musical interventions may be advantageous and can be useful in terms of promoting a positive psychosocial work environment, building positive resources in the workplace and even contribute to positive health outcomes. The participants reported positive change in psychosocial variables, overall health and in work engagement. The results are in line with similar findings in previous studies on choir singing and cultural activities (e.g. Grape et al. 2002; Cuypers et al. 2011; Bygren et al. 2009a, b), and thus with the concept of countervailing interventions.

The results should also be viewed in relation to the "broaden-and-build" theory (Fredrickson 2001), postulating that positive emotion influence the way individuals think and act, which in turn serve to build physical, intellectual and social resources. Participation in choir singing has been shown to induce positive emotions. For instance, Purchell and Kagan (2007) investigated the effect of a singing workshop in the workplace on well-being. The results showed that the workshops had a positive impact on participants' well-being, and the participants reported mood enhancement, happiness, perceived improved physical health, collectivity and confidence. These findings support the notion that countervailing interventions like SOW may serve to build and maintain resources in the workplace through arousing positive emotions, which in turn may contribute to counteract potential negative effects of high job demands in the work environment (Schaufeli and Bakker 2004). Consequently, combining knowledge from the field of arts and health, and occupational psychology, may provide an interesting and promising foundation for exploring new forms of interventions. We believe that countervailing interventions could be a part of a proactive approach to building healthy organizations. There are however many questions that are still to be answered concerning effectiveness, design and evaluation of countervailing interventions.

Although the findings from our study are interesting and can be said to provide some support for the concept of countervailing interventions, they also emphasize the need to further investigate specifically what aspects of the intervention result in positive outcomes for individuals. Is it related to the collective experience of singing in a choir? Did the competition against other department choirs have an effect? Did the participation in a choir influence individuals' self-efficacy? Is it the effect of having fun in the work place? Or were our results mainly attributable to a Hawthorn effect – the mere presence of professional musicians? These will be important research questions in our ongoing study. It is important to gain a greater understanding of these aspects. In addition, there is also a need to further explore the effects of the intervention in a time perspective. Are the observed effects on global health, commitment and engagement long term effects or will they simply wear off after a short while? Another important question is to what extent potential positive effects are transferrable to other forms of countervailing interventions.

Considering Potentially Negative Side Effects

In our study, participation in the intervention was offered to every employee in the organization; however, choir practice was set to after work hours. This might have had an impact on participation, and could have been an excluding factor for instance for people who commute or participate in other activities outside work. In interventions that involve musical or cultural participation, some individuals will never wish or be able to participate. An interesting point of discussion is whether this form of intervention, in addition to contributing to commitment and cohesion among the participants, also creates a larger gap between participants and those who do not wish or does not have the opportunity to participate. One should be aware of the possibility of unintended negative effect of the intervention on non-participants in terms of social exclusion, possible establishment of in-and-out groups, leaders neglecting important aspects of social support during the interventions etc.

In a Swedish study, the opportunity to participate in cultural activities was offered to some employees on a weekly basis in a period of 3 months. The researchers assessed emotional changes every week using a pre-post design.

Positive health effects were observed in the most enthusiastic participants; however, the same participants also reported a decrease in social support from colleagues (Theorell et al. 2009). Thus it is crucial to understand the effects on both participants and non-participants, and future research should therefore explore in what way implementation of these forms of interventions influence non-participants and group cohesion at work. An important aspect when designing cultural activities at work is that they are organized in a way that makes it possible and attractive for most employees to participate.

Research to Develop Efficient Countervailing Interventions

So, how do we go about developing efficient and successful countervailing interventions? There has to date been done little research on the effects of countervailing interventions (Kelloway et al. 2008). Consequently, knowledge of the effects of similar programs and what elements are important for success is limited. It is therefore important to further investigate what effects such interventions might have on the individual and in the working environment, and map out conditions where interventions have been successful. In intervention literature, although few studies on specific countervailing programs exist, there are some examples of studies that evaluate positive experiences in the work place such as work place fun and humor in the work place. Workplace "fun" has been found to have positive effects on individuals and has been positively related to job satisfaction and customer service quality (Karl and Peluchette 2006). Some researchers have also investigated stress moderating effects of humor in the workplace, but found no support for this (Martin 2001). The lack of research surrounding positive interventions illustrates the need for more research to find out if countervailing interventions may help prevent negative stress and ill health in the workplace, and if such programs have positive long term effects.

Kelloway et al. (2008) point out that the range of what could be considered countervailing interventions is broad. The SOW intervention involved music and singing, but there are many other possibilities in creating positive countervailing interventions. Accordingly, there is also a need for more research on potential forms of countervailing interventions to understand what works and to stake out efficient programs.

An interesting area of research that might provide some new answers is investigating the range of non-scientific health promotion and wellness programs in organizations. The idea of implementing activities or measures to promote employee health and well-being and improve work environment and motivate employees is not new. Dinners and lunches outside work hours, social and fun activities, competitions and physical activities are a just a few examples of measures that are common in work places to promote positive work environments and at the same time inspire and motivate employees. Aldana (2001) noted that roughly 90 % of organizations with more than 50 employees implement some sort of activity or program to promote health or well-being. Healthy workplace programs and activities are even promoted by HR-workers as a competitive advantage for the organization in the search for new employees (Grawitch et al. 2006). In spite of their prevalence and popularity, these types of measures are seldom evaluated and researched, even though they often are based on an underlying assumption that the activity or measure will lead to a change or improvement. There has to date been little research on the effects of such activities (Kelloway et al. 2008). Exploring and evaluating these forms of activities might uncover new knowledge on how to develop efficient countervailing interventions.

Evaluation Approaches for Countervailing Interventions

Another point of discussion is related to the way in which these forms of intervention should be evaluated. How do we evaluate countervailing interventions? In spite of few studies with positive findings concerning effectiveness of stress and health interventions, the intervention literature provides some good examples for evaluating interventions. Several researchers stress the importance of evaluating the implementation process as well as the effects of an intervention, and that effect should be measured through several follow up measurements (e.g. Saksvik et al. 2002; Nielsen and Randall 2012).

However, methods for evaluating interventions are mainly based on research on interventions implemented to prevent negative effects of stressors in the workplace. As discussed earlier, interventions are often directed towards solving problems that have been identified in the organization. An important aspect of evaluating the effectiveness of the intervention therefore involves assessing the intervention in terms of solving the problem. The purpose of the intervention is to eliminate the problem, and the effectiveness of the intervention is thus measured accordingly. Countervailing interventions such as SOW can be said to represent an entirely different frame of context, considering that they are not necessarily implemented on the basis of an existing problem in the organization, and that they also aim to investigate different outcome variables than what has been common (e.g. well-being, work engagement, etc.). This implies that the intervention process of countervailing interventions will differ, which also suggests that evaluating such interventions may call for a different approach. The premise of effectiveness does not depend upon the solving of a specific problem, but rather on enhancement of positive outcomes. In this sense one can argue that the outcome of such interventions appear to be more diffuse, and a challenge that arises in this regard is subsequently related to the way in which we measure success and effectiveness of these forms of intervention. As a part of a pro-active approach, countervailing interventions involve constantly working towards desired outcomes such as increased well-being or work engagement. Consequently, we believe that countervailing interventions represent more of a process perspective, and evaluation should therefore be more dynamic. A pre-post design may not be sufficient in order to observe long term effects, because the outcomes of such interventions are not necessarily clear cut.

In terms of outcome variables, promoting positive aspects of the work environment might have a different impact, and represent something qualitatively different than reducing the effect of negative aspects. For instance, research has shown that positive emotions are triggered by different factors than negative emotions, and that they also have different features (e.g. Fredrickson 2001). Also, several researchers draw a distinction between eustress and distress, that is, positive and negative responses to stressors (see Nelson and Simmons 2003). Empirical studies of hospital nurses revealed that nurses experienced both eustress and distress in response to their job demands. These stress responses were found to have different effects on the hospital nurses' perception of their own health. Another example is work engagement. The term has often been defined as the opposite of burnout (Maslach et al. 2001), but in recent years, research has shown that even though the concept is negatively related to burnout, there are different predictors predicting the two (Schaufeli and Bakker 2004). Taken together, such findings imply that positive states such as eustress and job engagement may have different patterns of causes and effects than negative states, something which underline that there is a need for different evaluation strategies. Such results also demonstrate the importance of investigating both positive and negative states because they often represent something qualitatively different.

In order to develop successful countervailing intervention programs, it is important to evaluate such measures in the right frame of context. A process evaluation of countervailing interventions may comprise many of the same questions that are asked in traditional process evaluations like support from managers, information, and participation, but also emotion-related questions may be included related to happiness, energy, and quality of life. Evaluating countervailing intervention programs on the premises of interventions based on a preventative or problem solving approaches may be inappropriate. On this basis, we argue that there is a need for an exploration of proper methods for evaluating countervailing interventions besides selecting different output variables.

Conclusions

The aim of this chapter was to explore and discuss the utilization of countervailing interventions. The chapter was not meant to provide a definite answer to effectiveness of specific countervailing intervention programs, but was rather intended as a catalyst of discussion and appeal for future research. We believe that building healthy organizations involves encompassing both a preventative approach in reducing potentially harmful aspects of the work environment, as well as a pro-active approach in terms of promoting positive aspects. Utilization of such interventions might provide a useful tool in health promotion and in building healthy organizations. We have in this chapter presented an example of a countervailing intervention. The results from our study indicate a range of possibilities with regard to interventions that incorporate a positive approach, which makes it a promising field for future study. Arguably, the need for further research to stake out successful and efficient forms of countervailing interventions is evident.

References

Aldana, S. G. (2001). Financial impact of health promotion programs: A comprehensive review of the literature. *American Journal of Health Promotion, 15*(5), 296–320. doi:10.4278/0890-1171-15.5.296.

Allen, N. J., & Meyer, J. P. (1997). *Commitment in the workplace: Theory, research, and application.* Thousand Oaks: Sage.

American Psychological Association. (1999). *What is a psychologically healthy workplace?* http://www.apahelpcenter.org/articles/article.php?id=34. Accessed 16 May 2009.

Bakker, A. B., & Derks, D. (2010). Positive occupational health psychology. In S. Leka & J. Loudmoth (Eds.), *Occupational health psychology* (pp. 194–224). Oxford: Blackwell Publishing Ltd.

Bygren, L. O., Konlaan, B. B., & Johansson, S. E. (1996). Attendance at cultural events, reading books or periodicals, and making music or singing in a choir as determinants for survival: Swedish interview survey of living conditions. *British Medical Journal, 313*, 1577–1580.

Bygren, L. O., Johansson, S.-E., Konlaan, B. B., Grjibovski, A. M., Wilkinson, A. V., & Sjöström, M. (2009a). Attending cultural events and cancer mortality: A Swedish cohort study. *Arts & Health, 1*(1), 64–73. doi:10.1080/17533010802528058.

Bygren, L. O., Weissglas, G., Wikström, B. M., Konlaan, B. B., Grjibovski, A., Karlsson, A. B., et al. (2009b). Cultural participation and health: A randomized controlled trial among medical care staff. *Psychosomatic Medicine, 71*(4), 469–473. doi:10.1097.

Carver, C. S., & Scheier, M. F. (1990). Origins and functions of positive and negative affect: A control-process view. *Psychological Review, 97*(1), 19–35.

Christensen, M. (2012). *Work and health in a changing world: The implications of job demands and resources for job satisfaction and health at work.* Trondheim: Norwegian University of Science and Technology.

Clift, S., & Hancox, G. (2001). The perceived benefits of singing findings from preliminary surveys of a university college choral society. *The Journal of the Royal Society for the Promotion of Health, 121*(4), 248–256.

Clift, S., Camic, P. M., Chapman, B., Clayton, G., Daykin, N., Eades, G., et al. (2009). The state of arts and health in England. *Arts & Health, 1*(1), 6–35. doi:10.1080/17533010802528017.

Cuypers, K. F., Knudtsen, M. S., Sandgren, M., Krokstad, S., Wikström, B. M., & Theorell, T. (2011). Cultural activities and public health: Research in Norway and Sweden. An overview. *Arts & Health, 3*(01), 6–26.

Fredrickson, B. L. (2001). The role of positive emotions in positive psychology. The broaden-and-build theory of positive emotions. *American Psychologist, 56*(3), 218–226. doi:10.1037//0003-066X.56.3.218.

Fredrickson, B. L., & Branigan, C. (2005). Positive emotions broaden the scope of attention and thought-action repertoires. *Cognition & Emotion, 19*(3), 313–332.

Fredrickson, B. L., & Losada, M. F. (2005). Positive affect and the complex dynamics of human flourishing. *American Psychologist, 60*(7), 678–686.

Fredrickson, B. L., Tugade, M. M., Waugh, C. E., & Larkin, G. R. (2003). What good are positive emotions in crisis? A prospective study of resilience and emotions following the terrorist attacks on the United States on September 11th, 2001. *Journal of Personality and Social Psychology, 84*(2), 365–376.

George, J. M., & Brief, A. P. (1992). Feeling good-doing good: A conceptual analysis of the mood at work-organizational spontaneity relationship. *Psychological Bulletin, 112*(2), 310–329.

Grape, C., Sandgren, M., Hansson, L. O., Ericson, M., & Theorell, T. (2002). Does singing promote well-being?: An empirical study of professional and amateur singers during a singing lesson. *Integrative Physiological and Behavioral Science, 38*(1), 65–74.

Grawitch, M. J., Gottschalk, M., & Munz, D. C. (2006). The path to a healthy workplace: A critical review linking healthy workplace practices, employee well-being, and organizational improvements. *Consulting Psychology Journal: Practice and Research, 58*(3), 129–147. doi:10.1037/1065-9293.58.3.129.

Hakanen, J. J., Bakker, A. B., & Demerouti, E. (2005). How dentists cope with their job demands and stay engaged: The moderating role of job resources. *European Journal of Oral Sciences, 113*(6), 479–487.

Hurrell, J. J., & Murphy, L. R. (1998). Occupational stress intervention. *American Journal of Industrial Medicine, 29*(4), 338–341.

Isen, A. M., Daubman, K. A., & Nowicki, G. P. (1987). Positive affect facilitates creative problem solving. *Journal of Personality and Social Psychology, 52*(6), 1122.

Karl, K., & Peluchette, J. (2006). How does workplace fun impact employee perceptions of customer service quality? *Journal of Leadership and Organizational Studies, 13*(2), 2–13. doi:10.1177/10717919070130020201.

Kelloway, E. K., Hurrell, J. J., & Day, A. (2008). Workplace interventions for occupational stress. In K. Naswall, J. Hellegren, & M. Sverke (Eds.), *The individual in the changing working life.* Cambridge: Cambridge University Press.

Kjeøy, N. (2009, November 27). Kultur gir bedre helse. *Adresseavisa,* p. 12.

Kreutz, G., Bongard, S., Rohrmann, S., Hodapp, V., & Grebe, D. (2004). Effects of choir singing or listening on secretory immunoglobulin A, cortisol, and emotional state. *Journal of Behavioral Medicine, 27*(6), 623–635.

Kuhn, D. (2002). The effects of active and passive participation in musical activity on the immune system as measured by salivary immunoglobulin A (SIgA). *Journal of Music Therapy, 39*(1), 30.

Luthans, F. (2002). The need for and meaning of positive organizational behavior. *Journal of Organizational Behavior, 23*(6), 695–706.

Martin, R. A. (2001). Humor, laughter, and physical health: Methodological issues and research findings. *Psychological Bulletin, 127*(4), 504–519. doi:10.1037/0033-2909.127.4.504.

Maslach, C., Schaufeli, W. B., & Leiter, M. P. (2001). Job burnout. *Annual Review of Psychology, 52*, 397–422. doi:10.1146/annurev.psych.52.1.397.

Nelson, D. L., & Simmons, B. L. (2003). Health psychology and work stress: A more positive approach. In C. Q. James & L. E. Tetrick (Eds.), *Handbook of occupational health psychology* (pp. 97–119). Washington, DC: American Psychological Association.

Nielsen, K., & Randall, R. (2012). Opening the black box: Presenting a model for evaluating organizational-level interventions. *European Journal of Work and Organizational Psychology,* 1–17. doi:10.1080/1359432x.2012.690556.

Norway. (2006). *Arbeidsmiljøloven.* Legislative document. http://www.lovdata.no/cgi-wift/wiftldles?doc=/app/gratis/www/docroot/all/nl-20050617-062.html&emne=arbeidsmilj%F8lov*&&. Accessed 17 Oct 2012.

Prior, R. (2010). Editorial. *Journal of Applied Arts and Health, 1*(1), 3–6.

Purcell, C., & Kagan, C. (2007). Joy at work: The impact of non-professional singing workshops on employee well-being. In *RIHSC annual conference, 2007.* Manchester: Research Institute for Health and Social Change (RHSC).

Reynolds, S. (1997). Psychological well-being at work: Is prevention better than cure? *Journal of Psychosomatic Research, 43*(1), 93–102.

Richardson, K. M., & Rothstein, H. R. (2008). Effects of occupational stress management intervention programs: A meta-analysis. *Journal of Occupational Health Psychology, 13*(1), 69–93.

Ruud, E., & Stige, B. (1994). *Kultur ger hälsa. Slutrapport* (Publikasjoner fra Finlands Unescokommisjon 70, pp. 79–103). Helsinki: Finlands Unesco-kommisjon.

Saksvik, P. Ø., & Gustafsson, O. (2004). Early retirement from work: A longitudinal study of the impact of organisational change in a public enterprise. *Policy and Practice in Health and Safety, 2*(2), 43–55.

Saksvik, P. Ø., & Tvedt, St. D. (2009). Leading change in a healthy way. *Scandinavian Journal of Organizational Psychology, 1* (1).

Saksvik, P. Ø., Nytrø, K., Dahl-Jørgensen, C., & Mikkelsen, A. (2002). A process evaluation of individual and organizational occupational stress and health interventions. *Work and Stress, 16*(1), 37–57.

Schaufeli, W. B., & Bakker, A. B. (2004). Job demands, job resources, and their relationship with burnout and engagement: A multi-sample study. *Journal of Organizational Behavior, 25*(3), 293–315.

Seligman, M. E. P., & Csikszentmihalyi, M. (2000). Positive psychology: An introduction. *American Psychologist, 55*(1), 5–14. doi:10.1037/0003-066X.55.1.5.

Theorell, T. (2009). *Noter om musik och hälsa*. Stockholm: Karolinska Institut University Press.

Theorell, T., Hartzell, M., & Näslund, S. (2009). A note on designing evaluations of health effects of cultural activities at work. *Arts & Health, 1*(1), 89–92. doi:10.1080/17533010802527993.

Turner, N., Barling, J., & Zacharatos, A. (2002). Positive psychology at work. In C. R. Snyder & S. J. Lopez (Eds.), *Handbook of positive psychology* (pp. 715–728). New York: Oxford University Press.

Vaag, J., Saksvik, P. Ø., Theorell, T., Skillingstad, T., & Bjerkeset, O. (2012). Sound of well-being – Choir singing as an intervention to improve well-being among employees in two Norwegian county hospitals. *Arts & Health,* 1–10. doi:10.1080/17533015.2012.727838.

Chapter 17
An Integrated Health Protection/Promotion Program Supporting Participatory Ergonomics and Salutogenic Approaches in the Design of Workplace Interventions

Robert A. Henning, David W. Reeves, and CPH-NEW Research Team

Abstract Since its founding in 2006, the Center for the Promotion of Health in the New England Workplace (CPH-NEW) has conducted evidence-based field research to determine how organizations can establish sustainable programs for planning and implementing integrated health promotion and health protection interventions with high levels of employee engagement. Salutogenic strengths of CPH-NEW's recommended programmatic approach are highlighted in this chapter, including how a small group of front-line employees work as a team to identify and prioritize health/safety issues/concerns, use participatory ergonomics to design and plan workplace interventions, and collaborate with management during intervention implementation and evaluation. A structured toolkit-based approach for designing workplace interventions is described in some detail to show how salutogenic principles and approaches can be systematically incorporated during intervention planning as part of a continuous salutogenic change process for healthy organizations. Research challenges associated with evaluating program effectiveness and sustainability are also discussed.

R.A. Henning, Ph.D. (✉)
Center for the Promotion of Health in the New England Workplace,
University of Connecticut, Storrs, CT, USA
e-mail: robert.henning@uconn.edu

D.W. Reeves, M.A.
Sirota, Purchase, NY, USA

Center for the Promotion of Health in the New England Workplace,
University of Connecticut, Storrs, CT, USA
e-mail: dreeves@sirota.com

CPH-NEW Research Team
Center for the Promotion of Health in the New England Workplace,
University of Connecticut, Storrs, CT, USA

University of Massachusetts-Lowell, MA, USA

G.F. Bauer and G.J. Jenny (eds.), *Salutogenic Organizations and Change:*   307
The Concepts Behind Organizational Health Intervention Research,
DOI 10.1007/978-94-007-6470-5_17, © Springer Science+Business Media Dordrecht 2013

Keywords Participatory ergonomics • Health promotion • Health protection • Salutogenesis • Cybernetics • Macroergonomics • Organizational learning • Program sustainability • Employee participation • Occupational safety and health • Integration • CPH-NEW • Sense of coherence

Healthy Organizations and Research Imperatives

An organization can be considered a healthy organization when it has become highly effective at being able to maintain and promote the health and wellbeing of employees along with the health of the organization itself. According to the salutogenic model of Antonovsky (1987), a healthy organization would aid employees in developing a strong sense of coherence (SOC) about their job and work environment in regard to these becoming more comprehensible, manageable and meaningful. From the shared systems perspective of macroergonomics (Hendrick and Kleiner 2002) and behavioral cybernetics (Smith and Smith 1987), a healthy organization is no accident and depends on good ergonomic design of physical and operational factors in the workplace. Achieving all this will depend on an organization being committed to a continuous process of health and safety improvement because there will always be changes internal and external to an organization that create new challenges, such as the introduction of new technologies, changes in global economics, and shifts in employee demographics. Healthy organizations will also show a readiness to engage in organizational learning (Haims and Carayon 1998) in order to meet and adapt to these new challenges, many of which will require complex sociotechnical changes involving both physical workplace changes and changes to work organization. Learning how to apply macroergonomics methods to address new safety challenges with technology is one example of where organizational learning can become critically important (Smith 2002).

Healthy organizations would adopt proactive and preventive (i.e., feedforward, Smith 2002) approaches to employee health/safety issues in addition to compensatory approaches, because compensatory approaches can never be fully effective. Proactive approaches require effective tracking and communication systems as part of any comprehensive employee health protection and promotion program and cannot depend on conventional surveillance of employee health outcomes for up-to-date tracking. Front-line employees can help out here by being engaged to identify operational hazards to health and safety because of their close familiarity with many aspects of their jobs not usually shared by either their supervisors or health and safety professionals (Smith 2002). Front-line employees can also be instrumental in recommending ideas to address workplace hazards of an operational nature as part of a hazard management program. In some cases it becomes necessary to also seek novel methods and expertise from outside the organization during intervention planning efforts (Smith 2002). In general, healthy organizations are committed to taking decisive action on a proactive basis, are willing to seek outside help and assistance, and welcome opportunities for organizational learning whenever confronted by difficult challenges that threaten the health or wellbeing of their employees.

Unfortunately, successful workplace interventions in healthy organizations are not likely to transfer to other organizations because of contextual differences in organizational design and culture (Hendrick and Kleiner 2002). An alternative to failing at attempts to "import solutions" is for an organization to apply best practices in planning and developing its own site-specific interventions. Best practices for such intervention planning and development would require a programmatic approach dedicated to the continuous improvement of the health, safety and wellbeing of employees. With this in mind, our research challenge has been to develop and field-test programmatic approaches that are based on best practices for continuously engaging employees in the identification and prioritization of health/safety issues/concerns as well as planning workplace interventions, and to also devise ways of gaining organizational support for approval, implementation and evaluation of these interventions in a sustainable manner.

Development and Testing of a Systems Approach for Continuous Improvement of Employee Health and Safety

Initial Combination of Participatory Ergonomics and Health Promotion (PExHP)

Starting in 2006, the Center for the Promotion of Health in the New England Workplace (CPH-NEW 2006), a NIOSH center for research excellence as part of the NIOSH Total Worker Health™ initiative with researchers from the University of Connecticut and the University of Massachusetts-Lowell, has engaged in a translational research effort to develop a new approach for helping organizations plan and implement workplace interventions to benefit worker health and health protection. This effort has had the following three main goals:

1. to improve worker health by combining health promotion and workplace health and safety interventions,
2. to promote a grass-roots, participatory approach that engages all levels of an organization in the design of effective workplace interventions, and
3. to create sustainable health promotion/protection programs through the collaboration of front-line employees and upper-management in intervention planning.

CPH-NEW researchers developed a structured and evidence-based programmatic approach to address three recognized shortcomings of conventional workplace HP programs: (1) a lack of sustainability, (2) little sense of employee ownership, and (3) the need for more effective integration of health promotion efforts with changes in work organization. When ergonomics approaches introduced through participatory ergonomics (PE) are combined with health promotion

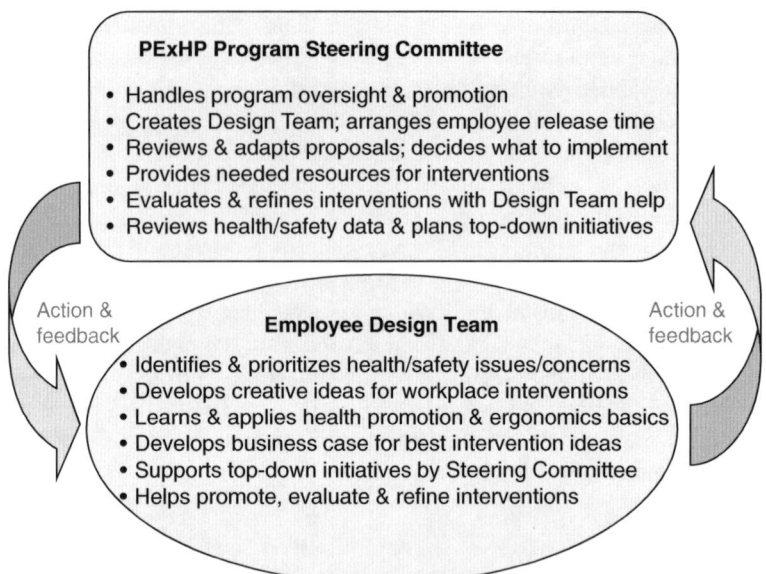

PExHP Program Steering Committee

- Handles program oversight & promotion
- Creates Design Team; arranges employee release time
- Reviews & adapts proposals; decides what to implement
- Provides needed resources for interventions
- Evaluates & refines interventions with Design Team help
- Reviews health/safety data & plans top-down initiatives

Action &
feedback   **Employee Design Team**   Action &
feedback

- Identifies & prioritizes health/safety issues/concerns
- Develops creative ideas for workplace interventions
- Learns & applies health promotion & ergonomics basics
- Develops business case for best intervention ideas
- Supports top-down initiatives by Steering Committee
- Helps promote, evaluate & refine interventions

Fig. 17.1 Feedback control dynamics in a PExHP program

(HP) approaches (Punnett et al. 2009), a beneficial synergism is expected that we have abbreviated as "PExHP" (Henning et al. 2009). The potential for synergistic benefits conforms to a systems understanding of human performance, where human behavior is strongly influenced by design factors in the work environment that include how the work is organized. Simply stated; employee health and safety are expected to benefit far more when behavior and lifestyle changes are not attempted in isolation from making changes to the workplace, with the converse also holding true. Therefore, the systems nature of PExHP interventions makes it more likely that the root causes of health/safety issues/concerns related to design factors can be identified and addressed, resulting in interventions that are proactive in nature.

PExHP Program Structure

The PExHP program structure consists of a "steering committee" with program oversight responsibility, and a "design team" that plans workplace interventions to address health/safety issues/concerns, as depicted in Fig. 17.1. A program facilitator meets regularly with the steering committee and the design team.

The design team is made up of 5–8 front-line employees who meet separately with the program facilitator. A design team works most effectively when its members share some of the same health/safety issues/concerns, and along with their peers stand to benefit from any resulting intervention. Design team members initially receive rudimentary training on ergonomics and health promotion principles, and then engage in intervention planning in much the same way that a group of employees functions in a participatory ergonomics program. This grassroots nature of the design team is an important feature of a PExHP program.

With the help of the program facilitator, usually a safety or health professional with appropriate background, temperament and training, design team members engage in the initial steps of intervention planning while working separately and autonomously from the program steering committee. This allows members of the design team to be more open with their peers when discussing health/safety issues/ concerns of a personal nature, and also maintain some degree of confidentiality when sensitive topics are being considered. This approach also fosters creativity during "brainstorming" sessions when the presence of a supervisor might prevent design team members from sharing undeveloped ideas or thoughts about interventions that might reflect on or impact management practices. For these same reasons, a facilitator must remain neutral throughout the intervention planning process in order to gain and maintain the trust of members of the design team. Finding a qualified facilitator internally may be easier to accomplish for a large company whereas a smaller company may need to hire a facilitator from the outside.

The steering committee has general oversight responsibility for the PExHP program and so must have some authority to approve interventions, and be capable of marshaling any needed resources for the implementation and evaluation of interventions. This requires that the program steering committee is made up of key personnel who are committed to improving employee health and safety. As per Henning et al. (2009), representation from all levels of the organization is recommended for a program steering committee, with a union leader included if a union is present.

Original Intervention Planning Process

The original intervention planning and design process tested in PExHP programs was structured as a somewhat generic seven-step planning process initiated only by the design team: (Step 1) Identify and a select a health/safety issue/concern, (Step 2) Gather information and analyze a health/safety issue/concern, (Step 3) Generate potential interventions, (Step 4) Select and plan an intervention, (Step 5) Meet with the steering committee to gain approval for the intervention, (Step 6) Implement the workplace intervention, and (Step 7) Evaluate the workplace intervention, and iterate the intervention design as needed. Consistent with best practices when planning new systems (Chapanis 1996), this was not a "forced march" through these seven planning and implementation steps. Design team members could revisit earlier planning steps to revise intervention plans whenever it was discovered that something important was overlooked in an earlier step. Once an intervention proposal was fully developed, it was presented to the steering committee for review and consideration. If it was found to be acceptable by the steering committee, and following any needed adaptations made in collaboration with the design team, the intervention was then implemented in much the same manner as any other project initiative within the organization. However, the design team could also be asked to help with its implementation and evaluation as part of an iterative design process for refining an intervention. For further details, please see Henning et al. (2009).

Development and Testing of a Toolkit for Establishing and Maintaining PExHP Programs

In late 2009 CPH-NEW initiated a 3-year translational effort to develop a Research-to-Practice (R2P) Toolkit that would provide a set of easy-to-use assessment instruments and protocols geared to the development of an in-house PExHP participatory program for the continuous improvement of employee health and safety. In contrast to the original PExHP program that was usually facilitated by researchers with doctorate degrees at field sites that were part of a larger study, the R2P Toolkit is intended to provide a safety or health professional (with the equivalent of masters-level professional training) with all of the necessary protocols and support materials needed to implement and maintain a healthy PExHP program. The design of the R2P Toolkit was initially based on lessons learned from CPH-NEW field studies, where the success of the PExHP integrated approach had been shown to depend on the training that is delivered to all levels of the organization, regular communication about the PExHP program during its start-up period, and regular meetings of the design team and steering committee.

The R2P Toolkit provides separate step-by-step guides and support materials for establishing a PExHP program that involve the following steps and associated activities over about a 5-month start-up period:

1. Initial contact and assessment of the host organization

    (a) Identify health champion to coordinate program start-up
    (b) Establish agreements regarding resources and preventing retribution
    (c) Conduct structured interviews with key personnel
    (d) Evaluate organizational readiness for a participatory program

2. Creation of the program steering committee

    (a) Begin organization-wide communication about the PExHP program

3. Assessment of employee health/safety issues/concerns

    (a) Conduct focus groups with front-line employees (optional)
    (b) Administer a baseline survey to all employees

4. Creation of the design team

    (a) Conduct teambuilding exercise
    (b) Provide training on ergonomics and health promotion

5. Begin intervention planning and implementation

   (a) Prioritize health/safety issues concerns
   (b) Plan and implement interventions using a structured planning tool

The baseline survey administered to all employees (the All-Employee Survey) was developed to provide feedback reports about employee health status and health/safety issues/concerns that can be shared as soon as possible with the steering committee and the design team. Feedback reports can build a readiness in the steering committee and organization to support interventions, and later can help focus intervention planning efforts by either the steering committee or design team on high priority health/safety issues/concerns. In some cases, comparisons with benchmark standards can be made to highlight health/safety areas in which the organization is underperforming. For further details about the All-Employee Survey, please see the section "Outcomes Evaluation".

Initial tests of the R2P Toolkit began at four field sites in 2010 and concluded in 2012.

An iterative design approach was employed to revise the R2P Toolkit based on any limitations or difficulties revealed by facilitators during field testing. Program facilitators reported several shortcomings of the original intervention design process. Design teams often rushed through the initial design steps, and this resulted in intervention proposals that were not well conceived nor fully developed. Field tests also showed that any time a program steering committee rejected an intervention proposal, this was perceived as a sign that the PExHP program was no longer supported by upper management and/or that the health/safety issue/concern being addressed was not considered important enough by management. In either case, this had a demoralizing effect on design team members, making it harder for the program facilitator to engage design team members in further intervention planning efforts.

Development of the Intervention Design and Analysis Scorecard (IDEAS) for More Structured Intervention Planning

Due to the abovementioned problems and limitations, CPH-NEW researchers developed a more structured planning approach that would meet the following scientific and programmatic needs discovered through field tests of the R2P Toolkit: (1) to address the root causes of health/safety issues/concerns, (2) to provide more balanced interventions in regard to application of both ergonomics and health promotion principles, (3) to provide more than one intervention option for the steering committee to consider for any specific health/safety issue/concern that is being addressed, and (4) to develop intervention proposals that are well grounded in business decision making practices by broadly considering the return-on-investment strengths and weaknesses so that these intervention proposals are tailored to survive a full review by the steering committee.

A new intervention planning tool was developed, the Intervention Design and Analysis Scorecard (IDEAS), based on best practices in systems engineering, macroergonomics, and management decision-making. It affords greater depth to the original seven-step design process by providing more structure within each planning step. The added structure of the IDEAS Tool is closely modeled after an intervention planning process developed for use by macroergonomics professionals as reported in a case study by Robertson and Courtney (2004). Unlike the approach developed by Robertson and Courtney, however, the IDEAS Tool does not assume ergonomics expertise on the part of the facilitator or design team members. The added structure provided by the IDEAS Tool supports a systems approach to intervention planning by placing a high priority on developing integrated health protection/promotion interventions that include (1) ergonomics approaches involving changes to the workplace or work organization and (2) health promotion approaches involving behavior, lifestyle changes, training or other approaches that typically do not require changes to the workplace or work organization.

Planning Steps in the Intervention Design and Analysis Scorecard (IDEAS)

The seven steps in the IDEAS planning process are shown in Fig. 17.2. The first four steps of the IDEAS Tool are described in some detail here in preparation for the section "Incorporation of Salutogenic Principles into the Intervention Planning Process" where we show how salutogenic principles are easily incorporated into this structured intervention planning process:

In IDEAS Step 1, the facilitator helps the design team engage in a systems analysis of the root causes of a health/safety issue/concern. Design team members are asked to identify as many contributing factors as possible by focusing on both ergonomics and lifestyle factors in a balanced manner.

In IDEAS Step 2, what had been identified as a high-priority issue/concern is transformed into an objective (or solution) for the intervention design effort. For example, if the issue/concern in IDEAS Step 1 was "20 % of employees have musculoskeletal injuries," the objective in IDEAS Step 2 might be "95 % of employees will be injury free." Once an objective has been decided upon, the facilitator leads the design team in a group "brainstorming" effort to generate a large number of possible activities that would contribute to achieving the objective (or sub-objectives, if this helps simplify planning efforts). Activities are generated until most of the important contributing factors identified in IDEAS Step 1 have been addressed, providing a balanced mix of both ergonomic and health promotion activities to consider using in IDEAS Step 3.

In IDEAS Step 3, the design team is asked to help create a set of "Key Performance Indicators" (KPIs) that are relevant to the objective (or sub-objectives) named in IDEAS Step 2. KPIs are the criteria that the design team will use to assess the

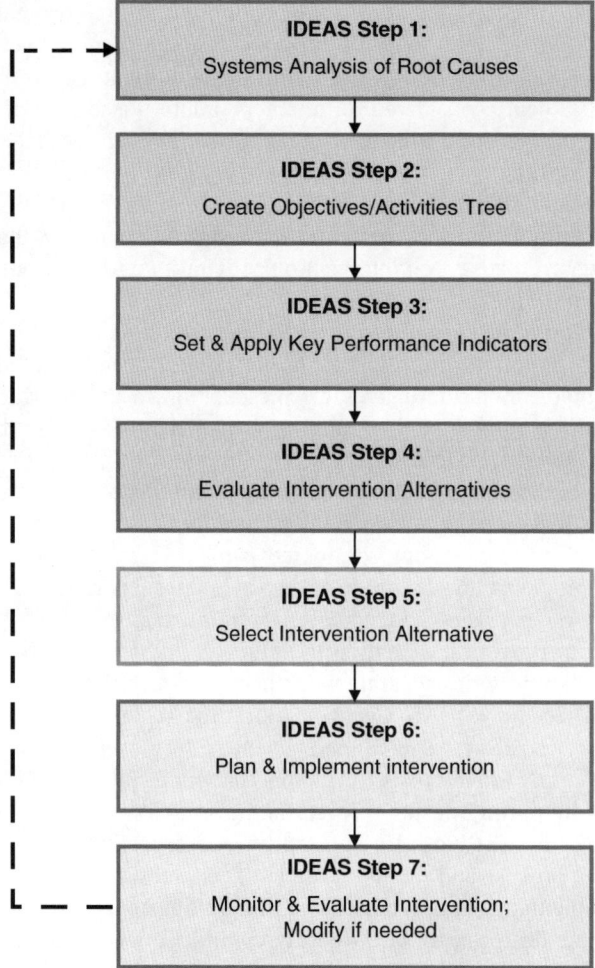

Fig. 17.2 Steps in the Intervention Design and Analysis Scorecard planning process. The program facilitator works with either the employee design team or steering committee in Steps 1–4. Steps 5–7 are dominated by steering committee but can benefit from collaborations with the design team

anticipated effectiveness of intervention activities to be considered. The design team generates KPIs in four categories:

1. Scope
2. Benefits/Effectiveness
3. Obstacles/Barriers
4. Resources/Costs

Once these KPIs are in place, the facilitator guides the design team through a process of systematically sorting through the list of potential intervention activities generated in IDEAS Step 2, and then selecting those activities that, either singly or in combination, would result in an effective and feasible "intervention alternative." Use of the KPIs helps the design team consider important trade-offs among the various activities being considered for an intervention. It also provides a means to incorporate recognized best practices of business planning and decision-making. For example, consideration of the scope of a potential intervention activity may reveal that an intervention activity is inferior to another intervention activity in terms of how many employees would be impacted. Alternatively, these considerations may suggest that several intervention activities would be needed to achieve the desired scope of an intervention.

In IDEAS Step 4, the design team uses the same KPIs generated in IDEAS Step 3 to compare intervention alternatives with each other. The goal is to select the three most viable intervention alternatives for presentation to the steering committee. Presenting multiple intervention alternatives is intended to increase the likelihood that one of the intervention alternatives will be supported by the steering committee. It also affords the steering committee the added flexibility of supporting a new subset of activities that the design team had not considered.

In IDEAS Step 5, the steering committee as the primary decision-making body in the PExHP program chooses which interventions to support as well as the nature and extent of these interventions, including their time course.

In addition to providing a facilitator's guide for using the IDEAS, the CPH-NEW R2P Toolkit provides separate worksheets for each IDEAS step. For example, the worksheet for IDEAS Step 1 supports the systems analysis of the root causes of a health/safety issue/concern by providing a graphical inverted tree diagram with empty fill-in boxes for factors that contribute to the issue/concern. In addition to supporting design efforts, the information captured in the IDEAS worksheets provides the basis for substantive and organized presentation of the entire planning process and the many trade-off choices that were made over the course of this planning. This is a useful starting point for a productive collaboration between the design team and steering committee whenever an intervention needs to be adapted. The IDEAS planning process therefore provides a complete site-specific business case for every intervention proposal. This context-specific approach to preparing a business case can be expected to have a better reception from management than a generic business case that is based on workplace interventions that were developed and implemented in different organizational contexts.

IDEAS Steps 6–7 largely consist of helpful checklists because it is assumed that most organizations already have project planning and implementation protocols in place. Nonetheless, the steering committee can greatly benefit from collaborating with the design team in IDEAS Steps 6 and 7; for example, by receiving assistance with assessment tools and in refining an intervention that has unexpected difficulties. It is desirable for both the steering committee and design team to retain a sense of "ownership" of any interventions that are implemented, consistent with best practices in macroergonomics (Brown 2002). This sense of ownership would also yield salutogenic benefits of increased comprehensibility, manageability and meaningfulness of organizational initiatives to improve employee safety, health and wellbeing.

A web-based version of the CPH-NEW R2P Toolkit, including the IDEAS Tool, is scheduled for release in 2013.

Linking PExHP to the Concept of Salutogenesis

Antonovksy (1996), in discussing how salutogenesis should be used to guide health promotion programs, provided an example of how one particular program would have benefited from the application of salutogenic principles and his SOC construct. Intervention researchers often make assumptions about what their participants need (e.g., support, training, etc.), and this can result in missed opportunities for introducing interventions that would have much greater impact. Antonovsky therefore recommends that researchers should first ask participants what would make their world more comprehensible, manageable and meaningful.

The very nature of the PExHP program participatory approach is seen as being intrinsically rewarding for employees by giving them the ability to institute meaningful change within their organization (Henning et al. 2009). Personal involvement in intervention planning is also likely to increase an individual's SOC through positive interactions with multiple stakeholders (e.g., supervisors, coworkers) during efforts to secure resources and needed approvals, and simply through meaningful involvement and control of one's safety and health. However, as described below, PExHP programs not only benefit individual SOC, they provide a macroergonomic framework to support salutogenic change in the workplace that can help any organization to become healthier.

Contributions of PExHP Programs to Individual Work-Related Sense of Coherence

In 1987, Antonovsky (1987) laid out a new model of salutogenesis in which job characteristics affect the three factors of SOC (comprehensible, manageable and meaningful) individually. The relevance of this new model to a PExHP program is clearly evident. Comprehensibility in Antonovsky's model was theorized to be affected by the job security and climate within the workplace. These two aspects of the work environment are fairly important, because without job security and high-quality communication, employees can begin to feel confused and uncertain about many aspects of the organization they work in, and these uncertainties undermine the comprehensibility of their work environment.

There are several aspects of PExHP programs that would reduce uncertainties in the working environment, and therefore increase comprehensibility. Top-down commitment to the PExHP program, efforts for continuous improvement with employee involvement, education about ergonomic and health promotion principles, acknowledgment of employee health/safety issues/concerns, and collaboration with a PExHP program steering committee would work to improve management-employee relations and employees' understanding of the workplace, and reduce uncertainty – all of which would benefit an employee's comprehensibility of his/her work environment. Research has shown that, indeed, a connection exists between the quality of a supervisor-subordinate relationship and an individual's SOC. Feldt et al. (2000) and also Rothmann et al. (2005) found that individuals who had more positive relationships with their supervisors also had a higher SOC.

To help strengthen the manageability factor of SOC, it is easy to see how the health/safety issues/concerns about a job could undermine an employee's sense of manageability. However, Antonovsky also pointed out that it is not just the demands of the job, but also the support that an individual receives which is important for developing a sense of manageability. Support for these relationships is reported by Rothmann et al. (2005) who found that lower demands in the workplace were related to higher levels of SOC. In addition, Albertson et al. (2001) found that support from coworkers was related to increases in SOC. There are many aspects of the PExHP program that would provide this support by helping employees address their health/safety issues/concerns and thereby increase employee perceptions of manageability in the workplace. These include: allocation of programmatic resources for continuous improvement of health and safety, training on ergonomic and health promotion principles, the availability of ergonomic and health promotion experts, opportunities for employees on the design team to prioritize and target health/safety issues/concerns, effective workplace interventions, employee involvement in the iterative design of interventions, and increased respect from management.

In regard to meaningfulness, Antonovsky indicated that meaningful participation in decision making was necessary for an individual to develop meaningfulness in their work. Subsequent research has supported the hypothesis that increases in meaningful decision making is related to increased SOC (Albertsen et al. 2001; Sagy and Antonovsky 2000). The very basis of the PExHP intervention design and implementation process is a partnership between management and front-line employees to improve the working environment, and this necessarily involves shared decision-making. There are several aspects of a PExHP program that particularly empower and involve employees in this shared decision process. These include being trained on ergonomic and health promotion principles before and during the design process, prioritizing health/safety issues/concerns, choosing activities for focused interventions, the ability to consult with experts, the sense of ownership of the program and any resulting interventions, and the collaborative decision-making process with the steering committee. All of these aspects of the PExHP program would contribute to employees developing a stronger perception of meaningfulness in the workplace.

Therefore, through active involvement of an employee on the design team in a PExHP program, or through indirect involvement by employees via interactions with design team members and an awareness of PExHP program activities, employees' work-related SOC is expected to increase based on the model put forth by Antonovsky (1987).

Incorporation of Salutogenic Principles into the Intervention Planning Process

As described above, a program facilitator in a PExHP program helps front-line employees engage in a structured intervention planning process through use of the IDEAS Tool. One way that the IDEAS planning process can be used to support salutogenic change in the workplace is to allow design team members to consider and prioritize both salutogenic issues/concerns and health/safety issues/concerns prior to IDEAS Step 1. Addressing salutogenic issues/concerns cannot be expected to involve the same risk reduction approaches that are conventionally used to address health/safety issues/concerns. For example, a salutogenic concern might be that a particular job has become less meaningful following the adoption of new automation technology. Having identified this salutogenic concern as a high priority, design team members would be able to then employ the structured intervention planning process offered by the IDEAS. Contributing factors to the salutogenic issue/concern would be identified in IDEAS Step 1; generation of activities that would contribute to whatever salutogenic objective or goal is agreed upon would occur in IDEAS Step 2. Thus, allowing salutogenic issues/concerns to be considered when issues/concerns are being prioritized is a simple and direct way to expand the domain of a PExHP program to include and address salutogenic issues/concerns.

A second way the IDEAS planning process can support salutogenic change in the workplace is for the facilitator to provide formal training on how to apply salutogenic principles when generating intervention activities in IDEAS Step 2. This would include training on how to incorporate salutogenic activities in interventions in a balanced manner along with ergonomic and health promoting activities. Whenever the workplace becomes more comprehensible, manageable and meaningful, this can be expected to have synergistic beneficial effects on employee well-being when combined with more conventional risk reduction activities.

A third way that the IDEAS planning process can support salutogenic change in the workplace is to factor in salutogenic considerations when setting KPIs in IDEAS Step 3. For example, the salutogenic benefit of "substantially contributes to job meaning" may be determined to be important enough to list as a KPI under the category of "Benefits/Effectiveness." Then later in IDEAS Step 3 when each potential intervention activity is being evaluated in relation to this KPI, this may reveal a lack of intervention activities with this salutogenic benefit and the need to return to IDEAS Step 2 to expand the list of potential intervention activities.

A fourth way that the IDEAS planning process can support salutogenic change in the workplace is for the program steering committee to decide to permanently add a new category of KPIs emphasizing salutogenesis, perhaps as a means to help achieve the organization's strategic plan, mission statement or new initiative. For example, a mission statement may include offering all employees an opportunity to have meaningful work. This expansion of the original prescribed KPI categories would have a large impact all subsequent intervention planning activities, consistent with the systems approach advocated by Bauer and Jenny (2007) in which management is engaged in setting salutogenic priorities at an organizational level.

Research on the Intervention Design Process
and PExHP Program Sustainability

Conducting research on PExHP programs brings unique challenges because the participatory nature of these programs and the intervention design process makes them inherently unpredictable. Not only are there significant differences between organizations in terms of their readiness or ability to implement a grassroots participatory approach to intervention planning (Reeves and Henning 2008), it is difficult to predict which health/safety issues/concerns will be prioritized by front-line employees functioning as a design team. An example of this from our field tests was that we expected the design teams at two field sites to focus on musculoskeletal disorders but instead they planned interventions on stress-related issues. Then there is the matter of offering unlimited flexibility in the design of the interventions themselves. Use of the IDEAS Tool opens up a wide range of options for an organization to choose from in regard to the scope and time course of any intervention. Unfortunately, all of these degrees of freedom and sources of variance complicate the scientific evaluation of program and intervention effectiveness.

Process Evaluation

It is important to include some form of process evaluation when assessing PExHP programs because of the extent of collaboration that must occur between the steering committee and the design team in order for the program to function effectively. When deciding which processes to measure, it is helpful to examine specific feedback control relationships that occur within these programs, consistent with behavioral cybernetic theory (Smith and Smith 1987; Smith et al. 1994, 1995; Haims and Carayon 1998; Smith 2002) and best practices in macroergonomics (Hendrick and Kleiner 2002).

Regarding control dynamics from the standpoint of the design team in Fig. 17.1, its members expect the steering committee to generally support design team autonomy during IDEAS Steps 1–4 but also to be responsive to any design team requests for assistance during this period, such as providing access to an external expert for consultation about intervention alternatives. In terms of the dynamics of the associated feedback control process involved here, any delayed response on the part of the steering committee can easily be misinterpreted by members of the design team; for example, as a sign that top-down support for the PExHP program has eroded.

Members of the design team are recruited to represent other employees as well as to reach out to them, and there are inherent control relationships of interest here. The ability of design team members to adequately represent other employees requires them to actively seek their opinions and ideas for interventions. The success and extent of these efforts depends in part on how well the PExHP program functions in regard to implementing interventions that address perceived health/ safety issues/concerns. Therefore, for this representative approach to succeed, members of the design team should have a sense of control over both their intervention planning efforts and the overall PExHP program but also not become overly burdened by functioning in this role.

To assess processes inherent to control dynamics like those described above and depicted in Fig. 17.1, CPH-NEW adapted a survey instrument developed by Matthews et al. (2011) to periodically assess the viability of the PExHP program from the perspective of the members of the design team. The following dimensions are evaluated: (1) involvement in design efforts, (2) knowledge base for ergonomics and health promotion, (3) managerial support, (4) employee supportiveness, and (5) unplanned consequences. High scores in all but the fifth dimension, which was included to assess possible adverse impacts, would reflect increased program health and viability.

The feedback control relationships shown in Fig. 17.1 can also be considered from the standpoint of the steering committee. A primary control action initiated by the steering committee is to request that the design team prioritize employee health/ safety issues/concerns and develop creative intervention ideas for consideration by the steering committee. Feedback to the steering committee from the design team in response to these control actions can take the form of regular reports by the program facilitator about the design team's progress in intervention planning. Providing too much information about the intervention planning activities of the design team could undermine the autonomy of the design team, and so feedback about planning progress is all that the steering committee needs to maintain effective oversight of the design team. The steering committee will eventually receive detailed feedback about earlier design team activities when IDEAS worksheets are shared during review of proposals. These will have captured process information regarding the planning considerations and decisions members of the design team made during their autonomous intervention planning period.

CPH-NEW researchers developed a software-based process tracking database tool to monitor and assess feedback control dynamics between the design team and steering committee during field tests of the R2P Toolkit. Measures developed by Haims and Carayon (1998) to track organizational learning were incorporated in this tracking system to assess PExHP program processes and planning progress. Additional measures were based on the quality (or compliance) of feedback, as defined in behavioral cybernetic theory (Smith and Smith 1987; Smith et al. 1995). Process assessments were made by the facilitator following each meeting of either the design team or steering committee. While only preliminary analyses have been conducted on these data, it would appear that these process measurements correlate with changes in the comprehensibility and manageability of ongoing design team activities, with greater manageability during training periods than during intervention planning and implementation efforts.

Gaining a better understanding of the organizational dynamics needed to support and sustain a participatory program for the continuous maintenance and improvement of employee health and wellbeing remains a work in progress for CPH-NEW

Table 17.1 Areas assessed in the All-Employee Survey

General physical and mental health	Pain/discomfort
Sleep quality and amount	Depression
Readiness to change lifestyle	Work stress
Work ability	Burnout
Organizational culture	Job satisfaction
Civility norms	Intent to turnover
Procedural justice	Work safety tension
Health/safety climate	Job content
Work-family conflict	Commute time
Sense of coherence	Demographics

researchers as we continue to study the impact of our research-to-practice programs on salutogenesis at the individual and organizational levels, and on members of both the design team and the steering committee.

Outcomes Evaluation

The start-up process for PExHP programs includes an initial administration of the All-Employee Survey as a baseline assessment of the content domains listed in Table 17.1. Information about any recent or ongoing organizational initiatives for health promotion and protection is obtained through structured interviews of key personnel. These same assessments can be repeated at a later date to assess PExHP program impact and effectiveness but preferably not before several intervention planning and implementation cycles have been completed. Additional items are added to the All-Employee Survey during re-administrations to assess employee awareness that certain interventions had occurred and their impact, as well as the overall effectiveness of the PExHP program.

Targeted pre- and post-intervention surveys are developed to evaluate the success of specific interventions and to provide data that would be useful in any iterative design effort of these interventions. These targeted surveys are much shorter than the All-Employee Survey. Consistent with participatory action research, members of the design team usually participate in the design of targeted surveys by identifying the major themes for inclusion, and in editing the wording of survey items to fit the workplace culture. Survey items can be based on the same KPIs that would have been used in IDEAS Step 3 for the intervention that is being implemented. After having been involved in the creation of targeted surveys, design team members usually develop a sense of "ownership" that motivates them to help administer these surveys through "snowball sampling," or by promoting general acceptance among their peers as a way to increase survey response rate. Targeted surveys are scored by the PExHP program facilitator to maintain confidentiality. CPH-NEW has selected a set of core survey items from the All-Employee Survey so that an abbreviated standardized assessment can occur alongside any more targeted items. These core items are selected based on their content and sensitivity to the intervention being evaluated. Inclusion of these core items helps maintain a systems approach in the evaluation of interventions by checking for impacts beyond what is anticipated. The steering committee can request that additional items be added to a targeted intervention survey, and may also decide to administer additional post-intervention assessments as part of an iterative design process to help refine the intervention.

Program Sustainability

Organizations will usually continue to invest in programs that yield results, and so any signs that a program will be sustained are some of the more unambiguous indicators of program effectiveness that a health promotion/protection program can have. This also suggests that researchers interested in evaluating program sustainability should seek to develop sets of indicators aligned to the priorities of the host organization. In addition to satisfying research needs, such assessments can also assist organizations engaged in the process of evaluating these programs. An example assessment here could be the level of employee engagement, either in planning interventions or participating in the interventions themselves. For research purposes, any evidence of long-term resource commitment by an organization to the PExHP program is considered a valid indicator of sustainability. Specific indicators of long-term commitment to a PExHP program would therefore include the following possibilities: (1) efforts to keep the PExHP program structure intact by maintaining or expanding the steering committee and design team, including plans for rotation of personnel or transferring program oversight responsibilities to a permanent committee, (2) recruitment of a permanent program facilitator, either internally or externally, (3) a commitment to maintaining or increasing the level of resource support to the program, (4) any promotional efforts about the program or interventions, and (5) any plans to expand the program to additional divisions or sites within a large organization. CPH-NEW has depended on structured interviews with key personnel as well as focus groups with design team members to collect data on these aspects of long-term commitment to a PExHP program. These interviews and focus groups are conducted by researchers with no involvement at the field site.

An example of long-term commitment to the PExHP program at one of our test sites was that the organization reassigned oversight responsibility for the PExHP program from the original dedicated steering committee to a standing committee that had other related oversight roles. This was considered a positive development in terms of PExHP program sustainability because the new oversight body was well established, had greater decision-making authority, and more access to resources. It is possible that a dedicated PExHP program steering committee may only be crucial during the start-up period when additional oversight is needed and there is still a need for the PExHP program to establish itself as a new and important initiative. While the eventual integration of a PExHP program into existing organizational structures that have better personnel reporting and accountability systems can be considered a positive development, we have found that this also necessitates additional training sessions for any members of the oversight body who are unfamiliar with how a PExHP program functions.

Acknowledgements Dr. Michelle Robertson, Liberty Mutual Research Institute for Safety and CPH-NEW Research Affiliate. Co-Principal Investigator R2P Toolkit Project.

Dr. Nicholas Warren, Associate Professor, Department of Community Medicine, University of Connecticut. Co-Principal Investigator R2P Toolkit Project.

Suzanne Nobrega, M.S., Department of Work Environment, University of Massachusetts-Lowell. Program Director R2P Toolkit Project.

Dr. Georg Bauer, Division of Public and Organizational Health, Institute of Social and Preventive Medicine, University of Zurich, and CPH-NEW Research Affiliate. Project consultant R2P Toolkit Project.

Elizabeth Erck, M.S., Mari Ryan, MBA, MHP, and Zandra Zweber, MA. Program facilitators R2P Toolkit Project.

Disclaimer:
This publication was supported by Grant Number 1 U19 OH008857 from the National Institute for Occupational Safety and Health. Its contents are solely the responsibility of the authors and do not necessarily represent the official views of NIOSH.

References

Albertsen, K., Nielsen, M. L., & Borg, V. (2001). The Danish psychosocial work environment and symptoms of stress: The main, mediating, and moderating role of sense of coherence. *Work and Stress, 15*, 241–253.

Antonovsky, A. (1987). Health promoting factors at work: The sense of coherence. In R. Kalimo, M. Eltatawi, & C. Cooper (Eds.), *Psychosocial factors at work and their effects on health* (pp. 153–167). Geneva: World Health Organization, WHO.

Antonovsky, A. (1996). The salutogenic model as a theory to guide health promotion. *Health Promotion International, 11*(1), 11–18.

Bauer, G., & Jenny, G. (2007). Development, implementation and dissemination of occupational health management (OHM): Putting salutogenesis into practice. In J. Houdmont & S. McIntyre (Eds.), *Occupational health psychology: European perspectives on research, education and practice* (pp. 219–250). Castelo da Maia: ISMAI.

Brown, O., Jr. (2002). Macroergonomic methods: Participation. In H. W. Hendrick & B. M. Kleiner (Eds.), *Macroergonomics: Theory, methods, and applications* (pp. 25–44). Mahwah: Lawrence Erlbaum Associates.

Center for the Promotion of Health in the New England Workplace (CPH-NEW). (2006). *A NIOSH center for research excellence as part of the NIOSH Total Worker Health™ initiative*. http://www.uml.edu/Research/centers/CPH-NEW. Center Co-Directors: Dr. Laura Punnett, University of Massachusetts-Lowell, and Dr. Martin Cherniack, University of Connecticut.

Chapanis, A. (1996). *Human factors in systems engineering*. New York: Wiley.

Feldt, T., Kinnunen, U., & Mauno, S. (2000). A mediational model of sense of coherence in the work context: A one-year follow-up study. *Journal of Organizational Behavior, 21*, 461–476.

Haims, M. C., & Carayon, P. (1998). Theory and practice for the implementation of "in-house" continuous improvement participatory ergonomics programs. *Applied Ergonomics, 29*, 461–472.

Hendrick, H. W., & Kleiner, B. M. (Eds.). (2002). *Macroergonomics: Theory, methods, and applications*. Mahwah: Lawrence Erlbaum Associates.

Henning, R. A., Warren, N., Robertson, M., Faghri, P., & Cherniack, M. (2009). Workplace health promotion through participatory ergonomics: An integrated approach. *Public Health Reports, 124*(Suppl 1), 26–35.

Matthews, R. A., Gallus, J. A., & Henning, R. A. (2011). Participatory ergonomics: Development of an employee assessment questionnaire. *Accident Analysis and Prevention, 34*, 360–369.

Punnett, L., Cherniack, M., Henning, R., Morse, T., Faghri, P., & The CPH-NEW Research Team. (2009). A conceptual framework for the integration of workplace health promotion and occupational ergonomics programs. *Public Health Reports, 124*(Suppl 1), 16–25.

Reeves, D. W., & Henning, R. A. (2008). Worksite measurement of organizational readiness for a participatory ergonomics intervention. In R. A. Henning (Chair), *Three interventions for workplace health: R2P strategies and participatory methodologies*. Symposium presented at Work, Stress and Health 2008. Washington, DC.

Robertson, M. M., & Courtney, T. K. (2004). A systems analysis approach to solving office work system health and performance problems. *Theoretical Issues in Ergonomics Science, 5*(3), 181–197.

Rothmann, S., Steyn, L. J., & Mostert, K. (2005). Job stress, sense of coherence and work wellness in an electricity supply organization. *South African Journal of Business Management, 36*(1), 55–63.

Sagy, S., & Antonovsky, H. (2000). The development of the sense of coherence: A retrospective study of early life experiences in the family. *Journal of Aging and Human Development, 51*(2), 155–166.

Smith, T. J. (2002). Macroergonomics of hazard management. In H. W. Hendrick & B. M. Kleiner (Eds.), *Macroergonomics: Theory, methods, and applications* (pp. 199–222). Mahwah: Lawrence Erlbaum Associates.

Smith, T. J., & Smith, K. U. (1987). Feedback-control mechanisms of human behavior. In G. Salvendy (Ed.), *Handbook of human factors* (pp. 251–293). New York: Wiley.

Smith, T. J., Henning, R. H., & Smith, K. U. (1994). Sources of performance variability. In G. Salvendy & W. Karwowski (Eds.), *Design of work and development of personnel in advanced manufacturing* (pp. 273–330). New York: Wiley.

Smith, T. J., Henning, R. A., & Smith, K. U. (1995). Performance of hybrid automated systems – A social cybernetic analysis. *International Journal of Human Factors in Manufacturing, 5*(1), 29–51.

Chapter 18
Participatory Intervention from an Organizational Perspective: Employees as Active Agents in Creating a Healthy Work Environment

Karina Nielsen, Maria Stage, Johan Simonsen Abildgaard, and Charlotte V. Brauer

Abstract While organizational level interventions are generally recommended and the interest in conducting such interventions is increasing, few descriptions of how researchers may develop and implement such interventions exist. In this book chapter we present the PIOP (Participatory Interventions from an Organizational Perspective) approach. It is an intervention framework that aims to improve employee well-being through changes in the way work is designed, organized and managed. Building on the job demands-resources model, and cognitive appraisal, conservation of resources, job crafting, and fit theories, an approach has been developed that focuses on building employees' resources through participatory processes. In this chapter, we describe the five phases in the PIOP approach and describe how participation is ensured in each phase. The five phases comprise: Initiation, screening, action planning, implementation and evaluation.

Keywords Organizational intervention • Cognitive theory • Job crafting • Participation • Process evaluation

K. Nielsen (✉)
Norwich Business School, University of East Anglia, Norwich Research Park, Norwich, NR4 7TJ, UK

The National Research Centre for the Working Environment, Copenhagen, Denmark
e-mail: k.nielsen@uea.ac.uk

M. Stage
The National Research Centre for the Working Environment, Lersø Park Allé 105, 2100 Copenhagen, Denmark
e-mail: mst@arbejdsmiljoforskning.dk

J.S. Abildgaard
University of Copenhagen, Øster Farimagsgade 2a, 1353 Copenhagen, Denmark
e-mail: Johan.Abildgaard@psy.ku.dk

C.V. Brauer
Postnord, Tietgensgade 37, 1566 Copenhagen, Denmark
e-mail: charlotte.v.brauer@post.dk

G.F. Bauer and G.J. Jenny (eds.), *Salutogenic Organizations and Change: The Concepts Behind Organizational Health Intervention Research*, DOI 10.1007/978-94-007-6470-5_18, © Springer Science+Business Media Dordrecht 2013

Background

In organizational research, participatory approaches to changing the way work is organized, designed and managed are generally recommended (Kompier et al. 1998; Kompier 2004; Nielsen et al. 2010c). In the participatory approach, employees are involved in: (1) planning the intervention design; (2) identifying areas for improvement initiatives; (3) developing action plans for improvement initiatives, (4) implementing improvement initiatives, and (5) evaluating the results of the intervention (Nielsen et al. 2010b). The outcomes of participatory interventions are increased social support, autonomy, and improved well-being (Nielsen and Randall 2012b). The participatory approach is believed to facilitate successful interventions for four reasons. First, it can help to optimize the fit of the intervention to the organizational culture and context. Making use of employees' job expertise and knowledge of the organizational context provides an important supplement to the expertise of intervention experts. Second, participation can smooth the change process and increase exposure to the intervention. As employees are involved in deciding the design and implementation they are more likely to feel ownership and actively support practical implementation. Third, it can be viewed as an intervention in its own right. The participatory approach can be seen as a working mechanism because employees are treated as co-learners in an empowerment process increasing respect, esteem and reward (Nielsen et al. 2010b; Nielsen and Randall 2012b). Four, the participatory approach may help enhance a positive collaborative climate between managers and employees. On the one hand, employees may get a better understanding of the strategic challenges faced by the organization, and on the other hand, managers may get a better understanding of the challenges employees face in daily working life. The development of shared goals may lead to an improved collaborate climate as this development may create an understanding of the role of employee representatives and the role of managers, respectively.

To date, limited research has explicitly focused on how we may ensure employee participation in the intervention process (Nielsen and Randall 2012b). In this book chapter we describe a participatory research approach that involves employees in the design, planning and implementation of organizational interventions. The PIOP approach, presented here, has been developed in an action research project together with The Danish Postal Service, targeting working conditions of mail delivery workers. In Denmark, the mail delivery workers are organized into work teams and our intervention was designed use this structure. The examples and experiences we present are based on this project. In the project, a research team at the National Research Centre for the Working Environment evaluated the project and an internal consultant employed at the postal service managed the process.

We will begin by describing some of the theoretical underpinnings of the approach and then describe the intervention phases making explicit how employee participation was sought at each phase.

Theoretical Framework

In an attempt to build a framework on which intervention activities should not only focus on minimizing risks as has been the case in previous organizational intervention research (Nielsen et al. 2010c) but also increase the resources of employees and ensure that the intervention fits the organizational context (Randall and Nielsen 2012), the intervention model was built on the job demands resources (JD-R) model (Bakker and Demerouti 2007), and cognitive appraisal (Lazarus and Folkman 1992), job crafting (Wrzesniewski and Dutton 2001) and fit theories (Kristof-Brown and Guay 2011).

Focusing on Resources in Addition to Adverse Working Conditions

According to the JD-R model, two underlying psychological processes determine the well-being of employees (Bakker and Demerouti 2007). First, the health impairment process suggests that a situation with high demands combined with inadequate resources will deplete employees' well-being. Over time this may lead to a negative spiral in which employees suffering from poor well-being will further deplete their available resources thus finding it increasingly difficult to deal with the demands of the job. Second, the motivational process assumes that resources have a motivational potential allowing individuals in possession of resources to mobilize their resources and gain more resources and as a result experience better well-being (Bakker and Demerouti 2007). According to Conservation of Resources (COR) theory (Hobfoll 1989) maximizing social job resources and task resources will have a positive effect on well-being because larger pools of resources enable the individual to protect themselves from resource depletion and deal with the demands of the environment. The mechanisms of the JD-R model have been validated in a recent review (Crawford et al. 2010).

Employees Actively Craft Their Jobs

Methods applied in organizational intervention research is based on the assumption that there exists an "objective" working environment that has a harmful effect on employees (Nielsen et al. 2010c) and that employees are passive recipients of the intervention (Kohler and Munz 2006); however, this assumption is in contrast to major psychological theory and research.

According to cognitive stress appraisal theory (Lazarus and Folkman 1992), individuals categorize their environment based on primary and secondary appraisal. Primary appraisal concerns the evaluation of whether an encounter is irrelevant (having no impact on well-being), benign-positive (potentially enhancing or pre-serving well-being) or harmful (potentially depleting well-being), secondary appraisal concerns the evaluation of what might and can be done to either enhance well-being (in a benign-positive situation) or prevent well-being depletion (in a harmful situation). Cognitive appraisal theory would suggest that it is important to measure whether the situation or a condition is appraised to be good or bad for the individual's well-being rather than trying to estimate an objective level of harm. Furthermore, an aspect of the psychosocial work environment, e.g. role conflict, can only be said to be harmful if the employee perceives a conflict and appraises it as a threat or a problem that is difficult to control (Lazarus and Folkman 1992). It also suggests that employees react to specific elements of the intervention based on their appraisal of it being beneficial or adverse to their health and well-being (Nielsen and Randall 2012a). Numerous studies have found support for the importance of cognitive appraisal in determining employee health and well-being (e.g. Daniels et al. 2004, 2006; Dewe 1989).

A central element of participation is the empowering process in which employ-ees take responsibility for improving their own work environment, rather than being passive recipients of change. In recent years, there has been an increasing interest in bottom-up job design with one particular form being job crafting (Grant and Ashford 2008; Grant and Parker 2009). Job crafting has been defined as "the physical and cognitive changes individuals make in the task or relational boundaries of their work" (Wrzesniewski and Dutton 2001, p. 179). Through job crafting, individuals actively strive to mobilize resources to fulfil their needs and thrive at work (Bakker and Demerouti 2007), and they proactively craft a job where they can use their skills and have opportunities to grow thereby increasing their well-being and creating meaningfulness in the job (Tims and Bakker 2010).

It has been suggested that organizations should develop interventions that allow employees to job craft collectively (Berg et al. 2010). Participatory interventions may be one way of encouraging employees to job craft collectively: Employees engaged in participatory organizational interventions may get new perspectives on their working life and learn how they can collectively question existing working procedures and craft their jobs not only to ensure their own goals and needs fulfil-ment but develop an understanding of how they may jointly obtain shared goals. An important aspect of participatory interventions is that employees should be made aware of how they can use the influence made available to them, i.e. that they must be proactive in influencing both intervention processes and outcomes. Although there have been no intervention studies explicitly aimed at increasing job crafting behaviors, Hasson et al. (2012) found that in some intervention groups, employees reported more changes than their managers (who were officially responsible for implementing intervention activities). They suggested this could be due to employees initiating their own activities, i.e. job crafting.

Fitting the Intervention to the Context and the People Within the Organization

Person-environment fit is broadly defined as the compatibility between an individual and the work environment that occurs when their characteristics are well-matched (Kristof-Brown et al. 2005, p. 281). Recently, this thinking has been transferred to organizational interventions suggesting that when developing intervention action plans, it is important to consider how the planned activities fit with the individuals' resources on the one hand, and the organizational context on the other (Randall and Nielsen 2012). In the PIOP approach we have taken this thinking one step further. In preparing our interventions we analyzed the fit of our intervention design to the organization and developed initiatives to develop these resources. We analyze the existing culture and the available resources within the organization to manage adverse working conditions and improve employee well-being: At the Organizational level we identify the formal structures for organizational development and employee support, at the Leader level we examine whether line managers are motivated and have the resources to manage the process, at the Group and Individual levels we explore whether groups of employees and also individual employees (e.g. union and health and safety representatives) have the resources necessary to engage in the intervention. We call this four level approach IGLO (Individual, Group, Leader, and Organization). The information obtained at this stage is used throughout the project to tailor the project to the organization.

Phases of the Participatory Intervention

The PIOP approach uses a systematic approach to the planning and implementation of the intervention project. The intervention is divided into five main phases as is common in organizational intervention research (Nielsen et al. 2010b). The five phases are: Initiation, screening, action planning, implementation, and evaluation. See Fig. 18.1 for an overview of the five phases.

Initiation Phase

During this first phase of the project, a steering group is established. It should consist of employee and management representatives. The steering group should guide and manage the intervention process and ensure that progress is made at all levels. It is therefore essential that the steering group has members from all relevant levels and functions. A typical steering group would thus include both senior and mid-level management, employee representatives, and representatives from the

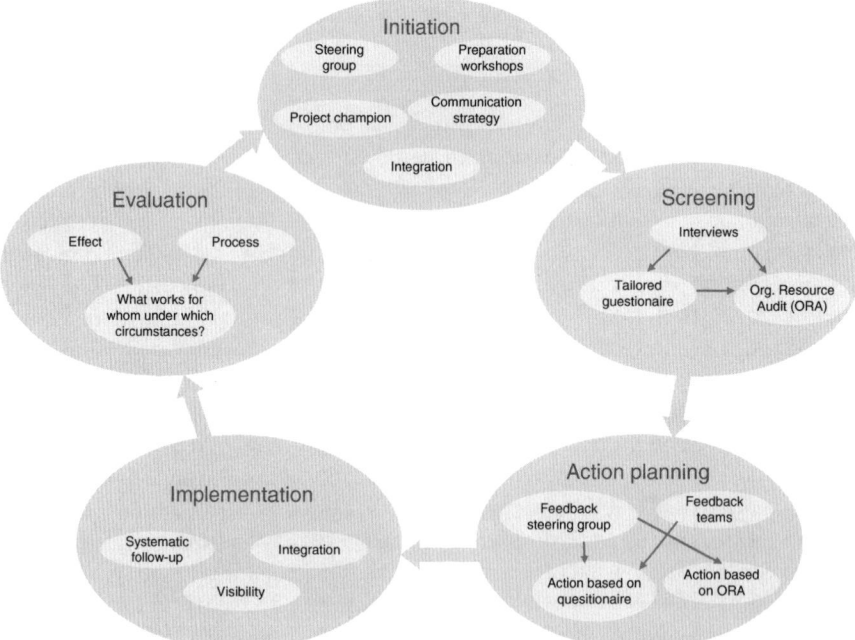

Fig. 18.1 PIOP model

organizational resource functions such as HR (both organizational development and communication) and occupational health. A project manager should be identified to manage the process.

The Steering Group

The steering group has two overall functions: An operational and a strategic. At the operational level, the steering group is responsible for daily progress of project activities, and at the strategic level, the steering group is responsible for the overall progress of the project. In larger organizations, it may be necessary to establish steering groups at different levels. It is our experience that it can be challenging to manage the group process in groups with more than 8–10 members.

The tasks of the operational steering group are:

- Develop a joint understanding of the definitions of well-being and psychosocial work environment and develop the overall objectives and aims of the intervention project.
- Plan and implement a communication strategy and plan on how to inform participants on (i) the content and the aims and objectives of the project, (ii) how they can gain influence over the project and provide feedback, and (iii) the progress of the project.

- Facilitate interviews with employees.
- Discuss and approve the screening tool and monitor the screening process.
- On an ongoing basis, evaluate the process and identify initiatives to ensure momentum.
- Decide on the strategy for feedback and approve feedback content.
- Discuss results of screening and determine a strategy for how improvement initiatives may be developed and implemented. A central element here is the discussion of how participation among employees not directly involved in the steering group is ensured.
- Ensure the participation of employees who are not involved in the steering group.

The tasks of the strategic steering group are:

- Identification of groups at risk that should take part in the project.
- Ensure that the aims and objectives of the project are aligned with the overall aims and objectives of the organization.
- Follow up on progress and if necessary provide additional resources for implementation.
- Reflect on the factors which facilitate or hinder the intervention process and take action to strengthen the intervention process.
- Evaluate how the intervention process is aligned with existing health and safety management procedures.
- Evaluate the strengths and weaknesses of the approach in the organizational context and examine how the strengths can be used better and weaknesses be addressed at a central level.
- Evaluate whether changes in existing health and safety management procedures should be introduced on the back of the project.

The Role of the Project Champion

A project champion should be appointed to manage the intervention project. A project champion can both be an internal or external HR or occupational health consultant. The competencies of the project champion include:

- Project management skills. The project champion manages the progress of the intervention project. This includes planning mile stones, ensuring mile stones are met and meetings are held as necessary.
- Process consultation skills. The project champion manages steering group meetings and workshops. It includes planning meetings and workshops, define the aims and objectives of these and make sure that the aims and objectives are met in the time allocated to meetings and workshops. This requires the skills to manage group processes and ensure that the goals of the meetings and workshops are reached.
- Knowledge of the intervention group. The project champion should have an understanding of the culture, competencies and skills of the intervention group. This understanding enables the project champion to tailor the process to the target group, e.g. in a group of employees with little education and who are not used

Fig. 18.2 Ownership model

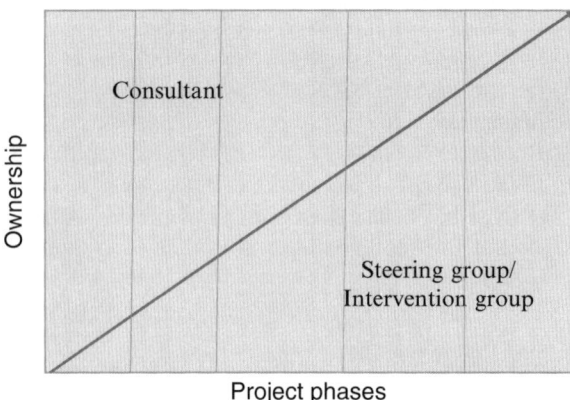

to discussing psychosocial issues it may be necessary to plan meetings differently than in a group of professionals.

- Knowledge of psychosocial issues and employee well-being. The project champion should also have an understanding of psychosocial issues and well-being in order to guide discussions. The project champion should provide neutral professional input to the participants' discussions on how to manage psychosocial issues and well-being. The expertise of the local context and the avenues for improvement initiatives rest with the intervention group.
- Navigator skills. The project champion holds many diverse roles. S/he is the driver of the process, owner of the project, observer of the intervention process, expert, and process consultant. This requires the project champion to be able to operate at many different levels at one time.

An important tool in the PIOP approach used to create awareness about the degree of participation is the ownership model (see Fig. 18.2). This model forms the basis for a discussion of the ownership of the steering group and the intervention group throughout the project's phases: Is it primarily the research team (in the case of an action research project) or the project champion that has primary ownership of the project? In the beginning of the project it is only natural that the project champion (together with the research team) has primary ownership as he or she is responsible for progress during the first phases. Screening and feedback requires expertise that steering group members do not necessarily possess, however, as the focus changes to that of developing, implementing and managing improvement initiatives, it becomes vital that responsibility shifts such that the intervention group, with the steering group in the lead, assumes responsibility for change. Real change and learning can only take place if it is initiated by the participants and they have gone through the process and acquired the necessary competencies to continually address the challenges they face at work. The ownership model helps to raise awareness of the level of ownership assumed by the steering group but can also help reveal discrepancies in perceptions of ownership among steering group members and thus it can open for a dialogue of what ownership means and how it should be operationalized in a particular project. Furthermore, the ownership model also allows for a dialogue about the competencies of members of the steering group and how the different competencies within the group can be applied to strengthen the collaboration of the group and ensure sustainable change processes.

Manager and Employee Workshops: Preparing for Participation

Numerous studies have shown that middle managers or employee representatives may not have the resources to engage in a participatory process (Biron et al. 2010; Nielsen et al. 2006, 2010a). Preparatory workshops for union representatives, health and safety representatives, and leaders at all levels (providing resources at the I and L level of the IGLO model) in the intervention group are conducted to ensure that a fit between the organizational members' resources and the demands put on them managing the intervention process. In the PIOP approach, workshops are conducted for the management team and for employee representatives separately.

Line managers are often the drivers of intervention projects but they are rarely included in the preparations of such projects. In the PIOP approach, a manager workshop is conducted with the managers in the intervention group. The objectives of the half-day workshop are to get managers: (1) to reflect on the overall objectives of the intervention to ensure they are understood and that managers buy into these, (2) to develop the goals of the intervention for the management team as a whole. The aim is to develop a shared understanding among managers how they can collectively use the intervention project to obtain a shared goal, (3) to develop their own individual goals for their team and help managers understand how they can use the project to develop their own employees, for example increase employees work engagement and collective job crafting behaviors, and (4) how the intervention can be used to develop their own leadership style.

Employee representatives, though they may be familiar with their formal roles such as union representatives or health and safety representatives, may not always feel equipped to engage in the intervention process (Nielsen et al. 2006). A 1-day workshop is conducted with the following content: (1) introduction of the project including a description of the central guiding elements such as participation, the job demands-resources model, the importance of fitting the intervention to the organization, and the IGLO concept, (2) discussions of their expectations of the project and their readiness for change, (3) discussions of their role as employee representatives and how this role influences their relations with colleagues and management. This includes a discussion of previous experiences with the role and common pitfalls and advantages of having a formal role, what the pitfalls and advantages are of participating in an intervention project that requires a close collaboration between managers and employee representatives.

Developing a Communication Strategy

Communication forms the basis of the participatory process. Without proper communication to provide an understanding of the aims and objectives of the project and ongoing updates about progress, employees are less likely to support the project because they do not notice any changes (Landsbergis and Vivona-Vaughan 1995), and if changes are not made explicit they are unlikely to change the cognitive appraisals of staff.

The communication plan is developed by the steering group, and it is therefore beneficial if a representative from the organization's communication department is a member of the steering group. This person can contribute with expert knowledge on communication processes, how to communicate in the local context, and can take on a role in ensuring communication material is developed and distributed.

Initially, the project should be presented at team meetings. The presentation should be held by the project champion such that participants are able to "put a face" on the project. Both employee and manager representatives should be available at these meetings, to show their commitment to the project, to answer questions from employees, and to get a feeling of the level of readiness for change in teams.

A communication strategy should be developed that focuses on three main areas:

1. Description of the intervention process, it goals, target areas, and the phases of the project. This element is important as employees need to understand the content of the project and can anticipate what is required of them at which point. It can help ensure ownership over and commitment to, for example, the completion of questionnaires and support in the implementation of action plans.
2. Description of the way in which participants can influence the project. All employees in the intervention group should have the opportunity to have their voice heard in terms the issues they believe need to be addressed by the project but also concerning the process.
3. Ongoing updates of the intervention progress. It should be made clear to participants where in the process the project is and what is currently being worked on. It is important to openly celebrate the "small successes", e.g. a high response rate or the completion of an action plan.

The communication strategy should include both written and oral means of communication and make use of existing information channels. Written material can be included in information in company newsletters, memos or a leaflet that introduces the project. Oral communication can be presented at meetings at all levels. Steering group members all play an important role in informing colleagues about the progress of the project and to help employees not part of the steering group understand what learning takes place in the steering group. It should be a fixed item on each steering group meeting agenda to discuss how the content of the meeting should be communicated to colleagues. A combination of oral and written information may help steering group members feel comfortable communicating, e.g. short description of what needs to be communicated together with answers to frequently asked questions; this increases the likelihood that all employees get the same information. It is equally

Plan of activities	Area
Who is the target group?	Employees in the area
What is the goal of communication	All employees know about the project and about progress. Employees get involved in the project and take responsibility for tasks within the project.
What is the content of communication?	Progress: At which phase is the project? What is being worked on in the team? What improvement initiatives are taken in the team? What are the effects of improvement initiatives?
Which media are used to communicate?	Oral information at team meetings Kaizen board Noticeboard: What are we working on right now? Letters to employees
Who is responsible for/participates in communication?	Members of the steering group –both employees and managers
How do we communicate in practice?	After each steering group meeting, members of the group get together to summarize what needs to be communicated and how. Improvement initiatives and other work going on as part of the project is a fixed item on the team meetings. Use of statements from the survey –where are we – are we making progress?
How much time is set aside?	Planning of the project is set to 1-2 days a month
What are the criteria for success?	Everybody needs to know the process and initiatives Everybody is involved to some degree
How do we ensure feedback and follow-up?	Project champion contacts the individual teams about progress. Every month teams are followed up on the suitability of current practices and ideas as to how the communication may be adjusted if necessary

Fig. 18.3 Example of communication plan

important to have visual reminders of the project. This could involve posters of the project with the aims and objectives and a timeline, where it is possible to follow progress. In Fig. 18.3, an example of a communication plan is depicted.

Integration into the Organizational Daily Life

The difficulties of integrating intervention projects into daily work practices are well-known. Managers and employees focus on what they perceive as core work activities and may resent taking time away from core tasks, seeing intervention projects as a nuisance to the completion of daily duties (Dahl-Jørgensen and Saksvik 2005). It is therefore important to ensure the integration of the project into to the daily work of the organization. This integration can be ensured at the practical level by integrating project activities into existing meeting structures, be it management meetings, team meetings, health and safety committee meetings, and/or worker councils. Such integration also helps emphasizing a central point in the PIOP approach: That the project should not be seen as an external, isolated, one-off event. Instead, the focus of the project is to change the way work is organized, designed and managed in order to improve productivity and employee well-being in the long term. These improvements are achieved by optimizing existing health and safety management practices and empowering employees to take responsibility for their own working life. When such discussions of working conditions and well-being become part of the daily procedures within the organization, they are more likely to have sustainable impact.

Screening Phase

During this phase, a systematic screening of the organization's demands and resources is conducted. Two different sets of screening are conducted: One of the working conditions of the intervention groups, and one of the resources available to staff within the organization.

The Tailored Questionnaire

Generally when conducting interventions to improve the psychosocial working environment, the recommendation is to conduct thorough screening to identify relevant factors to the group in question and target activities to the problems of the workplace as these will be more effective (Kompier and Kristensen 2001; Murphy and Sauter 2004). The challenges in capturing the local context using standardized questionnaires have previously been identified (Daniels et al. 2012). Standardized measures make it difficult to get an in-depth understanding of the complex situation in a given target group; to develop targeted interventions to change the way work is designed, organized and managed in that group (Dewe 1989). In a response to this challenge, Daniels et al. (2004) presented a cognitive model for how individuals appraise their situations. They suggested that assessment of working conditions should be made on the basis of employees' own categories and the language of employees should be used to describe those categories. Furthermore, they suggest using the response categories "problematic" and "good", which capture the employees' cognitive appraisal of their working environment. This approach also offers employees the opportunity to play an active role in developing the screening tool thereby ensuring ownership and relevance to the target group in question.

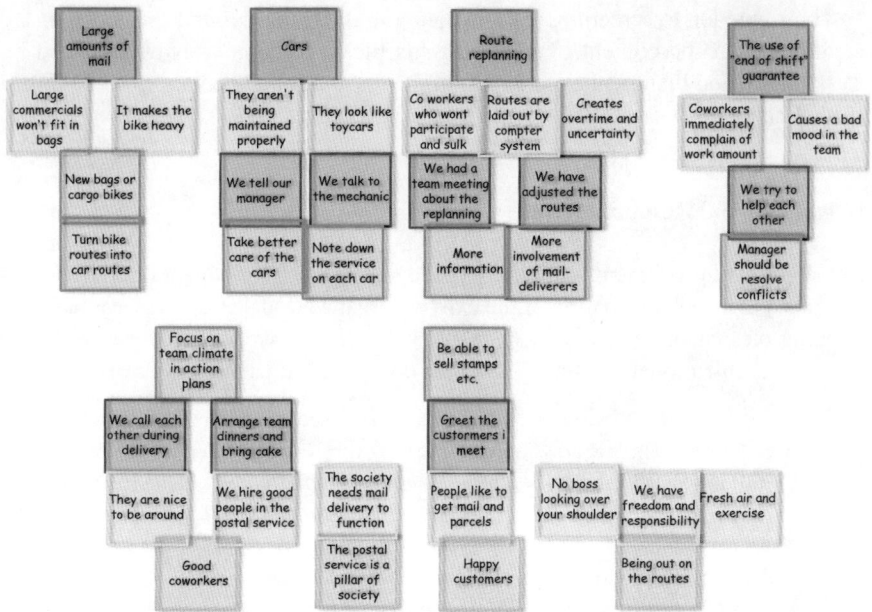

Fig. 18.4 Example of cognitive map

A two-step approach is used to develop a screening that examines the local context: Semi-structured interviews and a tailored screening tool.

The cognitive mapping approach (Harris et al. 2002) is used to develop a visual representation of the working life of employees. The interviews begin with open questions about the sources of engagement and burnout, i.e. the positive and the negative aspects of their job as operationalized in the JD-R model (Bakker and Demerouti 2007). Employees are then asked about which measures have been taken at different levels (Individual, Group, Leader or Organizational) to maximize resources and challenging demands and minimize adverse demands. All responses are written down on coloured sticky notes and placed on a large piece of paper. During the course of the interview, a map of perceived working conditions and improvement attempts is thus produced, providing the employee interviewed with a detailed understanding of his or her working life (for an example of a cognitive map see Fig. 18.4). The project champion and/or researchers then systematically analyze all resources/demands reported in the interviews in order to develop statements for use in the tailored screening tool. The reported aspects of the working environment are translated into neutrally worded items. These statements are then discussed in steering group meetings to ensure face validity. Also included in the screening tool are standardized measures of health and well-being. We used job insecurity (Hellgren et al. 1999), burnout (Kristensen et al. 2005; Schaufeli et al. 2006), work engagement (Schaufeli et al. 2006), and a single item of job satisfaction.

This approach to screening ensures that both the resources and the demands are identified, that the content of screening fits the local context as experienced by participants, and that local experiences of the resources and demands can be linked to well-being outcomes.[1]

Organizational Resource Audit

Developing improvement initiatives based on existing organizational resources requires a thorough evaluation of the existing organizational structures available for working on managing well-being, health and safety at work. For this purpose an audit of organizational resources (ORA) is conducted. Its main objectives are to:

- Map existing organizational resources that are used to manage employee health and well-being (e.g. HR and support personnel, HR programmes, employee well-being initiatives, man-hours available to conduct health and well-being activities, resource persons such as proactive managers, union representatives and health and safety representatives)
- Describe the formal and informal resources available to staff. This includes a description of the strategies and procedures of the organization with regards to well-being programmes as well as a description of the informal resources employees can, and do, draw upon e.g. colleagues, union representatives, and family.
- Describe the job functions relevant to managing health and well-being. This includes also a description of the specific content of the functions, for example, the training available to staff. A description of the monitoring of employee health and well-being of employees, i.e. description of the use of annual attitude surveys and registering sickness absence levels and how such data are used in health and safety management.
- Offer an evaluation of the current use of resources, i.e. a description of the effectiveness of monitoring systems, how the collected data is reported back to participants after collection and to what extent employees and managers feel the current improvement initiatives are implemented and successful?

A mixed methods strategy is used based on interviews with representatives of the different job functions to map the organizational resources. Representatives are identified at a steering group meeting. Subsequently, a snowball approach is used whereby each interviewed representative is asked to identify further functions needing to be interviewed. Interviews with employees and managers are conducted to get an understanding of how the health and well-being programmes and personnel are perceived. Organizational material is collected, e.g. annual attitude surveys and action plans, or descriptions of training programs and other relevant material.

---

[1] A similar approach to questionnaire development has been presented in reports commissioned by the UK Health and Safety Executive (Cox et al. 2002; Cox and Rial-Gonzalez 2000).

Finally, items are included in the questionnaire screening tool to explore how widely used the health and well-being systems are, e.g. are employees and managers aware of the functions, and do they approach them when necessary?

Overall, the ORA examines the degree to which the organization has a systematic approach to managing employee health and well-being: Which elements have been built into formal roles, structures, tools and processes? The ORA can be used to inform a discussion of whether the system could be structured differently, where improvements are needed, and can also be used to identify resources available to address the themes identified in the results of the tailored questionnaire survey. As such, this information is also very useful for the project champion and his/her possibility to tailor the process to the four IGLO-levels.

Action Planning Phase

During this phase two sets of action plans should be developed: One that addresses the results of the tailored questionnaire, and one that focuses on the results of the organizational resources audit.

Developing Improvement Initiative Based on Results of the Tailored Questionnaire

After completion of the tailored screenings and the ORA rapport, data are analyzed and results are presented to the steering committee. First, frequencies are calculated to investigate which aspects of work are perceived to be either problematic or positive by staff. Second, the identified demands and resources are linked to well-being outcomes by calculating the odds ratios of being burned out or engaged when a given factor is perceived as a problem or resource. This analysis strategy allows the steering group and teams to assess the frequency of a problem, as well as the risk it poses to affected employees.

Short reports to each work unit are produced. These consist of four sections, the first of which is a description of how the statistics should be read. The second section contains the health profile of staff (levels of work engagement, burnout, job satisfaction, and job insecurity). If possible comparisons to national representative data are included. The third section presents the job elements related to negative outcomes such as burnout, and/or positive outcomes such as work engagement and job satisfaction. In this section, frequencies and odds ratios for the whole department are presented.[2] To facilitate the presentation of data where specific working conditions appear to be a resource for some and a demand for

---

[2] Our reason for calculating odds ratios on departmental and not team data is because team size in our case was far too small to enable this type of analysis.

others, we visualized the odds ratios as "plus" signs (if related to work engagement) or "minus" signs (for statements related to burnout), for example an odds ratio of 5 between a job element and work engagement results in five plusses. The fourth and final section of the reports contains frequencies for each team. This part of the report helps individual teams detect whether any demands or resources are particularly prevalent and whether action needs to be taken, specifically targeting their team.

To interpret the results, steering group meetings are held in which managers and employee representatives together discuss the reports. The data have been prepared so each statement containing a work element included in the report is coloured according to the relation to well-being outcomes: Those related to negative outcomes such as burnout and job insecurity are coloured yellow, those related to positive factors such as work engagement are blue and the working conditions that are both a demand (if negative) and a resource (if positive) are colored green. Each statement is printed on a strip of paper so the steering committee members themselves can group the statements into themes. During this task the steering group is split up into smaller groups with representatives from each team working on their own team data. They are then given the task of both grouping the statements into larger clusters, and labeling these clusters (e.g. management, organizational changes, and team climate). This is done to facilitate the subsequent action plan development, ensuring that action plans target a wider range of working conditions. After agreeing on themes, participants add up the number of plusses and minuses to determine the importance of each theme. In Fig. 18.5, an example of thematic grouping is shown. The next step is presenting the themes at team meetings to give the team members the opportunity to discuss and adjust themes. Employee steering group members present the results in order to promote employee ownership of the process.

In order to develop action plans, steering groups or teams are advised to follow a series of steps (see Fig. 18.6). The aim of these steps is to develop the competencies needed to plan realistic improvements and improve their understanding of psychosocial issues and how these can be addressed in a systematic manner:

1. The first step includes prioritizing the themes and discussing the results, especially the severity of the issues raised: How many statements relate to the issue? How strongly is the theme linked to outcomes (based on the plusses and minuses)? How many perceive the theme as a problem? The team then discusses which of the themes are the most important for them to address, especially with regards to what is deemed qualitatively would lead to the greatest work life improvement. During these discussions it is noted if any themes need to be sent elsewhere in the system, e.g. to the management group or other teams. These discussions should also focus on possible opportunities and obstacles for addressing the issues and completing the action plan. This includes a discussion of whether the team has the competencies, resources and time to address the prioritized issues.

2. Next, the prioritized themes are discussed to get an understanding of whether an underlying factor is the cause of the problem/resource. A dialogue tool employed

Theme 1: Changes in the workplace

Working condition	Whole department problem	good	Burnout	Job Insecurity	Work engagement	Team 1 problem	good
Frequency of replanning of routes	73%	5%		- - -		46%	18%
Degree of influence on changes in the workplace	32%	27%	- - -	- - -		24%	37%
Degree of involvement in changes in the workplace	27%	27%		- - - -		20%	40%
Number of changes	50%	14%	- - - -	- - - - -	+++	27%	26%
Processes of merging teams	36%	18%			+++	31%	27%

Theme 2: Changes in the workplace

Degree of physical fatigue after a shift	55%	9%		- - - - - -		45%	23%
The work is physically demanding	27%	46%	- - -	- - - - -	+++	22%	58%
The degree of mental fatigue after work	14%	14%			++++	19%	42%

Theme 3: Tools and safety

The quality and condition of tools and vehicles	27%	14%		- - - - - -		24%	57%
The use of proper lifting technique	59%	5%	- - -	- - - - -	+++	32%	22%
The possibility to use correct lifting technique and follow safety guidelines	46%	14%			++++	16%	31%

Uncategorized

The time to speak to customers	27%	23%	- - -		+++++++	24%	34%
Follow-up on employee	41%	18%	- - -		+++	35%	32%

Fig. 18.5 Developing themes

Initiatives	Under standing	Goal	Action plan	Deadline Responsi-bility	Evaluation Effect
Theme from survey • Statement A • Statement B • Statement C etc. **Prioritization** • The numbers? (amount, strengths, percentages) • Can we change it? (time, people, competencies, culture) • What do we want to change? • Are the issues that we have to send elsewhere in the system?	Cause 1: _____ _____ _____ Cause 2: _____ _____ _____ Etc. **Brainstorming** • Why is this a problem? • What is the causeof the problem? • 5 x "Why?" • Herringbone	Overall goal: _____ _____ _____ Subgoal: _____	Kaizen (Plan Do Check Act)	Responsibility: _____ _____ Resources: _____ _____ People involved: _____ _____ _____ Timeline: _____ _____ _____ Evaluation: _____ _____ _____	• Has change happened? (in procedures, roles, methods, processes) • Has it solved the problem targeted?

Fig. 18.6 Framework for developing improvement initiatives

to examine this is "The Five Whys?". It is a method to dig into the causes of the themes, continually (five times) asking "Why?", and demanding further explanation and assessment of causality to the offered explanation of the problem. By investigating the underlying causes to problems, chances are that the following intervention activities will solve causes of problems instead of merely addressing the symptoms.

3. The goals and sub goals, deadlines, and responsible change agents are identified for each action plan.

4. The progress of action plans developed should be tracked in a visual fashion, such as on a Kaizen board[3] (Imai 1986). The action plans should be visible in the workplace and be subject to ongoing reevaluation as to whether the plan is effective or should be modified to reach the set goals. Evaluation should be specific: how can they tell that the goal and sub goals have been achieved?

Developing Improvement Initiatives Based on the Organizational Resources Audit

A report summarising the functions and the perceptions of their effectiveness is developed and fed back to the steering group. As with the results of the tailored questionnaire approach, themes are identified that need managing. It is important that HR and occupational health consultants are present as the responsibility for improvement initiatives is likely to rest, at least partially, on them.

As some improvement initiatives may need to be addressed at the higher levels or in other areas to address the issues identified in the audit, it becomes even more important to ensure that improvement initiatives are clearly visible to the intervention participants. Using the IGLO model, improvement initiatives may be best developed at four levels: At the Organizational level, procedures that need changing are identified and a plan made for the changes made including resources needed and deadlines for change. At the Leader level, managers identify how these changes are to be rolled out at their level. At the Group (team) level, employees are involved in the planning of changes that will alter their working procedures and discuss how they can support implementation of change. Finally, at the Individual level, participants consider whether they need to change their own working procedures to accommodate the change.

---

[3]Kaizen boards are a tool used in LEAN management to track progress of problem solving and improvement efforts. Reported issues are written on labels and placed on the board in a circular track of fields labeled "plan" (how to solve the problem), "do" (implement the plan), "check" (if the plan have the intended effect), "act" (upon the result). This Kaizen method (plan, do, check, and act) is thus a means of visualizing and tracking problem solving efforts in the workplace.

ORA action plan – an example: In an intervention group, one of the problems identified in the ORA were that the overtime regulations were not clear to all staff and this resulted in different operationalizations of the regulations across teams within the same area. To rectify the problems, actions were developed at three levels:

1. Organizational level: HR developed a working paper on the regulations including a clear description of how the regulations should be interpreted.
2. Leader level: In one of the regular, scheduled meetings between the management group and employee representatives, the regulations were discussed to ensure a shared understanding of the regulations and how they should be reinforced.
3. Team level: At a team meeting, team members discussed the working paper and the extent to which current team procedures adhered to the regulations or whether existing procedures needed changing.

Implementation Phase

Action plans should be visible, e.g. using existing tools to manage the way work is organized, designed and managed and should be discussed at every team meeting. When completed the action plan can be transferred to another board and thus provides an opportunity to mark and celebrate the "small successes".

It is also important that action plans, that are not local to the teams are discussed at team meetings to ensure employees are made aware of progress and have the opportunity for commenting on (lack of) progress and their experiences with the changes implemented, so if needed improvement initiatives can be initiated.

Minutes of meetings where progress has been discussed and not all participants have been present should be made freely available. Where such minutes are not possible, e.g. from management meetings it should be discussed how information relevant to the project is communicated. See Fig. 18.7 for an example of how the implementation phase can be made visual.

Evaluation Phase

During this last phase, a combined process and effect evaluation is conducted. The aim is to get a detailed understanding of how the intervention worked, why and under which circumstances, and for whom.

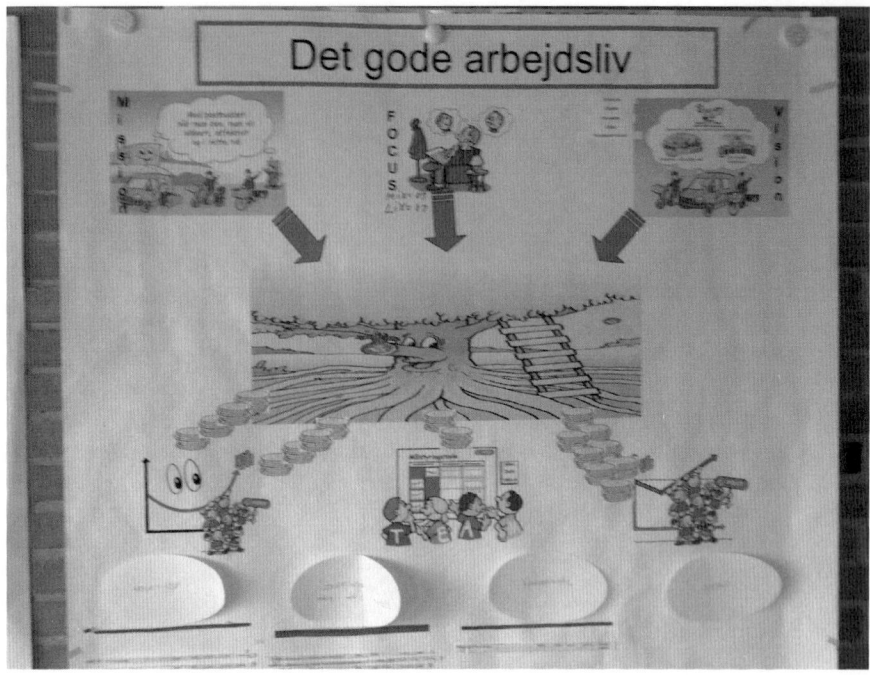

Fig. 18.7 Example of visual implementation

Effect Evaluation

The screening functions as a baseline measurement with a follow-up 12–18 months later including the same items. This makes it possible to evaluate effects at the targeted problem level, e.g. whether feedback on organizational change has become less of a problem and has weaker links to poor well-being but also whether overall improvements in well-being are reported, e.g. whether burnout and job insecurity decreased and work engagement and job satisfaction increased. Organizational data on performance, turnover and absence levels can be used to examine the effects of the intervention on "hard outcomes". In the current project, we also obtained organizational data concerning individual absence rates (both short- and long-term), quality (number of letters delivered to the correct address) and quantity (whether teams lived up to their budgets). We also included a measure of job crafting allowing us to determine whether job crafting had increased as a result of the participatory process (Nielsen and Abildgaard 2012).

Process Evaluation

The processes of the intervention is evaluated focusing on (1) the impact of the individuals' appraisals of the intervention project and the activities within the intervention, (2) the impact of the organizational context, both the organizational structure and culture and any concurrent events, such as downsizing, change of management or other organizational change which may have influenced the intervention progress, and (3) the impact of the intervention process itself, in terms of how the strategy chosen impacts on intervention outcomes and whether the intervention and its activities were implemented according to plan (Nielsen and Randall 2012a). The main objective of the process evaluation is to identify the working mechanisms of change: What were the drivers of change that can help explain the development in one phase and from one phase to another, e.g. which where the factors that enabled/hindered the translation of screening results into action plans? In the postal service projects we collected data on each element of the intervention. We used interviews, observations and quantitative process evaluation included in questionnaire follow-ups.

1. Interviews: We interviewed the steering groups about the experiences as members of the steering group: What had they learned from sitting in the steering group? Which tools had they felt were useful and which were less useful, e.g. communication plan and action planning tools? What did they think of the tailored questionnaire approach? We also interviewed managers and employees about (a) the information they had received about the project, for example, had they received information from members of the steering group, from their immediate manager, from their union representative? (b) their involvement in the project: Had they sought out information themselves? Had they been active in steering groups or ad hoc working groups? What were their experiences in participating in groups? What were their experiences participating in the project? E.g. concerning the use of the tailored questionnaire. (c) We asked about their experiences with developing and implementing action plans. Did they know about action plans? Had they been involved in developing and implementing action plans? What was the content of action plans? Did the action plans address the right problems? Did they see any changes as a consequence of the action plans (at the IGLO levels), i.e. did they perceive any changes in working procedures? (d) Had managers been supportive of the project and worked actively towards involving employees? (e) We also asked about the factors that had hindered or facilitated change (again at the IGLO levels) to test the fit of the intervention to the context.
2. Observations: Throughout the entire project we also made observations of what happened during the steering group meetings. This allowed us to examine how tools were perceived, how managers and employees interacted and how they perceived each other's roles and responsibilities. We were also able to perceive any changes during the project, for example, did employee representatives develop their role throughout their project? Did managers and employees representatives develop shared mental models on how to manage well-being in the workplace? (Did they develop a collaborative climate through the participatory approach? We made observations at the workshops to detect how the project and its tools were perceived by participants.
3. Questionnaire data: We measured participants' readiness for change at baseline in order to get target our communication plan and the participatory approach. In the follow-up questionnaires, we included information on: Line managers'

involvement in the project, the extent to which employees had participated actively in the project, changes in mental models (in talking about and managing well-being differently) (Randall et al. 2009). Furthermore, we collated data on the content and the progress of action plans. For each action plan, we asked whether participants knew about hem, had worked with them, whether they were visible on the Kaizen boards, and finally whether they felt the action plan had either improved or worsened their working conditions. We also asked some general questions about well the action planning and implementation had worked.

4. Organizational material: We collected relevant organizational data. For example, we collected the action plans based on this project but also those normally developed based on the annual attitude survey so that we could compare these and see whether there were any qualitative differences in the content and quality (e.g. level of detail).

Combining Process and Effect Evaluation

In order to get an understanding of *what* works for *whom*, *why* and *under which circumstances*, it is important to integrate process and effect evaluation. This integration requires the analysis of how we can explain the outcomes of the intervention through understanding the processes, for example, how does the level of participation and the nature of participation influence intervention outcomes, or how does the concurrent downsizing influence the intervention process and subsequently the outcomes of the intervention? It is also important to understand the effects in light of the changes in the context. For example, has the organizational context changed to such a degree that the effects are due to changes in this context, e.g. due to restructuring or an influx of additional resources?

Discussion

In this chapter, we have presented a participatory framework for developing and implementing changes in the way work is organized, designed, and managed in order to improve working conditions and employee well-being. We have described the theoretical background for the framework offering some insights into the mechanisms through which the framework may be effective. Acknowledging the current lack of explicit published knowledge on how to conduct participatory organizational interventions, we describe the phases of the framework, offering some tools that other researchers, HR and occupational health consultants may find useful when conducting organizational interventions. Based on the identified challenges in developing and implementing improvement initiatives we have introduced some methods that may be useful in our understanding of how we can make organizational interventions work. First, we have presented a tailored, participatory method to screen both resources and adverse demands of the job, taking into account the cognitive appraisals of staff. Second, we present a way of working with results to ensure that shared mental models of the issues in the specific group are developed and that detailed action is taken to improve the situation. Third, we propose methods for communication, ensuring that all employees are informed about the project and to some extent involved in the project. This latter approach is in line with the recent debate, that in order to ensure the benefits of participatory interventions, all employees need to be involved to some extent to ensure organizational learning (Nielsen and Randall 2012b).

References

Bakker, A. B., & Demerouti, E. (2007). The job demands-resources model: State of the art. *Journal of Managerial Psychology, 22*(3), 309–328.

Berg, J. M., Wrzesniewski, A., & Dutton, J. E. (2010). Perceiving and responding to challenges in job crafting at different ranks: When proactivity requires adaptivity. *Journal of Organizational Behavior, 31*, 158–186.

Biron, C., Gatrell, C., & Cooper, C. L. (2010). Autopsy of a failure. Evaluating process and contextual issues in an organizational-level work stress intervention. *International Journal of Stress Management, 17*(2), 135–158.

Cox, T., & Rial-Gonzalez, E. (2000). *Risk management, psychosocial hazards and work stress.* Copenhagen: World Health Organization, Regional Office for Europe.

Cox, T., Randall, R., & Griffiths, A. (2002). *Interventions to control stress at work in hospital staff.* Sudbury: HSE Books.

Crawford, E. R., LePine, J. A., & Rich, B. L. (2010). Linking job demands and resources to employee engagement and burnout: A theoretical extension and meta-analytic test. *Journal of Applied Psychology, 95*(5), 834–848.

Dahl-Jørgensen, C., & Saksvik, P. Ø. (2005). The impact of two organizational interventions on the health of service sector workers. *International Journal of Health Services, 35*(3), 529–549.

Daniels, K., Harris, C., & Briner, R. (2004). Linking work conditions to unpleasant affect: Cognition, categorization and goals. *Journal of Occupational and Organizational Psychology, 77*, 343–363.

Daniels, K., Hartley, R., & Travers, C. J. (2006). Beliefs about stressors alter stressors' impact: Evidence from two experience-sampling methods. *Human Relations, 59*(9), 1261–1285.

Daniels, K., Karanika-Murray, M., Mellor, N., & van Veldhoven, M. (2012). Moving policy and practice forward: Beyond descriptions of job characteristics. In C. Biron, M. Karanika-Murray, & C. L. Cooper (Eds.), *Improving organizational interventions on stress and well-being: Addressing process and context.* London: Psychology Press, pp. 313–332.

Dewe, P. (1989). Examining the nature of work stress: Individual evaluations of stressful experiences and coping. *Human Relations, 42*, 993–1013.

Grant, A. M., & Ashford, S. J. (2008). The dynamics of proactivity at work. *Research in Organizational Behavior, 28*, 3–34.

Grant, A. M., & Parker, S. K. (2009). Redesigning work design theories: The rise of relational and proactive perspectives. *Academy of Management Annals, 3*, 273–331.

Harris, C., Daniels, K., & Briner, R. (2002). Using cognitive mapping for psychosocial risk assessment. *Risk Management: An International Journal, 4*, 7–21.

Hasson, H., Gilbert-Ouimet, M., Baril-Gingras, G., Brisson, C., Vézina, M., Bourbonnais, R., & Montreuil, S. (2012). Implementation of an organizational-level intervention on the psychosocial environment of work. *Journal of Occupational and Environmental Medicine, 54*(1), 85–91.

Hellgren, J., Sverke, M., & Isaksson, K. (1999). A two-dimensional approach to job insecurity. Consequences for employee attitudes and well-being. *European Journal of Work and Organizational Psychology, 8*(2), 179–195.

Hobfoll, S. E. (1989). Conservation of resources: A new attempt at conceptualizing stress. *American Psychologist, 44*(3), 513–524.

Imai, M. (1986). *Kaizen: The key to Japan's competitive success*. New York: Random House.

Kohler, J. M., & Munz, D. C. (2006). Combining individual and organizational stress interventions. *Consulting Psychology Journal: Practice and Research, 58*(1), 1–12.

Kompier, M. (2004). Work organization interventions. *Sozial- und Präventivmedizin, 49*, 77–78.

Kompier, M., Geurts, S., Grundemann, R., Vink, P., & Smulders, P. (1998). Cases in stress prevention: The success of a participative and stepwise approach. *Stress Medicine, 14*, 155–168.

Kompier, M. A. J., & Kristensen, T. S. (2001). Organizational work stress interventions in a theoretical, methodological and practical context. In J. Dunham (Ed.), *Stress in the workplace: Past, present and future* (1st ed., pp. 164–190). London: Whurr.

Kristensen, T. S., Borritz, M., Villadsen, E., & Christensen, K. B. (2005). The Copenhagen Burnout Inventory: A new tool for the assessment of burnout. *Work and Stress, 19*(3), 192–207.

Kristof-Brown, A. L., & Guay, R. P. (2011). Person-environment fit. In S. Zedeck (Ed.), *APA handbook of industrial and organizational psychology* (pp. 3–50). Washington, DC: APA.

Kristof-Brown, A. L., Zimmerman, R. D., & Johnson, E. C. (2005). Consequences of individuals' fit at work: A meta-analysis of person-job, person-organization, person-group, and person-supervisor fit. *Personnel Psychology, 58*(2), 281–342.

Landsbergis, P., & Vivona-Vaughan, E. (1995). Evaluation of an occupational stress intervention in a public agency. *Journal of Organizational Behavior, 16*, 29–48.

Lazarus, R., & Folkman, S. (1992). *Stress, appraisal and coping*. New York: Springer.

Murphy, L. R., & Sauter, S. L. (2004). Work organization interventions: State of knowledge and future directions. *Sozial Praventivmedizin, 49*, 79–86.

Nielsen, K., & Abildgaard, J. S. (2012). The validation of a job crafting measure for blue collar workers. *Work and Stress, 26*(4), 365–384.

Nielsen, K., & Randall, R. (2012a). Opening the black box: A framework for evaluating organizational-level occupational health interventions. *European Journal of Work and Organizational Psychology*. doi:10.1080/1359432X.2012.690556.

Nielsen, K., & Randall, R. (2012b). The importance of employee participation and perception of changes in procedures in a teamworking intervention. *Work and Stress, 29*(91), 111.

Nielsen, K., Fredslund, H., Christensen, K. B., & Albertsen, K. (2006). Success or failure? Interpreting and understanding the impact of interventions in four similar worksites. *Work and Stress, 20*(3), 272–287.

Nielsen, K., Randall, R., & Christensen, K. B. (2010a). Does training managers enhance the effects of implementing teamworking? A longitudinal, mixed methods field study. *Human Relations, 63*(11), 1719–1741.

Nielsen, K., Randall, R., Holten, A. L., & González, E. R. (2010b). Conducting organizational-level occupational health interventions: What works? *Work and Stress, 24*(3), 234–259.

Nielsen, K., Taris, T. W., & Cox, T. (2010c). The future of organizational interventions: Addressing the challenges of today's organizations. *Work and Stress, 24*(3), 219–233.

Randall, R., & Nielsen, K. (2012). Does the intervention fit? An explanatory model of intervention success or failure in complex organizational environments. In C. Biron, M. Karanika-Murray, & C. Cooper (Eds.), *Improving organizational interventions for stress and well-being*. London: Routledge.

Randall, R., Nielsen, K., & Tvedt, S. D. (2009). The development of scales to measure participants' appraisals of organizational-level stress management interventions. *Work and Stress, 23*, 1–23.

Schaufeli, W. B., Bakker, A. B., & Salanova, M. (2006). The measurement of work engagement with a short questionnaire. *Educational and Psychological Measurement, 66*(4), 701–716.

Tims, M., & Bakker, A. B. (2010). Job crafting: Towards a new model of individual job redesign. *South African Journal of Industrial Psychology, 36*, 1–9.

Wrzesniewski, A., & Dutton, J. E. (2001). Crafting a job: Revisioning employees as active crafters of their work. *Academy of Management Review, 26*(2), 179–201.